Lonely Planet Publications
Melbourne | Oakland | London

D0066815

Damien Simonis

Venice

The Top Five

1 **Palazzo Ducale**
Tour La Serenissima's political heart (p58)

2 **Burano and Torcello**
Savour the islands' charm (p93)

3 **Basilica di San Marco**
See the marriage of East and West at Piazza San Marco's core (p51)

4 **Grand Canal**
Cruise along Main St, Venice (p108)

5 **Peggy Guggenheim Collection**
Gorge yourself on a feast of eclectic artworks (p68)

Contents

Published by Lonely Planet Publications Pty Ltd
ABN 36 005 607 983

Australia Head Office, Locked Bag 1, Footscray,
Victoria 3011, ☎ 03 8379 8000, fax 03 8379 8111,
talk2us@lonelyplanet.com.au

USA 150 Linden St, Oakland, CA 94607,
☎ 510 893 8555, toll free 800 275 8555,
fax 510 893 8572, info@lonelyplanet.com

UK 72–82 Rosebery Ave, Clerkenwell, London,
EC1R 4RW, ☎ 020 7841 9000, fax 020 7841 9001,
go@lonelyplanet.co.uk

The Author

Damien Simonis

As a young back-packer with not a word of Italian and barely two brass lire to rub together, Damien first landed in Venice back in his Dark Age. Enchanted by his first encounter with the city on water, he took away a treasure of confused and colourful images: majestic churches and palaces, twisting canals and narrow blind alleys, countless quaint bridges, ebullient produce markets and an inescapable sense of romance and mystery. He finally returned years later on assignment for Lonely Planet. Like an old flame never quite forgotten, the charming if aged queen of the sea again worked her magic. Things had changed. Italian had become Damien's second language, and so he began to see and hear the city in a closer, warts-and-all fashion. Having lived in Milan and distant Palermo, and crisscrossed the boot-like peninsula, he could put the unique one-time merchant empire into clearer context. Sure, cracks began to appear beneath the make-up, but that only endeared him more to the place, which he still visits as often as possible. As he learns to tread a finer path through the labyrinth of lanes (it's always fun to discover another short cut) and pot-ter about in boats on the lagoon, our man in Venice can only confess that he has become more hooked than ever. Even when at home in that other Mediterranean jewel, Barcelona, he can still taste that slightly bitter afternoon *spritz* as the sun goes down.

PHOTOGRAPHER
Juliet Coombe

Of the 120 cities Juliet has visited, Venice is still her true love, because of its unique, ethereal charm and theatrical setting. It may be one of the world's most photographed, filmed and written about places, but however many times she goes there, whether it be for Carnevale or the Mostra del Cinema di Venezia (Venice International Film Festival), she always finds something new to rekindle her passion for La Serenissima.

DAMIEN'S TOP VENICE DAY

After a long stretch and a little lazy staring out of my boutique hotel room window, it's time to get up for cappuccino, pastry and paper on the nearest square, in this case Campo Santa Maria Formosa. Suitably entertained by Prime Minister Berlusconi's latest capers, I wander the *calli* (streets) down to Riva degli Schiavoni to contemplate the busy lagoon spectacle before heading west to the Palazzo Ducale – a giddy trip down the Republic's glorious memory lane. Not wanting to overdo the sightseeing, I take the No 1 vaporetto to Rialto and disappear down the narrow lanes around the markets for some lunchtime *cicheti* (snacks) and wine at All'Arco. My favourite afternoon outing takes me across the lagoon to Burano and Torcello for a peaceful wander, coming back in time for an evening *spritz* before proceeding to a seafood splurge at, say, Trattoria da Remigio in Castello. Late in the night I can't resist sneaking back into a spectral Piazza San Marco after the cafés close and silence sets in. Glorious.

Introducing Venice

Perhaps Turner captured its essence best. Elusive, floating, enigmatic, Venice rides in a misty middle distance of muted colours and sounds, a dreamlike place that defies definition and beggars description. Anchored to the shimmering lagoon floor like some fantastical Gothic man-of-war, its slender bell towers like so many masts, it seems simultaneously to hover above the lightly ruffled water's surface, ready to slip quietly off into the Adriatic.

In this improbable city, built upon islets and platforms of countless pylons slammed over the centuries into the mud of the lagoon, people go about their business, traipsing along lanes and beside canals, up and down the countless bridges. The air hums to the sound of padding feet, chatter resonating off the walls along narrow, crooked streets and bustling, uneven squares.

The roads of Venice are made of water. Fire engines, police, ambulances and taxis tootle about as wheeled vehicles would elsewhere. Only here they are boats and the speed limit is 5km/h. Not that anyone seems to enforce the limit. Suntanned taxi drivers pound about in their expensive, oak-panelled vessels, dodging exasperated gondoliers with their boatloads of enthralled visitors.

Venetians are unperturbed. Used to the incredible, indigestible accumulation of natural and constructed beauty that surrounds them, and seemingly indifferent to the slow decay of that same beauty, they sometimes give the impression of being unaware that Venice has long ceased to be one of the centres of the European universe.

LOWDOWN

Population 64,000 (270,000 for whole municipality, including islands and mainland)

Time zone GMT/UTC plus one hour

3-star double room €150 to €200

Coffee at the bar Around 90c

Coffee on Piazza San Marco Up to €10!

Takeaway pizza slice €1.50 to €3

Gelato €1.50 to €2.50 (one or two flavours)

Vaporetto ticket €3.50 (single ride)

Consideration Walk single file (right side) along narrow streets to let people past in either direction– do NOT walk two abreast, as you annoy the hell out of locals trying to get about

Vaporetto etiquette If you're near the exit, get off at intermediate stops to let other passengers on and off. Better still, move inside. ('Down the back of the vaporetto' might be the conductor's cry!)

Venice was and remains a sore point with the rest of Italy, a source of envy and irritation. Throughout its history, rivals as varied as the popes, Milan, Genoa, Padua, Imperial Spain and the Turks sought to break the haughty masters of the Adriatic. Nowadays, other Italians consider the city to be as stuck-up as ever.

The city's builders seem to have delighted in variety: from the great mosaics of the Basilica di San Marco and Torcello to the sober Gothic majesty of the Frari, from the simplicity of Romanesque to the discipline of Palladio, from the sensuality of Veneto-Byzantine to the extremes of baroque, the concentration of architectural gems is astonishing. The same is true of its art– the march of past greats from the Venetian school seems infinite. Some of their works are scattered in galleries far from home, but the number of masterpieces by Tiepolo, Tintoretto, Veronese, Titian and others to be seen in the city is the equivalent of death-by-chocolate for art lovers.

There is more to Venice than history, art and architecture. Exploring the lagoon's islands is essential to a broader understanding of the whole. Contemplate Venice from the long Adriatic barrier that is the Lido and you can't help thinking the place a figment of your imagination. Over on Murano, glass-makers continue to create crystal dream-shapes at their blast furnaces, while on Burano a handful of dames still patiently sew together extraordinarily intricate lace. Back in town, Venetians also take leisure seriously, whether getting down to a succulent seafood meal by a canal or sidling up to a *bacaro* (old-style bar) for *cicheti* (bar snacks) and a glass of *prosecco* (sparkling white wine). Early-evening tipplers favour a *spritz*, a refreshing, fiery-red shot of *prosecco* mixed with soda and bitters.

But the proud city is slowly expiring. International organisations fight to preserve its monuments, and engineers debate how to stem Adriatic floods. Press coverage of the battle to clean the lagoon of toxic waste alternates with alarmed reports on building subsidence. Everyone, from the mayor of Venice to ministers in Rome, from art historians in Britain to architecture buffs in the USA, expounds unendingly about the need to do *something*.

Perhaps they have missed the point. The lifeblood of a city is its people, and the people of Venice are voting with their feet. Since the 1950s the population has more than halved. Housing is too expensive, transport too complicated, jobs too scarce. Talk to Venetians and you get the uncanny feeling you are on a sinking ship. One day it may truly be just a theme park open daily from eight till late – one former mayor even suggested establishing an entrance fee and imposing a daily limit on visitor numbers!

For the moment you can still feel the pulse, and Venice has returned from the brink of extinction before. In this elusive city, the tides rise and fall every six hours, pushing the water first this way then that along the canals. More than a 'sight', Venice seems to be time and motion itself.

ESSENTIAL VENICE

- Admiring the grandeur of Basilica di San Marco (p51), the city's awe-inspiring cathedral
- Cruising past the mansions that line the Grand Canal (p108)
- Taking a break on peaceful Burano (p93)
- Sipping a *spritz* (p160) on Campo Santa Margherita on a sunny afternoon
- Mucking about in a gondola (p246), a unique vessel designed for the lagoon city and a great way to be taken for a romantic ride

City Life

City Life

According to local writer Tiziano Scarpa, Venice is a fish. Look at a map and you can see what he means. To thrive, a fish needs nice clean water to flit about in. Has this one been left high and dry? Venice, with its crumbling walls, sometimes stinky canals and ever-present avalanche of tourists, continues to fascinate and enchant. But it has serious problems. Various physicians have been called to the patient's bedside. Many therapies have been applied, from cultural infusions to restoration campaigns. The patient is alive but not out of danger. Some observers insist that one day the city will become an open-air museum, the lifeblood of its people drained away elsewhere and a day charge applied at points of entry. Even former mayor Paolo Costa agreed the threat was real as he left office in early 2005. That's if the city isn't engulfed by its own poisoned waters first.

VENICE TODAY

What makes a city is not so much its monuments, art and glorious history. What makes a city is its inhabitants. Venice has no shortage of the aforementioned attributes, but its people are ebbing away like an outbound tide. International organisations and generations of politicians have kept applying Band-Aids to major sores, ranging from worsening tidal flooding to the need to restore the grand buildings and works of art that constitute Venice's fabulous legacy to the world. But next to nothing has been done to stop ordinary Venetians leaving. As the local resident population drops, the city's social infrastructure collapses. In southern Dorsoduro, where once there were half a dozen bakeries to choose from there is now one. Finding a shop that sells widgets is increasingly becoming a trial. Finding pizza by the slice is a cinch. As shops close and services disappear, it becomes harder to get things done and…more people leave.

Since the 1950s the population has dropped by two-thirds. Why? The city can be frustrating. You can't park your car outside the front gate (you can't park one anywhere!), and everything costs more because transport and distribution by boat is more costly and complex than on land. Jobs in anything other than the public service and tourism-related services are hard to come by. Indeed, most of the jobs outside tourism left for the mainland long ago.

Venice survives largely because of tourism, but the flip side is a constant run on local housing for use as hotel space and second homes. Buying is prohibitive and rents soar. When locals are evicted to make way for such development, they frequently throw in the towel and move to the mainland – less aesthetically pleasing but eminently more practical. Nothing (or little) is done to alleviate the distorting effects of these phenomena or to help Venetians stay.

Many people would love to remain, and many more non-Venetians would like to

HOT CONVERSATION TOPICS

- Will those lagoon barriers really keep the floods out? And will they ever be completed?
- Just what is the point in having a new bridge over the Grand Canal, even if they do ever manage to get it into place?
- The gondoliers' brief one-day strike in September 2004 against *moto ondoso* (damaging waves caused by speeding motorboats) seems to have done little to spur the city authorities to take action. The phenomenon damages building foundations, the lagoon and more peaceful vessels.
- Is it fair to evict Venetians so that buildings can be converted into hotels?
- It's wonderful to live in a city without car noise, but what a pain not to be able to park outside your front door!
- There's water, water everywhere, including sometimes the ground-floor hall.
- Does Venice really need a sub-lagoon metro system to Marco Polo Airport? Who will pay for it? And what's the point of the Tronchetto 'people mover' (monorail)?

RITES OF SPRING

Venetians have been celebrating the approach of spring with Carnevale since at least the 15th century. In those days private clubs organised masked balls, and popular entertainment included such fun as bull-baiting and firing live dogs from cannons! By the 18th century Venice was home to hedonism, and the licentious goings-on of Carnevale lasted two months.

Things quietened down after the city's fall to Napoleon in 1797, and Carnevale died when Mussolini banned the wearing of masks. Revived in 1979, it has become the world's best-known baroque fancy-dress party, as extravagant as Rio's Carnaval is riotous.

The festivities begin on a Friday afternoon with La Festa delle Marie, a procession through the city. This is a precursor to the official opening on Saturday, when a masked procession leaves Piazza San Marco around 4pm and circulates through the *calli* (streets). The next day there are jousts and other mock-military tournaments.

The following Friday evening's highlight is the Gran Ballo delle Maschere (Grand Masked Ball), which takes place in different locations each year – usually a suitably grand palace is chosen for the event, otherwise known as the Doge's Ball. Anyone with proper costume and mask who is able to dance the quadrilles and other steps of a few centuries ago may join in. Tickets can cost in excess of €200, plus the outlay for costume hire.

Saturday and Sunday are given over to musical and theatrical performances in Piazza San Marco and other locations. *Calcio storico* (a medieval approximation of football in period costume) matches are played on Piazza San Marco, also the scene for a parade of the best costumes in town (and they can be extraordinarily ornate). That parade is repeated on the following Tuesday.

Also on the Sunday a beautiful procession of decorated boats and gondolas bearing masked passengers wends its way serenely down the Grand Canal.

During the course of the festivities plenty goes on outside the main events. Street performers fill the main thoroughfares and squares. An ice-skating rink is sometimes set up in Campo San Polo. Whatever you do, make sure to pop into a pastry shop and stock up on *frittelle veneziane* (scrumptious sugar-coated deep-fried balls of dough made with raisins, rum and, depending on the cook's whim, other goodies).

move in. With world-class architecture, arts and Oriental studies faculties, among many others, Venice has a vibrant intellectual life, if on a modest scale. In what other city are people obliged by the lack of cars to get about mostly on foot? Apart from the benefits in terms of noise and air pollution, the absence of cars has helped preserve a social cohesion long lost in other centres. People greet each other in the streets and squares, and stop for a chat or a drink before continuing on their way. There is a spontaneity about the place that's absent in bigger, busier, more terrestrial urban centres. But for the majority of people all of this is not enough when the price to pay is sky-high rents, lack of job prospects and all the practical frustrations.

The city is not only under demographic assault. The very lagoon in which it stands and which protected the city for centuries is eating away at it. Floods, pollution and overfishing are all helping destroy the lagoon and its city. If nothing serious is done, we are told, Venice may well be uninhabitable before the century is out.

In the meantime, locals go about their business like phantoms in among the tourists. Although at times (especially on hot summer days) it seems impossible to even move for all the crowds, in general Venetians (and non-Venetians resident here) have developed coping mechanisms. It is as though they don't see all the day-trippers.

Seemingly unable to think of ways to attract more stable business and draw people back to live in Venice, the town authorities try to make up for it with a rich palette of cultural offerings. The six-month-long Biennale Internazionale d'Arte (Biennial International Art Exhibition) and its architecture equivalent in alternate years, coupled with the annual September film festival and frequent one-off exhibitions, are a treat for locals. But even there it is hard to escape the conclusion that it's all done to attract yet more tourism, a short-term boon to the coffers but a fickle beast.

More cynical locals are sure these and other ideas (such as proposals for a sub-lagoon metro to link the airport to Murano and Venice and a monorail train between Tronchetto and Piazzale Roma) are aimed simply at increasing the flow of tourists. Milk the cow while it's still alive seems to be the unspoken motto.

CITY CALENDAR

If you can manage it, timing your visit to coincide with one of the city's big shindigs will add an extra festive dimension to your discovery of Venice. Otherwise, as a general rule, the best time of year to visit is spring, from about April to June (although Easter is busy with school groups). July and August can be unpleasantly hot and muggy, and late autumn to December wet. If you don't mind the cold, you can get lucky in winter (around January-February) with crisp blue skies and a relative scarcity of tourists. See also Holidays, p255.

FEBRUARY
CARNEVALE
This is the major event of the year, when some Venetians and many outsiders don spectacular masks and costumes for a week-long party in the run-up to Ash Wednesday. The starting dates for Carnevale in the next few years are 21 February 2006, 13 February 2007 and 29 January 2008. See Rites of Spring, p9.

MARCH
SALONE NAUTICO DI VENEZIA
Since 2002 the Stazione Marittima (Ferry Terminal) has hosted this increasingly popular boat show. In 2005 the show was twinned with the big US Annual Fort Lauderdale International Boat Show. Venice seems to be looking out to sea again!

APRIL
FESTA DI SAN MARCO
The feast day of St Mark, the city's patron saint, when men give their beloved a bunch of roses, is on 25 April.

MAY
VOGALONGA
Meaning 'long row', this is a good-natured long-distance rowing regatta, held in the first half of the month. This event began in November 1974 and has developed into a friendly free-for-all, with 3000 to 5000 participants and around 1000 boats of all descriptions (powered by human muscle) participating in the 32km jaunt from the Bacino di San Marco up to Burano via Sant'Erasmo and back down to the Grand Canal via Murano and Cannaregio.

FESTA DELLA SENSA
This feast day falls on the second Sunday of May and marks the Feast of the Ascension (Sensa in Venetian). Already an important day in the Catholic calendar, it takes on a special significance in Venice. Every year since Ascension Day 998, when Venetian forces left to regain control of Dalmatia, the city has celebrated the Sposalizio del Mar (Wedding with the Sea) – see With This Ring I Thee Wet, p38.

LATE MAY–EARLY JUNE
PALIO DELLE QUATTRO ANTICHE REPUBBLICHE MARINARE
The former maritime republics of Amalfi, Genoa, Pisa and Venice take turns to host the colourful historic Regatta of the Four Ancient Maritime Republics, in which four galleons, crewed by eight oarsmen and one at the tiller, compete for line honours. The challenge will be held in Venice again in 2007.

REGATA DELLE CENTO VELE
The splendid Hundred Sails Regatta is held in summer (May-June) and involves traditional lagoon sailing vessels with triangular sails (this is lugsailing, or *vela al terzo*). The prize is the Coppa del Presidente della Repubblica (President's Cup). The boats also parade in the Bacino di San Marco and along the Grand Canal.

JUNE

VENEZIA SUONA

The streets and squares of Venice burst into musical life during Venice Plays, an annual music fest. Bands of all descriptions fill the evening air with good musical cheer on the third or final Sunday of the month. Performances run from 4pm to 10pm.

JUNE–OCTOBER-NOVEMBER

BIENNALE INTERNAZIONALE D'ARTE

This major international exhibition of visual arts started in 1895 and was held every even-numbered year from the early 20th century. The 1992 festival was postponed until 1993 so that there would be a festival on the Biennale's 100th anniversary in 1995. It is held in permanent pavilions in the Giardini Pubblici, and at other locations in Venice, including parts of the Arsenale, Palazzo Grassi and Palazzo Correr. In alternate years the Biennale Internazionale d'Architettura (Biennial International Architecture Exhibition), the architecture version, is staged. In 2003 a new element was added with the Festival Internazionale di Danza Contemporanea (International Festival of Contemporary Dance), held annually from mid-June for about six weeks.

JULY

FESTA DEL REDENTORE

The Feast of the Redeemer is marked by yet another regatta on the Grand Canal. The main celebrations, however, take place at the Chiesa del Redentore on Giudecca on the third weekend of the month. The Senato (Senate) ordered the construction of this church in 1577 in thanksgiving for the end of a bout of the plague. Every year thereafter, the doge (leader, duke), members of the Senato, other VIPs and sundry citizens celebrated by crossing the canal over a provisional pontoon bridge to give thanks. The doge is no more, but the tradition has continued. All sorts of boats fill the Canale della Giudecca to join in the festivities, as the city folk wander to and fro across the pontoon. The highlight is an extraordinary (and extraordinarily long) fireworks display above the Bacino di San Marco.

AUGUST-SEPTEMBER

MOSTRA DEL CINEMA DI VENEZIA

The Venice International Film Festival, Italy's version of Cannes, is organised by the Biennale committee and held annually at the Palazzo della Mostra del Cinema on the Lido.

TOP FIVE UNUSUAL EVENTS

- **Regata della Befana** The first of more than 100 regattas on the lagoon throughout the year is held on the day of the Epiphany (6 January), only this one features witches and broomsticks aboard the boats! In Italy, La Befana is a good, witch-like personage who, according to legend, accompanied the three wise men, distributing sweets to children everywhere, hoping that one would be Jesus. Italian children go to sleep on the night beforehand (the night the three wise fellows, according to tradition, arrived with gifts for the Christ child) wondering what La Befana will bring them. Traditionally, good children got sweets and naughty ones a lump of coal. In more modern times the lump of coal became a sticky sweetie. This used to be the main gift-giving feast, rather than Christmas. Babbo Natale (Father Christmas) is a foreign import that has, sadly, largely supplanted the Italian tradition.
- **Sagra di San Pietro di Castello** The busy Festival of St Peter of Castello takes place on the last weekend of June with music, drinking and eating at the steps of the church that was once the city's cathedral. It is one of the city's longest-standing and most traditional festivals.
- **San Pellegrino Cooking Cup** This rather bizarre and light-hearted series of races around the lagoon is held over the first weekend of July. Participants combine sailing with onboard cooking.
- **Sagra del Pesce (Fish Festival)** The island of Burano comes truly alive for a weekend in September (dates vary) for this annual fish festival. Stands sell fish and polenta, which is washed down with white wine and accompanied by traditional music. In the afternoon the city's only mixed men's and women's rowing regatta takes place off the island.
- **Festa del Mosto (Grape Juice Festival)** On the island of Sant'Erasmo, northeast of the city, where wine grapes are still grown – although the final product is hardly world-class – the grape harvest is celebrated in October (dates vary) with this festival dedicated to the fruit of the vine. Food, music and wine (fermented grape juice after all!) are part of the day's fun on Venice's 'garden island'.

SEPTEMBER
REGATA STORICA
This historic series of rowing races along the Grand Canal is preceded by a multifarious parade of boats, many decorated in 15th-century style and powered by crews in period costume. Venetians first organised a rowing race in 1274, and have been doing it ever since. This regatta, one of the most important, is held on the first Sunday of the month. The parade is followed by a series of four races in different categories. The races start at Castello and proceed west up the canal to the former convent of Santa Chiara, where the boats turn around a *bricola* (pylon) to pound back down to the finishing line at Ca' Foscari, cheered on by the locals. The main event is the men's *caorline* (broad, snub-nosed lagoon vessels) race – the men need all their muscle power to make these seaborne beasts surge ahead...

NOVEMBER
FESTA DELLA MADONNA DELLA SALUTE
This procession over a pontoon bridge across the Grand Canal to the Chiesa di Santa Maria della Salute on 21 November is to give thanks for the city's deliverance from the plague in 1630.

CULTURE
IDENTITY
Just what is a Venetian? Some would say an inward-looking and dying species. The lagoon city that spread its rule across northeast Italy, as well as territories up and down and beyond the Adriatic, for two and a half centuries, was once a proud and independent-minded place. With around 64,000 permanent residents (270,000 in the whole municipality, which encompasses the other lagoon islands – totalling around 32,000 – Chioggia, Mestre, Marghera and other bits of the mainland), Venice is not what it was. Back in the 1950s some 170,000 people were resident in the city itself. The downward demographic trend continues slowly – since 1993 the historic city has lost on average about 1000 residents a year, although that drain has slowed to a trickle since 2002. Nevertheless, some say the point of no return has already been passed.

The people of the Veneto region (population 4.54 million) in general have a reputation akin to that of the Scots – canny with money. They are said to be hard-working and thrifty but not necessarily the life of the party. The Venetians are a bit of a special case. The city long considered itself apart from the rest of Italy, and even today you get the feeling that the sentiment has changed little. There is a reserved air about the place – not unfriendly by any means, but slightly impenetrable. The impression is no doubt reinforced by the fact that, long ago stripped of its economic importance and overrun by *foresti* (non-Venetians), locals find themselves living in closed and ever-diminishing circles. That said, they can be extraordinarily welcoming once you have invested some time in the place.

LIFESTYLE
Living in Venice presents its challenges. To get anywhere you either walk or catch a ferry. The latter is frequently as time-consuming as the former, and so the city hums to the sound of padding feet. There are certain unwritten rules. Walking in single file in narrower streets allows more purposeful individuals to move ahead – a little like a human bus and taxi lane.

Commuting this way means you will sooner or later run into people you know. This can slow the day down, especially if you decide on a quick afternoon *spritz* (*prosecco*-based drink).

Even the simplest daily matters are approached differently. How much shopping you can do is limited by what you can carry – there are no weekend shopping excursions in the car. Locals still use the fruit and fish markets, abhorring the deep-frozen stuff. Moving house involves hiring a removals boat. If you have a large enough window overlooking a canal, so much the better – it's easier to hoist things up from the boat than to drag furniture around to a street entrance. Living on the ground floor is not a great idea – humidity and damp are constant companions, even without flooding.

The pace of life is refreshingly human, slowed down by the absence of cars (boats are not supposed to travel at more than 5km/h inside Venice proper). On summer weekends many locals chug out to the Lido for a day at the beach.

GONDOLAS & CO

There was a time when the only way to get about effectively in Venice was by boat. But things have gradually changed over the past few centuries as more and more canals and other waterways have been filled in and bridges have been added. Today Venice is really a pedestrian city and not, as often romantically imagined, a boat town. Of course, the canals are the only way to move goods around, but your average Venetian will walk to get from A to B. Only when they have to get from one end of town to the other will they bother with vaporetti, while the *traghetti* (commuter gondolas) come in handy for crossing the Grand Canal at strategic points and cutting down walking detours to bridges.

All this means that mucking about in a gondola is nowadays largely a tourist activity. Back in the 16th century someone calculated the number of gondolas in use in Venice and came up with the figure of 10,000. It would be interesting to know how they worked it out. At any rate, considerably fewer ply the canals today. There are about 400 licensed gondoliers, all men. They form a tight-knit guild and women appear not to be welcome. The few who have tried to get the license have all failed the exacting exam, although not a few sceptical tongues speculate that their only failing was simply being women.

Gondola owners used to paint their vessels every colour of the rainbow, and those with money to spare went to enormous lengths to bedeck them with every imaginable form of decoration. Finally, the Senato decided in 1630 that this was getting out of hand and decreed that gondoliers could paint their vessels any colour they wanted as long as it was black. Nothing has changed since.

No-one knows for sure the origin of the term 'gondola', but it seems probable that it came from the Near East. These people-movers don't just come in the standard size you see every day on the canals; special ones come out to play for regattas. They include the *dodesona* (with 12 oarsmen), the *quatordesona* (14 oarsmen) and the *disdotona* (18 oarsmen). The *gondolino da regata*, or racing gondola, is longer and flatter than the standard model.

More observant visitors will soon start to make out other types of vessel, used for work and pleasure. Perhaps the most common is the *sandolo* and its little brother, the *sandoletto*, with squared-off prow and stern. Two standing oarsmen power them along, although a skilled oarsman can row either one alone. The *vipera* is similar to the *sandolo* but pointed at each end – having no stern, it can be rowed in either direction. It was introduced by Austrian customs officials; if they suddenly found bandits scooting away behind them, it wasn't necessary to turn around to chase them! More common is the *mascareta*, used for pleasure-rowing about the lagoon.

Plying the canals is a series of heavy, sluggish-looking transport vessels powered with outboard motors. Known as *peate*, they are the city's workhorses and are used for everything from vegetable deliveries to house removals. The *bragozzo* is similar but sometimes has sails on two masts. Typical of light lagoon-going transport vessels is the *caorlina*.

In times past the construction and maintenance of all these vessels required the expertise of the *squerarioli*, master carpenters and shipbuilders, who often came from the mainland (as that is where the timber came from). *Squeri*, the small-scale shipyards where they carried out their trade, once dotted the city. By 1612 the *squero* near the Chiesa di San Trovaso (Map pp294–5) employed 60 masters and scores of apprentices, who built not only gondolas but also trading vessels. Run by the Della Toffola family and easily the most visible (and photographed) in Venice, it still does brisk business today. Only two other traditional *squeri* exist in Venice proper, that of the **Tramontin family** (Map pp294–5; Calle della Chiesa, Dorsoduro 1542) and, virtually next door, **Bonaldo** (Calle del Balastro, Dorsoduro 1545). The last great gondola builder, Nedis Tramontin, died in February 2005, but his son Roberto is keeping the family tradition alive. A further two relatively new *squeri* operate in Giudecca.

Making a good gondola is no easy task – seven types of wood are employed to make 280 pieces for the hull alone. Also, it has to be asymmetrical. The left side has a greater curve to make up for the lateral action of the oar, and the cross section is skewed to the right to counterbalance the weight of the gondolier.

Nowadays, a master craftsman can build a gondola in about a month. Your standard model costs from €20,000. If you want more fancy ornament, the price starts to rise. A really 'pretty' gondola can cost more than €50,000. Only senior and experienced gondoliers tend to go for such luxury. They do so in part as a sign of their standing within the profession and also in the hope of attracting more or better-off customers. A newly arrived gondolier, however, will satisfy himself with a simple, second-hand vessel to get started in the business. A gondola will last 20 to 30 years and, if it's well made, often longer.

FOOD

Some commentators, such as Venice's own historian Alvise Zorzi, claim that true Venetian cuisine has all but disappeared. Whether or not this is true is open to debate, and one hopes that Zorzi's faith in the rebirth of interest in good cooking (and eating!) will save any traditions that might have been on the verge of extinction.

Eating in Venice is more costly than elsewhere in Italy. This is partly due to the greater expense of waterborne transport. In some restaurants there is undoubtedly an element of cheek involved too, despite all protests to the contrary. Venetian restaurateurs are a little like farmers – always crying poor.

Traditional Venetian food revolves around products fished in the lagoon and out at sea. Remarkably, most of the products you see in the markets are still fished locally, and restaurant owners who know their stuff can tell instantly which critters have been caught in the vicinity. Much seafood is seasonal. Anything that's on menus year round is imported at least part of the time. That in itself is no problem, but often products are *surgelati* (deep-frozen) and largely tasteless. Better Venetian restaurants pride themselves on using only fresh fish and seafood bought that morning at the markets. For restaurant and café reviews, and practical information about eating in Venice, see p140.

Staples

The staple in northeast Italian cuisine is humble indeed – polenta. This maize-based stodge is to Venetians what couscous is to North Africans. It generally arrives at the table in the form of lightly grilled yellow slabs. A less common version is made of a fine maize and has the appearance of porridge. By itself it's pretty sad, but used to soak up sauces and the like during a meal it comes alive.

No man can live on polenta alone. Two dishes form the next basic rung up. *Risi e bisi* is a kind of risotto broth with peas. Despite the often lurid green appearance, it is tasty when properly prepared. Sometimes it's served with ham and parmesan cheese. In the Veneto, people tend to take their peas seriously – some towns even stage Sagre dei Bisi (Pea Parties). It takes all sorts.

Perhaps even more common is *pasta e fagioli* (in Venetian, *pasta e fasioi*). This is a peasant dish *par excellence* that people unable to afford much meat have been munching for centuries. To the basic mix of short pasta, dried *fava* beans, onion, olive oil, salt and pepper, you can add pretty much anything you want to liven it up.

City Life

CULTURE

Snacks & Starters

Cicheti (bar snacks) are a Venetian speciality. A classic *antipasto* (snack or starter) is *sarde in saor*, sardines fried in an onion marinade, a favourite since the 13th century. Anything fishy fried in *saor* tastes good. The secret is in the *saor* marinade, which comes out better still with a few *pinoli* (pine nuts). Onions played a big part in traditional Venetian cuisine as a preventative measure against scurvy, especially for those at sea.

Variations on the *baccalà* (dried cod) theme are legion. It is good served with polenta, which absorbs some of the fish's natural saltiness. A classic is *baccalà mantecato* (mashed cod prepared in garlic and parsley).

> ## FOREIGN TASTES & VEGANS BEWARE
>
> Venice is a small town and there is little in the way of foreign cuisine – about half a dozen restaurants spanning Japanese to Indian. Since 2003 a rash of kebab spots have opened up. Vegetarian restaurants are also thin on the ground (read: nonexistent), although a couple of places can accommodate most vegetarian needs. Vegans, however, will do it tough.

Another delicacy is *granseole* (large spider crabs that live at the bottom of the Adriatic), at their best from October to December. *Cape sante*, or coquilles St Jacques, often feature with pasta, but as a snack they're fried in olive oil and garlic, with parsley, lemon and a little white wine added at the last minute. *Moeche* (small shore crabs fished when shedding their shells, in March-April and November-December) are also good but tend to be expensive. *Peoci* (Venetian for mussels, known as *cozze* in Italian), *schie* (microscopic grey prawns) and other shellfish all feature prominently, and the list of bite-sized seafood items served up for *cicheti* is as long as the sea is deep. The Venetians also tend to have their own names for everything – the best advice is to get in there and pick and choose. Among the meat starters is *cotechino*, a type of pork sausage served with mustard. You could stand at an *osteria* (restaurant/bar) and make a whole meal of *cicheti*.

Verdure fritte (vegetables fried in breadcrumbs) are also good. A Venetian obsession is *articiochi* (the Venetian-dialect word for artichokes, which are *carciofi* in Italian; baby artichokes are called *castraure*). If you hang around produce markets you may well see buckets of carefully cut *fondi di articiochi* (artichoke hearts) in water. The height of the season is around June, and the best come from Sant'Erasmo. Locals swear that, fried with parsley and garlic and accompanied by a steak, *articiochi* will send your taste buds to heaven. They are right.

Primi Piatti (First Courses)

Risotto, basically a rice-based stew (think of the Spanish paella and you'll begin to get the idea), comes in many varieties. Among the possible ingredients are mushrooms, courgettes (zucchini), sausage, quail, trout and other seafood, chicken and spring vegetables. Not to be missed is *risotto in nero*, coloured and flavoured with *seppia* (cuttlefish) ink.

Only a few types of pasta, such as *bigoli* (a kind of thick, rough spaghetti), really have a long standing in the Venetian tradition. *Bigoli* is ideal for seafood sauces, which stick to it better than to other pastas. A classic is *bigoli alla busara*, with scampi and a mild red sauce. (Be careful when you talk about *bigoli*, as *bigolo* is also slang for a boy's naughty bit.) Gnocchi, made of potato, is strictly speaking a Veronese speciality but has been absorbed into the Venetian tradition.

Among the soups, the best known is *sopa de pesse* (in Italian is *zuppa di pesce*, fish soup).

Secondi Piatti (Second/Main Courses)

Seafood is popular but often expensive. The prices you see for some fish are per *etto* (100g). The cost of fresh fish is high, so cheap meals generally mean frozen fish is used. Common fish types include *branzino* (sea bass; good when boiled), *orata* (bream) and *sogliola* (sole).

Those not keen on seafood will on occasion be frustrated in Venice, as many *osterie* and restaurants specialise in watery delights and offer few, and in some cases no, meat alternatives.

This is not to say meat dishes do not exist. Of land-going critters, pork and its derivatives figure strongly in the more traditional foods, along with items such as *fegato* (liver) and even *milza* (spleen; an acquired taste) or *mammella di vacca* (cow udder). Don't worry – all the more standard cuts of *manzo* (beef), *agnello* (lamb), *vitello* (veal) and so on are available. Try boiled meats with *radicchio trevisano* (bitter red chicory), eaten baked, in risotto or with pasta.

If you were to try only one meat dish in Venice that you had never had before (or even if you had), it would have to be *carpaccio*. We all know that the Bellini was invented in the Cipriani family's Harry's Bar (see The Cocktail Circuit, p160), but less well known is that the idea to serve plates of finely sliced raw beef in a simple sauce was also 'cooked up' there. The sauce is a mix of mayonnaise, crushed tomato, cream, mustard and a dash of Worcestershire sauce. The Ciprianis named it after Vittore Carpaccio, because at the time the artist was the subject of a big exhibition in Venice. A common variation on the theme sees the beef slices bathed in lemon, *rucola* (rocket) and shavings of *grana* cheese.

SPORT

Venetians like their *calcio* (football) as much as any Italians, but fans have precious little to crow about at the moment. With their team, Venezia, languishing at the bottom of the second division and risking relegation, the island stadium at Sant'Elena can be melancholy.

Rowing is a more local passion, although clubs complain of declining interest. Nine rowing associations dot Venice, Mestre and the lagoon, and locals compete in frequent regattas all year round. Some of the most important are gala events (see the City Calendar, p10) and attract passionate local support. *Voga alla veneta* (Venetian-style rowing, ie standing up) is the local style, but Venice has produced world champions of *voga all'inglese* (the English seated version). *Voga alla vallesana* is a rowing style where one person uses two oars.

Venetians like sailing, too. *Vela al terzo* involves traditional, shallow-hulled lagoon vessels rigged up with vaguely triangular main sails. Yachting is virtually impossible in the treacherous lagoon.

See the Activities section of the Entertainment chapter (p173) for tips on getting involved in rowing, as well as other sporting activities.

LANGUAGE

Italian in Venice comes with its own unique flavour. Since the unification of Italy into one kingdom in the latter half of the 19th century, the issue of language has been vexed up and down the country. Venice is no exception.

Standard Italian, with its roots in the Tuscan dialect of Dante, is spoken by pretty much everyone but often with a strong local lilt. Influenced by Venessian (one of several dialects making up what linguists refer to as Venet, the language of the Veneto region), Venetians clip and chop consonants to some extent. *Ciao bello!* (hi handsome!) becomes *ciao beo!* in the local tongue. Many locals stick grimly to their dialect, although others tend to mix Venessian with Italian – giving Italian speakers from other parts of the country the impression at times that they understand everything, only to be confounded halfway through a sentence.

Documents from the time of the Republic show a disconcerting mix of Italian and Venetian (Venessian). Only with modern standardisation and universal schooling in the course of the 20th century have

TOP FIVE VENETIAN FOOD BOOKS

- *The Harry's Bar Cookbook* Arrigo Cipriani
- *The Da Fiore Cookbook* Damiano Martin and Dana Bowen
- *Veneto: Authentic recipes from Venice & the Italian Northeast* Julia della Croce
- *A Tavola con I Dogi. Storia con Ricette della Grande Cucina Veneziana* (Dinner with the Doges: History and Recipes of Great Venetian Cooking) Alvise Zorzi
- *Chow! Venice: Savouring the Food & Wine of La Serenissima* Ruth Edenbaum and Shannon Essa

dialects, or dialect-Italian mixes, been relegated to a clearly secondary place in Venice and elsewhere in Italy.

To start chatting in Italian, turn to the Language chapter at the end of this book (p266).

ECONOMY & COSTS

The fall of the Venetian Republic in 1797 had its economic fallout. The Austrians favoured their own Adriatic port, Trieste, over Venice, although they did establish the railway line that links the city with the mainland and Milan to this day. Inevitably, Venice stagnated. While Italy's northwest embarked on a programme of industrialisation in the 1880s, the northeast remained stubbornly rural and poor. Well after the end of WWI, more than 60% of the region's workforce was involved in agriculture.

Industrialisation came mainly with the creation and expansion of Porto Marghera in the 1920s. In the following decades, the port and the metallurgy, chemical and petrol industries became major employers. But it was only well after WWII that small-scale industry began to take off around the Veneto. By the late 1980s, only 7% of the population worked in agriculture, while 40% worked in manufacturing and 53% in services. The Veneto region contains around 8% of the country's population, but contributes 15% of exports (second only to Lombardy, which accounts for nearly 30%).

Tourism plays a pivotal role in the life of the Veneto, and above all in Venice. In 2004, according to regional statistics, nearly four million people overnighted in Venice. Estimates on day-trippers range from 15 million to 20 million a year!

Venice is the third most expensive city in Italy after Milan and Rome. Property prices are inflated by the hordes of holiday-flat owners and limited space. Rents, too, are high.

GOVERNMENT & POLITICS

Venice is the capital of the Veneto region (one of 20 regions in Italy), which extends west to Verona and the Lago di Garda and north into the Alps. The region is subdivided into seven provinces, of which the area around Venice – Venezia – is one (provinces are named after the main town in each). The other provinces are Belluno, Padova (Padua), Rovigo, Treviso, Verona and Vicenza.

Since 1927 the *comune*, or municipality, of Venice has comprised the islands of the lagoon (including Murano, Burano, Torcello, the Lido and Pellestrina), as well as Mestre, Porto Marghera and Chioggia on the mainland. Locals often divide the lot into three general areas: *terraferma* (mainland), *centro storico* (Venice proper, including Giudecca) and the *estuario* (all the remaining islands).

Traditionally, Venice is divided into six *sestieri* (municipal zones): San Marco, Castello, Cannaregio, Dorsoduro, Santa Croce (Santa Crose) and San Polo. Nowadays the territory of the *comune* is divided into 13 *quartieri* (quarters). The *sestieri* and the island of Giudecca (which is part of the Sestiere di Dorsoduro for administrative purposes) are grouped into the first two of these *quartieri*. The remaining 11 cover the lagoon islands and the mainland.

In April 2005 left-leaning philosopher Massimo Cacciari was elected for the third time as *sindaco* (mayor) of Venice in a neck-and-neck second ballot with judge Felice Casson, another left-wing candidate. The first round of these chaotic elections had seen 11 candidates stand.

Mistrust of government in Venice is as strong as anywhere in Italy. There is a feeling that little is done to address the city's acute long-term problems: diminishing population, flooding, pollution, and the extra-high cost of housing, exacerbated by the hotel-opening frenzy since the late 1990s. Rather than actively encouraging new businesses to set up in Venice and aiding people to get access to housing, Venice's town fathers, for all the noise they make, seem content to allow the city to slip further down the slope into an open-air museum.

Many Venetians want separation from the mainland parts of the Venice municipality. In the four referendums on the subject since 1979 the no vote has always won, but the gap has narrowed. Those in favour claim their city would be better served by a town hall that concentrates its energy and resources on solely Venetian issues.

ENVIRONMENT

Venice is under siege. For the most part, public attention to the city's ailments has focused on flooding and the chilling cry of *'Venezia sprofonda!'* ('Venice is sinking!').

THE LAGOON

For hundreds of years the city's greatest defence was its unique lagoon position. Now, the one-time guarantor of Venice's survival seems bent on the inexorable eradication of the city.

The territory of the Comune di Venezia extends over 457.5 sq km, of which 267.6 sq km are lagoon waters, canals and so on. On the mainland, the city's boundaries take in 132.4 sq km. The *centro storico* is just 7.6 sq km of land, while the remaining islands together total 49.9 sq km.

It is tempting when gazing across the lagoon to think of it as a simple extension of the sea. No impression could be more mistaken. The Adriatic forces its way into the lagoon through three *bocche di porto* (port entrances) that interrupt the bulwark of narrow sandbanks strung north to south in a 50km arc between the mainland points of Jesolo and Chioggia.

The lagoon was formed by the meeting of the sea with freshwater streams running off from several Alpine rivers. It is like a great shallow dish, crisscrossed by a series of navigable channels. These were either the extension of river flows or ditches created by the inflow of seawater. One of the deepest is the Grand Canal, which runs through the heart of the city. It is thought to have been an extension of the Brenta (which has since been diverted south).

Passarelle *(walkways)* are erected when acque alte *(high tides)* cause flooding in the city's main squares *(see opposite)*

No-one knew the lagoon better than the Venetians – whenever invaders threatened (such as in 1379–80, during the Battle of Chioggia), the Venetians would pull up buoys marking the course of navigable channels and so pretty much close access to the city. The channels are marked today by lines of *bricole* (wooden pylons).

More than 40 islands and islets dot the lagoon. The better-known ones include the Lido, Pellestrina, Murano, Burano and Torcello. The tinier ones have served as convents, quarantine stations, hospitals, madhouses and cemeteries. Today some belong to the city of Venice, while others are privately owned. One has become a luxury hotel. Some, such as San Michele, are easily accessible, while others have been abandoned to decay.

The 7.6 sq km of Venice today wasn't always there. The islands that together formed Rivoalto were a fraction of the area now covered. The very shallowness of the lagoon allowed the next step. Along the edge of the deeper channels, the inhabitants began to expand their

A SINKING CITY

Venice can be flooded by high tides. Known as *acque alte*, these mainly occur between November and April, flooding low-lying areas of the city such as Piazza San Marco. Serious floods are announced several hours before they reach their high point by 16 sirens throughout the city and islands. Although there is nothing new about the phenomenon (disastrous floods have been recorded since at least the 13th century), the wailing of the sirens is becoming an increasingly common part of the Venetian winter.

When floods hit, buy a pair of *stivali di gomma* (Wellington boots or gumboots) and continue sightseeing. *Passarelle* (raised walkways) are set up in Piazza San Marco and other major tourist areas of the city (you can pick up a map of them at the tourist office), and the floods usually last only a few hours. If the flood level exceeds 1.2m you can be in trouble, as even the walkways are no use then.

Since 1900 Venice has sunk by more than 23cm (some claim the real figure is much higher – anything up to 60cm), partly due to rising sea levels and partly due to subsidence. Climate change could cause a global rise in sea levels of 40cm to 60cm by 2100, which would make the city uninhabitable if no preventative measures are taken. Floods have become increasingly common and even occur out of the usual wet season.

Another major concern is water pollution. Until the years after WWII, the Adriatic Sea's tidal currents flushed the lagoons and kept the canals relatively clean (so clean that Venetian kids played in them until the end of the 1950s). But the dredging of a 14m-deep canal in the 1960s to allow tankers access to the giant refinery at Porto Marghera changed the currents. And the dumping of chemical waste from Porto Marghera has made things much worse. In the wake of the *Prestige* oil tanker disaster off Spain in 2002, single-hull tankers of the *Prestige* type were banned in the lagoon, and in 2005 worldwide.

As though pollution were not enough, the salt water – even when unpolluted – is corroding the foundations of the city's buildings (not to be confused with the city's pylon foundations, upon which the houses are built). Canalside buildings could start to collapse if nothing is done to combat the corrosion. Indeed, big problems have already revealed themselves. The Punta della Dogana has had to be shored up with injected cement. Gaping holes have appeared along some waterside walkways.

The good news, perhaps (many do not agree), is that a plan to install mobile flood barriers (known as the Mose project) at the main entrances to the lagoon, after decades of stalling over the pros and cons, seems to be going ahead. In 2002 the government in Rome approved the first phase around the Malamocco lagoon entrance (the main shipping lane into the lagoon), which will include a semicircular breakwater to reduce the effect of high seas pushed up the Adriatic by southerly winds, and a lock for waiting ships while the barriers are up. In all, 79 mobile barrier gates will be installed. They will be activated when floods of 1.1m above mean sea level (which occur on average about five times a year) threaten the lagoon. Work began in May 2003, and if all goes perfectly well the project could take eight years. Few believe it will be completed so quickly. Worse, many believe it will not work and that other measures (many would start by filling the petrol-tanker canal) are required.

The Mose project is the centrepiece of a wide series of measures aimed to protect the city. In 2003 work got underway to protect Piazza San Marco, one of the lowest and hence worst-affected spots in the city. The waterside will be raised to 1m above mean sea level, and subterranean rainwater run-offs will be repaired (often water bubbles up through these into the square).

Many remain sceptical about whether the system will even work (and about how and to whom the contracts have been awarded) but now that it is going ahead both its supporters and detractors will be praying it all works. If it fails, it will not only be an extraordinarily costly white elephant, but Venice's long-term fate could be sealed.

tiny islands. They did this by creating platforms on which to build new structures. Pine pylons were rammed into the muddy lagoon floor, then topped by layers of Istrian stone. The action of the sea water on the wood caused a process of mineralisation that hardened the structure, while the upper stone layers were impervious to the tides. It was an ingenious solution and the method has remained pretty much the same to the present day.

The lagoon, however, is under threat. Petrochemical waste is dumped into it from the Porto Marghera plants (only in 2004 did the regional president Giancarlo Galan take a stand on putting an end to the production of certain chemicals). The national society for oncological medicine declared in 2004 that Venice had become the leading city in terms of per capita cases of tumours. The extraction of fresh water from the beneath the lagoon has also contributed to subsidence problems in Venice.

The digging of a major transit channel for tankers in the 1960s and other interventions have radically altered natural flushing mechanisms. This and overfishing put pressure on the fragile marine life. And the rush of water from the sea into the lagoon through the deep channel is a big part of Venice's tidal problems.

The blatant disrespect of motorboat drivers for lagoon speed limits causes *moto ondoso*, the damaging waves that eat away at Venice's buildings but also destroy the *barene* (mud banks) that help keep the lagoon alive. Worse, giant cruise ships, instead of being slowly towed to their moorings, barge in under their own steam, causing heavy wave damage.

Huge sums are spent on preserving the *barene* – but little is done to bring the boat drivers to heel. Gondoliers (along with many others) protest against *moto ondoso* and in Mestre some organisations are clambering for a referendum on the shutting down of Porto Marghera's chemical operations. Ecologists and forward-thinking urban planners dream of reconverting the entire Porto Marghera industrial complex into environmentally friendly terrain, with hi-tech parks and other projects. But, for the moment, dreams they will remain. Motorboats also pollute, and in 2005 the first of four LPG stations was opened in the lagoon. Authorities hope that at least 20% of private motorboats will switch to this cleaner combustible fuel. At the 2005 Salone Nautica di Venezia a prototype hydrogen-powered vaporetto was also unveiled, although when such boats might go into service is anyone's guess.

If the lagoon and the many related environmental issues interest you, pop into **Punto Laguna** (Map pp294–5; ☎ 041 529 35 82; Campo Santo Stefano, San Marco 2949; ☯ 2.30-5.30pm Mon-Fri). It has a range of brochures, some in English, as well as videos and computers on which to search out specific information.

GREEN VENICE

Surprisingly for a city built out of the water, an extraordinary amount of greenery decorates Venice's private gardens. Public parks, however, are in short supply. The only ones of note are the Giardini Pubblici, created at the Castello end of town under Napoleon at the expense of a great deal of fine buildings, the rather small Giardini Papadopoli, near the bus station, and Parco Savorgnan, in Cannaregio.

Although there is frequent debate on recycling, refuse collection remains a basic affair. People leave plastic bags out on the street on collection nights and the lot is tossed into rubbish barges.

Arts & Architecture

Arts & Architecture

Venice was by tradition a city of practical people – merchants interested above all in the business of trade. This is not to say they were aesthetically indifferent; the reality is quite the opposite, as is evident in its periods of artistic greatness. In architecture in particular the city is adorned with an array of jewels that span early medieval Byzantine to the Renaissance splendour of Palladio.

In the visual arts the lagoon city was slower off the mark. The most glorious period came with the late Renaissance, taking in the 15th and 16th centuries and sputtering to a close in the early decades of the 17th century. Some masterly flashes followed in the form of the Tiepolos and Canaletto, but, like the Republic itself, the power and the glory belonged to the past. Venice attracted as well as bred artists – many big names came from surrounding mainland territories of the Veneto. Foreign visitors were not scarce either. Everyone from Albrecht Dürer to El Greco to Turner passed through.

Other arts, such as music and literature, seem to have excited Venetians less. A handful of exceptions tend to prove that rule.

The contemporary scene in a sense continues the historical trend. Reduced to a backwater when the Republic fell in 1797, Venice never completely recovered culturally. Sure, artists were at work through the 19th century and into the 20th century (as best seen in the Galleria d'Arte Moderna, p70), but true greatness rarely sparkled. The high notes of the art scene today come from the outside, particularly in the form of the temporary shows of the Biennale Internazionale d'Arte (Biennial International Art Exhibition; p11).

ARCHITECTURE

Of the early centuries in the life of Venice, no visible sign remains. The bulk of the city's surviving architectural testimony dates from the 11th century.

VENETO-BYZANTINE

East was West. That Venice stood apart from the rest of Italy is never clearer than in the city's monuments, whose inspiration is a mixture of Western and Byzantine influences. The obvious starting point is not in Venice at all, but on the island of Torcello. While Venice proper was still a motley collection of muddy refugee settlements, Torcello was a booming focal point. Its people raised the Cattedrale di Santa Maria Assunta (p93), a singular lesson in cross-cultural experimentation. Essentially following the Byzantine style that can be seen in the basilicas of Ravenna, its builders were also influenced by the Romanesque developments to the west. The iconostasis separating the central nave from the presbytery was a prime feature of Eastern Orthodox churches. The apses (dating to the 7th and 9th centuries) are the single clearest echo of the Romanesque style born in the Lombard plains to the west.

The real treasures are inside. Craftsmen from Ravenna created extraordinary mosaics, including the 12th- to 13th-century Madonna col Bambino (Madonna and Child) in the semidome of the central apse. Some art historians rate this work more highly than anything done in Constantinople itself.

TOP 10 NOTABLE BUILDINGS
- Basilica di San Marco (p51)
- Palazzo Ducale (p58)
- Chiesa di Santa Maria dei Miracoli (p77)
- Ponte di Rialto (p73)
- Arsenale (p80)
- Chiesa di San Giorgio Maggiore (p91)
- Libreria Nazionale Marciana (p57)
- Ca' Rezzonico (p63)
- Chiesa di Santa Maria della Salute (p65)
- Chiesa di Santa Maria Gloriosa dei Frari (p72)

Chiesa di Santa Maria del Giglio (p56), Sestiere di San Marco

Use of mosaics dates from Roman times and continued under the Byzantine Empire. In Venice the use of a gold background became the norm. Nowhere is that clearer than in the dazzling décor of the city's star attraction, Basilica di San Marco (p51). This also started off as a three-nave basilica when it was founded in the 9th century to house the remains of St Mark. Later, two wings were added to create a Greek-cross form, again a Byzantine idea (and based on the Church of the Holy Apostles in Constantinople). To the casual observer the clearest signs of its Eastern form are the five domes – add a couple of minarets and you could almost think yourself in Istanbul. Less visible from the outside, but still another characteristic that separates the basilica from Western churches, is the narthex (or atrium) wrapped around the front and side of the church up to the arms of the cross.

The basilica, with bits and pieces added on and redone over the centuries, is a bit of a hodgepodge. Romanesque elements are clear in the main entrances, and Gothic and even Renaissance contributions demonstrate the difficulty of easily categorising some monuments, built and altered over centuries.

ROMANESQUE

The architectural expression of Europe's reawakening, this style that swept across Western Europe made less of an impact on Venice. In some cases it was mingled with Byzantine building styles. Much of what was built in more purely Romanesque style was later demolished and replaced.

One reasonable surviving example is the Chiesa di San Giacomo dell'Orio (p71) in Santa Croce. Here you can see all the classic elements of the style. The Romanesque church tended to be squat and simple, with up to three apses. Decoration was minimal and the semicircle dominant. Doorways and windows, in the church as well as in the square-based and equally squat bell towers, were capped by semicircular arches. Architectural or sculptural ornament was otherwise virtually absent from most Romanesque buildings, at least in the earlier days. The pretty cloister at the Museo Diocesano d'Arte Sacra (p85), just east of the Palazzo Ducale, is a perfect specimen of Romanesque simplicity.

As the grander Gothic fad caught on, church authorities had few qualms about rebuilding churches from scratch, seeing little value in the Romanesque versions, judged too simple and modest for the Lord's houses. Oddly enough, the bell towers that stood beside them were frequently left intact.

GOTHIC

In the 13th century Gothic winds began to prevail in Venice, although the more sensual Byzantine aesthetic continued to inform artistic and architectural thinking. One way of identifying Venetian Gothic is by looking at the windows. Where you see them in clusters, with their tops tapering to a point, you can be reasonably sure the building you are looking at is Gothic (or perhaps a remake!). It is, however, a very Venetian twist on the theme – the shape of the windows is a hallmark of Byzantine and Eastern influences.

Of the city's great Gothic monuments, the Palazzo Ducale (p58) stands out. It is a remarkable creation and representative of the unique turn the style took in Venice. What you see is a mixed result: building started in the early 15th century, with several extensions and then reconstruction after fires in the late 16th century. The graceful porticoed façades facing the Bacino di San Marco and the square are given a translucent quality by the use of white Istrian stone and pink Veronese marble. Elsewhere the decoration is restrained. This is less the case on the side nearest the Basilica di San Marco: the carving on the Porta della Carta and the Arco Foscari are fine examples of the intricacy achieved in Gothic sculpture.

The two greatest Gothic churches in Venice were built earlier, at the height of the style's sway. The Chiesa di Santa Maria Gloriosa dei Frari (p72) was completed in 1443 (after a century's work), while the Chiesa dei SS Giovanni e Paolo (aka San Zanipolo; p82) was completed in 1368. Both are magnificent edifices on a Latin-cross plan. Decoration of both lasted long after construction was completed and reflects changing tastes. The Frari, a tower of elegance in brick, eschews almost completely the twisting lacelike external decoration typical of French and German Gothic. SS Giovanni e Paolo is partly decorated in marble and shows signs of the transition to the Renaissance. The churches are interesting for several reasons. Their relative sobriety of ornament underlines the fact that, throughout Europe, the Gothic style took many shapes and forms. These massive churches also symbolised the rivalry of two of Christendom's most important orders, the Franciscans (who built the Frari) and the Dominicans (who built SS Giovanni e Paolo).

THE POWER OF PALLADIO

Although Palladio (1508–80) was active in Venice, the greater concentration of his work is in and around Vicenza. Palladio's name has a far greater resonance for a wide audience than any of his contemporaries, largely because his classicism was later taken as a model by British and American neoclassicists. The White House in Washington, DC owes much to Palladio.

Palladio is best known for his villas (p234) in the Venetian hinterland. Of them, La Rotonda (p233), just outside Vicenza, is among the most famous. The villas were built for local nobility or those well-to-do Venetians who had turned their backs on the sea. They were conceived with a double role in mind – pleasure dome, and control centre over agricultural estates.

Steeped in the classicism of Rome that had inspired much Renaissance architecture, Palladio produced buildings rich in columns and triangular pediments and occasionally with a central dome (as in La Rotonda). Palladio's version of Renaissance architecture is often described as 'archaeological' due to his unswerving recourse to antiquity.

Palladio was made Venice's official architect on the death of Sansovino in 1570. His single greatest mark on the city was the Chiesa di San Giorgio Maggiore (p91) on Isola di San Giorgio Maggiore. Even in the distance, seen from Piazza San Marco, its majesty cannot fail to impress. He also built the Chiesa del Redentore (p90) on Giudecca and the magnificent façade of the Chiesa di San Francesco della Vigna (p83).

It is no accident that Palladio received commissions to work his particular magic in such relatively isolated corners of the city. Bereft of significant surroundings, these grand churches, with their weighty columns, high domes and strong classical façades, command respect – and are best contemplated at a distance. What's more, the conservative authorities in Palazzo Ducale had no intention of letting him loose in central Venice. Palladio was no conservationist nostalgic and would have demolished half the city to rebuild in his modern style had he been given half a chance.

Palladio died before finishing many of his projects, including Chiesa di San Giorgio Maggiore. For their completion we are largely indebted to Vincenzo Scamozzi (1552–1616), who faithfully carried out their designer's plans. Scamozzi did his own thing, too, designing the Procuratie Nuove in Piazza San Marco (completed by Baldassare Longhena).

Many architects at work in Venice were Lombards. Mauro Codussi (aka Coducci; c 1440–1504), from Bergamo, was responsible for the imposing façade of the 1483 Chiesa di San Zaccaria (p84), although much of the florid Gothic flavour (the apse is a good example) is the work of another architect, Antonio Gambello. Codussi also built several of the patrician families' grand *palazzi*.

RENAISSANCE

The Renaissance cracked over Italian and then European society like a burst dam. Revelling in the rediscovery of the greats of classical literature, philosophy, science and art, writers, thinkers and artists embarked on a frenzied study of the ancient and an impatient search for the new. This was most publicly reflected in construction.

If Gothic churches soared high into the heavens, reminding people of their smallness compared with the Almighty, Renaissance grandeur spread laterally, luxuriating in the power of the human mind and the pleasure of the human eye. While tall Gothic spires might be topped by the cross, a building such as the Libreria Nazionale Marciana is low, flat-roofed and topped by statues. It is a house of learning.

Of course, it is not as simple as that. Among the identifying signs in Venetian Renaissance building is a proclivity for spacious rounded arches on all levels (usually two but sometimes three storeys). Fluted half-columns often feature on the upper storey, but otherwise ornamentation is generally restrained. The classical triangular pediment borne by columns is another common touch, seen clearly at the front of Andrea Palladio's Chiesa di San Giorgio Maggiore.

During this period three of the city's master architects were from elsewhere. Jacopo Sansovino (1486–1570), whose real name was Tatti, was born in Florence, and lived and worked there and in Rome. Michele Sanmicheli (1484–1559) was from Verona, but he also was drawn to Rome. The sack of that city in 1527 spurred them both to leave. Sansovino moved to Venice and Sanmicheli back home. Both remained from then on in the service of the Republic. Palladio (1508–80) was from Padua; read more about him in The Power of Palladio, opposite.

Sansovino dominated the Venetian scene. He had a hand in 15 buildings, among them La Zecca (the Mint; p57), the Palazzo Dolfin-Manin (p111) on the Grand Canal, Ca' Grande (p117) and the Chiesa di San Francesco della Vigna (p83). Perhaps the most prominent testimony to Sansovino's work in Venice is his Libreria Nazionale Marciana (aka Biblioteca di San Marco, or Libreria Sansoviniana in memory of its creator; p57).

Sanmicheli's most important contribution to La Serenissima was Palazzo Grimani (built 1557–59; p111). The Republic's leaders kept him busy engineering defence works for the city and Venice's scattered possessions.

Quite a deal older than the others, Pietro Lombardo (1435–1515) was another out-of-towner. While he was chiefly a sculptor, his latter years were occupied principally with building. One pleasing result was the 1489 Chiesa di Santa Maria dei Miracoli (p77).

BAROQUE & NEOCLASSICISM

The 17th century in the Venetian building industry was dominated by Baldassare Longhena (1598–1682). A master of baroque, which took to florid ornament in seeming reaction to what some plainly considered the austerity of the Renaissance, Longhena cannot be said to have fallen for the most extreme of its decorative excesses.

His masterpiece is the Chiesa di Santa Maria della Salute (p65), the great dome of which dominates the southeastern end of the Grand Canal and not a few Venetian postcards. An octagonal church, its classical lines are a reminder of Palladio, but the sumptuous external decoration, with phalanxes of statues and rich sculpture over the main entrance, shows where Longhena was headed. To see where he ended up, you only need to look at the opulent façade of giant sculptures of the Ospedaletto (p86).

In Venice's last century of independence, neoclassicism came into vogue. One of the senior names of the period was Giorgio Massari (1686–1766). Inspired by Palladio, his more lasting works include the Chiesa dei Gesuati (p63), Palazzo Grassi (p118) and the completion of Ca' Rezzonico (p63) on the Grand Canal.

THE PRESENT DAY

Palladio frequently found himself up against the conservative habits of the town fathers. His plans for the Palazzo Ducale and for a new Rialto bridge were overruled. The attitude persists to this day but not necessarily with the same happy results. A design for a magnificent building on the Grand Canal by Frank Lloyd Wright and Le Corbusier's plans for a hospital in the area of the former Macello Comunale in Cannaregio are among many to have received the thumbs down.

It wasn't always thus, and some could even say Fascism wasn't all bad. Out on the Lido, the Palazzo del Cinema and former Casinò (the latter is now used for congresses) were built in under a year in 1937–38, double-quick time for structures that, in those days, were remarkable in their concept and used for staging grand congresses.

Venice, a labyrinth of canals, tight streets and urban-planning restrictions, leaves little room for innovative building. But lately the city appears to have been bitten by some kind of design flea – with notably little success or progress, however.

What was supposed to be a sparkling new addition to the city, the Ponte di Calatrava (p73), designed by Spaniard Santiago Calatrava and set to lie between Piazzale Roma and Ferrovia, is an elegant and airy bridge of glass and steel, a smallish leap into the 21st century – on paper. Already a source of controversy in Venice because of its apparent superfluity, the proverbial poo hit the fan when it was revealed in March 2005 that design faults could wind up leaving it half finished. Writs began flying, and Venetians looked set for a long and unhappy saga.

Meanwhile, what is happening at the Punta della Dogana? Milan-born Vittorio Gregotti, one of the country's leading architects, was charged with its remake after the last of the customs offices vacated the building in 2002. The Guggenheim Foundation was supposed to establish a modern-art museum here but the project fell through, leaving the future of the site up in the air and Gregotti somewhat irritated.

Outside the city, Frank Gehry has been given the go-ahead to transform Marco Polo airport with his Venice Gateway project, his first commission in Italy. A series of buildings seemingly half-covered in billowing drapes (or spinnakers according to the official interpretation) and what might pass for rigging will symbolise the air, the sea and the dynamism of the Veneto region. The project (which seems to be taking a while to get started) will add a water terminal, a five-star hotel, a shopping complex and a congress centre – and will surpass the wavy imagination of Gehry's Guggenheim project in Bilbao, Spain.

All this is not to say that nothing was ever done before. The best known of Venice's modern architects was Carlo Scarpa (1906–78). He designed the entrance to the Istituto Universitario di Architettura di Venezia in Santa Croce (p126) and redesigned the inside of several museums, most notably the Palazzo Querini Stampalia (p86). He also worked on pavilions for the Biennale in Castello from 1948 to 1978.

PAINTING & SCULPTURE

Venice's artistic golden era coincided with its expansion across northeastern Italy. It was a happy combination, for as Venice became the capital of a considerable land empire it attracted artists from its newly acquired territories. All of this happened as the winds of the Renaissance finally began to blow over the region in the first half of the 15th century. Many of the greatest names in Venetian art did not come from

Chiesa di San Stae (p72), Sestiere di Santa Croce

Venice, and many moved around in search of patrons, so that much of their work was either produced in other cities or has found its way to distant collectors' homes and galleries.

The Venetian Renaissance peaked with the 16th-century greats. A handful of geniuses studded the following centuries, which were otherwise increasingly lacklustre.

The arrival of Napoleon in 1797 was a disaster. In the years of his Kingdom of Italy (1806–14) he and his forces systematically plundered Venice and the region of their artistic treasures. Many were whisked away to Paris, while countless others were sold off at hasty auctions.

Venice sank into provincial obscurity and its art went with it. The 19th century was a mostly stuffy and academic time, and more adventurous outbursts through the 20th century, while interesting, rarely resulted in greatness. Today Venice largely wallows in its glorious past. A plethora of galleries flog a variety of lazy lounge-room art and unconvincing commercial contemporary stuff. Only a handful make a serious attempt to be at the cutting edge.

TOP FIVE MUSEUMS

- Palazzo Ducale (p58)
- Museo Correr (p57)
- Ca' Rezzonico (p63)
- Museo della Fondazione Querini Stampalia (p87)
- Museo d'Arte Orientale (p71)

Arts & Architecture

PAINTING & SCULPTURE

PRELUDE

Before the late flowering of the Renaissance here, Venice followed a largely pedestrian trail. The glory of its mosaic tradition (Venetian mosaicists worked in cities across the northern half of Italy) dominated the Middle Ages, and the likes of Paolo Veneziano (c 1300–62), perhaps Venice's most notable Gothic-era artist, could not break free from the Byzantine mould. His *Madonna col Bambino* (Madonna and Child; Gallerie dell'Accademia, p66) is a perfect example. The almost expressionless face of the Virgin Mary and the Christ child inside the almond with a gold background are typically Eastern iconic touches.

Some of Venice's best Gothic sculpture is represented in the tombs of the dogi (leaders, dukes) Michele Morosini and Marco Corner in the Chiesa dei SS Giovanni e Paolo. The latter was done by a Pisan, Nino Pisano (c 1300–68). Sculptors never achieved the renown of some of their counterparts elsewhere in Italy, notably Florence and Rome. Renaissance tombs of several dogi in the same church are among the city's most important Renaissance sculpture.

The real innovative impetus in painting came from the mainland. Tuscans such as Donatello and Filippo Lippi worked in Padua and influenced the work of Padua's Andrea Mantegna (1431–1506). Although Mantegna never worked in Venice, he became the conduit between that city and the fresh new Florentine artistic vision. He embraced the new idea of depicting perspective and injected a lifelike warmth and movement into his paintings.

The Renaissance was, in essence, a joyous rediscovery of classical models. They served as a launch pad to shoot away from the didactic but largely motionless world of Gothic art, itself an outgrowth of the still more instructive and exclusively religious Romanesque era.

This new wave brought another change. Although some Gothic-era artists had begun to sign their work, it was only with the Renaissance that painters and sculptors truly began to emerge from centuries of artisan anonymity. That said, artists continued to operate as small businesses, running workshops and often having only a supervisory role in the execution of many orders. For this reason, paintings are often attributed to an artist's workshop rather than the fellow himself. In some cases doubt remains over whose brushes were used. Although no longer anonymous, most artists are known to us by sobriquets – Veronese was from Verona, Tintoretto was the 'Little Dyer' because his father was a *tintore* (dyer).

Various Venetian painters, among them Jacopo Bellini (c 1396–c 1470) and Murano-born Antonio Vivarini (c 1415–c 1480) came into contact with Mantegna, but it was Antonio's brother Bartolomeo (c 1432–99) who picked up the baton. Altarpieces by him can be seen in the Santa Maria Gloriosa dei Frari (the Frari; p72), San Giovanni in Bragora (p83) and SS Giovanni e Paolo (p82) churches, as well as in the Gallerie dell'Accademia (p66). He filled his best and most lively paintings with a vivacious colour and crystal luminosity that were altogether new in Venice.

THE BELLINI BOYS & CO

Jacopo Bellini's sons Giovanni (1432–1516) and Gentile (1429–1507) proved less reticent about plunging into the new artistic wave than their father, who no doubt kept a keen eye on the order book and preferred to deliver what his clients wanted. Gentile had a crystal-clear eye for detail, evident in works such as *Processione a Piazza San Marco* (Procession to St Mark's Square; Gallerie dell'Accademia). A specialist portraitist in his early career, he was sent to Constantinople in 1479 to do Sultan Mehmet II's profile (now in London's National Gallery).

Giovanni shone out still more. The clarity of his characters, dominating their landscape backdrops, betrays Mantegna's influence, but Bellini extracts greater variety in tone and colour, creating a new softness and a meditative quality. He also experimented with oil, which would replace tempera (powdered pigments mixed with egg yolk and water). His works are scattered across the globe, but some can be admired in the Gallerie dell'Accademia, Museo Correr (p57) and elsewhere in Venice.

The following generation bubbled with enthusiastic artists. Among them were Vittore Carpaccio (1460–1526), Lorenzo Lotto (c 1480–1556), Cima da Conegliano (c 1459–c 1517) and Giorgione (1477–1510), the last two from the provinces. Carpaccio has left us some wonderful scenes that give us clues as to what the Venice of his day looked like, but the most extraordinary works come from Giorgione. He eschewed the usual route of the workshops, wrote poetry and music, and danced to his own tune. Credited with inventing the easel and teaching Titian, Giorgione was a man out of time. He painted *La Tempesta* (The Storm; Gallerie dell'Accademia) without having first drawn his subject – a striking step into new territory.

THE GLORY

Venice might have been slow to catch on to the Renaissance, but with the dawning of the 16th century came the immortals.

Titian (Tiziano Vecellio; c 1490–1576) was a 'sun amidst the stars', as one admirer put it. Born at Pieve di Cadore, Titian brought an unprecedented poetic approach to painting, full of verve and high drama. Confirmation of his status as leading artist of his day came in 1518 with the unveiling of his monumental *Assunta* (Assumption) in the Frari. His fame spread across Europe, and he executed portraits of the greatest leaders of his day, from Habsburg emperor Charles V to Francis I of France. Little of his work remains in Venice. A few pieces adorn the churches of Santa Maria della Salute (p65), I Gesuiti (p78) and San Salvador (p56). His most poignant work is in the Gallerie dell'Accademia. The *Pietà* (the dead Christ supported by the Virgin Mary), intended for his burial chapel, was finished by Palma il Giovane. Titian was carried off by the plague before he could finish it.

Titian was a hard act to follow, but he had fierce competition from Venice's Jacopo Robusti, aka Tintoretto (1518–94), and Paolo Caliari, or Veronese (1528–88).

Tintoretto is regarded as the greatest of all Mannerists in Italy, going beyond Michelangelo's lead away from the more classical Renaissance, and right up with the singular El Greco in Spain. Indeed the latter, who studied in Venice in 1560, may have encountered Tintoretto. Some of their works show surprising similarities.

Mannerism is one of those twilight phases in the history of art, falling between the splendours of the late Renaissance and the excesses that would come with baroque in the 17th century. It is characterised in painting by a yearning to break with convention and a certain wilful capriciousness in the use of light and colour. In his earlier stages, Tintoretto's paintings are dominated by muted blues and crimsons and spectral figures. He also relished three-dimensional panoramas – see his *Crocifissione* (Crucifixion; Scuola Grande di San Rocco, p75) – and a swift, airy brush stroke. Much of his work is

TOP FIVE GALLERIES

- Gallerie dell'Accademia (p66)
- Peggy Guggenheim Collection (p68)
- Galleria d'Arte Moderna (p70)
- Galleria Franchetti (p76)
- Scuola Grande di San Rocco (p75)

DIFFERENT STROKES FOR DIFFERENT FOLKS

Always in search of the new, Albrecht Dürer (1471–1528) left his native Nuremberg for Venice in 1494. Word of an artistic rebirth (the Renaissance) had reached his ears, and more intriguing news of perspective and a rediscovery of the classical world. Of all the local artists he met, Giovanni Bellini in particular took him under his wing. Dürer returned to Germany in 1495 but could not get Venice out of his system, returning in 1505, this time much fêted by the local German community. It has been said that these trips turned a Gothic painter into a Renaissance artist. Dürer also in no small degree set off what would later become quite a fashion, the pilgrimage from northern countries south to Italy in search of art, culture, light and inspiration.

The example was followed particularly by Anglo-Saxon artists and writers in the 19th century. Only now they came to capture their own images of the city rather than seek out local sages. William Turner (1775–1851) came three times (in 1819, 1833 and 1840), fascinated by the once-powerful merchant city that, like his native England, had built its greatness on its command of the sea. What stands out most in Turner's typically indistinct portraits of the city is his study of light. He painted views of the city at all times of day, capturing its spirit rather than its form. He once told John Ruskin that 'atmosphere is my style'. Ruskin loved it, but in London many critics loathed Turner's work. Nearly 40 years after Turner's last visit, American James Whistler (1834–1903) arrived in Venice in 1879, bankrupt and exhausted after a failed libel case brought against...John Ruskin. He stayed until the following year, rediscovering his verve and brush, painting the lagoon city prolifically, and returning to London with a formidable portfolio that re-established him.

Of all of the city's creative visitors, perhaps John Singer Sargent (1856–1925) was the most sedulous. Between 1880 and 1913 he was in Venice time and time again during extensive trips that took him and his canvases all over Italy. In 1908 Claude Monet turned up for a couple of months, and he too set feverishly to work, creating such memorable images as *Saint Georges Majeur au Crépuscule* (San Giorgio Maggiore at Dusk).

dominated by the dramatic use of shafts of light penetrating the dark. The Scuola Grande di San Rocco is a Tintoretto treasure chest, but also look for his masterpieces in the Palazzo Ducale (p58), the Gallerie dell'Accademia (p66) and elsewhere in the city.

Veronese, too, was busy in the Palazzo Ducale. His grand canvases are resplendent with lively colour and signal a penchant for architectural harmony. He liked to have all sorts of characters in his paintings, something that brought him uncomfortably close to the Inquisition. His *Ultima Cena* (Last Supper), done for the Chiesa dei SS Giovanni e Paolo, included figures the Inquisitors found impious, including a dog and a jester. It is unlikely that Veronese's defence of freedom of artistic expression won the day. The Inquisition was viewed unkindly by La Serenissima and so the latter decided on the face-saving solution of proposing another title for the painting, *Convito in Casa di Levi* (Feast in the House of Levi; now in the Gallerie dell'Accademia).

Other important artists of this epoch include Palma il Vecchio (1480–1528), originally from Cremona, and his grandson Palma il Giovane (1544–1628). Various works have been attributed to the former, but the younger Palma was more prolific. He finished Titian's final work, the *Pietà*. The Oratorio dei Crociferi (p78) is jammed with his work.

Another busy family were the Da Ponte, aka Bassano because they were from Bassano del Grappa (p238). Francesco Bassano il Vecchio worked in the first half of the 16th century. Four of his descendants stayed in the family trade: Jacopo (1517–92), Francesco Bassano il Giovane (c 1549–92), Leandro (1557–1622) and Gerolamo (1566–1621). Of the lot, Jacopo stands out. His works can be seen in his home town and the Gallerie dell'Accademia (p66).

ROCOCO & CITY VIEWS

The 18th century was marked by the steady decline of the Venetian Republic. In the arts, a handful of greats kept the flag flying before the end finally came.

Venice's greatest artist of the century and one of the uncontested kings of the voluptuous rococo style was Giambattista Tiepolo (1696–1770). Tiepolo lived most of his life in the lagoon city, but he spent his last years working for royalty in Madrid. You can see some examples of his work in the Chiesa dei Scalzi (p76), the Chiesa dei Gesuati (p63) and Ca' Rezzonico (p63). The Gallerie dell'Accademia has a fair smattering of paintings, too.

Tiepolo's son Giandomenico (1727–1804) worked with him to the end, returning to Venice after his father's death. Some caricatures of his, now housed in Ca' Rezzonico, presage the Spaniard Goya and the Frenchman Daumier.

On a completely different note, Antonio Canal, aka Canaletto (1697–1768), became the leading figure of the *vedutisti* (landscape artists). His almost painfully detailed *vedute* (views) of Venice, filled with light, were a kind of rich man's postcards. Many well-to-do visitors to 18th-century Venice took home such a souvenir. Canaletto was backed by the English collector John Smith, who lived most of his life in Venice, bringing the artist a steady English clientele. This led to a 10-year painting stint in London. Canaletto's success with foreigners was such that few of his paintings can be seen in Venice today.

Francesco Guardi (1712–93) became the Republic's chosen artist to paint official records of important events, such as the visit of Pope Pius VI. Guardi opted for a more interpretative, less photographic approach than Canaletto. His buildings almost shimmer in the reflected light of the lagoon. One of the few of his major works in Venice is the *Incendio di San Marcuola* (Fire at San Marcuola; Gallerie dell'Accademia).

Statue, Museo Archeologico (p57), Sestiere di San Marco

One of the rare women artists to achieve renown at this time was Rosalba Carriera (1657–1757), whose pastel portraits of the great and the good across Europe won her fame from an early age.

Born in Possagno, Antonio Canova (1757–1822) was the most prominent sculptor to emerge in late-18th-century Italy. He debuted in Venice but by 1780 had shifted to Rome, where he ended up doing most of his work. A few of his early forays, such as *Dedalo e Icaro* (Daedalus and Icarus), remain in Venice, in the Museo Correr. You could also head for Possagno (see p240).

TO THE PRESENT

Few Venetians stood out after the Republic's fall in 1797. Francesco Hayez (1791–1882) started in Venice but spent most of his life in Milan, where his work ranged from a strict neoclassicism to the more sentimental Romanticism.

Gino Rossi (1884–1947), whose career took him from Symbolism to a growing interest in Cubism, was one of Venice's biggest names in the first half of the 20th century. He frequently exhibited at the city's pre-WWI art expos in Ca' Pesaro.

One of the few noteworthy painters to emerge since WWII is Emilio Vedova (1919–). Setting out as an Expressionist, he joined the Corrente movement of artists, who opposed the trends in square-jawed Fascist art. Their magazine was shut down in 1940. In the postwar years Vedova veered more towards the abstract. Some of his works can be seen in the Peggy Guggenheim Collection (p68) and the Galleria d'Arte Moderna (p70).

Fabrizio Plessi (1940–), although born in Bologna, is seen by many Venetians as one of their own. He is known for his video art. Water is, appropriately, a central theme in his installations and sculptures, for which he combines all sorts of materials (anything from iron to straw) with videos.

LITERATURE

Venice does not enjoy a senior place in the history of Italian letters and has only occasionally taken centre stage in the minds of great writers from abroad. The lagoon city's mysterious location has, however, generated several strands of entertaining detective stories.

IN THE LIFE OF THE REPUBLIC

Not a great deal of literary consequence went on in medieval Venice. Francesco Petrarca (Petrarch; 1304–74), one of the 'big three' behind the birth of literary Italian in Florence, lived in Venice for some years, although he preferred Padua. He had already won fame for his sonnets in Italian, although he continued to write much in Latin as well.

One of the earliest Venetian writers of any importance was Leonardo Giustinian (1388–1446). A member of the Consiglio dei Dieci (Council of Ten) and author of various tracts in Latin, he is remembered for his *Canzonette* (Songs) and *Strambotti* (Ditties). They are a mix of popular verses wrought in an elegant Venetian-influenced Italian.

The shining literary light of early Renaissance Venice was Pietro Bembo (1470–1547), who in his *Rime* (Rhymes) and other works defined the concept of platonic love and, above all, gave lasting form to Italian grammar.

Bembo worked with Aldo Manuzio on a project that would help revolutionise the spread of learning – the Aldine Press (p127). From 1490 on, Manuzio and his family became the most important publishing dynasty in Europe. He produced the first printed editions of many Latin and Greek classics, along with a series of relatively cheap volumes of literature, including Bembo's *Cose Volgari* (Ordinary Things).

Playwright Carlo Goldoni (see p34) by far overshadowed the competition in the 18th century. Giorgio Baffo (1694–1768) is known above all for his risqué dialect verse (he was a pal of Casanova's and particularly enamoured of the female behind), while Francesco Gritti (1740–1811) satirised the decadent Venetian aristocracy. The bulk of the latter's work is collected in *Poesie in Dialetto Veneziano* (Poetry in the Venetian Dialect).

MODERN TIMES

EM Forster, better known for his Florentine introduction to *A Room With a View*, gave Venice a run in his first novel, *Where Angels Fear to Tread*. A young English widow flits off on the Grand Tour, marries an Italian (tut tut), dies tragically and leaves behind a young child being raised, much to the family's horror, as an Italian!

Henry James set his *Aspern Papers*, a brief tale of a literary researcher determined to get his hands on an American poet's love letters from his aged and reclusive one-time lover, in the lagoon city in the 1880s. Weightier is *The Wings of the Dove*, in which the penniless Merton Densher foists himself on the ailing heiress Milly Theale in the romantic setting of Venice. The hopes of Densher and his secret lover, Kate Croy, go rather awry.

If you were to pick up just one piece of fiction concerning Venice, Thomas Mann's absorbing *Der Tod in Venedig* (Death in Venice; 1912) should be it. The city itself seems to be the main protagonist, reducing Gustav von Aschenbach, its feeble human 'hero', to a tragic shadow.

Thudding heavily back to earth, Ernest Hemingway was in maudlin form when he penned *Across the River and into the Trees* in post-WWII Venice. It is hard not to imagine Hemingway seeing himself in his Colonel character, as he mooches about between lagoon hunts and monosyllabic trysts.

In 1963 a Venetian business association inaugurated the Campiello prize (won that year by Turin's Primo Levi for his *La Tregua*), which has become one of the country's most prestigious literary awards.

Among several scribblers at work today, Paolo Barbaro (Venetian by adoption) is one of the few Italian writers active in the city today. In *Venezia – La Città Ritrovata* (Venice Revealed), he struggles to come to terms with the wintry lagoon city after several years' absence.

In the latest wave of modern Italian literature is Tiziano Scarpa, whose first novel, *Occhi sulla Graticola* (Eyes on the Grate; 1996), set in the student ambience of the lagoon city, revolves around several love stories.

A modern hit was Ian McEwan's *The Comfort of Strangers*, an early novel (1981) in which an outsider rocks a marital boat.

Every night for 20 nights a man just diagnosed with an incurable disease writes a letter in Robert Dessaix's *Night Letters* (1997). The reader is swept up in a whirlwind of past and present, tale and musing.

Daughter of Venice (2002), by Donna Jo Napoli, is an intriguing story of a rich young girl in 16th-century Venice. The standard family plans of marriage or the convent were not for her, so she sneaks out into the streets of Venice, finds a tutor in Venetian and Latin, and in the process creates a hubbub.

In the same year Sally Vickers published her first novel, *Miss Garnet's Angel*, the twisting tale of a retired teacher and Communist who decides to set off and live in Venice for six months.

Cyprus-born Australian writer Donna Raven's first novel, *Daughter of Venice, The Last Queen of Cyprus* (2003) is an historical yarn on the life of Caterina Corner, made queen of Cyprus by Venice's wily diplomats (see A Queen Cornered, p129).

Several crime writers have found rich inspiration in Venice. Donna Leon's inspector Guido Brunetti resolves case after case in Leon's burgeoning series of detective stories, all set in the city. Try *A Venetian Reckoning, The Anonymous Venetian, Acqua Alta* and *A Sea of Troubles*. Michael Dibdin created another Venetian detective, Aurelio Zen, who tends to roam all over Italy. One book set in the detective's home town is *Dead Lagoon*.

MUSIC

Venice was the first European city to throw opera open to a broad audience by establishing public opera houses in the first half of the 17th century. Some important names were busy before this, too.

THE CLASSICS

Just because the first great names of Venetian music arose in the 17th century does not mean there was no music in Venice before. Church, court and popular music abounded, and some of it has been rediscovered. Massimo Lonardi, who plays the lute, has resurrected sounds of the past.

The greatest musical name to come out of Venice was Antonio Vivaldi (1678–1741), born in Castello. A gifted violinist from an early age, he completed his first important compositions in 1711. By the time he died he had left a vast repertory behind him; some 500 concertos have come down to us today. He was not simply prolific but also innovative, perfecting the three-movement concerto form and introducing novelties that allowed greater room for virtuoso displays. Surely his best-known concerto is *Le Quattro Stagioni* (The Four Seasons).

Overshadowed by the genius of Vivaldi was Tomaso Albinoni (1671–1750), something of a dilettante, who nevertheless produced a small body of exquisite music. Notable are the *Sinfonie e Concerti a 5*. His single best-known piece today is the airy *Adagio in G Minor*.

Bruno Maderna (1920–73), composer and conductor, was at the forefront of the avant-garde in 20th-century European classical music.

OPERA

Claudio Monteverdi (1567–1643), born in Cremona, is the father of modern opera. He cut his teeth as a composer at the court of the Gonzaga family in Mantova (Mantua) and his *Orfeo* (Orpheus; 1607) has been acclaimed as the first great opera. Monteverdi's relationship with the Gonzagas was unhappy, and he snapped up Venice's offer to make him music director at the Basilica di San Marco in 1613.

Until 1637 opera and most chamber music were the preserve of the nobility, performed in private sessions. This changed in Venice, which threw open the doors of the first public opera houses. Between 1637 and 1700 some 358 operas were staged in 16 theatres scattered across a city that at the time boasted a population of 140,000. As the only composer with any experience in the genre, the elderly Monteverdi wrote his two greatest surviving works, *Il Ritorno di Ulisse al suo Paese* (The Return of Ulysses) and *L'Incoronazione di Poppea* (The Coronation of Poppea). In each Monteverdi created an astonishing range of plot and subplot, with strong characterisation and powerful music. Although he was not Venetian, the city liked to consider him one of its own – he was buried with honours in the Frari.

Arts & Architecture

CINEMA

TOP FIVE CDS

- *Vivaldi: Four Seasons* Antonio Vivaldi (Boston Symphony Orchestra with Joseph Silverstein)
- *The Complete Concertos Opus 9 & Adagio for Organs & Strings* Tomaso Albinoni
- *Il Liuto a Venezia* (The Lute in Venice) Massimo Lonardi (16th-century Venetian music for lute)
- *Odissea Veneziana* (Venetian Odyssey) Rondò Veneziano
- *Venice Goes Ska* Ska-J

MUSIC IN VENICE TODAY

Venice's scene is dominated by opera and classical concerts by top Italian and foreign companies, who maintain full programmes at La Fenice (p172) and Malibran (p172) theatres.

On a cheesier note, baroque music groups regularly stage works by Vivaldi and company at various venues, mostly churches and other little-used religious locations, for tourists. One that has gone beyond that and produces its own compositions is Rondò Veneziano. It tours a lot and can be hard to catch in Venice.

Young folk left utterly indifferent by these offerings seek solace in a small local music scene. Jazz, blues and rock can all be seen in Venice and, more importantly, Mestre. Until 2002 Pitura Freska led the Venetian reggae wave. In its wake has come Ciuke e I Aquarasa, which does a mix of reggae, ragamuffin and rock, or what they call reggae 'n' roll. For a ska variant, try Ska-J.

Venice and the surrounding area have also produced notable jazz musicians, such as Pietro Tonolo and Massimo Donà.

For reviews of live-music venues, see p169.

CINEMA

Back in the 1980s a film archive in Venice found that the city had appeared, in one form or another, in 380,000 films (feature films, shorts, documentaries and so on). However, the city has starred in its own right in surprisingly few great flicks, tending rather to take bit parts.

From the early 1920s Venetians Othello and Casanova got their fair share of runs on the silver screen. A good one was the 1927 *Casanova* by Alexandre Volkoff.

As the German film industry collapsed in the wake of Hitler's rise to power, mostly shifting to Hollywood, Venice began to get a bit of a run there, too. Ernst Lubitsch's *Trouble in Paradise* (1932) has a lot to answer for. In his studio re-creation of the lagoon city, Lubitsch has a gondolier (dubbed with the voice of Enrico Caruso) singing that great Neapolitan song *O Sole Mio*. So that's where that irritatingly constant tourist request came from!

Orson Welles had a go at *Othello* in 1952, a film he shot partly in Venice but mostly in Morocco. The antithesis of this was standard Hollywood schmaltz, of which *Three Coins in the Fountain* (1954), directed by Jean Negulesco, is a fairly telling example. A year later, Katherine Hepburn fronted a more substantial production, David Lean's *Summertime*.

Morte a Venezia (Death in Venice), Luchino Visconti's 1971 rendition of the Thomas Mann novel, has a suitably ashen-looking Dirk Bogarde in the main role of Aschenbach. Perhaps less well known, but a better film, was Federico Fellini's *Casanova* (1977), starring Donald Sutherland. He was no stranger to Venice when he played Casanova. In 1973 he starred with Julie Christie in Nicolas Roeg's *Don't Look Now*. Based on a Daphne du Maurier novel, it shows Venice at its crumbling, melancholy best (or worst).

Venice has since made appearances in *Indiana Jones and the Last Crusade* (1989) and Woody Allen's *Everyone Says I Love You* (1996), while films set in the city include the dis-

TOP FIVE FILMS

- *The Wings of the Dove* Iain Softley
- *Morte a Venezia* (Death in Venice) Luchino Visconti
- *Pane e Tulipani* (Bread and Tulips) Silvio Soldini
- *The Venice Project* Robert Dornhelm et al
- *Othello* Orson Welles

appointing screen version of Ian McEwan's novel *The Comfort of Strangers* (1990), Oliver Parker's *Othello* (1995), and Henry James' *The Wings of the Dove* (1997), starring Helena Bonham-Carter. *Dangerous Beauty* (1998), directed by Marshall Herskovitz, is a raunchy and somewhat silly romp through 16th-century Venice seen through the eyes of a courtesan. Venice also has a bit part in the 2003 remake of *The Italian Job*, a heist story set mainly in Los Angeles that was funnier in its 1969 Roman guise with Michael Caine.

A charming Italian film, Silvio Soldini's *Pane e Tulipani* (Bread and Tulips; 1999) charts a housewife's unlikely escape from urban drudgery to the canals of Venice, where she embroils herself in all manner of odd occurrences.

Venice stars in several flicks by the city's controversial filmmaker and erotophile, Tinto Brass. Born in 1933 and trained as a lawyer, Brass has directed a mountain of films, some of them teetering on a razor's edge between serious cinema and porn. Whatever you make of his films, many agree that his vision of his home town is among the most acute (if you can see past the sex, that is). His latest effort, *Fallo!* (2003), is fairly vintage stuff. The title in Italian is a nice play on words, meaning at once phallus and do it!

On a rather different note, in 2004 Al Pacino starred as Shylock in Michael Radford's big-screen adaptation of *The Merchant of Venice*, which largely failed to meet expectations.

Almost 30 years after Donald Sutherland's rendition, Casanova got another outing in 2005 with the Swedish director Lasse Hallström's production of the same name, starring Australian Heath Ledger as the lover and Sienna Miller as the object of his desires.

THEATRE & DANCE

'Oh God,' Venetians groan as they peruse the programme at the city's main theatre, the Teatro Goldoni (p172), 'more bloody Goldoni!' The 18th-century playwright Carlo Goldoni (1707–93) bestrides the Venetian stage much as William Shakespeare dominates the English world's theatrical memory. Goldoni's stormy life saw him moving from one city to another, at times practising law but dedicating most of his energies to the theatre. Especially from 1748 the prolific playwright wrote dramas and comedies at an extraordinary rate.

Goldoni single-handedly changed the face of Italian theatre, abandoning the age-old commedia dell'arte, with its use of masks, a certain rigidity in storytelling and concentration on standard characters. This form of theatre had dominated the stages and public squares of Italy, and to a large extent France, for the previous couple of centuries, but Goldoni would have none of it. Instead, he advocated more realistic characters and more complex plots. *Pamela* (1750) was the first play to dispense with masks altogether.

Some of his most enduring works came during the 1750s and '60s. Among the best known are *La Locandiera* (The Housekeeper), *I Rusteghi* (The Tyrants; written in Venetian dialect) and *I Malcontenti* (The Malcontents). His decision to move to Paris was not an entirely happy one. With the exception of *Il Ventaglio* (The Fan), he produced little of note in the French capital, where, overtaken by the French Revolution, he lost his pension and died in penury.

Talking of theatre classics, Shakespeare's *The Merchant of Venice*, starring Shylock and a host of colourful characters, is mandatory reading for a distant Elizabethan view of what in those days must have seemed an extraordinarily exotic and bizarre city.

The modern theatre scene is not all Goldoni and Shakespeare reruns. Local theatre groups and a few small companies stage modern plays, both Italian and foreign, in Venice and Mestre. Tiny avant-garde and experimental theatrical hideaways lend a smidgen of local creativity, sometimes in dialect, to the Venice scene. For more information, see p171.

Since 2003 contemporary dance has received a thorough workout during the biennial arts and architecture extravaganzas with the Festival Internazionale di Danza Contemporanea (International Festival of Contemporary Dance).

History

History

To transport yourself back to the origins of La Serenissima Repubblica (the Most Serene Republic) – damp early days of refugees who chose the dubious swampy safety of the Venetian lagoon over the hazards of the lawless Italian mainland – get out of Venice. All the grand *palazzi* (palaces), busy canals and splendid squares – none of these existed in the beginning. Strike out for the distant scrub-covered flats of Torcello, in the north of the lagoon, where the first mainlanders sought haven as the edifice of empire and the rule of law on the mainland crumbled before the barbarian invasions at the beginning of the Dark Ages. That's how it began. Now let's wind forward a little.

THE RECENT PAST

In the summer of 2004 Venice was the scene of a wave of violent assaults…on statues. The crazed hammer attacks on the hands and arms of various pieces of public statuary around the city came to an end when the culprit, 'disturbed' according to the authorities, was arrested in July.

On 14 May 2003 Italian Prime Minister Silvio Berlusconi paid a quick visit to the lagoon city to mark what might be the end of the beginning. After 30 years of debate, bickering, slander and foot-dragging, the Italian government had finally decided to set in motion work designed to protect Venice from the increasingly damaging tidal floods.

Berlusconi unveiled the first stone in an ambitious project to protect the lagoon with a series of mobile flood barriers (among a battery of other measures), and work began. The environmental groups that claim the system will prove an expensive white elephant that may even do more harm than good attempted to block the project by legal means, but in December 2004 their case was thrown out of court. Work now continues apace, but completion is not due before 2011.

Water has dominated the history of the city from the beginning, and this particular phase of Venice's history started with record inundations on 4 November 1966. Never in living memory had such disastrous flooding been seen – the city looked set to be submerged. Ever since, debate has raged on how to protect the city, from the system of flood barriers now decided on, to lesser measures such as raising pavement levels.

The mayor from 2000 to 2005, Paolo Costa, supported the barriers project in tandem with other measures. His predecessor (and successor from April 2005), the charismatic left-wing philosopher Massimo Cacciari, sides with environmentalists, who regularly brandish impact studies showing the system cannot work. Venetians are more than sceptical about the whole thing.

Costa replaced Cacciari when the latter stepped down in 2000 in the hope of becoming president of the regional Veneto assembly. He failed in that attempt, as Berlusconi's right-wing Forza Italia party swept to power across the country and the president's position was taken by Giancarlo Galan (confirmed in regional polls in 2005). Cacciari returned to lecturing, but he couldn't resist the temptation to stand again for mayor in 2005, when Costa decided not to run for another term but to migrate to Strasbourg and a job as president of the European Transport Commission.

Berlusconi's 2003 visit to Venice was, as usual, a source of controversy. Since becoming prime minister in 2001, the media magnate turned self-appointed political white knight has made a lot of promises but seemed mostly intent on passing laws to serve his own complicated purposes. The social and political climate has heated up, with massive demonstrations,

c 1500 BC	25 March AD 421
Veneti tribes arrive in northeastern Italy	Traditional foundation date for Venice

bomb attacks and even the assassination of a senior government advisor. Venice got to feel some of the heat in August 2001, when a bomb ripped through the court buildings in Rialto just hours before Berlusconi was due to arrive for a lightning visit.

On, in retrospect, a lighter note of terror, seven young Venetian 'nationalists' invaded Piazza San Marco in May 1997 with a truck dressed up as an armoured vehicle and scaled the Campanile to place a home-made Venetian flag high up for all to see. The police were lying in wait and quickly hauled them off. The aim of this rather quixotic operation? A reminder to Venetians of their glorious past, exactly 200 years after the last doge (leader, duke) capitulated to Bonaparte and ended Venetian independence.

TOP FIVE HISTORY BOOKS

- *A History of Venice* John Julius Norwich
- *Francesco's Venice* Francesco da Mosto
- *Venice – The Biography of a City* Christopher Hibbert
- *Venice: Paradise of Cities* John Julius Norwich
- *The Venetian Empire – A Sea Voyage* Jan Morris

FROM THE BEGINNING

Legends suggest refugees from ancient Troy founded colonies in northeast Italy, just as the mythical Trojan Aeneas landed in what would one day become Rome. A more sober reading of events sees Celtic tribes, the Veneti, moving in from the east around 1500 BC. Founders of the city of Patavium and staunch allies of the Roman Empire, the Veneti would eventually be absorbed into the expanding empire and granted full Roman citizenship in 49 BC. For centuries thereafter they shared the empire's fate and lived mostly in peace, far from the frontier-expanding wars of the legions.

All good things come to an end, and by the opening of the 5th century AD, Italy was under threat as the empire slowly crumbled. In 402 Alaric led a Visigothic invasion through the province of Venetia. His hordes sacked the port and bishopric of Aquileia and pillaged cheerfully all the way to Rome. Many Veneti fled to the islands in the lagoon that stretches along part of the province's Adriatic coast, returning when the invaders were expelled. More barbarian invasions followed, the most terrible by Attila the Hun in 452, and refugees increasingly opted to stay on the islands. The nascent island communities elected tribunes and in 466 met in Grado, south of Aquileia. There they formed a loose federation and established a degree of self-rule. Little evidence supports Venice's traditional 'foundation' date of 25 March 421.

In the meantime the Western Roman Empire collapsed. Britain, Spain, Gaul and North Africa had all fallen, or were about to fall, into barbarian hands by 476, when the last, ineffectual emperor, Romulus, capitulated to the German Odoacer. Odoacer in turn was replaced by the Ostrogoth Theodoric, who proclaimed himself king in 493 and installed himself in Ravenna.

A DOGE IS BORN

In 540 the ambitious leader of the Eastern Roman Empire, Justinian, decided to turn the tide and recover Italy. Venetia (roughly equivalent to the modern Veneto region), the islands and Ravenna were quickly bound into the Eastern, or Byzantine, Empire, whose capital was Constantinople (modern Istanbul). The retaking of Italy and other former imperial territory proved costly and the successes short-lived, truncated by the Lombard invasion from France in 568. As the Lombards swept across the Po plains, refugees made for the islands in unprecedented numbers.

540	828
Byzantine occupation of Italy	Corpse of St Mark the Evangelist smuggled from Alexandria (Egypt) to Venice

WITH THIS RING I THEE WET

Pietro Orseolo's successful campaigns to subdue the Dalmatian coast and hamstring piracy earned him the title of Dux Dalmatiae. He and the nobles of Venice were so chuffed that in 998 they ordained that the events should be celebrated every year on the Festa della Sensa (Ascension Day).

The doge, accompanied by bishops, nobles and other important citizens, would sail out to the Lido on the ducal galley, the *bucintoro*, and carry out a brief ceremony: 'Oh Lord, keep safe your faithful mariners from storms, sudden shipwreck and the perfidious machinations of wily enemies.'

The ceremony developed in pomp and circumstance over the years and came to be known as the Sposalizio del Mar (Wedding with the Sea). It became customary for the doge to cast a ring into the waves just in front of the Chiesa di San Nicolò (at the northern end of the Lido) as part of this ritual. The ceremony is still carried out by the mayor today.

The new migrants settled primarily on Torcello, which would for some time remain the commercial centre of the islands, Malamocco (the southern end of what today is known as the Lido), Chioggia and Rivoalto. Rivoalto, subsequently known as Rialto ('high bank'), was no more than the highest of a small huddle of islets in the middle of the Venetian lagoon.

Anti-Byzantine uprisings had in part paved the way for the Lombards, and the Venetian lagoon communities were not immune to the spirit of rebellion. They named a certain Orso Ipato as their *dux* (leader, duke) in 726. *Dux* in Venetian dialect comes out as doge – and in this figure (another 117 dogi followed) would reside the office of head of the Venetian state for the ensuing millennium.

Various tales and legends surround the story of the creation of the first doge. It is equally possible that the *dux* was simply a military nomination by Constantinople. Some hold that Orso was preceded by two other dogi, beginning with Pauluccio Anafesto in 697.

Orso and some of his successors found it hard to resist turning their appointment into a hereditary monarchy. Such temptation had its price: Orso was assassinated, and two of his immediate successors were deposed, one of them blinded and sent into exile. Blinding became the common fate of later leaders who fell into disgrace. What slowly emerged was an electoral office, kept in check by two councillors and the Arengo (a popular assembly).

The Lombards were replaced by the Franks, who tried to invade the islands. They foundered in the lagoon, whose treacherously shallow waters only locals could navigate. In the end, Charlemagne, crowned Holy Roman Emperor in a muddy political deal with the Pope in Rome in 800, agreed to leave the so-called Duchy of Venetia to its own devices. It thus became the only part of northern Italy to remain anchored in the Byzantine sphere of influence.

THE REPUBLIC & ITS BODY SNATCHERS

The hero of the battle against the Franks was Agnello Partecipazio, from Rivoalto. He was elected doge in 809, and the cluster of islets around Rivoalto became the focus of community development. They were virtually impregnable to all who did not know how to navigate the deep-water channels that crisscross the lagoon. The duchy now began to come into its own. Its commercial and naval fleets were already the most powerful in the Adriatic, and Venetian ships were trading as far away as Egypt.

At home, Partecipazio had a fortress built on what would later be the site of the Palazzo Ducale. To the east, a church to St Zachariah (San Zaccaria) was going up at Byzantine expense. As the islands of Rivoalto were too small, too few and often too waterlogged for sustained settlement, land was drained and canals cleared. Most impressive of all, the land mass was extended by driving great clusters of wooden pylons into the muddy depths as foundations.

As Byzantine power waned, the duchy, which would become known as La Serenissima Repubblica, assumed greater autonomy. What it needed was a symbol to distinguish it from its official patrons in Constantinople. Legend had it (or was now cooked up) that the

1094	1171
Basilica di San Marco in its present form consecrated	After staged attack on Genoese in Constantinople, Byzantium orders arrest of all Venetians present in empire

Façade detail, Palazzo Ducale (p58), Sestiere di San Marco

evangelist St Mark (San Marco) had once visited the lagoon islands and been told by an angel that his body would rest there. A band of Venetian merchants decided to make true the prophecy and in 828 spirited the saint's corpse out of Alexandria, Egypt. To house the holy relics, the doge ordered the construction of a new basilica, which would rise next to the Palazzo Ducale. Thus was the Byzantine-imposed patron saint, St Theodore (San Teodoro or Todaro), upstaged. In Christian iconography St Mark is symbolised by a winged lion, an image soon appropriated by the city.

By the end of the century, local administration had been centred on Rivoalto (at the core of what, by the 12th century, would be known instead as Venezia, or Venice). A new series of bishoprics, independent but loyal to the Republic, was established to counteract leverage from Rome (ie the papacy) through the see of Aquileia. A board of *giudici* (judges) was created to curb abuses of power by the doge. None of this stopped Doge Pietro Candiano IV from trying to grab full power for himself. So incensed were the people that they burned down half of Venice before cornering the hapless would-be monarch in the flaming wreckage of the Palazzo Ducale and, with a stroke of the sword, sending him to his maker in 972.

Pietro Orseolo was elected doge in 991 and proved one of the Republic's most gifted leaders. By careful diplomacy he won the medieval equivalent of most-favoured-nation status in Constantinople *and* in much of the Holy Roman Empire. Constantinople went further before the century was out, virtually opening up all of the Orient (the lands east of the Mediterranean) exclusively to Venetian merchants. Placing trade before all other considerations, Orseolo also courted Muslim capitals from Damascus to Cordova (Córdoba).

Venice's growing prestige and prosperity could not have been better expressed than by the Oriental opulence of the Basilica di San Marco.

BYZANTIUM, BARBAROSSA & THE VENETIAN BLIND

In the wake of the First Crusade in 1095, Venice increasingly took part in naval operations in the Holy Land, almost always in return for trade concessions. But rivals Genoa and Pisa were also making their presence felt, and so Venice established the Arsenale, shipyards

1203–04	1295
Doge Enrico Dandolo leads Fourth Crusade and conquers Constantinople	Marco Polo returns home from China

in the Castello end of Venice that would become the greatest industrial site in medieval Europe. Here commercial and fighting ships could be constructed more efficiently than hitherto imaginable. Venice was going to need every last one of them.

Venetian participation in the First Crusade, although limited, spoiled relations with Constantinople. In 1171 the Byzantine emperor Manuele Comnenus staged an assault on the

A COMPLEX 'DEMOCRACY'

In early days the doge's power was circumscribed by two councillors and ultimately the will of the people, expressed by the Arengo, a popular assembly. This system proved too simple, and the Arengo gradually fell into disuse.

Instead there emerged a parliamentary body known as the Maggior Consiglio (Grand Council), made up of members of Venice's powerful and moneyed families. Technically at least, the approval of its 480 elected members was needed for any decision of moment. By 1340 it would have more than 1200 members. The Maggior Consiglio elected the doge by an incredibly complex balloting system described below. In 1298, franchise laws known as the Serrata del Maggior Consiglio (Closing of the Grand Council) effectively restricted access to the Maggior Consiglio or higher office to a caste of established noble families (although it allowed more numerous representation among these). Money alone did not constitute nobility (although this would change in the latter years of the Republic). By 1323 membership of the Maggior Consiglio had become permanent and hereditary.

The Quarantia (Council of Forty) was responsible for economic policy, while the 60-member Senato (Senate) dealt with lesser affairs. The decisions of either (which on occasion worked jointly) were ultimately supposed to be ratified by the Maggior Consiglio. In time, the Quarantia would evolve into the supreme judicial organ of the state.

The Quarantia elected three *capi* (heads) who were equivalent in status to the *consiglieri ducali* (doge's counsellors). Six of the latter were elected, one for each of central Venice's six *sestieri* (municipal divisions created in 1171). Terms lasted for a maximum of one year and *consiglieri* could not stand again for a minimum of two years.

The *consiglieri* and the three *capi della Quarantia* convened under the auspices of the doge to elaborate the bulk of policy, distributing tasks to the Quarantia and Senato. These 10 men together were known as the Signoria (Signory). With the passing of time, subcommittees evolved to deal with particular issues, often made up of *savii* (sages).

All positions were held by members of the ruling patrician class. From the 14th century some crumbs were also left to the rising middle class of *cittadini* (citizens). The biggest of them was the office of Gran Cancelliere (Lord High Chancellor), effectively the head of the civil service and superior in rank to the Senators. The Gran Cancelliere could be appointed only from among the ranks of *cittadini*.

Election of the Doge

The doge was elected by the Maggior Consiglio. His was theoretically a lifelong post but his power was heavily restricted. In an attempt to blunt family rivalries and corruption, the Venetians came up with an extraordinary system of indirect voting.

The people did not vote, although technically the Assemblea General, or Arengo, had to approve the Maggior Consiglio's choice. This body elected a commission that would then elect a candidate for doge. The members of the commission were in part elected by lottery. It worked a little like shuffling a deck of cards, picking some, and then repeating the process several times before arriving at the final choice of electoral commission. Records of the 1268 election (when the rules were tightened further) show how the vote went.

The Maggior Consiglio chose 30 members by lot, who in turn were reduced to nine by lot. These nine elected 40 members, who in turn were reduced to 12 by lots. The 12 elected 25, who were reduced to nine. These nine elected 45, in turn reduced to 11. These 11 voted for 41 members who then voted for a candidate for doge.

The 41 were locked away and proceeded with the complex electoral business. They each scribbled down the name of a candidate, and the names of all the proposed candidates were put in an urn. As each was pulled out, the candidate's suitability was discussed (if he or anyone from his family was among the 41, they had to leave the room while the deliberations continued). Then the candidate would be interviewed and voted on – if he got 25 votes, he became doge. If not, the electors went on to the next candidate. Lorenzo Tiepolo emerged as doge from the 1268 ballot; the process took 16 days from the death of his predecessor. In earlier times, the choice of the Maggior Consiglio then went before the Arengo, the people assembled in Piazza San Marco. This was rarely more than a rubber-stamp exercise.

Once elected, the doge had to sign a *promissione*, a contract defining the limits of his power. Initially a formality, the document had become a serious check on the doge's freedom of action by the mid-13th century.

1342	1409
One of the first recorded *acque alte* (high tides) inundates city	Jews obliged to wear a distinguishing 'O' sewn onto their clothes

newly formed Genoese colony in Constantinople, blaming it on the Venetians, who were promptly clapped into irons. A fleet sent to rectify this situation ended up sloping home ravaged by plague without having fired a shot. At about the same time Venice found itself joining the Lombard League of Italian city states and the papacy to oppose the designs of the Holy Roman Emperor, Frederick Barbarossa, on northern Italy. Venice was more or less at war on two fronts.

A series of reverses and excommunication convinced Barbarossa to back down. Venice was quick to seize the opportunity and staged an international public-relations coup by inviting Pope Alexander III and the repentant emperor to Venice in 1177. The spot where Barbarossa supposedly knelt before the Pope and was thus received back into the Christian communion is marked in the Basilica di San Marco to this day (although documents appear to show that both were lodged at the Benedictine monastery on the Isola di San Giorgio Maggiore and met there).

Again at peace with the Holy Roman Empire, Venice could turn its attention back to the East, where the events of 1171 had not been forgotten. When Doge Enrico Dandolo agreed to head the greatest armada yet put to sea in the service of God, few of the participants in this, the Fourth Crusade, could have known what he had in mind.

In fact, everyone involved in the negotiations of 1201 seems to have had something to hide. At any rate, Dandolo, who had lost his sight many years before, drove an extraordinary bargain: Venice would provide a fleet to carry 30,000 men (an unheard of number for such an undertaking) at a cost of 84,000 silver marks – approximately double the yearly income of the king of England at the time.

In the end, only one-third of the proposed forces turned up in Venice the following year, and their leaders couldn't pay. Venice had kept its side of the bargain. Did the wily 80-year-old Dandolo predict this situation? To compensate for their non-payment, he suggested the Crusaders help Venice out with a few tasks of its own on the way to Palestine. The most important of these involved a detour to Constantinople.

And so the war fleet pulled into the Golden Horn at the gates of Constantinople in 1203. In repeated assaults that lasted into the following year, Dandolo sacked and looted the city, put a Western (Latin) puppet emperor on the throne and had the figure of the doge declared 'Lord of a Quarter and a Half-Quarter of the Roman [ie Byzantine] Empire' – Venice's three-eighths of the spoils. The booty, including the four bronze horses that adorned the Hippodrome and would end up gracing the Basilica di San Marco, seemed boundless.

To what extent Dandolo was directly responsible for these events is unclear. Some historians suggest he did little more than play a skilful game as events unfolded, rather than plan the conquest of Constantinople. At any rate, Enrico Dandolo was for many the greatest doge to have lived. He managed to extract from this so-called Crusade more benefits for his city than anyone could have imagined. He died in a subsequent campaign in Constantinople and was buried in the city in whose capture and sack he had been instrumental.

The Eastern Empire later recovered its independence but remained a cripple among the world's powers. It is hardly surprising that it would later cave in to the green banner of Islam under the Ottoman Turks.

Venice was now at the head of a thriving commercial empire. The city's direct control of the Adriatic was undisputed. With subject cities and bases up and down the Adriatic, dotted about the Greek mainland, on Crete, Rhodes and Cyprus, in Constantinople and along the Black Sea coast, the banner of St Mark flew all over the eastern Mediterranean. The marketplaces around the Rialto teemed with produce from as far away as China – spices, silk, cotton and grain were all unloaded there for transport further on into Italy and Europe.

1479	1508
Peace treaty with Turkey after fall of several of Venice's Greek possessions	League of Cambrai formed against Venice

WAR, PEACE & THE BLACK DEATH

In the course of the 13th century Genoa's growing presence in the Black Sea and eastern Mediterranean began to upset Venice's applecart. The first scuffle came in the wake of riots between the Genoese and Venetian quarters in the Christian enclave of Acre in Palestine. This ended in an ignominious defeat for Genoa off the coast of Acre in 1258.

Three years later, Venice's luck began to look distinctly pear-shaped. In Constantinople the Byzantines, with Genoese connivance, overthrew the Latin emperor, threatening Venice's possessions and trade routes. Venice later suffered a heavy reverse at the battle of Curzola (Korc) on the Dalmatian coast, where the Republic lost 65 out of 95 vessels and the Genoese took 5000 prisoners (among them Marco Polo).

The conflict would simmer throughout the 14th century, also marked by a long spat with the Papal States over control of Ferrara and a rebellion at home in 1310. This was ruthlessly crushed and in its aftermath the Consiglio dei Dieci (Council of Ten) was set up to monitor security. It ultimately became a kind of CIA-cum-cabinet. From then the Consiglio, whose members were elected in rotation from the Maggior Consiglio, wove an intelligence network in the city and throughout Europe unequalled by any of the Republic's rivals.

Venice also found itself embroiled in a short, sharp fight against the Scaliger family, who from Verona had come to control Vicenza, Padua, Treviso, Parma and Lucca. Venice found plenty of allies willing to put an end to this dangerous expansion, and by the end of it all Venice had acquired its first mainland territories, land up to and including Treviso. For the first time Venice could now secure its own supplies of staples for a population that numbered around 200,000 (three times the population today). On the other hand, the maritime republic would never again be able to remain aloof from the intrigues of mainland politics.

At the same time, trade had never been better. The invention of the compass and the introduction of the rudder on boats had greatly improved seamanship. Commercial vessels were larger and voyages more frequent. The removal of a Moroccan blockade of the Strait

---

POLOS APART

For Venice, 1261 was a disastrous year. It had lost control of a trade nerve centre in Constantinople, and Venetian merchants were debarred from Black Sea trading bases. The new regime in Constantinople declared open season on Venetian traders, labelling them pirates. When captured, they routinely had their eyes put out and noses lopped off.

The change in circumstances caught up with the Polo brothers, Nicolò and Matteo, trading with the Mongol Khan's representatives in the Crimea. They decided the best option was to head east and so went deeper into the unknown, ending up at the court of Kublai Khan. According to some accounts they were in Beijing (the winter residence); others talk of the Khan's summer residence, Shang-tu (aka Xanadu).

The brothers returned to Venice in 1269 but two years later set off again, this time with Nicolò's 20-year-old son, Marco.

For the next few years, the Polos trundled around the Orient making a stash in the jewellery business. It took several years of overland travel from the Gulf of Iskenderun (Turkey) to China, but eventually they made it to Shang-tu. There Marco entered the Khan's service and travelled extensively in China for the following 17 years.

The Polos' return was somewhat disastrous, for they were robbed of much of their fortune in Trebizond (Trabzon in modern Turkey). No-one even recognised them when they finally made it home.

Marco's tales of adventure were the talk of the town, but sceptics began to consider them rather tall and they came to be known as *il milione* (the million) because there were so many. Three years after coming home, Marco was captured by the Genoese in the naval battle of Curzola and hauled off to a Genoese prison. There he dictated his Eastern adventures to a scribbler called Rustichello. Marco called his memoirs *Il Milione*. Freed in 1300, he returned to Venice and settled down to a quiet life. His book, known as *The Travels of Marco Polo* in English, has been the subject of constant speculation ever since his death in 1324.

1609	1670
Galileo Galilei demonstrates his telescope to the Signoria	Crete, the last Venetian stronghold outside the Adriatic, falls to Turks after a 25-year struggle

Rainwater wells (see p131) on the courtyard inside the Palazzo Ducale, Sestiere di San Marco

of Gibraltar had opened the way to more regular trading with Flanders and England. The only serious cloud on the horizon was Genoa.

But before Venice and Genoa could even begin to grapple properly, their merchant vessels had brought back from the Black Sea a most miserable import. The rats on board the vessels of 1348 were carrying the Black Death. The effect on Venice was as horrific as anywhere, with as many as 600 people dying every day. Up and down the canals, barges plied their sorry trade: *'Corpi morti! Corpi morti!'* ('Bring out your dead!') the steersmen cried.

The two powers barely paused to absorb this blow. In 1372 an incident in Cyprus sparked their last and most devastating duel. The climax came in 1379, when a Genoese fleet appeared off the Lido and took Chioggia. On Genoa's side were Padua and Hungary, busy devastating Venetian mainland territories. It was one of Venice's darkest hours.

The city worked day and night to build new ships and defences on and around the islands, especially on the Lido, San Giorgio Maggiore and Giudecca. Incredibly, the Genoese opted to starve out Venice – a decision that served only to grant the city precious time. The Venetian commander, Vittore Pisani, turned the tables by laying siege to Chioggia, but his forces were inadequate. All of Venice prayed for the return of Carlo Zeno's war fleet, which had been sent out long before the siege to patrol the Mediterranean. His appearance on the horizon at the beginning of 1380 spelled the end for the Genoese.

TURKEY ON THE MARCH

By the time the Turks marched into Constantinople on 29 May 1453 and snuffed out Byzantium, Venice had in most respects reached the apogee of its power. The Venetian zecchino had largely replaced the Florentine fiorino as the European currency of reference, and Venetian was widely spoken across the eastern Mediterranean. Local historian Alvise Zorzi recounts that a Venetian ambassador was told by a Turkish minister prior to an audience with the Grand Sultan, 'Go ahead and speak Venessian, the Grand Lord will understand'!

Since the Battle of Chioggia, the Republic had largely kept out of naval conflicts. In a series of rapid conquests early in the 15th century, it acquired a land empire stretching from

1684–87	1718
Venice joins European alliance against Turks; Francesco Morosini embarks on series of short-lived reconquests in Turkish-held Greece	Treaty of Passarowitz leaves Venice with its Italian mainland possessions, parts of Dalmatia and Istria, Corfu and a few Greek bases

Gorizia in the east to Bergamo in the west. Venice allowed the conquered cities to retain their own statutes and long had popular support from its new subjects, who found Venetian rule less capricious than that of the average Italian despot (to which they had earlier been accustomed). The local noble families, shunted aside, were clearly less enthusiastic. For the next 2½ centuries they would mostly live in peace under the standard of the winged lion, sporadic wars with Milan and other disgruntled neighbours notwithstanding.

Greek refugees poured into Venice after the fall of Constantinople and confirmed the Republic's reputation as the most Eastern of Western cities and also as one of the most tolerant (the Orthodox population was given its own church). La Serenissima's ambassadors hammered out commercial treaties with the victorious Sultan Mehmet II but were soon confronted with a harsh new reality. By 1500 the Turks had taken most of Venice's Greek possessions.

Venice's blackening mood was not helped by news of the discovery of the New World by Columbus in 1492 and Vasco de Gama's sailing around the Cape of Good Hope from India to Portugal in 1498. The Atlantic would in time overshadow the Mediterranean, with predictable consequences for Venetian trade.

Of more immediate concern was the formation of the League of Cambrai against Venice. Pope Julius II had decided that Venice was too powerful and drummed up support from France, the Holy Roman Empire (in the person of the Habsburg ruler of Austria, Maximilian), Spain and several Italian city-states. In return for cutting Venice to pieces, all were promised rich territorial rewards. In April 1509 French forces marched on Venetian territory, and within a year Venice had lost virtually all its land empire. The coalition, however, fell apart and by 1516 Venice had fully recovered its territories.

But La Serenissima, like the rest of Italy, was being increasingly overshadowed by Europe's great nation-states: France, Henry VIII's England, and the Habsburg Empire, stretching from Austria to Spain and taking in the new American colonies. More than ever, Venice had to tread a subtle line to ensure survival against the unquestionably greater powers around it. And so it adopted a policy of armed neutrality, attempting to stay out of bloody European squabbles.

For some years the Republic was able to avoid trouble from Turkey, too, which was otherwise engaged in Eastern Europe (Vienna came within an ace of falling to Suleiman the Magnificent in 1529). But it was only a matter of time. In 1537 Suleiman tried and failed to take Corfu. Frustrated, he quickly swallowed up a series of small Venetian-run Greek islands and two remaining bases in the Peloponnese. He then took Cyprus, an act that finally spurred united action by Christian powers. Venice, Spain and the Papal States vowed to assemble a fleet every year and return to the fight until 'the Turk' was destroyed.

THE PRINCE OF PLEASURE

Never was a hedonist born at a better time and in a more appropriate place. Eighteenth-century Venice had turned its back on the arduous business of running a merchant empire and maintaining a fighting fleet. Rather, it had converted itself into the pleasure capital of Europe. Into this world was born Giacomo Casanova in 1725. He was orphaned as a young boy and educated in law in Padua. Already a known rake and by all accounts (largely his own, although no-one ever contested his claims) one of the world's great lovers, Casanova got lucky when he befriended an elderly Venetian patrician, who set him up in an all-expenses-paid apartment. Venice was a licentious place, but not everything went. Denounced for an evening of foursomes with the French ambassador and a couple of nuns, Casanova wound up in the Piombi (the Leads) for his moral 'outrages'. Sentenced to five years, after 15 months he became one of the only men to escape this prison, and made for Paris. There he made his fortune and continued his adventures, fathering children (including, it appears, one by one of his daughters), contracting venereal diseases (despite his occasional use of a linen prototype of the condom) and studiously avoiding commitment. He wound up an elderly librarian in a castle in Bohemia, the ideal location for him to write (in French) his 3000-page memoirs. The fall of Venice to Napoleon in 1797 depressed him greatly – he predicted in letters that the city, stripped of its possessions and no longer a capital, would waste away. He himself passed on the following year.

1797	1846
The 1000-year La Serenissima Repubblica comes to an end as Napoleon arrives in Venice	First train crosses new rail bridge connecting Venice with the mainland

In 1571 a huge allied fleet led by Don John of Austria (much of it provided by Venice) routed the Turks off Lepanto in Greece. Venice urged its allies to press the victory home but in vain. Seeing allied resolve so brittle, Venice had little choice but to sue for a separate peace.

The watchword in the remaining years of the century was caution. Venice had by now embarked on the most illustrious period of its diplomatic career. In other words, from here on its single greatest weapon would be lots of fast talking.

DECLINE & FALL

As the 17th century dawned, Venice began a slow decline. Although eastern Mediterranean commerce had not been eliminated by the new Atlantic trade routes, Venice was suffering, which was due in part to its loss of territory to the Turks and the revocation of its trade privileges. The city's well-heeled nobs wallowed in luxury, but in the face of the great nations and empires around it, Venice had neither the will nor the manpower to equip great fleets, let alone armies.

Venice's policy of maintaining neutrality wherever possible helped turn it into a den of espionage. A rather absurd Spanish conspiracy of 1618 to seize the city from the inside was merely one example among many of the plotting that characterised life in the city.

The Consiglio dei Dieci, in its role as the state's security service, had plenty to do in these years of intrigue. Its spy network within and beyond the Republic was one of the most effective in the world. It needed to be. In the case of the 1618 plot the Consiglio, once it had been informed and gathered evidence, quietly dispatched about 300 conspirators. The Consiglio worked fast and without ceremony. Trials, torture and executions were all generally carried out in secret. That said, compared with its neighbours to the east and west, Venice remained a haven of tolerance.

Venice did what it could to avoid costly conflict, but in 1645 the Turks landed on Crete and launched a 25-year campaign to conquer the island. Venice then joined a coalition of Christian countries in a series of campaigns against the Turks in the late 17th century, but the gains were short-lived. With the signing of the 1718 Treaty of Passarowitz, Venice was left in control of its mainland empire, which included Brescia, Bergamo, Cremona, Verona, Vicenza, Padua, Treviso and the Friuli area. In addition, it had Istria, Dalmatia, parts of coastal Albania, Corfu and a spattering of other Ionian islands.

But Venice was a shadow of its former self. Its once proud navy was already in the 17th century obsolete and underequipped. The shipbuilders of the Arsenale and their techniques had long been eclipsed by their counterparts in England, France and the Netherlands. The great commercial families that made Venice's wealth and provided many of its most illustrious characters had lost interest in the sea. They neither traded nor had any desire to endure the rigours of naval life. These tasks they left mostly to the minority communities resident in Venice, such as the Greeks and Armenians. The nobles, or at least those who had not become impoverished, looked instead to their mainland estates.

Venice managed to tootle along unmolested until French revolutionary troops under Napoleon appeared. On 12 May 1797, with Napoleon's guns ranged along the lagoon, the panicking Maggior Consiglio voted the Republic out of existence. Napoleon was charmed by his new acquisition, describing Piazza San Marco as the 'finest drawing room in Europe'.

For six months the Republic lived as a puppet 'democracy' under the French. In January 1798 Venice and most of the Veneto, along with Istria and Dalmatia, passed to Austria. Venice became a playing piece to be shunted around among the great powers. For an eight-year interlude it was tied to Napoleon's Kingdom of Italy before reverting to Austria in 1814.

FROM AUSTRIAN RULE TO UNITED ITALY

What did the Austrians ever do for Venice? They built the rail connection with the mainland, dredged and deepened entrances to the lagoon to ease shipping access, implemented a street-numbering system and invented the *spritz*. The Venetians were not impressed and in

1866	14 July 1902
Venice and Veneto join Kingdom of Italy	Collapse of Campanile di San Marco, rebuilt 10 years later

Façade detail, Palazzo Ducale (p58), Sestiere di San Marco

1848 joined the long list of rebels who rose up against the established order across Europe. The Republic was again proclaimed and the city held out until August of the following year. The return of the Austrians proved to be of limited duration. Five years after the proclamation of a new united Italian kingdom in 1861, Venice and the Veneto joined it.

During the last decades of the 19th century the city was a hive of activity. Increased port traffic was coupled with growing industry. Canals were widened and deepened, and pedestrian zones were laid out. Tourism took off around the turn of the century, as the fine hotels along the Grand Canal came into their own. And by 1922 La Biennale, or the Esposizione Internazionale d'Arte (International Art Expo), was firmly in place as an added attraction.

During WWI, after their disastrous 1917 defeat in the Battle of Caporetto, the Austro-Hungarian forces were halted on the road to Venice by navy marines. Air raids on the city started in May 1915, two days after Italy declared war on Austria, and continued intermittently until 1918. Although in general they caused little damage or loss of life, one bomb dropped in 1915 and intended for the train station hit the Chiesa dei Scalzi and damaged works by Giambattista Tiepolo (these were moved to the Gallerie dell'Accademia, where they can be seen today). A 1916 bomb damaged the Chiesa di Santa Maria Formosa.

Under Mussolini a road bridge was built parallel to the railway bridge, and this marked the shift of industry to what is now 'greater' Venice: Mestre and Porto Marghera. Later these areas would bear the brunt of Allied bombing campaigns during WWII, although Venice itself came out of it unscathed. As elsewhere in post-war Italy, Venice struggled along in penury. But Harry's Bar was still in action and Hemingway was one of several celebrities to spend time here. The guns silent, Venice the charmer soon started working her magic.

By the mid-1950s things were beginning to look up, but new challenges lay ahead. The population of 170,000 started to move, slowly at first and then with increasing rapidity. Venice is pretty but also pretty inconvenient. People left in search of work on the mainland. As tourism began to take off and outsiders began to buy property in Venice for conversion into hotels and holiday residences, Venetians began to find the cost of living increasingly untenable. The process has continued to this day. One can only ask if the city, once the heart of a great trading empire, is destined, one way or another, to sink back into the lagoon from which it emerged in the dark years following the eclipse of the Roman Empire.

27 February 1918	May 2003
Austro-Hungarian planes drop almost 300 bombs on Venice	After decades of debate, work starts on lagoon barriers to prevent disastrous floods

Sights

Sights

The grandest surprise for the casual stroller in Venice is that the city is not completely teeming with outsiders in the manner of a wheat field swarming with locusts. Certainly, the main trails linking the train station to Piazza San Marco and the vaporetti of the Grand Canal are a year-round stage for the incessant, awkward pageant of international tourism. But most of Venice's visitors get little further – many are in town too briefly to venture into the unknown; others are simply too bemused by the tangle of lanes and canals that twist and bend around the cityscape like an Escher drawing. It is an uncommon pleasure to lose yourself in the backstreets and marvel in comparative calm at the many faces of this unique creation.

Of course, you will want to poke around the great monuments and art centres as well, and these are explored in this chapter. Make time to visit the outlying islands too – each is possessed of its own peculiar charm.

This chapter is divided into sections covering Venice's six *sestieri*, the 12th-century old municipal divisions, and sections on the surrounding islands and the mainland.

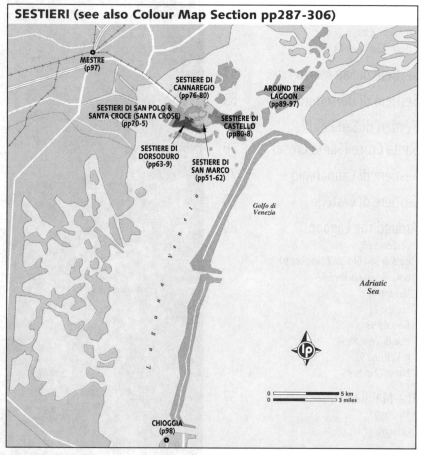

SESTIERI (see also Colour Map Section pp287-306)

MESTRE (p97)

SESTIERE DI CANNAREGIO (pp76-80)

AROUND THE LAGOON (pp89-97)

SESTIERI DI SAN POLO & SANTA CROCE (SANTA CROSE) (pp70-5)

SESTIERE DI CASTELLO (pp80-8)

SESTIERE DI DORSODURO (pp63-9)

SESTIERE DI SAN MARCO (pp51-62)

Golfo di Venezia

Adriatic Sea

Laguna Veneta

CHIOGGIA (p98)

0   5 km
0   3 miles

ITINERARIES

You could cobble together an endless variety of itineraries through the city. See the Walking chapter (p114), which contains detailed itineraries linking all the main sights of Venice proper, and not a few minor ones that are not covered in this chapter.

One Day

If you're only in town for a day and it's your first ever visit, you will find it hard to resist the obvious. Instead of the classic stroll from the train station to Piazza San Marco, you could catch the vaporetto down the Grand Canal to Accademia and visit the Gallerie dell'Accademia, followed by the Peggy Guggenheim Collection. Proceed to the grand Chiesa di Santa Maria della Salute. After visiting this church, catch a vaporetto across the mouth of the canal to San Marco, where you can finally see what you have been waiting for: the famous square and its extraordinary basilica. If you have time and energy you could explore the innards of the Palazzo Ducale and head up to the top of the Campanile for views over the city.

If you have been to Venice before and seen the big sights, you could devote a day to something different – pick one of the *sestieri* for some exploration or 'do' the island trio of Murano, Burano and Torcello.

Three Days

In three days you can get a more solid idea of the city. You could start with the one-day itinerary outlined above. The second day could be devoted to the islands of Murano, Burano and Torcello, while the final day could be dedicated to any of a number of projects. Take a vaporetto to Rialto, for instance, and explore the produce markets and shops in this area before settling in to an early lunch. Proceed through the busy lanes towards the Chiesa di Santa Maria Gloriosa dei Frari (the Frari) and the nearby Scuola Grande di San Rocco. After such a culture hit you might wander into Campo Santa Margherita for a drink, followed by a lazy stroll through Dorsoduro.

One Week

Take the above three-day programme and add a day to explore Cannaregio, including its Ghetto. Another day could be dedicated to the Lido, especially in summer when you might want some beach time. The following day could easily be spent exploring some of Castello, from the grand Chiesa dei SS Giovanni e Paolo to the curious Museo dell Icone or Museo Storico Navale. A final day (not necessarily the last) should be kept aside for a mainland excursion, say to Padua or Verona.

ORGANISED TOURS

You can join free tours for a biblical explanation of the mosaics in the Basilica di San Marco. They are arranged by the Patriarcato (the church body in Venice) and take place in Italian at 11am Monday to Saturday. Tours in English are at 11am on Monday, Thursday and Friday, and in French at the same time on Thursday. This timetable is subject to change. For more information, call ☎ 041 270 24 21 from 10am to noon, Monday to Friday.

Consult *Un Ospite di Venezia*, available from tourist offices, for details of other tours of Venetian churches and sights. The Azienda di Promozione Turistica (APT) has an updated list of authorised guides, who will take you on a walking tour of the city. Many museums, such as the Palazzo Ducale, can organise guided tours at a price. A couple of museums, including the Museo Archeologico and the Libreria Nazionale Marciana, offer free tours.

Travel agencies and hotel-reception staff all over central Venice can put you on to a range of city tours, or at least give you some brochures to point you in the right direction. **Venice Events** (☎ 041 523 99 79; www.veniceevents.com; Frezzaria, San Marco 1827; adult/student & senior/6-15yr/under 5yr €20/15/10/free; ☻ 11.15am Mon, Tue, Thu & Fri Apr-Oct, 2pm Sat & Sun Nov-Mar) runs a Venice Past and Present tour from Piazza San Marco to the Arsenale.

Sights

It includes entry to the Basilica if crowds permit. Venice Events also runs tours less frequently in the Rialto area and around the Chiesa dei SS Giovanni e Paolo. Call to book your place on each tour. Similarly priced and focused, although some of the routes are different, are walks presented by **Venice Walks & Tours** (☎ 041 520 86 16; www.tours-italy.com).

Want to be guided but remain alone? One option is the **Planetaudio** (www.planetaudioguide .com) handheld audio sets. You rent these GPS handsets for €15 a day. As you approach a sight, the handset tunes in to the relevant recorded commentary. You can also search for and listen to whatever commentary you choose. With the accompanying map, you can follow commentated itineraries to key parts of the city. If you want a break, just switch it off – you can't do that with human guides! You can hire the audio sets at the tourist offices in Piazza San Marco, Piazzale Roma and the Venice Pavilion (see p262). Languages catered for are Italian, English, French, German and Spanish. You need to leave your passport as a guarantee that you'll return the item when you've finished.

RiViviNatura (Map pp294–5; ☎ 041 296 07 26; www.rivivinatura.it, in Italian; Calle dei Vitturi, San Marco 2923) organises offbeat day tours around the lagoon. There are various options and, depending on the kind of boats used (from large traditional *bragozzi* under sail to a vaporetto), these trips can cost up to €55 per person (more if you want lunch thrown in). Trips can be organised year round, but you need to get in touch to see what can be tailor-made to your needs. The company is also developing a range of tours within Venice itself. Note that it might not always be easy to get English-speaking guides.

Grand Canal Tour (☎ 041 521 06 32; meeting point Alilaguna pier, San Marco; admission €30; ⏰ 11.30am year round & 1.30pm Apr-Oct) is a one-hour boat tour running up the Grand Canal, across to Porto Marghera, along the southern side of Giudecca and back to the starting point just off Piazza San Marco. A minimum of two people is required for the tour to take place. Several languages are catered for. The same company offers four-hour boat tours to Murano, Burano and Torcello. Tours cost €20 per person, and leave at 9.30am and 2.30pm from April to October and at 2pm from November to March. A minimum of four people is required.

Città d'Acqua (☎ 041 93 68 33; www.veniceitineraries.com; Centro Internazionale Città d'Acqua, Officina Viaggi, Via Col Moschin 14, Mestre; per person with minimum 40-person group €75, with minimum 10-person group €95; ⏰ variable) runs its singular Maree Veneziane (Venetian Tides) tours exploring various parts of the lagoon, including the Arsenale (otherwise virtually impossible to visit), Malamocco, Le Vignole and Giudecca.

SPECIAL TICKETS

A **Museum Pass** (adult/student 15-29yr €15.50/10) covers admission to Palazzo Ducale, Museo Correr, Museo Archeologico, Libreria Nazionale Marciana, La Torre dell'Orologio, Ca' Rezzonico, Museo Vetrario on Murano, Museo del Merletto on Burano, Palazzo Mocenigo, Casa di Goldoni and Ca' Pesaro. The ticket is valid for three months and can be purchased from any of these museums. A **Museum Card** (adult/student/child €11/5.50/3) covers Palazzo Ducale, Museo Correr, Museo Archeologico and Libreria Nazionale Marciana only.

Further options include a combined ticket (adult/student €8/4.50) for Ca' Rezzonico, Palazzo Mocenigo and Casa di Goldoni, and a second combined ticket (adult/student €6/4) for the Murano and Burano museums. When Palazzo Fortuny at last fully reopens there will be a combined ticket (adult/student €6/4) for it and Ca' Pesaro. Another cumulative ticket (adult/child €11/5.50) groups the Gallerie dell'Accademia, Ca' d'Oro and Museo d'Arte Orientale.

An organisation called **Chorus** (☎ 041 275 04 62; www.chorusvenezia.org), involved in the upkeep of Venice's most significant churches, offers visitors a special ticket (adult/senior & student under 30yr €9/6) providing admission to 15 churches. The ticket is valid for a year. Otherwise, admission to individual churches costs €2.50. The churches concerned are the Frari, Santa Maria del Giglio, Santo Stefano, Santa Maria Formosa, Santa Maria dei Miracoli, San Polo, San Giacomo dell'Orio, San Stae, Sant'Alvise, Madonna dell'Orto, San Giovanni Elemosinario, Gesuati, San Pietro di Castello, Redentore and San Sebastian. The ticket is available from any of the churches. Among the most worthwhile are Santa Maria Gloriosa dei Frari, Santa Maria dei Miracoli, San Giacomo dell'Orio, Santo Stefano, San Polo and San Sebastian.

A handful of museums and galleries offer reductions for students and seniors regardless of where they are from. It never hurts to ask.

Eolo (☎ 049 807 80 32; www.cruisingven ice.com; Via Croce Rossa 1181, Padua) takes you on board the like-named 1946 *bragozzo*, a typical heavy-hulled lagoon sailing vessel, for six-day trips around the lagoon. Especially tempting is the Cooking and Lagoon tour, six days of lazy sailing around lesser-known nooks of the Venetian lagoon and eating fine food on board. These tours are for six to 10 people.

The **Associazione Sant'Apollonia** (☎ 041 270 24 64) can be contacted for guided visits of several churches off-the-beaten tourist track, including the Cattedrale di Santa Maria Assunta in Torcello, Chiesa di San Pantalon, Chiesa dei Carmini and the Chiesa di San Salvador.

Waterfront scene, Sestiere di San Marco (below)

Through **M.A.C.S.** (☎ 348 341 83 92, 349 230 69 42) Manuel Vecchina and his associates run two main tours. One covers a round of typical Venetian *osterie* (restaurant/bars; €30 per person including food), but more intriguing are evening walking tours based on tales and legends of ghosts and other shiver-inducing types (€20 per person). Tours are conducted in English and are based on tales vividly recounted by Alberto Toso Fei in *Venetian Legends and Ghost Stories* and *Veneziaenigma*. Check out Toso Fei's website, www.venetianlegends.it, too. M.A.C.S. can provide wheelchair assistance for those with walking difficulties (not fully handicapped).

SESTIERE DI SAN MARCO

Eating pp142–4; Shopping pp178–81; Sleeping pp194–6; Walking pp114–21

Orientation

Largely cobbled together over the centuries by reclaiming (or simply creating) land from the salty lagoon waters, San Marco is named after the grand basilica. The area is separated from Castello, which occupies the tail of this fish-shaped city, by the waterways of Rio di Palazzo della Paglia, which runs just behind the Palazzo Ducale and Basilica di San Marco, and its continuation in the Rio di San Zulian, Rio della Fava and finally Rio del Fontego dei Tedeschi, which empties into the Grand Canal just north of the Ponte di Rialto. San Marco's other boundary is the serpentine swing of the Grand Canal between the Rialto and the Bacino di San Marco.

The glory of the Republic is long past, but Piazza San Marco remains the city's symbolic heart, a grand ceremonial space. To its north a web of narrow *calli* (streets) winds north towards the Ponte di Rialto. The heart of this labyrinth is known as Le Marzarie and has long been home to stores of all sorts. Most now cater to tourists and many sell the kind of gewgaws you are going to wish you hadn't bought. But there are also fashion stores, delicatessens, and a sprinkling of hotels and eateries.

West of Piazza San Marco, on and around Frezzaria and Salizada San Moisè is the city's chichi shopping scene. Just about every name in Italian fashion has set up around here.

BASILICA DI SAN MARCO Map p296

☎ 041 522 52 05; www.basilicasanmarco.it; Piazza San Marco; admission free; ⏰ 9.45am-5.30pm Mon-Sat, 2-4.30pm Sun & holidays; 🚊 Vallaresso/ San Marco

The Basilica di San Marco is at once a remarkable place of worship and a singular declaration of commercial-imperial might. The basilica embodies a unique blend of architectural and decorative styles, dominated by Byzantine and ranging through Romanesque and Gothic to Renaissance.

TOP FIVE FOR CHILDREN

- Grand Canal (p108)
- Museo Storico Navale (p85)
- Telecom Future Centre (p62)
- Giardini Pubblici (p85)
- Campanile, Basilica di San Marco (p55)

BASILICA DI SAN MARCO

0 _____ 30 m

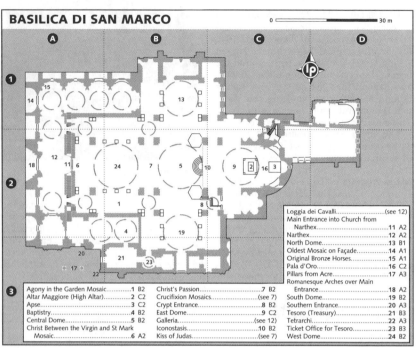

Loggia dei Cavalli	(see 12)
Main Entrance into Church from Narthex	11 A2
Narthex	12 A2
North Dome	13 B1
Oldest Mosaic on Façade	14 A1
Original Bronze Horses	15 A1
Pala d'Oro	16 C2
Pillars from Acre	17 A3
Romanesque Arches over Main Entrance	18 A2
South Dome	19 B2
Southern Entrance	20 A3
Tesoro (Treasury)	21 B3
Tetrarchi	22 A3
Ticket Office for Tesoro	23 B3
West Dome	24 B2

Agony in the Garden Mosaic	1	B2
Altar Maggiore (High Altar)	2	C2
Apse	3	C2
Baptistry	4	B2
Central Dome	5	B2
Christ Between the Virgin and St Mark Mosaic	6	A2
Christ's Passion	7	B2
Crucifixion Mosaics	(see 7)	
Crypt Entrance	8	B2
East Dome	9	C2
Galleria	(see 12)	
Iconostasis	10	B2
Kiss of Judas	(see 7)	

Building work on the first chapel to honour the freshly arrived corpse of St Mark (see Making His Mark, p54) began in 828, but the result disappeared in a fire in 932. The next version didn't have a much happier run, for in 1063 Doge Domenico Contarini decided it was poor in comparison to the grander Romanesque churches being raised in mainland cities and had it demolished.

The new basilica, built on the plan of a Greek cross with five bulbous domes, was modelled on Constantinople's Church of the Twelve Apostles (later destroyed) and consecrated in 1094. It was built as the private ducal chapel and was only made Venice's cathedral in 1807. But no-one was in any doubt that this was the city's principal church. Thus symbolically tied to the power of the doge (leader, duke), this state of affairs was an eloquent expression of the uncomfortable position of the Church in Venice, which had no intention of allowing its state interests to be subordinated to the Church (and hence the Roman Empire).

For more than 500 years the dogi enlarged and embellished the basilica, adorning it with an incredible array of treasures plundered from the East, in particular Constantinople, during the Crusades.

The arches above the doorways in the façade boast fine mosaics. The one at the left, depicting the arrival of St Mark's body in Venice, is the oldest, completed in 1270. Above the doorway next to it is a later (18th-century) mosaic depicting the doge venerating St Mark's body. The mosaics on the other side of the main doorway date from the 17th century. The one at the right shows the stealing of St Mark's corpse, while next to it the Venetians receive the body. The three arches of the main doorway are decorated with Romanesque carvings from around 1240.

The only original entrance to the church is the one on the south side that leads to the baptistry. It is fronted by two pillars brought to Venice from Acre in the Holy Land in the 13th century. The Syriac sculpture *Tetrarchi* (Tetrarchs), next to the Porta della Carta of the Palazzo Ducale, dates from the 4th century and is believed to represent Diocletian and his three co-emperors, who ruled the Roman Empire in the 3rd century AD.

On the Loggia dei Cavalli above the main entrance are copies of four gilded bronze horses: the originals, on display inside, were stolen when Constantinople was sacked in 1204, during the Fourth Crusade. Napoleon removed them to Paris in 1797, but they were returned after the fall of the French Empire. It didn't occur to anyone to send them on to the original owner, the (by now) Muslim Istanbul.

Through the doors is the narthex, or vestibule (a typical Byzantine element), its domes and arches decorated with mosaics dating mainly from the 13th century. The oldest mosaics in the basilica, dating from around 1063, are in the niches of the bay in front of the main door from the narthex into the church proper. They feature the Madonna with the Apostles. Look for the red marble spot in the floor. This marks where Pope Alexander III and Barbarossa supposedly kissed and made up in 1177 (see p39).

The interior of the basilica is dazzling: if you can take your eyes off the glitter of the mosaics, admire the 12th-century marble pavement, an infinite variety of geometrical whimsy interspersed with floral motifs and depictions of animals, made wavy by subsidence in parts. The lower level of the walls is lined with precious Eastern marbles, above which the extraordinary feast of gilded mosaics begins. Work started on them in the 11th century. Those in the baptistry and side chapels date from the 14th and 15th centuries, and mosaics were still being added or restored as late as the 18th century.

Notable mosaics are the 12th-century Ascension in the central dome; those on the arch between the central and west domes, dating from the same period and including Christ's Passion, the kiss of Judas and the Crucifixion; the early-12th-century mosaics of the Pentecost in the west dome; the 13th-century lunette over the west door showing Christ between the Virgin and St Mark; the 13th-century depiction of Christ's agony in the garden, on the right-aisle wall; the early-12th-century mosaics in the north (left-transept) dome portraying the life of St John the Evangelist; those in the east dome depicting the religion of Christ as foretold by the prophets (12th century); 12th-century mosaics in the south (right-transept) dome depicting a series of saints; and those between the windows of the apse depicting St Mark and three other patron saints of Venice, which are among the earliest mosaics in the basilica.

SAN MARCO TRANSPORT

Vaporetti No 1 and N stop at various points along the Grand Canal on their run between the train station and Piazza San Marco. Stops include Rialto, Sant'Angelo, San Samuele, Santa Maria del Giglio and Vallaresso. No 82 stops at Rialto, San Samuele and San Marco. For more information, see p246.

Separating the main body of the church from the area before the *altar maggiore* (high altar) is a magnificent, multicoloured marble iconostasis (another Byzantine element not generally present in Western churches). Dividing the iconostasis in two is a huge cross of bronze and silver. To each side, the Virgin Mary and the Apostles line up. In a crypt beneath the majestic marble *altar maggiore* lie the remains of St Mark (or so they say).

Behind the altar is one of the basilica's treasures, the exquisite Pala d'Oro (adult €1.50; ⏰ 9.45am-5pm Mon-Sat, 2-5pm Sun & holidays Apr-Sep, 9.45am-4.45pm Mon-Sat, 1-4.45pm Sun & holidays Oct-Mar), a gold, enamel and jewel-encrusted altarpiece (measuring 384cm by 212cm) made in Constantinople for Doge Pietro Orseolo I in 976. It was enriched and reworked in Constantinople in 1105, enlarged by Venetian goldsmiths in 1209 and reset in the 14th century. Among the almost 2000 stones that adorn it are 526 pearls, 320 emeralds, rubies, amethysts, sapphires, jasper, topaz and coralline. Depicted in the altarpiece are, along the

IT'S FREE

For one week of the year (usually in spring), entry to *musei statali* (state museums) throughout Italy is free. Since dates change, it is impossible to plan a trip around this, but keep your eyes open. Admission to all state museums is free for EU citizens under 18 and over 65. In Venice only a few museums are concerned: the Gallerie dell'Accademia, the Ca' d'Oro and the Museo d'Arte Orientale. Admission is also free for non-EU citizens aged 12 and under.

It costs nothing to wander into the Basilica di San Marco (although various attractions inside entail a charge), and the same goes for many of the lesser churches.

Sights

SESTIERE DI SAN MARCO

top, scenes from the life of Christ and beyond, ranging from the entry into Jerusalem to the death of the Virgin Mary, interrupted by an image of the Archangel Michael. Further down is an image of Christ Pantocrator surrounded by the four Evangelists. On either side are angels, the 12 Apostles and prophets. At the bottom appears the Virgin Mary flanked by the Eastern Emperor and Empress. The whole is framed by New Testament scenes.

The Tesoro (Treasury; admission €2; 9.45am-5pm Mon-Sat, 2-5pm Sun & holidays Apr-Sep, 9.45am-4.45pm Mon-Sat, 1-4.45pm Sun & holidays Oct-Mar), accessible from the right transept, contains most of the booty from the 1204 raid on Constantinople, including a thorn said to be from the crown worn by Christ. Some extraordinary 10th- to 11th-century chalices, made of sardonyx, alabaster, glass and silver, figure among the most beautiful pieces, along with some stunning icons and a 14th-century reliquary box that belonged to Holy Roman Emperor Charles V.

Through a door at the far right end of the narthex, stairs lead to the Galleria (aka Museo di San Marco; admission €3; 9.45am-5pm Apr-Sep, 9.45am-4.45pm Oct-Mar), which contains the original gilded bronze horses and provides access to the Loggia dei Cavalli (Horses Loggia). The Galleria affords wonderful views of the church's interior, while the loggia has equally splendid vistas of the piazza.

The basilica's mosaics are best seen when illuminated: on weekdays from 11.30am to 12.30pm and during some of the weekend Masses. You can try booking an entry time to the basilica at least two days in advance on the Web at www.alata. it (if it's working!) to avoid queuing. Access to the crypt and baptistry is possible only if you have specific permission from the church administrators.

To avoid the disappointment of being turned away at the door, dress appropriately for a religious building – no-one with bare shoulders or knees will be admitted. Note that, given the volume of visitors, a set route has been instituted and, apart from visits to the Loggia dei Cavalli, the Tesoro and the Pala d'Oro, you will probably find yourself being bustled through the main part of the church in 15 minutes or so.

If you are carrying a backpack or any other kind of bag, you must store it at the deposit located at a side entrance of the **Ateneo di San Basso** (Map p296; Calle San Basso; 9.30am-5.30pm), just off

MAKING HIS MARK

The story goes that an angel appeared to the Evangelist Mark when, while on his way to Rome from Aquileia, his boat put in at the islands that would, centuries later, constitute Rialto. The winged fellow informed the future saint that his body would rest in Venice (which didn't exist at this point!). When he did die some years later, it was in Alexandria, Egypt. In 828, two Venetian merchants persuaded the guardians of his Alexandrian tomb to let them have the corpse, which they then smuggled down to their ship in port, covered in pork to dissuade customs inspections (Egypt was then a largely Muslim country).

Why would anyone bother with such strange cargo? In those days, relics (bits and pieces of saints, real or purported) had enormous value in Christian countries, so the robbers probably saw a fast buck in the operation. Secondly, any city worthy of the name had a patron saint of stature. Venice had St Theodore (San Teodoro or Todaro), but poor old Theodore didn't really cut the mustard. An Evangelist, though, would be something altogether different. Did Doge Giustinian Partecipazio order this little body-snatching mission? We will never know. Whatever the truth, it seems that *someone's* putrid corpse was transported to Venice and that everyone rather liked to think St Mark was now in their midst. St Theodore was unceremoniously demoted, and the doge ordered the construction of a church to house the newcomer. That church later evolved into the Basilica di San Marco. St Mark was symbolised in the Book of Revelation (the Apocalypse) as a winged lion, and this image came to be synonymous with La Serenissima Repubblica (the Most Serene Republic).

Legend also has it that, during the rebuilding of the basilica in 1063, the body of St Mark was hidden and then 'lost' when its hiding place was forgotten. In 1094, when the church was consecrated, the corpse (which must have been a picture of frailty by this time) broke through the column in which it had been enclosed. 'It's a miracle!' the Venetians cried. Or dodgy plasterwork? St Mark had been lost and now was found. A grateful populace buried the remains in the crypt, beneath the basilica's high altar. Or did they? According to one story the remains were at some point sent back to Egypt, to Cairo, where they supposedly lie in a Coptic church!

Piazzetta dei Leoni. Storage is free, but there's a one-hour limit. You will not be allowed into the basilica with any bags, so don't join the queue in the hope of circumventing this rule. In the Ateneo di San Basso a video on the basilica (several languages catered for) is shown.

CAMPANILE Map p296

Piazza San Marco; adult/child €6/3; ⊙ 9.45am-8pm Jul-Sep, 9.30am-5pm Apr-Jun, 9.45am-4pm Oct-Mar; 🚢 Vallaresso/San Marco

The 99m-tall Campanile di San Marco stands apart from the church. It was raised in the 10th century and served the faithful for a good nine centuries. Then suddenly, on 14 July 1902, it just fell in a heap. The town fathers vowed to rebuild it brick by brick *dov'era, com'era* ('where it was and as it was'), which they did over the following 10 years. Alterations had already been made in the 12th and 16th centuries. On the second occasion, a statuette of the Archangel Gabriel was positioned at the tip of the tower to serve as an elaborate weather vane. Oddly, the tower contains just one bell, the Marangona, rather miraculously the only one to survive the collapse. The bell was brought to Venice from the East in the Middle Ages and no-one knows when it was made. It maintains a rare sound from another age.

In more grisly times past, particularly unfortunate criminals might be condemned to be strung up in a gibbet suspended high on the south face of the bell tower. There they would stay day and night, exposed to the elements, until their sentence was completed or they expired.

Take the lift to the top, from where there are spectacular views across the entire city.

CHIESA DI SAN BARTOLOMEO

Map p296

Campo San Bartolomeo 5178; admission free; ⊙ 10am-noon Tue, Thu & Sat; 🚢 Rialto

Long the parish church of the German community related to the nearby Fondaco dei Tedeschi, the church has undergone numerous reincarnations. Evidence suggests there was a church on this spot in the 9th century, but what you see today is the result of reworking in the wake of the building of the Ponte di Rialto and later changes. Much of the artwork inside is signed by Palma il Giovane.

Campanile (left), Sestiere di San Marco

CHIESA DI SAN MOISÈ Map p296

Campo di San Moisè; admission free; ⊙ 9.30am-12.30pm Mon-Sat; 🚢 Vallaresso/San Marco

Legend has it that the first church in this spot was founded in the 8th century, but the rather unrestrained baroque façade you see today is a product of the 1660s. Inside, among the more interesting works on view is Tintoretto's *La Lavanda dei Piedi* (The Washing of the Feet), in the sanctuary to the left of the main altar, and Palma il Giovane's *La Cena* (The Supper), on the right side of the church.

NO-NOS IN PIAZZA SAN MARCO (AND ELSEWHERE)

Stretching out for a rest on the ground, settling in for a picnic and littering Piazza San Marco are all offences attracting €50 fines. Similar fines are applied to anyone caught swimming in the Bacino di San Marco, or wandering around (anywhere in town) in swimming attire or bare-chested. Riding a bicycle (hardly a good idea anyway), inline skating or using any other wheeled mechanism is also prohibited throughout the city and punishable with similar fines.

CHIESA DI SAN SALVADOR Map p296

☎ 041 523 67 17; www.chiesasansalvador.it;
Campo San Salvador 4835; admission free; ☺ 9am-noon & 4-6pm Mon-Sat, 4-6pm Sun Jun-Aug,
9am-noon & 3-6pm Mon-Sat, 3-6pm Sun Sep-May;
🚤 Rialto

Built on a plan of three Greek crosses laid end to end, San Salvador is among the city's oldest churches, possibly dating from the 7th century (although the bulk of what you see dates from later periods). The present façade was erected in 1663. Among the noteworthy works inside is Titian's *Annunciazione* (Annunciation), at the third altar on the right as you approach the main altar. Behind the main altar is another of his contributions, the *Trasfigurazione* (Transfiguration). A stone funerary monument to Caterina Corner, unhappy Venetian Queen of Cyprus (see A Queen Cornered, p129), is on the right side of the transept.

To the right of the church is the former monastery of the same name, now owned by the national phone company Telecom, which has installed an interesting interactive communications museum there (see p62).

CHIESA DI SAN VIDAL Map pp294-5

Campo di San Vidal 2862; admission free; ☺ 9am-noon & 3.30-6pm Mon-Sat; 🚤 Accademia

No longer a functioning church, San Vidal has found a use as home to one of the many baroque-music groups active in Venice. If you find it open (hours are subject to whim), the main object of interest inside is the Carpaccio above the main altar.

CHIESA DI SANTA MARIA DEL GIGLIO Map pp294-5

Campo di Santa Maria del Giglio 2541; admission €2.50 or Chorus ticket; ☺ 10am-5pm Mon-Sat, 1-5pm Sun; 🚤 Santa Maria del Giglio

Also known as Santa Maria Zobenigo, this church's baroque façade is a fanciful atlas, centuries old, featuring maps of European cities as they were in 1678. The façade also hides the fact that a church has stood here since the 10th century.

The church is a rather small affair, but it's jammed with an assortment of paintings. Of particular interest is Peter Paul Rubens' *Madonna col Bambino e San Giovanni* (Madonna and Child with St John), the only work of his in Venice. Behind the altar lurk Tintoretto's typically moody depictions of the four Evangelists.

Outside, the oddly out-of-place brick structure in the middle of the *campo* (square) was the base of the church's bell tower, knocked down in 1775 because it was in danger of falling over of its own accord.

CHIESA DI SANTO STEFANO
Map pp294-5

Campo Santo Stefano 2773; admission to church free, admission to museum €2.50 or Chorus ticket; ☺ 10am-5pm Mon-Sat, 1-5pm Sun; 🚤 Accademia

When you walk in here, look up at possibly the finest timber ceiling (*a carena di nave* – 'like an upturned ship's hull') of any church in Venice. Then head for the small museum to the right of the altar, where a collection of Tintoretto's paintings has been crammed. Among the most notable are the *Ultima Cena* (Last Supper), *Lavanda dei Piedi* (Washing of the Feet) and *Orazione nell'Orto* (Agony in the Garden).

FONDACO DEI TEDESCHI Map p296

Salizada del Fontego dei Tedeschi 5346; admission free; ☺ 8.30am-6.30pm Mon-Sat; 🚤 Rialto

From the 13th century onwards the German trading community occupied a *fondaco* (or *fontego*, an accommodation and storage facility for foreign merchants) on this privileged site. After a fire in 1505, the present building was erected in under three years (by 1508) – not bad going.

It looks sombre now, but imagine the exterior adorned with frescoes by Giorgione and Titian. (You can see some fragments in the Ca' d'Oro, p76). When they turned up at the Palazzo Ducale to collect their payment of 150 ducats, the two artists were told their work was worth only 130 ducats. Incensed, they insisted on an independent appraisal, which confirmed the original figure. The artists were told that more than 130 ducats couldn't be arranged, so they could take it or leave it. Perhaps such penny-pinching lay partly behind Titian's increasing tendency to accept commissions from abroad!

Inside, the building is simple but dignified. The Germans used the porticoed floors above the courtyard as lodging and offices, storing their merchandise below. They even had their own well, which remains. The courtyard was covered over in 1937 and the building is now the central post office.

LIBRERIA NAZIONALE MARCIANA

Map p296

☎ 041 240 52 11; www.museicivicivenezian.it; Piazza San Marco 52; admission see Special Tickets; 🕐 9am-7pm Apr-Oct, 9am-5pm Nov-Mar; 🚇 Vallaresso/San Marco

Across Piazzetta San Marco from the Palazzo Ducale lies the gracious form of what Palladio described as the most sumptuous palace ever built. Designed by Jacopo Sansovino in the 16th century, the building occupies the entire west side of the *piazzetta* and houses the Libreria Nazionale Marciana (National Library of St Mark, aka Biblioteca di San Marco or Libreria Sansoviniana, after its architect) and the Museo Archeologico. The library extends around the corner on the waterfront into what was once La Zecca, the Republic's mint. For more on the Libreria Nazionale Marciana and the Museo Archeologico, see Museo Correr below. Admission to both is through that museum.

MUSEO CORRER Map p296

☎ 041 240 52 11; www.museicivicivenezian.it; Piazza San Marco 52; admission see Special Tickets; 🕐 9am-7pm Apr-Oct, 9am-5pm Nov-Mar; 🚇 Vallaresso/San Marco

Begun by a certain Corsican general and his lackeys as a ballroom but not completed until halfway through the 19th century under Austrian rule, the Ala Napoleonica is now home to the Museo Correr, dedicated to the art and history of Venice.

Once inside upstairs, you turn right into a hall lined with statuary and bas-reliefs by Canova. More of his creations adorn the following couple of rooms, known as the Sale Neoclassiche (Neoclassical Rooms). Keeping the statues company is an assortment of 19th-century paintings (including some works by Hayez), books, documents, medallions, musical instruments, and other bits and bobs.

From here you slide on into the rooms dedicated to Civiltà Veneziana (Venetian Civilisation), where you can inspect coins and standards of the Republic, model galleys, maps, navigational instruments and a display of weaponry from bygone days.

You are then encouraged to continue straight on to the Museo Archeologico, crammed mostly with Greek and Roman statues, along with a vast collection of ancient coins and ceramics. Some, but by no means all, of the material was collected in the Veneto. A couple of rooms are devoted to ancient Egyptian and Assyro-Babylonian objects. Free guided tours are offered in English at 11am on Saturday, and in Italian at noon on Saturday and noon and 3pm on Sunday. You will be asked to show your ticket here, as you will again in the adjoining Libreria Nazionale Marciana.

You enter the **library**, in a sense, through the back door. The Sala della Libreria (Library Room) is the main reading hall, built in the 16th century to house the collection of some 1000 codices left to the Republic by Cardinal Bessarione in 1468. The ceiling was decorated by a battalion of artists chosen by Titian and Sansovino, the architect. Veronese was considered the best; his three contributions form the second line of medallions after you enter.

The Vestibolo (Vestibule) follows. The centrepiece of its ceiling ornamentation is *Sapienza* (Wisdom) by Titian. The ancient statues cluttering the floor were part of a wider collection placed here late in the 16th century. Most were later shunted

Sights

SESTIERE DI SAN MARCO

STOP THE PIGEONS!

If you get the impression that there are more pigeons in Piazza San Marco than inhabitants in the whole of Venice, you're right. Officials estimate the pesky pigeon population at around 100,000 (but how do you count them?). Tests have shown that around 15% of the flock have salmonella and can pass it on to their hapless human victims.

Attempts to deal with these flying rats have all ended in abject failure. An effort to sterilise them with chemically treated birdseed failed because they didn't swallow it. Equally unsuccessful has been the supposed ban on feeding the little beggars. There is purportedly a hefty fine for this activity, but to judge by the (two licensed) birdseed vendors and the throngs of delighted tourists allowing birdies to poop on their shoulders (they say it brings good luck) for that memorable Piazza San Marco photo, that rule died at birth. Another idea that has been around for years is to introduce trained falcons to chase the pigeons away.

Worse than the poop on the people is that on the monuments – the acid in bird droppings eats away at the stone. People in restoration pull their hair out at the thought of the vast sums spent on restoring monuments, only to see the work imperilled by the toilet habits of these gormless creatures. Don't feed them!

over to what would eventually become the Museo Archeologico. Finally you arrive at the top end of the fine entrance stairway – a twin to the Scala d'Oro in the Palazzo Ducale across the square.

Free guided tours of the library are available in Italian and English at 10am, noon, 2pm and 3pm at weekends.

You now backtrack to the armoury in the Museo Correr. The western corridor of the Ala Napoleonica contains further baubles relating to the Civiltà Veneziana collection. About halfway along, a stairway leads up to two other collections. The modest Museo del Risorgimento, on the 2nd floor, traced the fall of the Venetian Republic and Italian unification. It has been closed for years and is opened only occasionally to house temporary exhibitions. The Arte Antica collection is a kind of Noah's Ark of largely second-rate art, starting with 14th-century Byzantine painters and proceeding to Gothic art, with a series of rooms given over to Flemish and German paintings, and a room with eight works that came out of the Bellini workshop.

After going back downstairs, you turn left to walk through the remainder of the Civiltà Veneziana collection and so return to the ticket counter. In this section you can view paintings of Venetian scenes, society games and a large collection of *bronzetti* (miniature bronzes), produced mostly in Padua and depicting everything from frogs to gods.

MUSEO DELLA MUSICA Map pp294-5

☎ 041 241 18 40; Campo San Maurizio 2761; admission free; ✆ 9.30am-8.30pm; 🚢 Santa Maria del Giglio

Housed in the restored neoclassical Chiesa di San Maurizio, this collection of rare and in many cases rather curious instruments spans the 17th to the 19th century. Accompanied by informative panels on the life and times of Antonio Vivaldi, the collection will appeal to music lovers. On sale is a huge range of music by, among others, er, Vivaldi. Concerts are sometimes held here in summer (May to October).

PALAZZO CONTARINI DEL BOVOLO
Map p296

☎ 041 271 90 12; Corte del Bovolo 4299; adult/child €3/2.50; ✆ 10am-6pm Apr-Oct, 10am-4pm Sat & Sun Nov-Mar except Christmas & Carnevale periods; 🚢 Rialto

This intriguing Renaissance mansion, hidden down narrow lanes off Campo Manin, takes its name from the dizzying external spiral (*bovolo* in Venetian) staircase. Built in the late-15th century, the palace maintains a hint of the Gothic in its arches and capitals. You can enter the grounds and climb the staircase, but it is perfectly visible from outside. The prize, however, for bothering to climb the staircase is the wonderful view from the top.

PALAZZO DUCALE Map p296

☎ 041 271 59 11; www.museicivicivveneziani.it; Piazza San Marco 1; admission see Special Tickets; ✆ 9am-7pm Apr-Oct, 9am-5pm Nov-Mar; 🚢 Vallaresso/San Marco

The Doge's Palace, a unique example of Venetian Gothic fantasy, was, along with its simpler predecessors, the political heart of La Serenissima for most of the Republic's existence. As the palace's name suggests, the doge called it home, but in its halls and dependencies were also housed all the arms of government, not to mention the prisons.

Established in the 9th century, the building began to assume its present form 500 years later, with the decision to build the massive Sala del Maggior Consiglio to house the members of the Maggior Consiglio (Grand Council), who ranged in number from 1200 to 1700. The hall was inaugurated in 1419. The whole thing rests on what amounts to a giant raft of pylons and stone blocks rammed into the muddy depths of the lagoon.

The palace's two magnificent Gothic façades in white Istrian stone and pink Veronese marble face the water and Piazzetta San Marco. Much of the building was damaged by fire in 1577, but it was successfully restored by Antonio da Ponte (who also designed the Ponte di Rialto). Thankfully,

---

QUEUE JUMPING

You can book tickets for the Palazzo Ducale (including the Secret Itineraries tour; see p60) the Gallerie dell'Accademia and Ca' Rezzonico at Weekend a Venezia (www.weekendavenezia.com). This can be handy for avoiding queues at ticket counters. You pay a service fee of €1.98 for each ticket.

Basilica di San Marco (pp51–5), Sestiere di San Marco

Palladio's pleas to have the burnt-out hulk demolished and replaced by another of his creations fell on deaf ears.

From the loggia looking onto the *piazzetta* death sentences would be solemnly read out between the ninth and 10th columns from the left, both of them darker than the remaining columns. The sentences were usually carried out between the columns on the *piazzetta*. On occasion, the condemned person might be offered one last chance to avoid the chop. They would be directed to the third column on the seaward side of the Palazzo Ducale from the corner of the *piazzetta*. Arms tied behind their back and facing the column, they had to try to turn around the column without falling off the low marble step at its base (no longer visible). They say that no-one ever managed it and that out of this rather macabre bit of Venetian humour was born a popular kids' challenge.

You enter the palace through the waterfront entrance. Infrared audioguides, which pick up an audio-loop commentary, can be hired near the ticket desk for €5.50. Beyond the ticket office and to the left is the **Museo dell'Opera**. It contains 42 capitals that once adorned the porticoes of the palace and have slowly been replaced by copies to protect the originals from further deterioration. Careful observation reveals a wealth of sculptural whimsy. On one are depicted

eight emperors and kings, from Priam of Troy to Julius Caesar. The message appears to be that, compared with the illustrious lagoon Republic, they were rather small fry.

When you leave the museum you emerge into the main courtyard. The two 16th-century wells in the middle are the most exquisite in the city. Access to Antonio Rizzi's magnificent marble Scala dei Giganti (Giants' Staircase) at the northeastern end is closed, but you can view it easily enough. It is topped by Sansovino's statues of Mars and Neptune, behind which the swearing-in ceremony of the doge took place. Here he would be presented with his ducal cap and swear fidelity to the laws of the Republic.

To continue, climb the Scala dei Censori (Censors' Staircase) to the Piano delle Logge. The floor of the loggia is a classic *terrazzo alla Veneziana* (see Of Floors & Walls, p87), of which you will see more inside the building. Wander along this gallery to the loggia that looks out over Piazzetta San Marco. When you have finished here, head back to the Scala dei Censori and beyond to Sansovino's grand Scala d'Oro (Golden Staircase). Just before you climb these stairs up to the next floor, you pass a *bocca della verità* (mouth of truth), into which people placed denunciations against wayward citizens.

Halfway up the first flight of the Scala d'Oro, turn right and then continue up more stairs to reach the series of rooms comprising the Appartamento del Doge (Doge's Apartments). Among these, the grand Sala delle Mappe (Map Room) contains maps dating from 1762 depicting the Republic's territories and the voyages of Marco Polo. Also here is the standard of the last doge, Manin. You pass through several smaller rooms on the left wing before reaching the long hall known as the Sala dei Filosofi (Philosophy Room), so called because portraits of great philosophers once hung here. Of particular interest is Titian's *San Cristoforo* (St Christopher), a fresco above a side stairwell (signposted) and one of the few works to survive the 1577 fire. They say he finished this fresco in just three days. More rooms follow in the right wing. Continue through these, cross the Sala delle Mappe again and turn upstairs to the next floor.

The highest echelons of the government met in these rooms of the palace. You enter the Sala delle Quattro Porte (The Four Doors Room, named for obvious reasons), where ambassadors would be requested to await their audience with the doge. Palladio designed the ceiling and Tintoretto added the frescoes. Titian's memorable *Il Doge Antonio Grimaldi in Ginocchio Davanti alla Fede, Presente San Marco* (Doge Antonio Grimaldi Kneels Before the Faith in the Presence of St Mark) dominates the wall by the entrance.

Off this room is the Anticollegio (College Antechamber), which features four Tintorettos and Veronese's *Ratto d'Europa* (Rape of Europa). Through here is the splendid Sala del Collegio (College Room), the ceiling of which features a series of works by Veronese and a few by Tintoretto. Next is the Sala del Senato (Senate Room), graced by yet more Tintorettos. Senators met here in the presence of the doge and the Signoria (Signory; a council that advised the doge on policy), which sat on the high tribune.

Veronese was again at work in the Sala del Consiglio dei Dieci (Council of Ten Room). This council came to wield considerable power, acting as the Republic's main intelligence-gathering agency. The next room is known as the Sala della Bussola (Collection-Box Room). Note the small box in the wall. Members of the Consiglio dei Dieci picked up denunciations left here – they were poked though a hole on the other side of the wall, rather like the way you would post a letter.

From here you follow a set of stairs on the right to the Armeria (Armoury), what is left of the palace's once considerable collection of arms. After this, you turn left down one flight of the Scala dei Censori and turn right into the Andito del Maggior Consiglio (Corridor of the Grand Council), a narrow L-shaped corridor (also known as the Liagò) off which is the Sala della Quarantia Vecchia (Old Council of Forty Room). This body oversaw administrative matters regarding the city. In the small Sala dell'Armamento (Armaments Room) next

SECRET ITINERARIES

Lesser-known areas of the Palazzo Ducale, including the original Prigioni Vecchie (Old Prisons), can be visited on the Itinerari Segreti (Secret Itineraries) tour (☎ 041 520 90 70; adult/student/child €12.50/7/4; ☉ tours in English 9.55am, 10.45am & 11.35am, Italian 9.30am & 11.10am, French 10.20am, noon & 12.25pm). Buy tickets for the tour at the Palazzo Ducale ticket desk, which is also the tour departure point.

The 1½-hour tour is an intriguing look at the underside of the palace and the workings of government in the days of La Serenissima. You are taken first through some administrative offices, small rooms in which the Republic's civil servants beavered away. You then get to pass through a torture chamber, the Sala dei Tre Capi del Consiglio dei Dieci (Room of the Three Heads of the Council of Ten) and the Inquisitors' office.

After all this, the route winds upstairs to the Piombi (Leads), prison cells beneath the roof of the building. Here prisoners froze in winter and sweltered in summer. Giacomo Casanova got five years here for his apparently wayward and reckless lifestyle. The guide will show you how he made his escape. You also get an explanation of the engineering behind the ceiling of the immense Sala del Maggior Consiglio below.

The toughest prisoners ended up in the Pozzi (Wells), two bottom storeys of dank cells at (but, contrary to popular belief, not below) water level. They are closed to the public, but from all accounts, by the rather dismal standards of the Middle Ages, they could have been worse.

The ticket for this tour is separate from the normal €11 ticket. Both admit you to the Palazzo Ducale, but if you want to visit the Museo Correr and other museums on the standard ticket *and* do the Itinerari Segreti, you'll have to pay for both. You must book your place on the tour.

door you can see the remains of Guariento's 14th-century fresco *Paradiso* (Heaven), damaged in the 1577 fire.

On the other side of the corridor is the immense Sala del Maggior Consiglio (Great Council Room). This is dominated at one end by Tintoretto's replacement *Paradiso*, one of the world's largest oil paintings, measuring 22m by 7m. Among the many other paintings in the hall is a masterpiece, the *Apoteosi di Venezia* (Apotheosis of Venice) by Veronese, in one of the central ceiling panels. Note the black space in the frieze on the wall depicting the first 76 dogi of Venice. Doge Marin Falier would have appeared here had he not been beheaded for treason in 1355.

The room off the northwestern corner of the Sala del Maggior Consiglio housed the Quarantia Civil Nuova (New Civil Council of Forty), a kind of appeals court, while beyond lies the Sala dello Scrutinio (Ballot Room), where elections to the Maggior Consiglio were held. It is lined with stirring and bloody battle scenes.

From the northeastern end, a trail of corridors leads to the small, enclosed **Ponte dei Sospiri** (Bridge of Sighs; Map p296). Before you reach the bridge, you pass through three small rooms, the last of which contains a small collection of paintings by Hieronymus Bosch (c 1450–1516). He must have been doing drugs!

The bridge is split into two levels, for traffic heading into and out of the **Prigioni Nuove** (New Prisons; Map p296), built on the eastern side of Rio di Palazzo della Paglia in the 16th century to cater for the overflow from the Prigioni Vecchie (Old Prisons) within the Palazzo Ducale. The bridge is presumably named after the sighs that prisoners heaved as they crossed it on their way into the dungeons.

You wind your way through the cells of the Prigioni Nuove (the building is now also known as the Palazzo delle Prigioni and occasionally hosts period-music concerts, see p170); they are small and dank, but not too bad by the standards of the times. Of course, they are cleaned up and airy now, but wouldn't have been much fun when overcrowded with sick and unhappy prisoners on a bread-and-water diet.

Re-emerging from the prison, you again cross the Ponte dei Sospiri to end up in the offices of the Avogaria Comun (Venetian magistracy) and the Sala dello Scrigno (Room of the Coffer). Here the Libro d'Oro

(Golden Book) was kept. The Libro identified those noble families of impeccable Venetian descent who had the right to join the Maggior Consiglio. Interclass weddings were forbidden and a vigilant watch was maintained for fraudulent attempts to pass off unsuitable persons as nobles.

The last office you pass through before arriving back in the courtyard is the Milizia da Mar (Marine Militia). An office of 20 senators was set up in 1545 to organise the rapid equipping and manning of emergency war fleets whenever the need arose. The organisation began here. You then pass through a shop and downstairs to a café that leads onto the courtyard.

Exit the courtyard by what was traditionally the main entrance, Giovanni and Bartolomeo Bon's 15th-century Porta della Carta (Paper Door), to which government decrees were fixed (hence the name).

PALAZZO FORTUNY Map pp294-5
☎ 041 520 09 95; www.museiciviveneziani.it; Campo San Beneto 3780; adult/senior & student €4/2.50; ☼ 10am-6pm Tue-Sun; ⚓ Sant'Angelo
You'll recognise this building instantly by its two rows of *hectafores*, each a series of eight connected Venetian-style windows. Mariano Fortuny y Madrazo, an eccentric Spanish painter and collector, bought the building at the beginning of the 20th century. He left his works here and, together with another 80 by the Roman artist Virgilio Guidi, they make up the bulk of the Museo Fortuny. After years spent firmly shut, some rooms of the *palazzo*, holding part of the collection, are now open. Temporary exhibitions are also held in an exposition space downstairs from the museum proper. At the time of writing, it was still uncertain when the museum would be open in its entirety.

PALAZZO FRANCHETTI Map pp294-5
☎ 041 240 77 11; www.istitutoveneto.it; Campo Santo Stefano 2842; adult/student €7/5; ☼ 2-7pm Mon-Sat, 11am-7pm Sun & holidays; ⚓ Accademia
After three years of painstaking restoration work, the magnificence of this great patrician house, which from 1922 until 1999 was home to a private bank, was revealed to the public late in 2004. The 16th-century mansion is now owned by the Istituto Veneto di Scienze, Lettere ed Arti (The Veneto Institute of the Sciences, Letters and Arts, founded by the Austrians

in 1838), which plans to have a full, rotating programme of expositions here. From the entrance off the *campo* a grand 19th-century staircase winds up to the noble 1st floor (where the exhibitions are held). A series of magnificent halls, especially the central one and the three overlooking the Grand Canal, form the stage for exhibitions. Unfortunately, you can't visit the next floor, because it is rented to the World Health Organization. When you're finished, head for the peaceful canalside garden.

PONTE DELL'ACCADEMIA Map pp294-5
Campo San Vidal & Campo della Carità;
🚇 Accademia
Built in 1930 to replace a 19th-century metal structure, the last of the Grand Canal bridges was supposed to be a temporary arrangement until a satisfactory design for a more permanent structure was produced. All that seems to have been forgotten, and the municipality is forever having to patch this timber job up. From the middle, the views in both directions along the Grand Canal are spellbinding. One of the most common images from Venice is the view of the Chiesa di Santa Maria della Salute from this spot. The bridge links the *sestiere* of San Marco with Dorsoduro. In front of you when you cross the bridge are the Gallerie dell'Accademia (p66).

TEATRO LA FENICE Map pp294-5
🕾 041 78 66 11; www.teatrolafenice.it; Campo
San Fantin 1965; tours adult/student & senior €7/5;
🕑 varies; 🚇 Santa Maria del Giglio
First raised in the twilight years of La Serenissima, in 1792, and rebuilt after fires in 1836 and again in 2003, this is one of the world's great opera stages. Emperor Napoleon enjoyed a show here in December 1807, and many of the greats of European opera have performed here in the two centuries since. The building today is a careful reconstruction of the opera house raised in 1837, incorporating the latest in theatre technology and with room for 1000 spectators (somewhat more than in the pre-fire theatre). Materials and methods employed in the original were, where feasible, again employed in the decoration of this phoenix. You may visit the magnificent opera during the day by joining a tour. You must book by phone or in person and you should reckon on a couple of days' waiting time.

Tour times are volatile – you will be told when you book the times and days tours are available. See also p172.

TELECOM FUTURE CENTRE Map p296
🕾 041 521 32 00; www.futurecentre.telecomitalia
.it, in Italian; Campo San Salvador 4826; admission
free; 🕑 10am-6pm Tue-Sun; 🚇 Rialto
Set up in the 15th-century cloisters of the adjacent Chiesa di San Salvador and nerve centre of the city's telephone services, this museum of the future shows us how we might communicate decades from now – a little science-fiction fantasy in the heart of the venerable historic city. There are lots of hands-on interactive displays and gadgets here. How we will spend countless hours of our lives creating MMMails personalities, personal TV shows on the Web or converting written messages in to the artificially spoken word. As if we didn't spend enough time already with our TVs, computers and mobiles!

TORRE DELL'OROLOGIO Map p296
www.museicivicimagneziani.it; Piazza San Marco;
🕑 due to reopen 2005; 🚇 Vallaresso/San Marco
The Clock Tower, an early-Renaissance gem on the north flank of Piazza San Marco, is a fitting timepiece for the grand square. The clock and its tower were considered such a work of genius that, it is said, their designer was blinded to prevent him repeating the feat anywhere else! The blue enamel and gold-leaf clock face shows not only the time but the position of the sun, the lunar phases and the signs of the zodiac.
On the small terrace atop the tower, two dark bronze Mori (Moors, so called because of the patina of the bronze rather than intentional design by their makers in 1497) strike the hour on a huge bell. At midday and midnight, a hammer strikes the same bell no less than 132 times! On rare occasions (the Epiphany and the Ascension) you can also see 18th-century wooden statues of the Three Wise Men preceded by an angel parade past a statue of the Virgin Mary and child on the level below the Mori. Restoration work on the tower and its mechanisms was due for completion by the end of 2005. The work on the clock mechanisms is being backed by the Swiss watch people Piaget, so there should be no problems with the clock running slow. When all is ready, small groups will be able to book visits.

SESTIERE DI DORSODURO

Eating pp144–6; Shopping pp181–3; Sleeping pp196–8; Walking pp121–4

Orientation

Let's assume you are on the Ponte dell'Accademia, having come through Campo Santo Stefano. On the other side of the bridge you are in Campo della Carità. Now it's time for some serious art appreciation, with the Gallerie dell'Accademia and the Peggy Guggenheim Collection the main attractions. Between them cluster a hive of small private galleries.

The *sestiere* occupies the southern flank of Venice, looking onto the broad Canale della Giudecca and receiving the full force of the sun (blistering in summer and blissful in winter) throughout the day. The district is mostly quiet and residential, with the one major exception of Campo Santa Margherita, *the* nightlife hub of the city.

CA' REZZONICO (MUSEO DEL SETTE-CENTO VENEZIANO) Map pp294-5

☎ 041 241 01 00; www.museicivicivenezianz.it; Fondamenta Rezzonico 3136; adult/student/child €6.50/4.50/2.50, see also Special Tickets; ☼ 10am-6pm Wed-Mon Apr-Oct, 10am-5pm Wed-Mon Nov-Mar; ⚓ Ca' Rezzonico

This superb 17th- to 18th-century mansion, facing the Grand Canal, houses the Museum of the 18th Century. Designed by Longhena and completed in the 1750s by Massari, it was home to several notables over the years, including the poet Robert Browning, who died here. The museum includes a collection of 18th-century art and furniture, and is worth visiting just for the views over the Grand Canal.

A broad staircase by Massari ascends from the ground floor to the *piano nobile* ('noble' or 1st floor). This leads to the Salone da Ballo (Ballroom), a splendid hall dripping with frescoes and richly furnished with 18th-century couches, tables and ebony statues. There follows a series of rooms jammed with period furniture, *objets d'art* and plenty of paintings.

Particularly noteworthy is Tiepolo's ceiling fresco in the Sala del Trono (Throne Room), the *Allegoria del Merito tra Nobiltà e Virtù* (Allegory of Merit Between Nobility

and Virtue). Tiepolo contributed several other frescoes and paintings, as did his son Giandomenico (look out for his fresco cycle, taken from the Tiepolo house at Zianigo, near Mira on the mainland). Other represented artists include Pietro Longhi, Francesco Guardi, Rosalba Carriera and Canaletto.

CHIESA DEI CARMINI Map pp294-5

☎ 041 522 65 53; Campo dei Carmini 2617; admission free; ☼ 2.30-5.30pm Mon-Sat; ⚓ Ca' Rezzonico

What remains of the original 14th-century Byzantine and then Gothic church sits a little uneasily beside the richer, and perhaps less digestible, ornament of the 16th and 17th centuries. Among the paintings on view are several works by Cima da Conegliano and Lorenzo Lotto.

CHIESA DEI GESUATI Map pp294-5

Fondamenta Zattere ai Gesuati 909; admission €2.50 or Chorus ticket; ☼ 10am-5pm Mon-Sat, 1-5pm Sun; ⚓ Zattere

Built for the Dominicans (who had replaced the suppressed order of the Jesuits, or Gesuati, on this spot in 1668) by a team of architects under Giorgio Massari from 1726 to 1735, this imposing church is more properly known as the Chiesa di Santa Maria del Rosario. It contains three ceiling frescoes by Tiepolo telling the story of St Dominic – the appearance to the saint of the Virgin Mary, the institution of the rosary (hence the church's official name) and St Dominic in glory. Tiepolo also had a hand in the frescoes in the dome, while Tintoretto left behind a *Crocifissione* (Crucifixion) in his typically flowing reds and blues on the left side of the church nearest the altar. The statues and sculpture lining much of the interior are by Gian Maria Morlaiter (1699–1781).

DORSODURO TRANSPORT

All Grand Canal vaporetti stop at Accademia, while the No 1 also calls at the Ca' Rezzonico and Salute stops. Along the southern flank of the *sestiere*, a branch line of the No 82 and the N night vaporetti call at Zattere and San Basilio. Nos 61 and 62 also call at Zattere and San Basilio. For more information, see p246.

Chiesa di Santa Maria della Salute (opposite), Sestiere di Dorsoduro

Virtually next door is the little-visited **Chiesa di Santa Maria della Visitazione** (Map pp294–5), also called Santa Maria degli Artigianelli, which has a curious 15th-century chessboard timber ceiling with numerous scenes depicting the Visitation and a series of portraits of saints and prophets. Opening hours are erratic.

CHIESA DELL'ARCANGELO RAFFAELE
Map pp294-5
Campo Anzolo Rafael; admission free; ⏱ 9am-noon & 4-6pm Mon-Sat; 🚊 San Basilio
The two towers of this stout church can be seen from all over southern Dorsoduro. The church was initially raised in the 7th century and for a long time was the focus of community life for the fishing families who once lived around here. The present church dates to the 17th century. The series of paintings inside above the main entrance has been attributed to the Guardi brothers, but no-one is sure which one – the *vedutista* (landscape artist) Francesco or his lesser-known elder brother Gian Antonio (1699-1760)!

CHIESA DI SAN NICOLÒ DEI MENDICOLI Map pp294-5
☎ 041 528 45 65; Campo San Nicolò; ⏱ 10am-noon & 4-6pm Mon-Sat; 🚊 San Basilio
Although it has been fiddled with over the centuries, the church still preserves elements of the 13th-century original. The portico attached to one side was used to shelter the poor. The whole area was fairly downtrodden and known for its *mendicoli*, or beggars. The church's tiny square, bound in by the canals and featuring a pylon bearing the winged lion of St Mark (one of the few not to have been destroyed under Napoleon), is at the heart of one of the oldest parishes in Venice.

CHIESA DI SAN PANTALON Map pp294-5
☎ 041 523 58 93; Campo San Pantalon 3700; admission free; ⏱ 3-6pm Mon-Sat; 🚊 San Tomà
The stark, unfinished brick façade dates from the 17th century, although a church was here as early as the 11th century. Inside, the greatest impact comes from the 40 canvases representing the *Martirio e Gloria di San Pantaleone* (Martyrdom and Glory of St Pantaleone), painted for the ceiling by Giovanni Antonio Fumiani. The artist died in a fall from scaffolding while at work and is buried in the church. Veronese, Vivarini and Palma il Giovane have works here, too. Head for the Cappella del Sacro Chiodo (Chapel of the Holy Nail) to see the greatest concentration of works. To better observe the ceiling and Veronese's *San Pantaleone Risana un Fanciullo* (St Pantaleone Heals a Boy), stick coins into the slot machine to turn on the lights.

When you've finished in the church, take a stroll off to the right down a dogleg blind alley to Campiello Ca' Angara. On the wall that marks the end of the alley (Nos 3717 and 3718) is a sculpted medallion of what could be a Byzantine ruler, dating perhaps to the 8th century. That is one of the remarkable things about Venice – what would anywhere else have long been removed and put behind glass in a museum here remains in the streets.

CHIESA DI SAN SEBASTIAN Map pp294-5
Campo San Sebastian 1687; admission €2.50 or Chorus ticket; ⏱ 10am-5pm Mon-Sat, 1-5pm Sun; 🚊 San Basilio
Veronese's final resting place, this Renaissance remake of an earlier church is often attributed to Antonio Scarpagnino (c 1505–49).

Inside, Veronese went to town, decorating the interior with frescoes and canvases that cover a good deal of space on the ceiling and walls. The organ is his work, too, with scenes from Christ's life on its shutters. The ceiling paintings together seem to exude a pallid, yellowish light. Titian left a notable item here as well – his *San Nicolò* (St Nicholas), first on the right as you enter the church.

CHIESA DI SANTA MARIA DELLA SALUTE Map p296

☎ 041 522 55 58; www.marcianum.it/salute, in Italian; Campo della Salute 1/b; sacristy €1.50; ☯ 9am-noon & 3.30-6pm; 🚢 Salute

Possibly the city's most familiar silhouette (viewed from Piazzetta San Marco or the Ponte dell'Accademia), this bulging baroque beast is one of Longhena's masterpieces. Seen from close up, it's difficult to take it all in, but Longhena knew what he was doing and deliberately designed a monument to be admired from afar.

Longhena was commissioned to build the church in honour of the Virgin Mary, to whose intervention was attributed the end of an outbreak of plague in 1630. The ranks of statues that festoon the exterior culminate in one of the Virgin Mary on top of the dome. As is often the case in Venice, the church is built not on solid land but on what amounts to a huge raft of, it is said, a million tightly knit pylons hammered into the lagoon floor.

The octagonal form of the church is unusual. Longhena's idea was to design it in the form of a crown for the Mother of God. The interior is flooded with light pouring through windows in the walls and dome. Dominating the main body of the church is the extraordinary baroque *altar maggiore*, into which is embedded a Cretan icon of Mary.

Of the paintings in the church proper, only Titian's *Pentecoste* (Pentecost) is of particular note, but admission to the sacristy is worth shelling out for: the ceiling is bedecked with three remarkable Titians. The figures depicted are so full of curvaceous movement they seem to be caught in a washing machine! The three scenes are replete with high emotion, depicting the struggles between *Caino e Abele* (Cain and Abel), *David e Golia* (David and Goliath) and finally Abraham and his conscience in *Il Sacrificio di Isaaco* (The Sacrifice of Isaac).

The eight medallions by Titian, depicting saints, are small but intriguing. St Mark seems to be winking in amusement to himself, while you could swear that, under his swirling beard, St Jerome (San Girolamo) is having a quiet chuckle.

The other star of the sacristy is Tintoretto's *Le Nozze di Cana* (The Wedding Feast of Cana), filled with an unusual amount of bright and cheerful light by Tintoretto's rather morose standards.

Every year, on 21 November, a procession takes place from Piazza San Marco to the church to give thanks for the city's good health. The last part of the march takes place on a pontoon bridge thrown out between the Santa Maria del Giglio *traghetto* (commuter gondola) stop and the church.

FONDAZIONE BEVILACQUE E LA MASA Map pp294-5

☎ 041 520 77 97; www.bevilacqualamasa.it, in Italian; Palazzetto Tito, Fondamenta Gherardini 2826; admission free; ☯ noon-6pm Wed-Mon; 🚢 Ca' Rezzonico

This private foundation, with its HQ in a charming *palazzo* that was once home to the artists Ettore and Luigi Tito, stages regular exhibitions on the 1st floor, ranging from single artists to photography.

GALLERIA DI PALAZZO CINI

Map pp294-5

☎ 041 521 07 55; www.cini.it; Piscina Forner 864; adult/student €6.50/5.50; ☯ 11am-7pm Tue-Sun; 🚢 Accademia

After the overwhelming parade of Venetian masters in the nearby Gallerie dell'Accademia (p66) comes this small but curious collection of Tuscan intruders. Oddly, the main façade of this 16th-century building looks over the Rio di San Vio rather than the Grand Canal. Spread out over two floors are around 30 works, mostly from the 14th and 15th centuries. You'll see a handful of works by Lippi, Piero della Francesca (*Madonna col Bambino*, or Madonna and Child), Botticelli (*Il Giudizio di Paride*, or The Judgment of Paris) and Beato Angelico. Mixed in are some fine pieces of 15th-century Venetian furniture, porcelain, and other odds and ends.

Opening periods can be vague. The tendency seems to be to shut down in July-August and December-February.

GALLERIE DELL'ACCADEMIA

Map pp294-5

☎ 041 522 22 47, bookings ☎ 041 520 03 45; www.gallerieaccademia.org, in Italian; Campo della Carità 1050; adult/EU citizen 18-25yr/under 12yr & EU citizen (and those of certain other nations) under 18yr or over 65yr €6.50/3.25/free, see also Special Tickets, video guide €6, audio guide €4; ☯ 8.15am-2pm Mon, 8.15am-7.15pm Tue-Sun; 🚇 Accademia

The single greatest repository of the finest in Venetian art lies here. The former church and convent of Santa Maria della Carità, with additions by Palladio, houses a swath of works that follows the progression of Venetian art from the 14th to the 18th centuries. Work on the renovation and expansion of the gallery (which at present displays about 400 works) was launched in early 2005. When completed (due in 2008), another 250 works in storage will be added to the display in what has been dubbed the Grandi Gallerie dell'Accademia. The Accademia delle Belle Arti art school that occupied the ground floor until 2003 has moved to the renovated Ospedale degli Incurabili (Map pp294–5; p123) on Fondamenta Zattere, liberating much-needed space.

In 1750 the rococo painter Gian Battista Piazzetta founded the art school that later became the Accademia, Venice's official arbiter of artistic taste. The collection of paintings was assembled in 1807 and opened to the public 10 years later. The first works came from churches and other religious institutions suppressed during the brief but violent years of Napoleonic rule. Later additions came from private collections. In 1878 the galleries were hived off from the art school and passed into state control. Acquisitions have continued ever since.

Ticket in hand (the ticket office is in a booth outside), you head inside and upstairs to Sala (Room) 1, where the galleries' more or less chronological display begins. You are in what was the main meeting hall of the Scuola Grande di Santa Maria della Carità, the oldest of the Scuole Grandi (see When School Was Cool, p74). The magnificent timber ceiling is divided into squares; at the centre of each is a sculpted face – every one different – of an angel. The room is given over to religious art of the 14th century, including Paolo Veneziano's *Madonna col Bambino e i Due Commitanti* (Madonna and Child with Two Donors).

Sala 2, designed by Carlo Scarpa and with an unusual black *terrazzo alla Veneziana* floor (see Of Floors & Walls, p87), includes a couple of works each by Giovanni Bellini, Vittore Carpaccio and Cima da Conegliano. Note the commonality in themes adopted by all three in their depictions of the Madonna and child (for instance, the musicians at the Madonna's feet).

View from the tip of the Sestiere di Dorsoduro across the Canale della Giudecca (p63)

The most enthralling of the works is, however, Carpaccio's altarpiece *Crocifissione e Apoteosi dei 10,000 Martiri del Monte Ararat* (Crucifixion and Apotheosis of the 10,000 Martyrs of Mt Ararat). The story goes that some 10,000 Roman soldiers sent to quell rebellion in Armenia instead converted to Christianity. The Emperor was unimpressed and sent more troops. They were ordered to subject the 10,000 to the same trials that Christ had suffered if they didn't change their minds. The result was a massacre. The painting, representing a kind of collective sainthood, was a departure from the standard depiction of one or two saints in religious painting. The soldiers all have the appearance of Christ, while their executioners appear in the garb of nasty Turks – no doubt reflecting Venetian and European feelings towards the infidels of their own time.

More works by Giovanni Bellini and Cima da Conegliano adorn Sala 3.

In Sale 4 and 5 you can enjoy a mixed bag, including the work of some non-Venetians. These include Andrea Mantegna's *San Giorgio* (St George) and works by Cosmè Tura, Piero della Francesca and Jacopo Bellini. In Bellini's pieces, note the comparative stiffness of his characters, a faithful reflection of a painting style still crossing over from earlier Gothic tenets. Bellini's son Giovanni has 11 paintings here, and the greater suppleness and reality of expression is clear – take, for instance, the remarkable *Madonna col Bambino tra le Sante Caterina e Maddalena* (Madonna and Child Between Saints Catherine and Mary Magdalene).

The most striking paintings in these rooms are the two rare contributions by Giorgione, *La Tempesta* (The Storm) and *La Vecchia* (The Old Woman). Both are way ahead of their time. Look at the latter closely. The lines and brush strokes, the look in the eyes, indeed the very subject matter, would be more at home in a collection of 19th-century portraiture.

In Sala 6 are works by Tintoretto and Veronese, and one by Titian. In Tintoretto's *La Creazione degli Animali* (The Creation of the Animals) you can see the thick, splashy paint strokes that characterised much of this Mannerist painter's work. His use of muted crimsons and blues in this and other works reminds one of Spain's El Greco. Or rather, in Tintoretto's work you can see support for the claim that El Greco took with him to Spain a good deal of what he had learned in Venice.

The main interest in Sale 7 and 8 is Lorenzo Lotto's *Ritratto del Giovane Gentiluomo nel Suo Studio* (Portrait of a Young Gentleman in His Studio). What's the lizard doing on his desk? Others represented here are Titian, Palma il Vecchio and even the Tuscan Giorgio Vasari, better known for his history of great Italian artists. Sala 9 is a shop selling souvenirs and books.

In Sala 10 you are confronted by some major works, one of the highlights of which is Veronese's *Convito in Casa di Levi* (Feast in the House of Levi). Originally called *Ultima Cena* (Last Supper), the painting's name was changed at the behest of the Inquisition (see p29). The room also contains one of Titian's last works, *Pietà*. The almost nightmarish quality of the faces has a Goyaesque touch and reflects, perhaps, the fact that Titian was working on it during an epidemic of the plague. Indeed he died before finishing the work. Finally, there are some remarkable Tintorettos dedicated to the theme of St Mark. The *Trafugamento del Corpo di San Marco* (Stealing of St Mark's Body) is a mighty example of this artist's daring with a brush.

Another fine Tintoretto is his *Crocifissione* (Crucifixion) in Sala 11, where you can also admire frescoes by Giambattista Tiepolo salvaged from the Chiesa dei Scalzi after an Austrian bomb missed its target (the nearby train station) in 1915 and hit the church. Another of his works, the long frieze *Castigo dei Serpenti* (Punishment of the Snakes), was for 60 years rolled up and stashed away in a church in the town of Castelfranco, which explains the damage evident today. It had once adorned the Chiesa di SS Cosma e Damiano in Giudecca.

Sala 12 contains minor 18th-century landscape paintings, while Sala 13 has works by Jacopo Bassano, Palma il Giovane, Tintoretto and Titian. Sale 14, 15, 16 and 16a are of less interest, although a few minor Giambattista Tiepolos appear. Sala 17 is crammed with small works, including a rare (in Venice) couple by Canaletto. Francesco Guardi, Pietro Longhi, Marco Ricco and Rosalba Carriera (with several portraits) also figure here, as do some studies by Giambattista Tiepolo.

Works by minor Veneto *vedutisti* line the walls of Sala 18, while Sala 19 is given over to 15th- and 16th-century artists – thus breaking the chronological order established so far.

Just as you might have thought the exhibition was losing steam, you enter Sala 20. The crowd scenes, splashes of red and activity pouring from the canvases in this cycle dedicated to the *Miracoli della Vera Croce* (Miracles of the True Cross) come as quite a shock. They were carried out by Vittore Carpaccio, Gentile Bellini and others for the Scuola di San Giovanni Evangelista, which is home to a relic of the true Cross. Today, much of their fascination lies in the depiction of a Venice of centuries ago, with gondolas tootling about, classic Venetian chimneys in evidence everywhere and a faithful depiction of the timber Rialto bridge that preceded the present one.

Carpaccio's extraordinary series of nine paintings recounting the life of St Ursula (Santa Orseola) follows in Sala 21.

Sala 22 hosts a few neoclassical sculptures, while Sala 23 is actually the former Chiesa di Santa Maria della Carità. Several works from the Bellini workshops are on display. The area is often used for temporary expositions, too. The last room (Sala 24) was the Sala dell'Albergo (a kind of reception area of what was the Scuola Grande di Santa Maria della Carità), and is dominated by an exquisite timber ceiling and Titian's *Presentazione di Maria al Tempio* (Presentation of Mary at the Temple).

In each of the rooms there are detailed description sheets in English and Italian – remember to put them back before proceeding to the next room! When the galleries are crowded, the queues outside can be a pain – a ceiling of 300 visitors at any one time is imposed (see Queue Jumping, p58).

If you want more, it is possible to see another 88 works of Veneto art spanning the 15th to the 18th centuries in the Quadreria on the 2nd floor, but only at weekends by appointment (☎ 041 522 22 47).

PALAZZO DARIO Map pp294-5
Ramo Ca' Dario 352; 🚤 Salute
You can get some impression of this late-Gothic mansion (aka Ca' Dario) from the rear, but to really appreciate it you need to see the façade – a unique Renaissance marble facing that was taken down and reattached in the 19th century – from the Grand Canal. The building looks a little unsteady, and many Venetians view it with misgiving, given that most of its owners –

right from the man who had it built in 1479, Giovanni Dario – seem to have met mysterious or miserable ends, lost fortunes or simply become frightfully ill. Just spending time here seems to be tempting fate. One week after renting the palace for a holiday in Venice, The Who's bass player John Entwhistle died of a heart attack in Las Vegas in June 2002, just as the newly reformed band was set to embark on a tour of the USA. In spite of the place's macabre track record, Woody Allen was rumoured to be interested in buying it only a month after Entwhistle's demise, having bargained the price down from US$11 million to US$6 million. By all accounts his superstitions got the better of him.

PALAZZO ZENOBIO Map pp294-5
☎ 041 522 87 70; Fondamenta del Soccorso 2597; admission by donation; ☯ call to book tours; 🚤 San Basilio
This grand baroque structure has housed the Collegio Armeno dei Padri Mechitaristi (Armenian College of Mechitarist Fathers) since the mid-19th century. The structure is the handiwork of Antonio Gaspari, but apart from the grand curved tympanum, the exterior of the building tells you little. To behold the Sala della Musica (Music Room), also called the Sala dei Specchi (Hall of Mirrors) is to witness Gaspari's voluptuous décor at its baroque, baubly extreme. This and adjacent rooms are handsomely decorated with frescoes depicting scenes from ancient mythology. The building is a world unto itself, with dormitories, classrooms, grand kitchen and halls used for expositions. The exuberant garden is sometimes the scene of private receptions, concerts and the like. Guided visits can be organised by calling ahead.

PEGGY GUGGENHEIM COLLECTION
Map pp294-5
☎ 041 240 54 11; www.guggenheim-venice.it; Palazzo Venier dai Leoni, Fondamenta Venier dai Leoni 701; adult/senior/student €10/8/5; ☯ 10am-6pm Wed-Mon; 🚤 Accademia
Peggy Guggenheim called the unfinished, truncated Palazzo Venier dai Leoni home for the 30 years until her death in 1979. She left behind a collection of works by her favourite modern artists, representing most of the major movements of the 20th century.

Miss Guggenheim came into her fortune in 1921 and set off for Europe from North America with no particular aim. During the 1930s she developed a voracious appetite for contemporary art (and some of the artists!). She opened an art gallery in London in 1938, the Guggenheim Jeune, and embarked on a programme of collection that continued well into 1940. Seemingly oblivious to the conflagration raging around her, she decided to return to New York from Paris only when the Nazis were at the city gates. In New York she opened the Art of this Century gallery in 1942 but five years later decided to return to Europe. By 1949 her home and museum in Venice was open to the public. The Palazzo Venier dai Leoni was so called because, it is said, the Venier family kept lions here. Peggy herself preferred the company of dogs – many of them are buried alongside her own grave in the sculpture garden.

The bulk of the collection is housed in the east wing. It is the pleasing result of an eclectic collector's whim, and the list of greats of 20th-century art is long. Early Cubist paintings include Picasso's *The Poet* (1911) and *Pipe, Glass, Bottle of Vieux Marc* (1914), and Georges Braque's *The Clarinet* (1912). Look out also for Picasso's *Sulla Spiaggia* (On the Beach; 1937) in the main entrance. There are a couple of Kandinskys, including his *Upward* (1929). Interesting works from Spain include Dalí's *Birth of Liquid Desires* (1932) – a classic example of his psycho-sick 'eroticism' – and Miró's *Seated Woman II* (1939).

It wouldn't be right if Max Ernst, Guggenheim's husband and doyen of Surrealism, were not represented. Among his many paintings on show is the disturbing *Antipope* (1942). Other names to look for include Jackson Pollock (his 1946 *Circoncisione* looks painful!), Mark Rothko, Willem de Kooning, Paul Delvaux, Alexander Calder, Juan Gris, Kurt Schwitters, Paul Klee, Francis Bacon, Giorgio de Chirico, Piet Mondrian and Marc Chagall. The sculpture garden is sprinkled with works by, among others, Henry Moore and Jean Arp. The pieces on display in the garden change regularly. Some are part of the museum's permanent collection, but others come from the Raymond & Patsy Nasher Sculpture Collection in Dallas, USA.

The rear of the mansion hosts a separate collection of Italian futurists and other modern artists from the peninsula, collected

Palazzo Dario (opposite), Sestiere di Dorsoduro

by Gianni Mattioli and now incorporated into the Guggenheim collection. Artists include Umberto Boccioni (in particular his mesmerising *Materia*, a powerful portrait of the artist's mother done in 1912), Giorgio Morandi and Giacomo Balla, and there is one early work by Amedeo Modigliani.

Temporary exhibitions are held in the new wing on the western side of the garden. A highly agreeable café overlooks the garden.

SCUOLA GRANDE DEI CARMINI
Map pp294-5

☎ 041 528 94 20; Campo Santa Margherita 2617; adult/student €5/4; ☉ 9am-6pm Mon-Sat, 9am-4pm Sun Apr-Oct, 9am-4pm Nov-Mar; 🚣 Ca' Rezzonico

Just before you bump into the church of the same name at the southwestern end of Campo Santa Margherita, you pass on the right this *scuola*, with numerous paintings by Tiepolo and others. Tiepolo's nine ceiling paintings in the Salone Superiore (Upper Hall) depict the virtues surrounding the Virgin in Glory. The monochrome paintings downstairs are striking, and a rare display of black and white on canvas in Venice. The ceiling *boiseries* (intricately carved timber) are of extraordinary richness, while Longhena's Scalone (grand staircase linking the ground with the 1st floor) is a bubbling baroque tunnel. The building façades have also been attributed to Longhena. For more on *scuole*, see When School Was Cool, p74.

SESTIERI DI SAN POLO & SANTA CROCE (SANTA CROSE)

Eating pp146–50; Shopping pp183–7; Sleeping pp198–200; Walking pp125–9

Orientation

These two *sestieri* have been lumped together because they form a neat whole, sandwiched in between Piazzale Roma and the Ponte di Rialto. Its character changes enormously from the quiet back lanes of Santa Croce (Santa Crose) to the busier area around the Istituto Universitario di Architettura di Venezia. Around the Ponte di Rialto a web of lanes converging on the produce markets of Rialto is peppered with shops of all sorts and some wonderful old-time eateries. The bulk of sights is made up of churches, religious confraternities and 18th-century mansions. Most notable are Ca' Pesaro, the Frari and the Scuola Grande di San Rocco, a Tintoretto feast.

CA' PESARO Map pp290-1

☎ 041 524 06 95; www.museiciviciveneziani.it; Fondamenta di Ca' Pesaro, Santa Croce 2076; adult/senior, student & child €5.50/3, see also Special Tickets; ⏱ 10am-6pm Tue-Sun Apr-Oct, 10am-5pm Tue-Sun Nov-Mar; 🚊 San Stae

The main façade of this restored mansion fronts the Grand Canal. Home to the **Galleria d'Arte Moderna** (Modern Art Gallery) since 1902, Ca' Pesaro was designed for one of Venice's senior families by Longhena, in a muted baroque style much influenced by the Renaissance ideas of Sansovino, and finished in 1710 by Antonio Gaspari, after Longhena's death. He died worrying about the mounting bills! The Pesaros were succeeded by the Gradenigo family, the Armenian Mechitarist Fathers (who turned it into a college before moving to Palazzo Zenobio in Dorsoduro) and then the Bevilacqua family, who turned it over to the Venice town hall for use as an art gallery.

The collection includes works purchased from the Biennale art festival, and an eclectic array of Italian and international modern art. The *androne* (main ground-floor hall) is typical of the great patricians' mansions in Venice. You can look out over the Grand Canal from one side, while the inland end fronts onto a sunny courtyard dominated by a monumental fountain. A handful of statues and sculptures by 20th-century Italian artists are littered about, and temporary exhibitions are held in a side hall. As you head up the grand stairway to the 1st floor you will pass a large bronze cast of Auguste Rodin's *Il Pensatore* (The Thinker; originally conceived in 1880).

The bulk of the works are on the 1st floor. The central grand hall, or *portego*, is typical of Venetian mansions. Facing the Grand Canal and the rear courtyard, it is the main artery off which branch other rooms. While wandering around and looking at the art on the walls, don't neglect the fine frescoes from the original building on the ceilings of many rooms and the admirable *terrazzo alla Veneziana* floors (see Of Floors & Walls, p87). The building faithfully reflects the grandeur to which the Republic's senior families were accustomed.

The art starts with late-19th-century Venetian works (such as Giacomo Favretto's scenes from Venice) and broadens into a series of works from the same period by other Italians. After that it gets more interesting, with works from the early Biennale years and the 1930s, such as Klimt's *Judith II (Salomé)*, and artists including Kandinsky, Chagall, Matisse, Paul Klee and Spain's Joaquim Sorolla. Next come striking sculptures by the Milanese Adolfo Widt, and then the eclectic De Lisi collection, with works by De Chirico, Miró, Kandinsky and Yves Tanguy, among others. The following two rooms are again dedicated to Italian works from the interwar years. Max Ernst, Henry Moore and others follow in a room

---

SAN POLO & SANTA CROCE TRANSPORT

A plethora of vaporetti call at Piazzale Roma and across the Ponte dei Scalzi at Ferrovia, putting you in (or very close to) the northwestern corner of Santa Croce. Otherwise, the No 1 calls at Riva de Biasio, San Stae (the N stops here too), San Silvestro and San Tomà (No 82 and N call here as well). The Rialto stop, although on the other side of the canal, is also handy (Nos 1, 4, 82 and N). For more information, see p246.

dedicated to the 1940s and 1950s. The final two rooms again return to Italian, and more specifically Venetian, art of the 1950s.

Proceed upstairs to the **Museo d'Arte Orientale** (Museum of Oriental Art), one of the most important collections in Europe of Edo-period art and objects from Japan. During a two-year world tour in the 1820s, Count Enrico di Borbone amassed a store of Japanese arms and light armour (the samurai preferred ease of movement over heavy protection, judging their best defence to be their fencing skills) dating from the 17th to the 19th century. The display is also replete with porcelain, art and all sorts of elegant household objects, from snuff boxes to ladies' toiletry cabinets. The whole scene is fascinating, as the collection has been left much as it was organised in 1928, giving it a delightfully musty feel.

CASA DI GOLDONI Map pp294-5
☎ 041 275 93 25; www.museiciviciveneziani. it; Calle Nomboli, San Polo 2794; adult/senior, student & child €2.50/1.50, see also Special Tickets; ☻ 10am-5pm Mon-Sat Apr-Oct, 10am-4pm Mon-Sat Nov-Mar; ⚎ San Tomà

This is where Venice's greatest playwright, Carlo Goldoni, was born in 1707. The 15th-century Gothic-era house is worth a quick visit, and Goldoni fans will find a host of material on the playwright's life and works displayed in its otherwise fairly bare rooms. The entrance is the most striking part of the house, with its quiet courtyard, private well and stone stairway in Istrian stone. The display across the rooms on the 1st floor illustrates the history of Goldoni's theatrical activities in Venice.

CHIESA DI SAN GIACOMO DELL'ORIO
Map pp290-1
Campo San Giacomo dell'Orio, Santa Croce 1457; admission €2.50 or Chorus ticket; ☻ 10am-5pm Mon-Sat, 1-5pm Sun; ⚎ Riva de Biasio

The charming, leafy *campo* is graced by the modest outline of one of Venice's few good examples of Romanesque architecture, the Chiesa di San Giacomo dell'Orio. The initial 9th-century church was replaced in 1225. The main Gothic addition (14th century) is the remarkable wooden ceiling *a carena di nave* (in the style of an upturned ship's hull). It is one of several examples in Venice

and, for anyone who has tramped around the great churches of Spain, starkly reminiscent of the Muslim-influenced *artesonado* ceilings. Among the intriguing jumble of works of art are a Byzantine column in green marble, a 13th-century baptismal font and a Lombard pulpit perched on a 6th-century column from Ravenna.

CHIESA DI SAN GIOVANNI DECOLLATO Map pp290-1
☎ 041 97 25 83; Campo San Giovanni Decollato, Santa Croce; ☻ 10am-noon Mon-Sat; ⚎ Riva de Biasio

Long shut and disused, this modest little church (San Zan Degolà, or St John the Headless, in Venetian, known in less blood-curdling fashion in English as St John the Baptist) has been reborn as a home for Russian Orthodox services. It is curious to wander in here and be transported to the eastern reaches of Europe for a moment. Some 14th-century frescoes remain. On the south wall facing the *campo* is a small, sculpted medallion of a lopped-off head. Logic suggests it represents that of St John, but the popular tale in Venice suggests it represents that of Biasio, the horrible butcher of children whose story is recounted briefly on p125.

CHIESA DI SAN GIOVANNI ELEMOSINARIO Map p300
Ruga Vecchia San Giovanni, San Polo 477; admission €2.50 or Chorus ticket; ☻ 10am-5pm Mon-Sat, 1-5pm Sun; ⚎ Rialto

You easily stride right past this beautiful little Renaissance church, built by Antonio Abbondi after a disastrous fire in 1514 destroyed much of the Rialto area. The church and its separate bell tower are camouflaged by the surrounding houses, so their presence comes as a bit of a surprise. The frescoes inside the dome are by Pordenone, as is one of two altarpieces. Another fresco is by Titian.

CHIESA DI SAN POLO Map pp294-5
Campo San Polo 2115; admission €2.50 or Chorus ticket; ☻ 10am-5pm Mon-Sat, 1-5pm Sun; ⚎ San Tomà

Although of Byzantine origin, this church has lost much of its attraction through repeated interference and renovation. Worst of all, the pile-up of houses between it and the Rio di San Polo has completely obscured its façade. It is, however, worth taking the time to wander inside if you enjoy the art of Tiepolo. A whole cycle of his, the *Via Crucis* (Stations of the Cross), hangs in the sacristy. With them are other paintings and some wonderful ceiling frescoes. In the main body of the church are works by Tintoretto and Palma Il Giovane.

CHIESA DI SAN ROCCO Map pp294-5

☎ 041 523 48 64; Campo San Rocco, San Polo 3053; admission free; ⊙ 7.30am-12.30pm & 3-5pm Mon-Sat, 8am-12.30pm & 3-5pm Sun & holidays Apr-Oct, 7.30am-12.30pm Mon-Fri, 8am-12.30pm & 2-4pm Sat, Sun & holidays Nov-Mar; ⚑ San Tomà

You are likely to wander out of the Scuola Grande di San Rocco (p75) wondering what hit you. Maybe that's why there's no charge to enter this church across the way. Although built at about the same time as the *scuola*, the church was completely overhauled in the 18th century – hence the baroque façade (easily identified by all the statues in niches and wall sculpture). It has a somewhat neglected feel inside but contains several paintings of interest to those who have not overdosed, including some by Tintoretto on the main-entrance wall and around the altar.

Palazzo dei Dieci Savi (p74), Sestiere di San Polo

CHIESA DI SAN STAE Map pp290-1

Campo San Stae, Santa Croce 1981; admission €2.50 or Chorus ticket; ⊙ 10am-5pm Mon-Sat, 1-5pm Sun; ⚑ San Stae

A simple house of worship dedicated to St Eustace, this church is a little deceptive. The elaborate exterior (finished in 1709) hides an austere interior. Among its art treasures are Tiepolo's *Il Martirio di San Bartolomeo* (The Martyrdom of St Bartholomew).

CHIESA DI SANTA MARIA GLORIOSA DEI FRARI Map pp294-5

Campo dei Frari, San Polo 3004; admission €2.50 or Chorus ticket; ⊙ 9am-6pm Mon-Sat, 1-6pm Sun; ⚑ San Tomà

If you have seen Notre Dame in Paris or Cologne's Dom, you might be asking yourself what is so Gothic about the Frari. Built for the Franciscans in the 14th and 15th centuries of brick rather than stone, and bereft of flying buttresses, pinnacles, gargoyles and virtually any other sign of decoration inside or out, it is indeed a singular interpretation of the style. Nevertheless, some features give it away, among them the Latin-cross plan (with three naves and a transept), the high vaulted ceiling and its sheer size. A look inside is a must on any art-lover's tour of the city.

A curious element is the presence in the middle of the central nave of the *coro* (choir stalls). This is a common feature in Spain, but the stalls in most churches beyond the Iberian Peninsula tend to be kept out of the way (behind the altar, off to the side or high up at the bottom end of the cross floor plan). Was the idea an import or is it coincidence?

The simplicity of the interior (a red-and-white marble floor, with the same colours dominating the walls and ceiling) is more than offset by the extravagance of decoration in the form of paintings and funereal monuments. Titian is the main attraction. His dramatic *Assunta* (Assumption; 1518) over the high altar, praised unreservedly by all and sundry as a work of inspired genius, represents a key moment in his rise as one of the city's greatest artists.

Another of his masterpieces, the *Madonna di Ca' Pesaro* (Madonna of Ca' Pesaro), hangs above the Pesaro altar (in the left-hand aisle, near the choir stalls). Also of note are Giovanni Bellini's triptych in the apse of the sacristy, Donatello's statue of *Giovanni Battista* (John the Baptist) in the first chapel to the right of the high altar, and Vivarini's *Sant'Ambrogio in Trono e Santi* (St Ambrose Enthroned and Saints) in the second-last chapel to the left of the high altar.

FONDACO DEI TURCHI Map pp290-1

☎ 041 275 02 06; www.museiciviciveneziani.it; Salizada del Fontego dei Turchi 1730; admission free; ⏲ 10am-6pm Sat-Sun; ⚓ San Stae

This 12th-century mansion belonged to the dukes of Ferrara until it was handed over in 1621 for use as a warehouse and way station for Turkish merchants (who operated here in spite of the centuries of at times vicious antagonism). The building now houses the **Museo Civico di Storia Naturale** (Natural History Museum).

In Venice and across the Middle East and beyond, these warehouses were set up both to house foreign merchants and to store their goods. The word *fondaco* (*fontego* in Venetian) spread, and places where Western merchants stayed and worked came to be known in Arabic as a *funduq*, from Aleppo in Syria to Alexandria in Egypt. In Arab countries, *funduq* has come to mean hotel.

The Fondaco dei Turchi was rented out to the Turks until 1858, long after the demise of La Serenissima. Although it dates to the 12th and 13th centuries, the place was restored in appalling taste in the mid-19th century. It was a little like plastic surgery gone wrong. Original features in the façade were sacrificed to the architectural fancies of the time – the odd crenellations are, for example, an unhappy addition.

On the 2nd floor of the now partially reopened museum is an imaginative display dedicated to a series of archaeological expeditions in the Sahara desert of Niger in the 1970s. What is now all rock and sand was, 100 million years ago, a verdant biosphere inhabited by dinosaurs, giant crocodiles and a host of animals and flora. The two most outstanding finds are an Ouransaurus and remains of a 12m-long prehistoric crocodile skeleton. Downstairs you'll find a little aquarium dedicated to Venetian coastal sea specimens.

PALAZZO MOCENIGO Map pp290-1

☎ 041 72 17 98; www.museiciviciveneziani.it; Salizada di San Stae 1992; adult/senior, student & child €4/2.50, see also Special Tickets; ⏲ 10am-5pm Tue-Sun Apr-Oct, 10am-4pm Tue-Sun Nov-Mar; ⚓ San Stae

This mansion belonged to one of the most important families of the Republic. Originally a Gothic pile, it was overhauled in the 17th century and is typical of Venetian patricians' lodgings. The 16th-century philosopher Giordano Bruno was hosted here for a time by the Mocenigo family, who then betrayed him and handed him over to the Inquisition. (He was subsequently tortured and burnt at the stake in Rome for heresy.) The mansion now houses a modest museum, with clothes, period furnishings and accessories from the 17th century. It is interesting for the hints it gives you of how the other half lived in the twilight years of La Serenissima.

Sweeping stairs take you up to the *piano nobile*, divided in typical Venetian fashion. A *portego* (central hall) divides the floor in two and is graced with period furnishings and portraits of various Mocenigo greats (the family provided seven dogi). The five big portraits are of rank outsiders, such as Charles II of England. Not all of the furnishings belonged to the Mocenigo family, who stopped living here in 1945.

PONTE DI CALATRAVA Map pp290-1

Ponte di Calatrava, Santa Croce/Cannaregio
⚓ **Piazzale Roma/Ferrovia**

The Spanish architect's daring, luminous design for Venice's fourth pedestrian bridge, linking the train station with Piazzale Roma, is a fantasy of glass, stone and steel. It is also an incredible cock-up. After repeated delays in putting the bridge in place between the two concrete ends built on either side of the canal, it was discovered in March 2005 that they had been botched and the centrepiece could not be slotted in. Subject of controversy from the beginning (why a bridge so close to the Ponte dei Scalzi?), the bridge has become the subject of writs, anger and not a little humiliation for its godfather, Mayor Paolo Costa, who left office in 2005. Whether or not you will be able to see the completed bridge when you have this in your hands is a moot point.

PONTE DI RIALTO Map p296

⚓ **Rialto**

Given Rialto's importance from the earliest days of the Republic, it is hardly surprising that the city's first bridge over the Grand Canal was built here. The crossing had quite a chequered history before Antonio da Ponte (Anthony of the Bridge) built this robust marble version. Commissioned in

1588, it cost 250,000 ducats, an enormous sum in those days. When it was finally completed in 1592, all concerned must have been happy with the result – which has lasted nicely in the four centuries since.

The first bridge was little more than a dodgy pontoon arrangement thrown across the canal around 1180. A more permanent wooden structure was built in 1265, but it was cut in two in 1310 as Baiamonte Tiepolo and his fellow rebels beat a hasty retreat on horseback (see Knocking Rebellion on the Head, p120). The bridge was repaired, but it collapsed in a heap in 1444 under the weight of a crowd straining to watch the wedding procession of the Marquis of Ferrara. It was again rebuilt, as a timber drawbridge, before finally being dismantled and replaced by da Ponte's version.

RIALTO Map p300
🚊 Rialto

Rivoalto (later contracted to Rialto), the highest spot in the collection of islets that formed the nucleus of the lagoon city, was one of the areas of first settlement – although the more active part was initially on the San Marco side of the bridge. The San Polo side slowly gained the ascendance and became the centre of trade and banking for the Republic. This is where dosh traded hands, voyages were bankrolled, insurance was arranged and news (or gossip) was exchanged.

The area continues to buzz with the activity of the daily produce and fish **markets** – why break the habit of 700 years?

The **Fabbriche Vecchie** (Old Buildings; Map p300), along the Ruga degli Orefici, were created by Scarpagnino in 1522. They were designed to accommodate markets at ground level and house offices in the upper levels. Next door is the **Palazzo dei Dieci Savi** (Palace of the Ten Wise Men; Map p300). The Dieci Savi administered taxes (the building now houses the Magistrato alle Acque, or water administration). The **Fabbriche Nuove** (New Buildings; Map p300), running along the Grand Canal, went up in 1555 to designs by Sansovino and became home to magistrates' courts. Other magistrates, the 'chamberlains', were housed in a separate Renaissance edifice, the curious, five-sided **Palazzo dei Camerlenghi** (Map p300), designed by Guglielmo dei Grigi. At ground level were prisons for common offenders.

The **Pescaria** (Fish Market; Map p300), which extends into Campo delle Beccarie, was rebuilt in neo-Gothic style in 1907. They have been selling fresh fish here since 1300. While in Campo delle Beccarie, spare a thought for the Querini family. One wing of their house still looks onto the square, but the rest was demolished in 1310 in reprisal for having backed the revolt against Doge Pietro Gradenigo.

From the docks all around Rialto, crusader fleets set sail. While men and provisions were gathered, various knights and other notables stayed in hostels just behind the Fabbriche Nuove. Many others camped out on Giudecca or around the Chiesa di San Nicolò on the Lido. Before heading off, they heard their last Mass on

WHEN SCHOOL WAS COOL

The name *scuola* (school) as applied to the great confraternities in Venice is perhaps misleading to a modern reader. In an era when the welfare state had not even been dreamed of, the *scuola* served as a community and religious association. Its lay members formed a *confraternita* (brotherhood) under a patron saint and, apart from acting as a religion-based club, they dealt with such matters as financial assistance to the families of members fallen on hard times. The *scuola*, along with the parish church, formed the backbone of local social life and was regulated by the *mariegola* (from the Latin *matricula*), a kind of club rulebook.

The division between the rich and powerful big six (the Scuole Grandi, dedicated to San Marco, San Rocco, San Teodoro, San Giovanni Evangelista, Santa Maria della Misericordia and Santa Maria della Carità – the latter swallowed up into the Accademia in the 18th century) and the rest (the Scuole Minori) was decreed in the 15th century. The Scuola dei Carmini was added to the big league in 1767. The smaller *scuole* totalled about 400, many without a church or even a fixed headquarters. Pretty much all the city's workers' and artisans' guilds had their own *scuola* and patron saint, with whom they identified strongly. As club, welfare centre and rallying point for the big parades and religious events in the city, the role of the *scuola* in Venetian society cannot be underestimated.

Early in the 19th century, most of the *scuole*, as religious institutions, were suppressed by Napoleon's administrators. Some of the richer ones (and they were well endowed) lost a good number of their works of art and precious artefacts in the course of what can only be described as heavy-handed plundering by the French. Only a few of the *scuole* were later resurrected. Some are now used, among other things, to host exhibitions and concerts.

land for some time in the **Chiesa di San Giacomo di Rialto** (Map p300). Virtually in the middle of the market, off the Ruga degli Orefici, it was supposedly founded on 25 March 421, the same day as the city.

Across the square from the church is a statue of a man bent beneath the weight of a staircase. Sculpted in 1541, the staircase allowed officials of the Republic to climb onto the adjacent trunk of an ancient column to proclaim official decrees. Known to Venetians as **Il Gobbo** (The Hunchback; Map p300), the statue also represented the finishing line for criminals sentenced to be paraded and flogged through the streets from Piazza San Marco. On reaching Il Gobbo they would kiss the statue, thus marking the end of their torment. The Church disapproved and eventually ordained that the prisoners should kiss a small cross etched for the purpose into a pillar to the left of Il Gobbo.

SCUOLA GRANDE DI SAN GIOVANNI EVANGELISTA Map pp290-1

☎ 041 71 82 34; Campiello della Scuola 2454; adult/child €5/1.55; ⏱ 9am-12.30pm Tue-Thu; 🚈 Ferrovia

Hidden behind what is to all intents an open-air iconostasis and thus set back from the street is one of the six major Venetian *scuole*. Like the Scuola Grande di San Rocco (see below), the plan is typical of the big schools, with an assembly hall (here divided in two by a line of columns) and a grand staircase up to the 1st-floor hall, which contains an altar used for religious services. Codussi designed the original interior, and Massari restyled the main hall in sumptuous fashion in 1727. Many of the major works of art once housed here have been moved to the Gallerie dell'Accademia.

Opposite the *scuola* stands the **Chiesa di San Giovanni Evangelista** (Map pp294–5), which was closed for restoration at the time of research.

SCUOLA GRANDE DI SAN ROCCO

Map pp294-5

☎ 041 523 48 64; www.scuolagrandesanrocco.it; Campo San Rocco, San Polo 3052; adult/18-26yr/ under 18yr €5.50/4/free; ⏱ 9am-5.30pm Easter-Oct, 10am-4pm Nov-Easter; 🚈 San Tomà

Scarpagnino's Renaissance façade (exhibiting a hint of the baroque to come), with its white-marble columns and overbearing magnificence, seems uncomfortably

Chiesa di Santa Maria Gloriosa dei Frari (p72), Sestiere di San Polo

squeezed into the tight space of the narrow square below it. Whatever you make of the exterior of this *scuola* dedicated to St Roch, nothing can prepare you for what lies inside.

St Roch was born in 1295 in Montpellier, France, and at the age of 20 began wandering through southern France and Italy helping plague victims. He died in 1327 and a cult soon developed to celebrate his memory. His body was transferred to Venice as a kind of plague-prevention measure in 1485 (you can never be too careful when it comes to the plague).

After winning a competition (Veronese was among his rivals), Tintoretto went on to devote 23 years of his life to decorating the school. The overwhelming concentration of more than 50 paintings by the master is altogether too much for the average human to digest. Chronologically speaking, you should start upstairs (Scarpagnino designed the staircase) in the Sala Grande Superiore (Upper Great Hall). Here you can pick up mirrors to carry around to avoid getting a sore neck while inspecting the ceiling paintings, which depict Old Testament episodes. Around the walls are scenes from the New Testament. A handful of works by other artists (such as Titian, Giorgione and Tiepolo) can also be seen. To give your eyes a rest from the paintings, inspect the woodwork below them – it is studded with curious designs, including a false book collection.

Downstairs, the walls of the confraternity's assembly hall feature a series on the life of the Virgin Mary, starting on the left wall with the *Annunciazione* (Annunciation) and ending with the *Assunzione* (Assumption) opposite.

SESTIERE DI CANNAREGIO

Eating pp150–3; Shopping p187; Sleeping pp200–2; Walking pp130–4

Orientation

Long the swampiest part of Venice and unpleasantly malarial to boot, the area owes its name to the *canne* (reeds) that grew in abundance here. For most people, this *sestiere* represents their first contact with Venice. Trains pull into Santa Lucia station and disgorge passengers into this corner of town. Covering the whole northwest sector of Venice above the Grand Canal, and bordering the *sestieri* of Castello to the east and San Marco to the south, it is a curious mix.

The main drag to San Marco has a tacky, cheap-souvenir feel to it, lined with shops and restaurants that in most cases have an eye on the quick euro and hope to attract new arrivals who haven't yet had a chance to learn better. The area near the train station is laden with quick-fix hotels – some good, but many a dreary choice.

Away from the inevitable hubbub along the main drag, hidden in the streets and canals away from the Grand Canal side of the *sestiere* are a mix of off-the-beaten-track churches and a hive of nocturnal activity around Fondamenta della Misericordia. This is also where you'll find the city's one-time Jewish Ghetto.

CA' D'ORO Map p300

☎ 041 523 87 90, bookings ☎ 041 520 03 45; www.cadoro.org, in Italian; Calle di Ca' d'Oro 3932; adult/student/under 12yr & EU citizen (and those of certain other nations) under 18yr or over 65yr €5/2.50/free, see also Special Tickets; ☾ 8.15am-2pm Mon, 8.15am-7.15pm Tue-Sun; ☲ Ca' d'Oro
This magnificent Gothic structure, built in the 15th century, got its name (Golden House) from the gilding that originally decorated the sculptural details of the façade. The façade, visible from the Grand Canal, stands out from the remainder of the edifice, which is rather drab by comparison.

Ca' d'Oro houses the **Galleria Franchetti**, an impressive collection of bronzes, tapestries and paintings. The 1st floor is devoted mainly to religious painting, sculpture and bronzes from the 15th and early 16th

centuries. One of the first items you see is *San Bartolomeo,* a polyptych recounting the martyrdom of St Bartholomew. Take a closer look at the detail: the violence is remarkable, as is the saintly indifference with which Bartholomew seems to accept his torment!

On the 2nd floor are a series of fresco fragments saved from the **Fondaco dei Tedeschi** (p56). All but one are by Titian. The other, a nude by Giorgione, is the most striking. Also on this floor is a collection including works by Tintoretto, Titian, Carpaccio, Mantegna, Vivarini, Signorelli and van Eyck.

A big incentive for visiting is the chance to lean out from the balconies over the Grand Canal on the 1st and 2nd floors.

CHIESA DEI SCALZI Map pp290-1

Fondamenta dei Scalzi 55; admission free; ☾ 7-11.45am & 4-6.45pm Mon-Sat, 7.45am-12.30pm & 4-7pm Sun & holidays; ☲ Ferrovia
Virtually next to the train station, this is a rare baroque extravagance. Longhena designed the church, but the baroque façade was done by Giuseppe Sardi. The abundance of columns and statues in niches is a deliberate echo of the particularly extravagant baroque style often employed in Rome. The Carmelites, who had moved here from Rome several years before, specifically requested that it be so. The voluptuous decorative spin continues within – the altar is a good example of baroque clearly heading for the extremes of rococo. Damaged frescoes by Tiepolo appear in the vaults of two of the side chapels. The last doge, Ludovio Manin, who presided over the dissolution of the Republic in 1797 before the threat of Napoleon and died in ignominy five years later, is buried here before the main altar on the left.

CHIESA DELLA MADONNA DELL'ORTO Map pp290-1

Campo della Madonna dell'Orto 3520; admission €2.50 or Chorus ticket; ☾ 10am-5pm Mon-Sat, 1-5pm Sun; ☲ Madonna dell'Orto
Architecture fans should find the exterior of this church intriguing. Elements of Romanesque remain (the inner arch over the main entrance, for instance) in what is largely a 14th-century Gothic structure in brick. That changes were made a century later is clear from the series of statues in niches

above the two lower wings of the façade and from the triangular finish at the top. The five statues crowning the façade were added in the 18th century.

Tintoretto was a parishioner and, although he used a good deal of his creative genius filling the Scuola Grande di San Rocco with his paintings, he found time to execute works for this church, too. Among them are the *Giudizio Finale* (Last Judgment), the *Adorazione del Vitello d'Oro* (Adoration of the Golden Calf) and the *Apparizione della Croce a San Pietro* (Vision of the Cross to St Peter). On the wall at the end of the right aisle is the *Presentazione di Maria al Tempio* (Presentation of Mary at the Temple). Tintoretto is buried with other family members in the church.

In the Cappella di San Mauro is the whitestone statue of the *Madonna col Bambino* (Madonna and Child) after which the church is named. The statue was supposedly found in a nearby garden in 1377 and brought here amid considerable excitement.

CHIESA DI SAN GEREMIA Map pp290-1
☎ 041 71 61 81; Campo San Geremia 274; admission free; 🕙 8.30am-noon & 4-6.30pm Mon-Sat, 9.30am-12.15pm & 5.30-6.30pm Sun & holidays 🚊 Ferrovia

This otherwise uninspiring 18th-century church contains the body of St Lucy (Santa Lucia), who was martyred in Syracuse in AD 304. Her body was stolen by Venetian merchants from Constantinople in 1204 and moved to San Geremia after the Palladian church of Santa Lucia was demolished in the 19th century to make way for the train station.

CHIESA DI SAN GIOVANNI GRISOSTOMO Map p300
☎ 041 522 71 55; Salizada San Giovanni Grisostomo; admission free; 🕙 8.30am-12.15pm & 3.30-7pm Mon-Sat, 10.15am-12.15pm & 3-7pm Sun & holidays; 🚊 Rialto

This church was remodelled on a Greekcross plan by Codussi in 1504. Since 1977 it has housed an icon of the Virgin Mary that attracts a lot of the local faithful. With all the burning incense and candles, to wander in here is to feel yourself transported to a mysterious church of the Orthodox East. Notable is Giovanni Bellini's *San Gerolamo e Due Santi* (St Jerome and Two Saints).

CHIESA DI SAN MARCUOLA
Map pp290-1
☎ 041 71 38 72; Campo San Marcuola 1758; admission free; 🕙 3-6pm Mon-Sat; 🚊 San Marcuola

Although a church has been here since the 9th century, what you see was cobbled together (and not quite completed) in the 18th century by Giorgio Massari and Antonio Gaspari. Inside is an *Ultima Cena* (Last Supper) by Tintoretto. His Christ and apostles are spotlighted against a black background, giving the meal an extraordinary air.

CHIESA DI SANTA MARIA DEI MIRACOLI Map p300
Campo dei Miracoli 6074; admission €2.50 or Chorus ticket; 🕙 10am-5pm Mon-Sat, 1-5pm Sun; 🚊 Fondamente Nuove

It looks like an elaborate box containing the most refined of chocolates. Pietro Lombardo was responsible for this Renaissance jewel, which is fully covered inside and out in marble, bas-reliefs and statues. They say the marble came from leftovers originally destined for use in the Basilica di San Marco, but regardless of where it came from or was meant to go, the result is richly intense but without the flowery motifs that would come later with baroque. The timber ceiling is also eye-catching. Pietro and Tullio Lombardo did the carvings on the choir stalls.

CHIESA DI SANT'ALVISE Map pp290-1
Campo Sant'Alvise 3025; admission €2.50 or Chorus ticket; 🕙 10am-5pm Mon-Sat, 1-5pm Sun; 🚊 Sant'Alvise

Built in 1388, this church plays host to a noteworthy Tiepolo, the *Salita al Calvario* (Climb to Calvary), a distressingly human

Sights

SESTIERE DI CANNAREGIO

CANNAREGIO TRANSPORT
Vaporetti allow you several approaches to the area. Apart from the Ferrovia stop, where an abundance of lines call, there are only two Grand Canal stops – San Marcuola (Nos 1 and 82 and N) and Ca' d'Oro (No 1 and N). Lines 41, 42, 51 and 52 wing around from Ferrovia into the Canale di Cannaregio and then on around the *sestiere's* northern lagoon shore to Fondamente Nuove, where you can also pick up vaporetti for Murano and other islands in the northern half of the lagoon. For more information, see p246.

depiction of one of Christ's falls under the weight of the cross. The ceiling frescoes are a riot of colour.

I GESUITI Map p300

☎ 041 528 65 79; Salizada dei Specchieri 4880; admission free; ☉ 10am-noon & 4-6pm; 🚊 Fondamente Nuove

The Jesuits took over this church, more properly known as the Chiesa di Santa Maria Assunta, in 1657 and ordered its reconstruction in the Roman baroque style. The conversion was completed by 1730. The façade is impressive enough – in fact, as is often the case with such sights in Venice, it seems out of place, as though it's bursting for more space to allow a greater appreciation of its splendour.

No-one could accuse the Jesuits of sober tastes. Inside, the church is lavishly decorated with white-and-gold stucco, white-and-green marble floors, and marble flourishes filling in any empty slots. Tintoretto's *Assunzione della Vergine* (Assumption of the Virgin), in the northern transept, is a remarkable exception to his usual style – think of the darkness of his images in the Scuola Grande di San Rocco and you wonder where all the lightness and joy came from in this painting. Maybe there was some role-swapping going on, as Titian's *Martirio di San Lorenzo* (Martyrdom of St Lawrence) is an uncharacteristically stormy and gloomy piece (it's the first painting on the left as you enter the church). Of course, the subjects of each painting make the respective results quite logical.

MUSEO EBRAICO Map pp290-1

☎ 041 71 53 59; www.ghetto.it; Campo del Ghetto Nuovo 2902/b; adult/student €3/2, tours incl admission €8.50/7; ☉ 10am-7pm Sun-Fri except Jewish holidays Jun-Sep, 10am-4.30pm Sun-Fri Oct-May, tours of Ghetto & synagogues half-hourly to hourly from 10.30am Sun-Fri except Jewish holidays; 🚊 Guglie

A modest collection of Jewish religious silverware can be found at the Jewish Museum. Opened in 1955, it has been enriched down the years with donations of material used in private prayer and to decorate synagogues. The guided tours (in Italian or English; other languages if booked in advance) of the Ghetto and

three of its synagogues (Schola Canton, Schola Italiana and then the Schola Levantina in summer or the Schola Spagnola in winter) that leave from the museum are highly recommended. You can also enquire at the museum about guided tours to the Antico Cimitero Israelitico (Old Jewish Cemetery; Map pp302–3) on the Lido. See also the boxed text, opposite.

ORATORIO DEI CROCIFERI Map p300

☎ 041 271 90 12; Campo dei Gesuiti 4095; admission €2; ☉ 3.30-6.30pm Fri & Sat Apr-Oct; 🚊 Fondamente Nuove

Virtually across the road from the grand Gesuiti church is this tiny 12th-century oratory, once part of a medieval hospice that has long since ceased to exist. It appears the brothers of the Crociferi order who set up here came from Rome. The hospice had a dual role, as was common at the time: to give shelter to pilgrims and provide assistance to the sick. In the 16th century the whole complex was renovated and Palma il Giovane hired to plaster the walls of the oratory with paintings and frescoes depicting events in the history of the hospice and of the order, along with more standard scenes from the Christian tradition.

PALAZZO LABIA Map pp290-1

☎ 041 78 12 68; Campo San Geremia 275; admission free; ☉ 3-4pm Wed-Fri; 🚊 Guglie

Now the Venice office of the RAI, Italy's national radio and TV organisation, this was once a grand 17th-century family residence. It boasts several frescoes by Giambattista Tiepolo inside, but you need to phone ahead to arrange an afternoon visit. The Labia family had arrived in Venice from Spain and planned to make a hit among the local aristocracy. The frescoes are said to represent his greatest secular commission.

The grand ballroom, a two-storey-high space characterised by a gamut of architectural trompe l'oeil trickery, is the framework for two giant frescoes depicting the meeting of Anthony and Cleopatra and the Cleopatra's banquet. In the latter fresco, Tiepolo included a portrait of himself as one of the dignitaries invited along. The ceiling fresco represents the victory of Bellerophon over Time.

The Labia family quickly established a reputation in Venice for their lavish lifestyle.

THE JEWS OF VENICE

The first records of Jews in Venice go back to the 10th century. The early Jews were Ashkenazi of German and Eastern European origins. Even at this early point, acquiring Venetian citizenship was all but impossible, and so outsiders had to content themselves with regularly renewing their residence permits. In 1382, the Maggior Consiglio decreed that Jews could operate as moneylenders. Indeed, it encouraged them.

As refugees of various nationalities crowded into Venice during the dark days of the League of Cambrai (see p44), the Republic decided on 29 March 1516 that all Jews residing in Venice should be moved to one area. The Getto Novo (New Foundry) was considered ideal, being far from the city's power centres and surrounded by water – a natural prison. The Ashkenazis' harsh Germanic pronunciation gave us the word *ghetto*. It should be emphasised that, although Venice gave us the word, the concept was an old one, as Jews living in Spain in earlier centuries well knew.

Jews could move freely through the city only if they wore a yellow cap or badge. At midnight a curfew was imposed. Gates around the Ghetto Nuovo were shut by Christian guards (paid for by the Jewish community) and reopened at dawn.

Excluded from most professions, Jews had few career options. Most tried to get along as moneylenders or in the rag trade. Two of the 'banks' from which moneylenders used to operate remain in evidence on Campo del Ghetto Nuovo, the Banco Rosso and Banco Verde (Map pp290–1). A third option was medicine. Jews who had lived in Muslim Spain or in the Middle East had benefited from the advances in the Arab world on this front and were considered better doctors than their Christian counterparts. Jewish doctors were allowed, in emergencies, to leave the Ghetto during curfew. It sounds bad, but everything is relative. Jews who made it to Venice were not persecuted and were free to practise their religion. Compared with their brethren in much of the rest of Europe, Venice's Jews were doing OK.

A quick look around will show you how small the Ghetto was. And the population, already in its thousands, was growing. In 1541, waves of Levantine Jews from Spain and Portugal made their way to Venice. Here there was a difference – they came with money, as many were wealthy merchants with contacts in the Near East.

Extreme overcrowding combined with building-height restrictions had already created 'skyscrapers' around the Campo del Ghetto Nuovo – some apartment blocks have as many as seven storeys, but with low ceilings. On top of three of them were built three modest *schole*. The Schola Tedesca (German Synagogue) is above the building that now houses the Museo Ebraico. Virtually next door is the Schola Canton (Corner Synagogue) and further around is the Schola Italiana (Italian Synagogue; all Map pp290-1). The last is the simplest; the largely destitute Italian Jews concerned had come from Spanish-controlled southern Italy. From the outside, the synagogues can be distinguished from the residential housing by the small domes that indicate the position of the pulpit. In the case of the German and Italian ones, the rows of five larger windows are another clear sign.

When the Levantine Jews began to arrive, even the town authorities had to admit there was no more space and ceded another small area to the Jews – the Getto Vecchio (Old Foundry). So of course it came to be known as the Old Ghetto, although the converse was true (the foundry was old but the Jewish community was new). Here the Spanish and Portuguese built their two synagogues (Schola Levantina and Schola Spagnola; see the Museo Ebraico, opposite), considered the most beautiful synagogues in northern Italy.

A final small territorial concession was wrung from the town authorities when a street east of the Ghetto Nuovo, subsequently known as the Calle del Ghetto Nuovissimo (Very New Ghetto Street), was granted to the Jews.

From 1541 until 1553, the Jewish community thrived. Their money and trade were welcome in Venice, and they also built a reputation for book printing. Then Pope Julian banned such activities. From then on, things started to go downhill. To top it off, the plague of 1630 left fewer than 3000 Jews alive.

In 1797 Napoleon abolished all restrictions on Jews. Later, under the Austrians, they enjoyed considerable liberty, if not complete freedom from prejudice. After Venice was annexed to the Kingdom of Italy in 1866, all minorities were guaranteed full equality before the law and freedom of religious expression.

Mussolini's rise to power spelt trying times for Jews in Italy. The 1938 race laws imposed restrictions, but the real torment only came in November 1943, when the puppet Fascist government of Salò declared Jews enemies of the state. Of Venice's 1670 remaining Jews, quite a few were rounded up and sent to the Italian concentration camp of Fossoli (outside Modena). They were even marched out of the Casa Israelitica di Riposo rest home (Map pp290–1) on Campo del Ghetto Nuovo; the home's wall bears a memorial to the victims. The next stop for about 200 of them was a death camp in Poland. Altogether, about 8000 Italian Jews were killed in the Holocaust.

Of the 500 or so Jews still living in Venice, only about 30 remain in the Ghetto. For more on the Ghetto, you can look online at www.ghetto.it.

A story recounts that on one evening they hosted a grand dinner party. As the meal came to an end, in a grand gesture the master of the house had all the gold cutlery thrown out the window into the canal, declaring: *'Le abbia o non le abbia, sarò sempre un Labia'* (a nice word game, the gist of which is that, 'whether I have it' – the gold cutlery – 'or not I will always be a Labia'). The guests were suitably impressed, but the story goes that Signor Labia had been careful to have nets laid out at the bottom of the canal earlier that day…

PALAZZO VENDRAMIN-CALERGI
Map pp290-1

☎ 041 529 69 90; Campiello Vendramin 2040; admission free; tours 10.30am Sat; 🚢 San Marcuola
The canalside façade of this one-time patrician mansion is a masterpiece of restrained Renaissance elegance, behind which lurk the gambling rooms of the city's casino. The composer Richard Wagner expired here in 1883. You can wander into the ground-floor area during casino hours but you'll have to fork out to see the gaming rooms, where formal dress is obligatory. To tour the rooms Wagner took while in Venice, you must book a place on Friday between 10am and noon for the tour that takes place at 10.30am on Saturday.

SESTIERE DI CASTELLO
Eating pp153–5; Shopping pp188–9; Sleeping pp202–12; Walking pp134–8

Orientation
The fish's tail stretches east from San Marco, and contains a mix of the major monuments (such as the grand Chiesa dei SS Giovanni e Paolo) and posh waterfront hotels facing the Bacino di San Marco. The defensive walls of the city's once mighty shipyards, the Arsenale, dominate the centre of Castello; east of here the district trails out into a mix of intensely Venetian, lively 'suburbs' and quiet extremities, such as the leafy Sant'Elena and sleepy San Pietro.

ARSENALE Map p298
☎ 041 270 95 46; Campo Arsenale 2407; admission depends on exhibitions; 🕐 depends on exhibitions; 🚢 Arsenale

For centuries the crenellated walls of the Arsenale hid from view the feverish, infernal activity of the city's shipwrights, busy churning out galleys, merchant ships and other vessels at a pace unmatched anywhere in Europe. Thousands of *arsenaloti* (Arsenale workers), each specialising in certain trades, beavered away in assembly-line fashion hundreds of years before the industrial era.

The dockyards are said to have been founded in 1104, although some historians think it may have happened a century later. What became known as the Arsenale Vecchio (Old Arsenal; Map p298) is the core of the complex. Within it was a special storage area for the *bucintoro*, the doge's ceremonial galley (used on important occasions, such as the Sposalizio del Mar – see With This Ring I Thee Wet, p38).

As the Republic's maritime needs grew and shipbuilding requirements changed, so the Arsenale was enlarged. In 1303–04 came the first expansion, known as La Tana (Map p299). Occupying almost the whole length of the southern side of the Arsenale, it was refashioned in 1579 by Antonio da Ponte. The Arsenale Nuovo (New Arsenal; Map p299) was added in 1325, followed in 1473 by the Arsenale Nuovissimo (Very New Arsenal; Map p289). When, in the 16th century, production of *galeazze* (much larger war vessels with a deeper draught) got under way, further workshops and construction sheds (Map p289) were added, along with the Canale delle Galeazze. The whole was, unsurprisingly, walled in and top secret. The *arsenaloti* were relatively well paid and tended to be faithful to the doge and the State throughout the history of the Republic. This was proven on several occasions when they were called to arms in times of unrest or rebellion.

The Arsenale was as close as Venice (or anyone for that matter, until the 18th century) came to industrial production. And to late-medieval eyes it must have made an enormous impression, with all its boiling black pitch, metalworking and timber cutting. Dante was so awestruck he used it as a model scene for hell in his *Divina Commedia* (Divine Comedy; Canto XXI, lines 7–21).

As well as shipyards, the Arsenale served as a naval base. An emergency reserve fleet of at least 25 vessels was always kept ready to set sail from inside the Arsenale, either as a war fleet or as merchant ships. As the centuries progressed, although the shortage of raw materials (especially timber) became a problem, more often than not the Republic's difficulty was finding crews. Eventually, it was obliged to employ slaves, prisoners and press gangs to fill the personnel gaps.

At its peak the Arsenale covered 46 hectares, was home to 300 shipping companies and employed up to 16,000 people. In 1570, when requested to produce as many ships as possible for an emergency fleet, the Arsenale put out an astounding 100 galleys in just two months. The following year at the Battle of Lepanto, the last great sea struggle fought mainly with oar power and a stunning defeat of the Turks, more than half the allied Christian fleet (which included Imperial Spain) was provided by Venice.

For most of its history, Venice relied on one form or another of rowing vessel, often combined with sail. In battle, such galleys were often more manoeuvrable. By the 17th century, however, the nimble, all-sail vessels being produced in England and Holland began to show their superiority. The Arsenale never fully made the switch and, when it tried, its products often proved inferior. By this time, Venetians were increasingly turning away from the sea anyway, and the practice of buying or renting foreign vessels (and sometimes their crews) grew more common. Venice was growing soft and its people were becoming landlubbers. By the time La Serenissima fell in 1797, naval production had all but ceased. Various minor modifications were made to the Arsenale in the course of the 19th century and the area remains in the Navy's hands, although much of it is now used as exhibition space.

The land gateway, surmounted by the lion of St Mark, is considered by many to be the earliest example of Renaissance architecture in Venice; it was probably executed in 1460. Later, a plaque was installed commemorating the victory at Lepanto in 1571. The fenced-in terrace was added in 1692. At the foot of the statues (each with allegorical meaning) is a row of carved lions of varying size and type. The biggest of them, in regally seated pose, was taken as booty by Francesco Morosini from the Greek port of Piraeus. This must have required quite an effort. On its right flank is a series of Viking runes. Attempts to decipher them have brought mixed results, although by one account they are an 11th-century 'Harold

Fishing on the Arsenale (opposite), Sestiere di Castello

was here'–style piece of graffiti left behind by Norwegian mercenaries who apparently took control of Piraeus at the time.

Over the past few years, large (and for a long time largely neglected) parts of the Arsenale have been taken over and partly restored by the city's Biennale organisation for conversion into gallery and exhibition space. These areas include the former Corderia (where ships' cables were made), the Artiglierie (guns) and various wharfs. Exhibitions thus provide ample opportunity to get inside the Arsenale, although parts remain naval property and thus out of bounds. It is possible to enter via the main entrance, although more often than not entry to exhibitions is from Campo della Tana. You pass through the lofty shipyard buildings, now empty but for the massive pillars that hold up the roof. Following these you can then head outside to view the Darsena Grande (aka Darsena Nuova; Map p299), still home to coastguard and *carabinieri* (military police) vessels.

CASTELLO TRANSPORT

Vaporetti Nos 41 and 42 run clockwise and anticlockwise around the Castello district on their circular routes. Nos 51 and 52 do the same thing but include the Lido in their travels. They call at San Zaccaria, the main Castello stop near Piazza San Marco and calling point for various lines, including Nos 1, 5, 20 and 82, N and a branch of the LN. Giardini is the main stop for the Biennale grounds (the Biennale stop operates only during the festival). For more information, see p246.

CATTEDRALE DI SAN PIETRO DI CASTELLO Map p299

Campo San Pietro; admission €2.50 or Chorus ticket; ⏱ 10am-5pm Mon-Sat, 1-5pm Sun; 🚤 San Pietro

Although it's overshadowed by the Basilica di San Marco in the heart of town, this church, sitting in easy somnolence on the far-removed island of San Pietro, was in fact Venice's cathedral from 1451 to 1807. Indeed the island, originally known as Olivolo, was among the first areas to be inhabited.

In 775 the original church here was the seat of a bishopric. Between then and the 16th century it underwent several transformations. Its present appearance is basically a post-Palladian job, taking its cue in part from Giudecca's Chiesa del Redentore, with a monumental façade dating to the end of the 16th century. Palladio had initially been awarded the contract in the 1550s, but the death of the patriarch when the architect was two years into the project led to a halt in work that lasted beyond the genius's death. His successors largely respected his initial ideas.

Inside, various hands were at work at one point or another, including that of Longhena, who was responsible for, among other things, the baroque main altar. Legend says that the strange *Trono di San Pietro* (St Peter's throne) was used by the Apostle Peter in Antioch and that later the Holy Grail was hidden in it. This is all rather unlikely, as the seatback of the throne is made up of a Muslim tombstone, postdating the Apostle's death by quite a number of centuries. But hey, never let the facts get in the way of a good story. The throne is located between the second and third altars on the right side of the church as you enter.

Today San Pietro rests in easy retirement, with its blinding white campanile of Istrian stone by Codussi (finished in 1490) leaning at an odd angle, and the former patriarchate dozily crumbling away next door. The latter was used as a barracks for a while and is now partly occupied by, strictly speaking, illegal apartments.

CHIESA DEI SS GIOVANNI E PAOLO

Map p300

☎ 041 523 59 13; Campo SS Giovanni e Paolo; admission €2.50; ⏱ 9.30am-7pm Mon-Sat, 1-7pm Sun; 🚤 Ospedale

This huge Gothic church (aka San Zanipolo in Venetian), founded by the Dominicans, rivals the Franciscans' Frari (p72) in size and grandeur. Work started on it in 1333, but it was not consecrated until 1430. The similarities between the two are all too evident. The use of brick and modest white stone refinements around windows and doorways is a clear point they have in common. A particular departure here, however, is the way in which three chapels, each of different dimensions, have been tacked – it seems almost willynilly – onto the church's southern flank.

The vast interior, like that of the Frari, is divided simply into an enormous central nave and two aisles, separated by graceful, soaring arches. The red-and-white chessboard floor is a further demonstration of the contemporaneity of the two buildings.

A beautiful stained-glass window made in Murano in the 15th century fills the southern arm of the transept with light. A host of artists contributed to its design, including Bartolomeo Vivarini, Cima da Conegliano and Girolamo Mocetto. It owes some of its brilliance to restoration carried out in the 1980s. Below the window and just to the right is a fine *pala* (altarpiece) by Lorenzo Lotto. On the opposite aisle wall, below the organ, is a triptych by Vivarini. Noteworthy, too, are the five late-Gothic apses, graced by long and slender windows. Look out for Giovanni Bellini's polyptych of *San Vincenzo Ferreri* (St Vincent Ferrer) over the second altar of the right aisle.

In the Cappella del Rosario (Rosary Chapel), off the northern arm of the transept, is a series of paintings by Veronese, including ceiling panels and an *Adorazione dei Pastori* (Adoration of the Shepherds) on the western wall.

The church is a veritable ducal pantheon. Around the walls, many of the 25 tombs of dogi were sculpted by prominent Gothic and Renaissance artists, in particular Pietro and Tullio Lombardo.

At the back of the church runs the narrow Calle Torelli, also known as Calle Cavallerizza, after stables that once stood here. It may seem incredible now, but there was a time when nobles got around town on horseback, and these stables could house about 70 of the beasties. In 1755 Giacomo Casanova was arrested in a house along this street and led off to the Piombi, the rooftop prisons of the Palazzo Ducale.

CHIESA DI SAN FRANCESCO DELLA VIGNA Map p298

☎ 041 520 61 02; Campo San Francesco della Vigna 2786; admission free; ⏲ 8am-12.30pm & 3-7pm; 🚤 Celestia

Palladio was responsible for the high-and-mighty façade of this Franciscan church, which takes its name from the vineyard that once thrived on the site. The remainder was designed by Sansovino. The bell tower at the back seems to all intents and purposes the twin of the Campanile di San Marco. Inside, just to the left of the main door, is a triptych of saints by Antonio Vivarini. The Cappella dei Giustiniani, to the left of the main altar, is decorated with splendid reliefs by Pietro Lombardo and his school. Off the left (northern) arm of the transept you can enter the Cappella Santa, which houses a *Madonna col Bambino e Santi* (Madonna and Child with Saints) by Giovanni Bellini. From here you can admire the leafy cloisters, too.

CHIESA DI SAN GIORGIO DEI GRECI
Map p298

☎ 041 522 65 81; Campiello dei Greci; admission free; ⏲ 9am-1pm & 3-4.30pm Wed-Sat & Mon, 9am-1pm Sun; 🚤 San Zaccaria

Greek Orthodox refugees who fled to Venice from the Ottoman Turks were allowed to raise a church, 'St George of the Greeks', here in 1536. It is intriguing above all for the richness of its Byzantine icons, iconostasis and other artworks. The separate, slender bell tower, completed in 1603, began to lean right from the start.

CHIESA DI SAN GIOVANNI IN BRAGORA Map p298

☎ 041 520 59 06; Campo Bandiera e Moro 3790; admission free; ⏲ 9-11am & 3.30-5.30pm Mon-Sat; 🚤 Arsenale

Antonio Vivaldi was baptised in this church. Among the works of art inside is a restored triptych by Bartolomeo Vivarini, the *Madonna in Trono tra I Santi Andrea e Giovanni Battista* (Enthroned Madonna with St Andrew and John the Baptist). In the peaceful square just south of the church, Campiello del Piovan, the architect Giorgio Massari was born at No 3752.

CHIESA DI SAN LIO Map p296

Campo San Lio; admission free; 🚤 Rialto

Worth a peep in this 11th-century church, if you find it open, is the magnificent ceiling fresco by Giandomenico Tiepolo, the *Gloria della Croce e di San Leone IX* (The Glory of the Cross and St Leon IX). On the left as you enter by the main door is a work by Titian, the *Apostolo Giacomo il Maggiore* (Apostle James the Great). Many years later, Canaletto was baptised and, eventually, buried in this, his parish church.

CHIESA DI SAN MARTINO Map p298

☎ 041 523 04 87; Campo San Martino 2298; admission free; ⏲ 9am-noon & 4.30-7.30pm; 🚤 Arsenale

The ceiling fresco depicting the *Gloria di San Martino* (Glory of St Martin) attracts the eye in here. A further treasure are the

THE INFAMY OF FAMAGUSTA

Keep an eye out for the monument to Marcantonio Bragadin in the Chiesa dei SS Giovanni e Paolo. It is on the wall of the southern aisle, virtually opposite the westernmost pillar. The monument is singular for its content, rather than for any artistic merit.

Bragadin was the commander of the Famagusta garrison in Cyprus, the last to fall to the Turks in 1570. Promised honourable terms of surrender after having endured a long siege, Bragadin decided to call on the Turkish commander Mustafa and present him with the keys of the city. Mustafa lost his head, as it were, and lopped off Bragadin's ears and nose. Several hundred Christians in the vicinity also lost their heads, rather more literally. The postbattle massacre that until now had been avoided suddenly swept like a storm across the city.

While the population of Famagusta was decimated, Bragadin rotted for a couple of weeks in prison. He was then hauled about the town under the crushing weight of sacks of stone and earth. After various other humiliations, he was tied to a stake in the execution square and skinned alive. According to one account, he passed out only when they reached his waist. The corpse was then beheaded and quartered, and the skin stuffed with straw and paraded about town. Mustafa then took it home as a trophy to present to the sultan. Some years later, a Venetian trader with considerable courage managed to steal it from the arsenal of Constantinople and return it to the Bragadin family in Venice. The remains have been in the Chiesa dei SS Giovanni e Paolo since 1596.

Chiesa di San Giovanni in Bragora (p83), Sestiere di Castello

canvases by Palma il Giovane showing Jesus being flogged and on the way to Calvary. The only problem is that these are in the small choir stalls behind the altar and are generally unreachable. You can glimpse them from in front of the altar! There was a church here as early as the 7th century, built by mainland refugees fleeing Lombard invaders, but what you see today was built according to plans by Sansovino and completed in 1654. Well, almost. The façade in Istrian marble was only added in 1897. The church is named after St Martin of Tours (AD 316–97), a Hungarian who wound up as a priest after a stint in the Roman army in Gaul (France). He was the first Christian saint to die a natural death and not as a martyr.

CHIESA DI SAN ZACCARIA Map p298
☎ 041 522 12 57; Campo San Zaccaria 4693; admission to Cappella di Sant'Anastasia €1; ☽ 10am-noon & 4-6pm Mon-Sat, 4-6pm Sun; ⛴ San Zaccaria

If the Basilica di San Marco was the doge's private chapel, this was his parish church (eight dogi are buried here). The Renaissance façade is the handiwork of Antonio Gambello and Codussi. Gambello started off in a Gothic vein but was already influenced by Renaissance thinking. The lower part of the façade in marble is his work. When Codussi took over he favoured white Istrian stone, and the clean curves at the top mark his take on the Renaissance.

Inside, the mix of styles could not be clearer. Against a backdrop of classic Gothic apses, the high cross vaulting of the main body of the church is a leap of faith into the Renaissance. The church has an even longer history and its earliest version dates to the 9th century.

On the second altar to the left after you enter the church is Giovanni Bellini's *La Vergine in Trono col Bambino, un Angelo Suonatore e Santi* (The Virgin Enthroned with Jesus, an Angel Musician and Saints). You cannot miss it. It exudes a light and freshness that the surrounding paintings seem deliberately to lack.

The **Cappella di Sant'Anastasia** is off to the right. It holds works by Tintoretto and Tiepolo, as well as magnificently crafted choir stalls. After walking through it, you then pass through another chapel to reach the **Cappella di San Tarasion** (also called Cappella d'Oro) in the apse. Its vaults are covered in frescoes and the walls are decorated with Gothic polyptychs. Twelfth-century mosaics also survive, and you can wander downstairs to the 10th-century Romanesque crypt, left over from an earlier church on the site.

CHIESA DI SANTA MARIA DELLA VISITAZIONE Map p298
☎ 041 523 10 96; Riva degli Schiavoni 4149; admission free; ☽ closed; ⛴ San Zaccaria

More simply dubbed La Pietà, this church is best known for its association with the composer Vivaldi, who was concertmaster here in the early 18th century. Look for the ceiling fresco by Tiepolo. For many years the church was the scene of regular concerts of Vivaldi's music. The concerts have been transferred for a time to another location (see p170) and until then the church and instruments are off limits.

CHIESA DI SANTA MARIA FORMOSA
Map p296
Campo Santa Maria Formosa 5267; admission €2.50 or Chorus ticket; ☽ 10am-5pm Mon-Sat, 1-5pm Sun; ⛴ San Zaccaria

Rebuilt in 1492 by Mauro Codussi on the site of a 7th-century church, this house of worship bears a curious name stemming from the legend behind its initial foundation. San Magno, bishop of Oderzo, is said to have had a vision of the Virgin Mary on this spot. Not just any old vision, however: in this instance she was *formosa* (beautiful, curvy), which hardly seems in keeping with standard views of Our Lady. The inside of the church was damaged when an Austrian bomb went off in 1916. Among the works of art to survive is an altarpiece by Palma il Vecchio depicting St Barbara, among other saints, and the body of Christ in his mother's arms. Just to the right of the main door (as you face it from the inside) is a 16th-century Byzantine icon, *Santa Maria di Lepanto* (St Mary of Lepanto). Next to the first chapel on the same side of the church is displayed an 8th-century Egyptian Coptic garment, claimed to be the veil of St Marina.

GIARDINI PUBBLICI & BIENNALE

Map p299

🚊 Giardini

Creation of these, the most extensive (if slightly tatty) public gardens in the city, was ordered by Napoleon in 1807. They were officially opened in 1811, just three years before his demise. In the gardens you'll find shaded benches, a few *giostre* (swings and other kids' rides) and a snack bar/restaurant. You may have noticed during your Venetian strolls that there is a surprising amount of greenery, mostly in the form of private gardens (so much so that there is a coffee-table book entitled *Secret Gardens in Venice*, by Cristiana Moldi-Ravenna, Gianni Berengo Gardin and Tudy Sammartini).

Also here are the national pavilions of the Biennale Internazionale d'Arte, Venice's contemporary-arts fest held from June to November every two years (see p11). Together the pavilions form a kind of mini-compendium of 20th-century architectural thinking. Standing well away from the historic centre and thus uninhibited by concerns about clashing with it, the site's pavilions are the work of a legion of architects. Carlo Scarpa contributed in one way or another from 1948 to 1972, continually updating the labyrinthine Italian Pavilion and building the Venezuelan one (1954). He also did the Biglietteria (ticket office) and entrance courtyard. Other interesting contributions are James Stirling's 1991 Padiglione del Libro (Book Pavilion), Gerrit Rietveld's Dutch Pavilion (1954), Josef Hoffman's Austrian Pavilion (1934) and Peter Cox's Australian Pavilion (1988), which backs onto a canal.

MUSEO DELLE ICONE Map p298

☎ 041 522 65 81; www.istitutoellenico.org, in Italian; Ponte dei Greci 3412; adult/student €4/2; ⏱ 9am-5pm; 🚊 San Zaccaria

Also known as the Museo dei Dipinti Sacri Bizantini (Museum of Holy Byzantine Paintings) and attached to the Chiesa di San Giorgio dei Greci (p83), this museum is housed in the Istituto Ellenico (Hellenic Institute). The building was for more than two centuries a hospice for poor and ailing Greeks. Here you can explore the curiosities of Orthodox religious art. On display are some 80 works of art and a series of other items, including the letter from Doge Leonardo Loredan granting the Greeks permission to build their church in Venice. Foremost among the artworks are two 14th-century Byzantine icons, one representing Christ in glory and the other the Virgin Mary with the baby Jesus and Apostles. Many of the remaining works were produced by or for the Greeks in Venice and elsewhere in northern Italy.

MUSEO DIOCESANO D'ARTE SACRA

Map p296

☎ 041 522 91 66; Fondamenta di Sant'Apollonia 4312; admission free, donations welcome; ⏱ 10.30am-12.30pm Mon-Sat; 🚊 San Zaccaria

Housed in a former Benedictine monastery dedicated to Sant'Apollonia, this museum has a fairly predictable collection of religious art. More interesting is the exquisite Romanesque cloister you cross in order to get to the museum. It is a rare example of the genre in Venice. The cloister is often open much longer hours than the museum. The building next door was a church until 1906, and now houses exhibition spaces.

MUSEO STORICO NAVALE Map p298

☎ 041 520 02 76; Riva San Biagio 2148; admission €1.55; ⏱ 8.45am-1.30pm Mon-Fri, 8.45am-1pm Sat; 🚊 Arsenale

Lovers of model boats, from ancient war vessels to modern battleships, will want to call in here. There's plenty of stuff related to Venetian history on the high seas in this former grain silo. Spread over four floors, the museum traces the maritime history of the city and of Italy. There are some wonderfully complex models of all sorts of Venetian vessels, but also ancient triremes, Asian men o' war, WWII warships and ocean liners. The ground floor is devoted mainly to weaponry (the usual stuff: cannons, blunderbusses, swords and sabres). Most curious are the 17th-century diorama maps of Venetian ports and forts across the city's one-time Adriatic and Mediterranean possessions.

On the 1st floor is a model of the sumptuous *bucintoro*, the doge's ceremonial barge, in among the many large-scale model sailing vessels. Napoleon's French troops destroyed the real thing in 1798. The 2nd floor is mostly given over to Italian naval history and memorabilia, from unification to the present day. Up on the 3rd floor is a room containing a few gondolas, including Peggy Guggenheim's. A small room set above the 3rd floor is dedicated to – wait for it – Swedish naval history. Curious.

The ticket also gets you entrance to the **Padiglione delle Navi** (Ships Pavilion; Map p298; Fondamenta della Madonna), near the entrance to the Arsenale. Of the various boats on display, the most eye-catching is the *Scalé Reale*, an early-19th-century ceremonial vessel last used in 1959 to bring the body of the Venetian Pope Pius X to rest at the Basilica di San Marco. It was also used to ferry King Vittorio Emanuele to Piazza San Marco in 1866 when Venice joined the nascent Kingdom of Italy.

EAST FLEES WEST

Venice's fame for comparative tolerance by medieval standards did not extend to making things easy for newcomers. By the time Constantinople fell to the Ottoman Turks in 1453, there was already a Greek community in Venice. The collapse of Byzantium led thousands to flee to La Serenissima. Considered schismatics by the Catholic hierarchy, they were long obliged to worship in private houses. The Greeks wanted to build their own house of worship, independent of the authority of the Venetian patriarch or Rome, but the best they could do was borrow a Catholic church from 1456. In 1498 they were allowed to establish a confraternity. Only in 1514 did they finally receive permission to build their own church, which was completed in 1577. The community thrived from then until the fall of Venice in 1797 to Napoleon. By the end of WWII only 30 Orthodox Greeks remained in the city. In 1958 the Istituto Ellenico, dedicated to Byzantine studies, opened in the premises of what had been the Orthodox Greek confraternity.

OSPEDALETTO Map p298

☎ 041 270 90 12; Barbaria delle Tole 6691; guided visit to Sala da Musica €2; ◷ 3.30-6.30pm Thu-Sat; 🚊 Ospedale

Longhena's baroque Chiesa di Santa Maria dei Derelitti (also known as the Ospedaletto, or Little Hospital) is the focal point of a hospital for elderly and poor patients built centuries earlier on this spot (it also served for a time as an orphanage). The façade is one of the most exuberant bursts of baroque in the city, with giant figures leaning out over the narrow street below. Inside are some fine works by Giambattista Tiepolo and Palma il Giovane.

In an annexe is the elegantly frescoed **Sala da Musica** (Music Room). Most of the frescoes, which celebrate in allegorical form the importance of music, were done by Jacopo Guarana. Here young female orphans learned to sing and play musical instruments, in many cases becoming virtuosi performers. The *putte* or *figlie del coro* (choir girls) were a highly Venetian phenomenon. From around the early 17th century the state not only took in orphan girls (as well as illegitimate girls and daughters of families fallen on hard times) but also paid for their education here and in three other religious institutions around the city (including the **Chiesa di Santa Maria della Visitazione** – see p84 – where Vivaldi was concert master). The bulk of that education served a purpose. Dedicating their time to music, the girls came to form an important part of the city's musical repertory, much admired by locals and foreign visitors to the city alike.

PALAZZO QUERINI STAMPALIA

Map p296

☎ 041 271 14 11; www.querinistampalia.it, in Italian; Campiello Querini Stampalia 5252; adult/student & senior €6/4; ◷ 10am-6pm Tue-Thu & Sun, 10am-10pm Fri & Sat; 🚊 San Zaccaria

The last of this branch of the Querini family ordained that his mansion should become home to a foundation of the same name, which it has been since the 1860s.

Never judge a book by its cover. The outer shell of this building dates from the first half of the 16th century, but the inside could not be more surprising. In the 1940s Carlo Scarpa redesigned the entrance and garden; he then did the 1st floor (which houses the foundation's library) in 1959.

Scarpa decided to have some disciplined fun with shape, and, in the garden in particular, took inspiration from the Arab emphasis on geometric patterns. It may or may not appeal, but it does make a refreshing change. After all, there is little that is 'modern' in Venice.

On the 2nd floor is the **Museo della Fondazione Querini Stampalia**. The core of the collection is made up of period furniture that mostly belonged to the Querinis, portraits of more illustrious family members and various papers. Among the some 400 paintings, mostly minor works, is an interesting *Presentazione di Gesù al Tempio* (Presentation of Jesus at the Temple) by Giovanni Bellini. The poor child looks like a long-suffering mummy, standing up improbably in his tightly wrapped swaddling clothes. And what's the guy on the right looking at? Well you, actually.

Just before you get to the Bellini is a small annexe off a large hall. It contains a long series (around 70 paintings in all) by Gabriele Bella (1730–99) depicting *Scene di Vita Veneziana* (Scenes of Venetian Life). The style of painting is rather naive, if not downright childlike, but the series provides an intriguing set of snapshots of life in Venice's last century under the dogi.

Another room towards the end of the permanent exhibition is devoted to works of Pietro Longhi. It also contains some good examples of traditional Venetian furniture, characterised by its engraved and lacquered wood with painted floral motifs. Quite a few hotels have adopted a watered-down version of the style.

Further rooms range from the Stanza Nuziale (Nuptials Room), decorated with classic Venetian furniture, to the Sala delle Porcellane (Porcelain Room), which boasts the Sèvres collection acquired in 1795–96 by Alvise Querini, the Venetian Republic's last ambassador in Paris before Venice fell to Napoleon. Musical instruments, medallions, coins, tapestries, miniature artillery models, sketches and engravings complete the eclectic collection.

On Friday and Saturday evenings (at 5pm and again at 8.30pm) there are half-hour concerts of 14th- to 18th-century music. The ground-floor café (which you can enter without visiting the *palazzo*) serves light meals and has a boisterous student atmosphere.

RIVA DEGLI SCHIAVONI Map p298
San Zaccaria

The waterside walkway west from Rio Ca' di Dio to the Palazzo Ducale in San Marco is known as the Riva degli Schiavoni. Schiavoni, meaning Slavs, referred to fishermen from Dalmatia (in the former Yugoslavia) who, from medieval times, used to cast their nets off this waterfront. For centuries, vessels would dock here amid all the chaos you might expect from a busy harbour.

Sights

SESTIERE DI CASTELLO

OF FLOORS & WALLS

As you wander about the Palazzo Querini Stampalia (opposite), observe the floor. The smooth, speckled surface, a classic *terrazzo alla Veneziana*, could almost be a mottled carpet if it weren't a little more solid than pile. In fact it's the result of combining finely fragmented marble chips with plaster and then laying this mixture down.

Why not straight marble floors? Virtually the entire city is built on foundations of timber pylons and has all the resulting problems of subsidence that you would expect. Movement is often greater than in more stable mainland environments. Great slabs of marble have no give – they would just crack open. This mixture, when hardened, has all the feel and solidity of marble, but greater elasticity. And when cracks do appear, all you need to do is mix up a batch of the marble-plaster goo, smooth it over and allow it to dry. You don't want it to dry out completely, though. Treatment with linseed oil at least once a year is needed to keep it in good shape and to allow it to be polished.

You will no doubt have noticed this type of floor in the Palazzo Ducale, Museo Correr and some other sites – you may well have it in your hotel room! It is not so apparent in the Palazzo Querini Stampalia, but if you get to see inside other houses or manage to stay in a hotel or mansion of sufficient history, you will often see how much these floors undulate with time – a lot better than breaking up altogether.

While on the subject of home-maintenance issues, you may also have noticed that the classic Venetian colour is a burnt reddish-orange. Innumerable houses are 'painted' this way. Only it isn't really paint. A straight coat of red paint quickly fades and streaks with all the rain and humidity inevitable in the lagoon. Traditionally, the outside walls of houses were coated in a mixture of paint and crushed red bricks. Once applied and dry, it lasts much longer than standard wall paint.

Boat crews, waterfront merchants, nobles, gendarmes and crooks, dressed in all manner of garb reflecting the passing parade of Greeks, Turks, Slavs, Arabs, Africans and Europeans, all jostled about these docks. It is perhaps hard to imagine the seemingly chaotic rows of galleys, galleons and, later on, sailing vessels competing for dock space or moored further out in the Canale di San Marco. Or the confusion of rigging and containers of all sorts, the babble of languages, and the clang and clatter of arms and cooking pots as locals or seafarers prepared impromptu meals for those just arrived. The assault on the senses must have been something.

Today it remains busy, but the actors have changed. The galleons of yore have been replaced by ferries and a growing armada of mega-yachts, the exotic crews and merchants by gondoliers and not-so-exotic tourists. Instead of impromptu food stalls and the smell of cooking meat, there are ice-cream stands and tourist tat. The linguistic babble remains as confusing as ever. Some of the grand old mansions now function as pricey hotels for the well-heeled out-of-towner. Petrarch, one of Italy's greatest writers and a friend of Venice, found lodgings for a time at No 4175, east of Rio della Pietà.

SCUOLA DI SAN GIORGIO DEGLI SCHIAVONI Map p298

☎ 041 522 88 28; Calle dei Furlani 3259/a; admission €3; ☽ 9.30am-12.30pm & 3.30-6.30pm Tue-Sat, 9.30am-12.30pm Sun Apr-Oct, 10am-12.30pm & 3-6pm Tue-Sat, 10am-12.30pm Sun Nov-Mar; ⛴ San Zaccaria

Venice's Dalmatian community established this religious school in the 15th century and the building was erected in the 16th century. The main attraction is on the ground floor, where the walls are graced by a series of superb paintings by Vittore Carpaccio depicting events in the lives of the three patron saints of Dalmatia: George, Tryphone and Jerome. The image of St George dispatching the dragon to the next life is a particularly graphic scene. Scattered about before the dragon are remnants of its victims – various limbs, the half-eaten corpse of a young woman and an assortment of bones.

Members of the *scuola* gathered upstairs for meetings and religious services. Delicate timber décor and the heavy exposed beams of the ceilings complete the scene.

SCUOLA GRANDE DI SAN MARCO

Map p300

☎ 041 529 43 23; Rio dei Mendicanti 6776; admission free; ☽ 8.30am-2pm; ⛴ Ospedale

Standing at right angles to the main façade of the Chiesa dei SS Giovanni e Paolo is the eye-catching marble frontage of this *scuola*. Pietro Lombardo and his sons all worked on what was once one of the most important of Venice's religious confraternities. Codussi put the finishing touches on this Renaissance gem. Have a closer look and, apart from the predictably magnificent lions, you will notice the sculpted trompe l'oeil perspectives covering much of the lower half of the façade. Inside, the timber beams of the ceiling are held up by two ranks of five columns. The staircase to the upper storey is closed.

Nowadays the *scuola* is the main entrance to the Ospedale Civile. Beyond, in what were the Convento dei Domenicani and the Chiesa di San Lazzaro dei Mendicanti, is the hospital proper. You can wander just inside the entrance of the former *scuola* itself, although technically you're not really supposed to if you're not here on the business of ill health. You won't get past the desk in any event. Groups can, theoretically, arrange visits by calling ahead.

STATUE OF BARTOLOMEO COLLEONI

Map p300

Campo SS Giovanni e Paolo; ⛴ Ospedale

Presiding over the grand canalside square is the proud equestrian statue of Bartolomeo Colleoni, a self-indulgent mercenary commander who from 1448 commanded armies in the name of the Republic. It is one of only two such works in the city, a magnificent piece by the Florentine Verrocchio (1435–88). Although Colleoni was of the military school that tended to organise things so that they lived to fight another day, he remained faithful to La Serenissima. On his death in 1474, he bequeathed 216,000 gold and silver ducats and considerably more in property to Venice, on one condition – that the city erect a commemorative statue to him in Piazza San Marco. The Senato took the money but cheated, placing the grand statue here instead. After all, the wise rulers of Venice reasoned after Colleoni's death, the name San Marco appears in the *scuola grande* on the square (see above). Still, Colleoni can rest easy that the Republic didn't scrimp on the statue itself.

AROUND THE LAGOON

Eating pp155–7; Shopping pp189–90; Sleeping pp212–15

Venice goes beyond the six *sestieri*. Indeed, it didn't even begin on the islands that constitute them. Though most of the city's visitors don't bother, it's a worthwhile exercise to get out to at least some of the islands.

Orientation

The island of Giudecca is virtually a part of Venice, forming a vaguely banana-shaped basin to the south of the city. A few kilometres to the east starts the long protective strip of the Lido, Venetians' local beach and sea wall. Below it stretches the razor-thin and equally long sea barrier of Pellestrina island. The most visited islands lie to the north. Murano, of glass-making fame, is first up, while further off lie the pastel-coloured Burano, known for its fishing and lace-making, and the now nearly abandoned Torcello, important for its impressive cathedral and mosaics. Several other islands are dotted about to the north and south of Venice and merit a visit.

GIUDECCA

Originally known as *spina longa* (long fishbone) because of its shape, Giudecca's name probably derives from the word Zudega (from *giudicato* – the judged), applied to rebellious nobles banished from Venice proper. There are variations on this story – the most likely seems to be that as early as the 9th century, families who had been exiled earlier (and, one assumes, unjustly) were given land on Giudecca by way of compensation. Until that time, the only inhabitants had been a handful of fishermen and their families. Some historians beg to differ with this and assert that the island's name comes from a period when many of Venice's Jews lived on it before being forced into the confines of the Ghetto.

By the 16th century the island had been extended through land reclamation to reach something approaching its present form. Merchants set up warehouses, and a flourishing local commercial life made Giudecca a prime piece of real estate. Elite families (such as the Dandolos, Mocenigos and Vendramins) bought up land to build their homes-away-from-home, facing Venice to the north and ending in luxuriant gardens looking south to the open lagoon. Several religious orders also established convents and monasteries here.

When the Republic fell in 1797, everything changed. The noble families slipped away as their fortunes declined. The religious orders were suppressed and the convents closed. The face of the island gradually changed through the 19th century. Replacing the pleasure domes and religious retreats came prisons, barracks and factories, and, with the latter, working-class housing grids. Descendants of the workers who powered the factories remain in the modest low-level housing, but most of the factories have long since been closed down.

Giudecca is a strangely melancholy place. A few boatyards keep busy with repair work, while a handful of shops and eateries

Boating near Isola di San Michele (p92)

survive on a modest local trade and the few tourists who stop long enough to want to eat here. The women's prison (which was a convent for reformed prostitutes until 1857) is still in operation. Mild building activity suggests that more life is perhaps coming to Giudecca; slightly more affordable housing than in central Venice is an attraction. Mind you, there is something for everyone, as VIPs such as Elton John also buy up getaway properties here.

CHIESA DEL REDENTORE Map pp302-3
Campo del SS Redentore 194; admission €2.50 or Chorus ticket; ⏰ 10am-5pm Mon-Sat, 1-5pm Sun; 🛳 Redentore

With the passing of a bout of plague in 1577, the Senato commissioned Palladio to design a church of thanksgiving. The following year, the doge, members of the Senato and a host of citizens made the first pilgrimage of thanksgiving, crossing from Zattere on a pontoon bridge of boats and rafts.

Work on this magnificent edifice was completed under Antonio da Ponte (better known for his Ponte di Rialto) in 1592. The long church was designed to accommodate the large numbers of pilgrims who, from 1578 onwards, made the annual excursion. The pilgrimage still takes place today on the third Saturday in July, and it remains one of the most important events on Venice's calendar.

Inside the church are a few works by Tintoretto, Veronese and Vivarini, but it is the powerful façade that most inspires observers. Indeed, although it is uncertain why the site was chosen, there is no doubt that its open position makes the church easy to observe and admire from just about anywhere on the Fondamenta Zattere across the Canale della Giudecca. The classical cleanness of the design reminds one, if on a considerably grander scale, of the Venetian villas on the mainland (see p234).

CHIESA DELLE ZITELLE Map pp302-3
Fondamenta delle Zitelle; admission free; ⏰ 10am-noon Fri & Sat; 🛳 Zitelle

Designed by Palladio in the late 16th century, the Chiesa di Santa Maria della Presentazione, known as the Zitelle, was a church and hospice for poor young women (zitelle means 'old maids', which is presumably what many of them remained). It is now used for conferences.

CHIESA DI SANT'EUFEMIA Map pp302-3
☎ 041 522 58 48; Fondamenta Sant'Eufemia; 🛳 Palanca

A simple Veneto-Byzantine structure of the 11th century, this church's main portico was actually added in the 18th and 19th centuries. Down Fondamenta Rio di Sant'Eufemia are the one-time church and convent of SS Cosma e Damiano. They were turned into a factory and the bell tower into a smokestack.

TRANSPORT AROUND THE LAGOON

While vaporetti are something of an option in Venice itself and walking is often faster and more interesting, you clearly need to use the ferries to get around the islands. Lines 41, 42, 82 and N serve Giudecca regularly, the easiest approaches being from Ferrovia, Piazzale Roma and San Zaccaria. You can reach the Lido by vaporetti Nos 1, 51, 52, 61, 62 and 82, N and the vehicle ferry (No 17) from Isola del Tronchetto.

The other islands require a little more effort. The DM line runs from Tronchetto via Piazzale Roma and Ferrovia to all stops in Murano. No 5 runs directly from San Zaccaria in summer. Otherwise the most regular services are the 41 and 42, most easily picked up at Fondamente Nuove. You can get to Burano with the LN lines, either from Fondamente Nuove via Murano and Mazzorbo, or the longer trip from San Zaccaria via Lido and Punta Sabbioni. From Burano the T vaporetto runs every half-hour to Torcello. For San Servolo and San Lazzaro, take the No 20 from San Zaccaria. The No 13 vaporetto runs to Le Vignole and Sant'Erasmo from Fondamente Nuove via Murano (Faro stop).

You can get to Pellestrina using the No 11 Lido–Pellestrina bus-and-vaporetto line. If you've hired a bicycle, you can take it across on the vaporetto for €1 (or a combined fare of €4.10 for passenger and bike if you haven't got a day ticket).

For Chioggia, bus No 11 leaves from Gran Viale Santa Maria Elisabetta, outside the tourist office on the Lido; it boards the car ferry at Alberoni and then connects with a steamer at Pellestrina that will take you to Chioggia. The trip costs €5 (if you haven't got a day ticket). Alternatively, you can adopt a more prosaic approach and catch a bus from Piazzale Roma (€4, one hour). In summer the Linea Clodia ferry runs directly from in front of the Pietà church (Chiesa di Santa Maria della Visitazione, p84). Once you're in the town, city bus Nos 1, 2, 6 and 7 connect Chioggia with Sottomarina (a 15-minute walk), the town's beach. For more transport information, see p246.

MULINO STUCKY Map pp302-3

Fondamenta San Biagio; 🚲 **Palanca**

The striking neo-Gothic hulk of the best-known factory complex on the island, the Mulino Stucky, was built in the late 19th century and employed 1500 people. The windowless brick structure, built on an iron frame, looks like a cathedral to industry and is hard to miss when looking across from the western end of the Zattere. It was shut in 1954 and sat long in dignified silence. In 2000 the buildings were saved from the wrecking ball as a plan to restore them and create a luxury hotel for the Hilton chain, apartments and a congress centre got under way. Completion is due in 2006.

ISOLA DI SAN GIORGIO MAGGIORE

CHIESA DI SAN GIORGIO MAGGIORE

Map pp302-3

☎ 041 522 78 27; church free, bell-tower lift €3; 🕑 9.30am-12.30pm & 2.30-6.30pm May-Sep, 9.30am-12.30pm & 2.30-4.30pm Oct-Apr; 🚲 San Giorgio

Palladio's grand church occupies one of the most prominent positions in Venice and, although it inspired mixed reactions among the architect's contemporaries, it had a significant influence on Renaissance architecture. Built between 1565 and 1580, it is his most imposing structure in Venice. The façade, although not erected until the following century, is believed to conform to Palladio's wishes. The massive columns on high plinths, the crowning tympanum and the statues all contain an element of sculptural chiaroscuro, if such a term is permissible, casting strong shadows and reinforcing the impression of strength. Indeed, facing the Bacino di San Marco and the heart of Venice, its effect is deliberately theatrical. Inside, the sculptural decoration is sparse, the open space regimented by powerful clusters of columns and covered by luminous vaults.

San Giorgio Maggiore's art treasures include works by Tintoretto: an *Ultima Cena* (Last Supper) and the *Raccolta della Manna* (Shower of Manna) on the walls of the high altar, and a *Deposizione* (Deposition) in the Cappella dei Morti. Take the lift to the top of the 60m-high bell tower for an extraordinary view.

FONDAZIONE GIORGIO CINI

Map pp302-3

☎ 041 524 01 19; www.cini.it; adult/senior & 7-12yr/under 7yr €12/10/free; 🕑 10am-4.30pm Sat & Sun by one-hour guided visit only; 🚲 San Giorgio

Behind Palladio's grand church extend the grounds of the former monastery. Established as long ago as the 10th century by the Benedictines, it was rebuilt in the 13th century and then restructured and expanded in a series of projects that spanned the 16th century, finishing with the library built by Longhena in the 1640s.

The Cini clan (with interests in the Porto Marghera industrial complex, Adriatic shipping and more) set up the Fondazione Giorgio Cini and bought the island in 1951 (saving the monastic complex from a slow death by neglect) and by 1960 had largely restored the site. The foundation runs various scholarly centres here.

Visits take you first to the Chiostro dei Cipressi (named after the four cypress trees in the cloister), the oldest extant part of the complex, completed in 1526 in an early Renaissance style. One side is flanked by the cells of 56 Benedictine monks who long lived here. Next you pass to the Chiostro del Palladio (designed by the Renaissance star) on the site of the grand Medici library that had been destroyed by fire.

The library had been a donation from Cosimo de' Medici, exiled from Florence in 1433 and head of the dynasty that would preside over that city's destiny for centuries. The Benedictines of the Isola di San Giorgio Maggiore were long the traditional hosts of prestigious foreign dignitaries. The exiled Cosimo was one of the most prestigious, and proved one of the most generous to his benefactors during and after his one-year sojourn in La Serenissima.

Palladio also designed the monumental refectory, in which a grand painting by Veronese depicting the *Nozze di Cana* (Wedding at Cana) once took pride of place. It now hangs in the Louvre. Like so many of the city's artworks, it fell into the greedy hands of Napoleon after the Republic's fall in 1797, and was cut in two, rolled up and packed off to Paris, where it has remained. After visiting the refectory, you are taken up a grand staircase in restrained baroque by Longhena and into his magnificent library.

Finally you stroll through the gardens to the outdoor Teatro Verde, built in the 1950s and sometimes used for summer performances, although in 2005 its immediate future was unclear.

Languages catered for include Italian, English, French and German. Groups of at least 15 can also arrange to visit on weekdays. Enter the door to the left of the main church entrance.

ISOLA DI SAN MICHELE

CIMITERO Map p289
☎ 041 72 98 11; admission free; ◷ 7.30am-4pm Oct-Mar, 7.30am-6pm Apr-Sep; 🔬 Cimitero

The city's cemetery was established on San Michele under Napoleon (even the Venetians can't complain that the diminutive Corsican did nothing for them) and is maintained by the Franciscans. The **Chiesa di San Michele in Isola**, begun by Codussi in 1469, was among the city's first Renaissance buildings, built in sober style of white Istrian stone. The quiet cloister is attractive and worth a peek. Among those pushing up daisies here are Ezra Pound, Sergei Diaghilev and Igor Stravinsky. Look for their graves in the northeastern sector of the (signposted) island; they are in the 'acatholic' (read Protestant and Orthodox) sections. Vaporetto lines 41 and 42 from Fondamente Nuove stop here.

MURANO

The people of Venice have been making crystal and glass since the 10th century. The bulk of the industry was moved to the island of Murano in 1291 because of the danger of fire posed by the glass-working kilns.

Venice had a virtual monopoly on the production of what is now known as Murano glass, and the methods of the craft were such a well-guarded secret that it was considered treason for a glass-worker to leave the city. See The Noble Art of Glass-Blowing, p188.

The incredibly elaborate pieces produced by the artisans can range from the beautiful to the grotesque – but, as the Italians would say, *i gusti son gusti* (each to his own). Watching the glass-workers in action in shops and factories around the island is certainly interesting. You can see them in several outlets along and off Fondamenta dei Vetrai. Look for the sign 'Fornace' (Furnace).

Palazzo da Mula (Map p301), near the Ponte Vivarini, the only bridge to span the Canal Grande di Murano, sometimes plays host to exhibitions. More often than not the subject is...glass.

CHIESA DEI SS MARIA E DONATO
Map p301
☎ 041 73 90 56; Campo San Donato; admission free; ◷ 9am-noon & 3.30-7pm Mon-Sat, 3.30-7pm Sun; 🔬 Museo

This is a fascinating example of Veneto-Byzantine architecture. Looking at the apse, however, it is impossible not to see Romanesque influences too. Founded in the 7th century and rebuilt 500 years later, the church was originally dedicated to the Virgin Mary. It was rededicated to St Donato after his bones were brought here from the Greek island of Cephalonia, along with those of a dragon he had supposedly killed (four of the 'dragon' bones hang behind the altar). The church's magnificent mosaic pavement (a very Byzantine touch) was laid in the 12th century, and the impressive mosaic of the Virgin Mary in the apse dates from the same period.

MUSEO DEL VETRO Map p301
☎ 041 73 95 86; www.museiciviciveneziani.it; Fondamenta Giustinian 8; adult/senior, student & child €4/2.50, see also Special Tickets; ◷ 10am-5pm Thu-Tue Apr-Oct, 10am-4pm Thu-Tue Nov-Mar; 🔬 Museo

The Glass Museum has some exquisite pieces. The building, set in a peaceful garden, is a grand 15th-century affair that from 1659 until the early 19th century was the seat of the Torcello bishopric (until its dissolution) and then became Murano town hall. The museum was installed here in 1861, mostly on the 1st floor. On the ground floor is a display of ancient glass artefacts, mostly unearthed in tombs in Dalmatia and dating to the 1st and 2nd centuries (the art of glass-blowing had taken off in Palestine in the 1st century BC). Upstairs you can turn right into a room where glass-making is explained. At left is the frescoed Salone Maggiore (Grand Salon), with a display of all sorts of exquisite pieces from the 19th and 20th centuries. The surrounding annexes are dedicated to displays from preceding centuries, starting with the 15th.

Across Canale di San Donato is one of the few private mansions of any note on the island, the 16th-century **Palazzo Trevisan.**

BURANO

Famous for its lace industry, Burano is a pretty fishing village with a busy populace of around 5000. Its streets and canals are lined with bright, pastel-coloured houses, and they say the bonbon colours have their origins in the fishermen's desire to be able to see their own homes when heading home from a day at sea. Regardless of the reasons, the bright, cheerful colours are engaging. Given the island's distance from Venice (around 40 minutes by vaporetto), you really do get the feeling of having arrived somewhere only fleetingly touched by La Serenissima.

Give yourself time to wander into the quietest corners and shady parks. Walk over the wooden bridge to neighbouring Mazzorbo, a larger island with little more than a few houses, a couple of trattorie, market gardens (the artichokes are a local speciality) and open green space. They also fish *moeche* (soft-shell crabs) here. A snooze in the grass takes you light years away from the marvels of Venice and somehow puts them into a harmonious perspective.

If you plan to buy lace on the island, choose with care and discretion, as these days some of the cheaper stuff is imported from Asia. That said, you can still occasionally see women working away at their latest, frilliest creations in the shade of their homes and in the parks.

CHIESA DI SAN MARTINO Map p304
☎ 041 73 00 96; Piazza Galuppi; admission free;
⏲ 9am-noon & 3-6pm Mon-Sat; 🚊 Burano
This 16th-century church is worth a quick look, in particular for the *Crocifissione* (Crucifixion) by Giambattista Tiepolo.

MUSEO DEL MERLETTO Map p304
☎ 041 73 00 34; www.museicivicieneziani.it; Piazza Galuppi 187; adult/senior, student & child €4/2.50, see also Special Tickets; ⏲ 10am-5pm Wed-Mon Apr-Oct, 10am-4pm Wed-Mon Nov-Mar; 🚊 Burano
Housed on the top floor of the island's one-time lace school (it closed in 1970), here you will see pieces of handiwork that are little short of mind-boggling in the intricacy

of their design. Everything from shawls to tablecloths, from gloves to napkins, is on show. Some of the 17th-century pieces, with complex relief detail and clearly the result of long and painstaking labour, are truly remarkable. In the last room hang sundry diplomas and prizes awarded at international exhibitions from the 19th century on. Recognition for the quality of the islanders' work came from as far off as Paris and Boston.

TORCELLO

This delightful island, with its overgrown main square and sparse, scruffy-looking buildings and monuments, was at its peak from the mid-7th century to the 13th century, when it was the seat of the bishop of mainland Altinum (modern Altino, now disappeared) and home to some 20,000 people. Rivalry with Venice and a succession of malaria epidemics systematically reduced the island's splendour and population. Today, some 17 souls call Torcello home. In its now nearly abandoned state, the island gives us some idea of how things might have looked at the outset of settlement in the lagoon.

When you get off the vaporetto, you have little choice but to follow the path along the canal that leads to the heart of the island in a leisurely 10 minutes. Around the central square is huddled all that remains of old Torcello – the lasting homes of the clergy and the island's secular rulers.

A combined ticket for the Cattedrale di Santa Maria Assunta and Museo di Torcello costs €6 and can be purchased at either place.

CATTEDRALE DI SANTA MARIA ASSUNTA Map p304
☎ 041 270 24 64; Piazza Torcello; cathedral €3, bell tower €2, or combined ticket; ⏲ 10.30am-6pm Mar-Oct, 10am-5pm Nov-Feb; 🚊 Torcello
The island's ancient Veneto-Byzantine cathedral, Venice's first, was founded in the 7th century. What you see today dates from the first expansion of the church in 824 and rebuilding in 1008, making it about the oldest Venetian monument to have remained relatively untampered with.

The three apses (the central one dates back to the original 7th-century structure) are Romanesque in inspiration and underline

Fruit seller, Lido di Venezia (below)

its intermarriage of building styles. A jewel of simple, early-medieval architecture, the interior is still more fascinating for its magnificent Byzantine mosaics.

On the western wall of the cathedral is a vast mosaic depicting the Last Judgment. Hell (lower right side) doesn't look any fun at all. Sceptics in the 21st century may grin knowingly, but such images inspired sheer terror in the average resident of Torcello back in the 12th and 13th centuries, when the mosaics were put together.

The greatest treasure is the mosaic of the *Madonna col Bambino* (Madonna and Child) in the half-dome of the central apse. Starkly set on a pure gold background, the figure is one of the most stunning works of Byzantine art in Italy. And if you need more confirmation of the church's Eastern influences, have a look at the iconostasis set well before the altar.

Climb the bell tower for fine lagoon views (the tower closes half an hour before the church does from March to October).

In front of the cathedral entrance are the excavated remains of the 7th-century circular **baptistry**. Steps lead down into a small pool, a standard early-Christian model for baptistries. It was later demolished and replaced several times until in the 19th century these remains were uncovered. Fragmentary remains of construction on the site of the baptistry go back to the 4th century, indicating that the island was already inhabited under the Roman Empire.

Adjacent to the cathedral, the **Chiesa di Santa Fosca** (10am-4.30pm) was founded in the 11th century to house the body of St Fosca.

MUSEO DI TORCELLO Map p304

 041 270 24 64; Piazza Torcello; admission €2, or combined ticket; 10.30am-5.30pm Tue-Sun Mar-Oct, 10am-5pm Tue-Sun Nov-Feb; Torcello

Across the square from the cathedral in the 13th-century **Palazzo del Consiglio** is this museum dedicated to the island. On the ground floor are some sculptural fragments from the cathedral, a 6th-century holy-water font and a curious display of Byzantine objects from Constantinople. Upstairs, among a series of rather dark religious paintings, many from the workshops of Veronese, are all sorts of odds and ends, including a 7th-century lead seal. The museum's ancient artefacts are held in the **Palazzo dell'Archivio**, just opposite the Palazzo del Consiglio. They include Roman bronze implements and figurines, some funerary stelae (inscribed, upright stone columns) and statuary, and other bits and pieces. The Roman items were mostly unearthed at the now-vanished Altino, on the mainland, but some objects have found their way into the collection without having anything to do with Torcello or the surrounding area.

The rough-hewn stone chair outside is known as the **Sedia d'Attila** (Attila's Seat). Why is anyone's guess, and even the use to which the seat was put is a mystery. It is surmised that magistrates sat here to pass judgment.

LIDO DI VENEZIA

The main draw here is the beach, but the water ain't that great and the public areas of the waterfront can be less than attractive.

You pay a small fortune (up to €10 for a sun-lounger and €60 for a basic changing room per day) to rent a chair, umbrella and changing cabin in the more easily accessible and cleaner areas of the beach. That said, it is not entirely clear what, if anything, is done if you choose to plonk your towel close to the water's edge (a town ordinance technically forbids obstruction of the open beach area between the rows of cabins and the water).

The Lido forms a land barrier between the lagoon and the Adriatic Sea. For centuries, the dogi made an annual pilgrimage to the Chiesa di San Nicolò (off Map pp302–3), at the northern end of the island, to fulfil Venice's traditional Sposalizio del Mar (Wedding with the Sea; see With This Ring I Thee Wet, p38). The church today is a relatively uninteresting 17th-century structure. One of the city's defensive forts was nearby.

A few hundred metres to the south of the church lies the **Antico Cimitero Israelitico** (Old Jewish Cemetery; Map pp302–3; adult/student €8.50/7; 1hr Italian & English tours 2.30pm Sun Apr-Sep). You can turn up at the gates or buy tickets in advance at the Museo Ebraico (see p78) to tour the burial ground, said to be the second-oldest Jewish cemetery in Europe after that in Worms (Germany). The cemetery is open only on Sunday for these organised visits.

The Lido became a fashionable seaside resort at the end of the 19th century, and its more glorious days are depicted in melancholy fashion in Thomas Mann's novel *Der Tod in Venedig* (Death in Venice). A wander around the streets between the Adriatic and the Santa Maria Elisabetta vaporetto stop will turn up occasional Art Nouveau (what the Italians refer to as Liberty style) and even Art Deco villas. One of the most extravagant is the **Hungaria Palace Hotel** (Map pp302–3; Gran Viale Santa Maria Elisabetta 28).

Today the island is fairly laid-back for most of the year, but it's crowded on summer weekends with local and foreign sunseekers. The beaches are frankly better on the northern coast of the mainland (Cavallino, Jesolo and farther along the coast as far as Bibione), but the Lido is easier to reach. The place fills up for the Mostra del Cinema di Venezia (Venice International Film Festival), which takes place every year from late August to September. The cinema-fest is hosted in the snappy Palazzo della Mostra del Cinema (Map pp302–3).

On the lagoon side, you can see the nearby Isola di San Lazzaro degli Armeni (see p97). Closer to the shore is the former leper colony of Isola del Lazzaretto Vecchio.

Bus B from Gran Viale Santa Maria Elisabetta, or your bicycle, will take you to Malamocco (off Map p288), in the south of the island. Arranged across a chain of squares and some canals, the old heart of this town is far more reminiscent of Venice than the late-19th-century seaside conceits at the northern end of the island. The original settlement of Malamocco, besieged by the Frankish ruler Pepin in the early years of the Republic, is believed to have been an island off the Lido and has long since disappeared.

The first thing you should do on arriving at the Lido is hire a bike at **Anna Garbin** (Map pp302–3; Piazzale Santa Maria Elisabetta 2/a; hire per day €9-10), just off Gran Viale Santa Maria Elisabetta, a couple of minutes from the main vaporetto stop. This will allow you to explore the island, as well as (for the energetic) Pellestrina and even Chioggia to the south.

PELLESTRINA

Separated from the southern tip of the Lido by the Porto di Malamocco, one of the three sea gates between the Adriatic and the lagoon, Pellestrina (off Map p288) is shaped like an 11km-long razor blade. Small villages of farmers and fishing families are strung out along the island, protected on the seaward side by the Murazzi, a remarkable feat of 18th-century engineering, although they don't look much to the modern eye. These sea walls, designed to keep the power of the sea over the lagoon in check, once extended without interruption some 20km from the southern tip of Pellestrina to a point well over halfway up the coast of the Lido. The Pellestrina stretch and part of the Lido wall remain. They were heavily damaged during the 1966 floods and partially restored in the 1970s. Long stretches of sparsely populated grey-sand beaches separate the Murazzi from the sea on calm days. Venetians occasionally make the effort to come here for a meal at one of the handful of small family restaurants, known for their excellent seafood.

MINOR ISLANDS

San Francesco del Deserto

The Franciscans built themselves a **monastery** (☎ 041 528 68 63; www.isola-sanfrancescodeldeserto.it; admission free, donations appreciated; 🕙 9-11am & 3-5pm Tue-Sun) on this island about 1km south of Burano to get away from it all. The island (Map p288), on which evidence of an earlier Roman presence has also been found, makes an enchanting detour while exploring the islands of the lagoon. Legend has it that Francis of Assisi himself landed here, seeking shelter after a journey to Palestine in 1220. The Franciscans deserted the island (hence the name) in 1420, as conditions had become difficult and malaria was rampant.

Another branch of the order reoccupied the island later that century, and in the 18th century they were succeeded by yet another reforming branch of the Franciscans. These various groups were united by Pope Leo XIII in the 19th century into the order of the Frati Minori and, except for an interruption under Napoleon, they have remained ever since. The monastery complex retains some of its 13th-century elements, including the first cloister. It is advisable to call before heading out, especially if you are in a group. If you turn up within the hours outlined a tour should take place, but it depends on whether or not a brother is free.

The only way to get there is to hire a private boat or taxi from Burano, or row your own! Ask around at the vaporetto stop. You will be looking at about €80 for up to four passengers for the return trip and a 40-minute wait time.

Le Vignole & Sant'Erasmo

Welcome to the Venetian countryside! Together these two islands almost equal Venice in size, but any comparison ends there. Sparsely inhabited, these largely rural landscapes are covered in fields, groves and vineyards rather than endless monuments.

The southwestern part of Le Vignole (Map p288) is owned by the military and contains the best preserved of a scattering of old forts, the 16th-century **Forte Sant'Andrea**. Generally, you have to content yourself with a distant view of the fort from the lagoon, but it may become possible to visit, as the Venice municipality is looking at taking it over from the state. In the meantime, you can sometimes organise private visits (☎ 368 320 68 46). The low-level cannons pointing out to sea, combined with a chain across to the (now gone) Forte di San Nicolò on the Lido, rendered entry into the heart of the lagoon by enemy warships virtually impossible. The island long produced most of the doge's wine, and its 50 inhabitants still live mainly from agriculture.

Together with Le Vignole, Sant'Erasmo (Map p288) was long known as the *orto di Venezia* (Venice's garden). About 1000 people live on the island, many around the Chiesa ferry stop. For most of its history the island has had a predominantly agricultural vocation, although the Roman chronicler Martial records the presence of holiday villas belonging to the well-to-do of the now-disappeared mainland centre of Altinum (Altino). Until the 1800s the island bore the direct brunt of Adriatic rollers, but subsequent construction of dikes at the Porto del Lido lagoon entrance favoured the build-up of sediment that created Punta Sabbioni and largely closed the island off from the sea.

It is about a half-hour walk from the Chiesa stop to the more southern Capannone stop, and another 15 minutes east to what remains of the round Torre Massimiliana, a 19th-century Austrian defensive fort. The small nearby beach and restaurant become a weekend summer focal point for young and restless Venetians, who parade around in speedboats with music blaring, much as their young landlubber confrères do in wide-wheeled cars.

A RIVAL FOR CASANOVA?

Lord Byron spent a good deal of time seeking spiritual solace with the Mechitarist Fathers on the island of San Lazzaro, but more seeking earthly ecstasy in Venice. One night, he was in such exultant mood after a night with a mistress that he leapt into the Grand Canal and swam home. The only problem was the danger of gondoliers bumping into him. So, it is said, he repeated the exploit the following night, but carried a flaming torch in one hand so that he could be seen! He found the city (struggling under Austrian occupation) an inexhaustible source of carnal amusement. Of Venetian women (and it appears he knew quite a few) he said: 'Some are countesses, and some are cobblers' wives, some noble, some middling, some low – and all whores.' A real charmer, what?

San Clemente, San Servolo & San Lazzaro degli Armeni

The island of San Clemente (Map p288) was once the site of a hospice for pilgrims returning from the Middle East. Later, a convent was built and from 1522 it was a quarantine station. The plague that devastated Venice in 1630 was blamed by some on a carpenter who worked on San Clemente, became infected and brought the disease over to the city. The Austrians turned the building into a mental hospital for women (the first in Europe), and until 1992 it still operated in part as a psychiatric hospital. The entire island is now a luxury hotel (see San Clemente Palace, p214), but to Venetians 'going to San Clemente' still means only one thing.

San Servolo (Map p288) shared these hospital functions from the 18th century until 1978. From the 7th to the 17th centuries Benedictine monks had a monastery here, bits of which still remain in the former hospital. Now the island is home to various cultural institutions, including the Centro Europeo de Venezia per i Mestieri della Conservazione del Patrimonio Architettonico, a rather long-winded way of saying the Venice European Restoration Centre.

Of the islets scattered about south of Venice, the most important is San Lazzaro degli Armeni. In 1717 the Armenian order of the Mechitarist Fathers (named after the founding father, Mechitar) was granted use of the island, which centuries before had been a leper colony and earlier still the site of a Benedictine hospice for pilgrims. The Mechitarists' **monastery** (Map pp302–3; ☎ 041 526 01 04; adult/student & child €6/3; ☼ tours only 3.25-5pm) became an important centre of learning and repository of Armenian culture, which it remains to this day.

After wandering around the peaceful cloister you are taken to the church, sparkling with mosaics and stuffed with paintings (the Armenian monastery was the only one in Venice spared from pillaging by Napoleon). From there you are led to the 18th-century refectory and then upstairs to the library. The latter is divided into several rooms. The first, by which you enter, is lined by cabinets with all sorts of odds and ends, including antiquities from Ancient Egypt, Sumeria and India. The precious collections of books are followed by a room dedicated mostly to Armenian art and artefacts.

An Egyptian mummy and a 15th-century Indian throne dominate a room dedicated to the memory of Lord Byron, who stayed on the island in search of a little (much-needed) inner peace. True to his eccentric nature, he could often be seen swimming from the island to the Grand Canal. Lastly, a circular room contains precious manuscripts, many of them Armenian and one dating as far back as the 6th century!

THE MAINLAND

Eating pp157–8; Sleeping pp215–16; Shopping p190

MESTRE

There's not a lot to come to Mestre for, although a stroll around the central Piazza Ferretto can be pleasant enough. The one exception is the **Centro Culturale Candiani** (Map p305; ☎ 041 238 61 11; www.comune. venezia.it/candiani, in Italian; Piazzale Candiani; admission prices depend on exhibitions; ☼ 10am-1pm & 4-8pm Tue-Sun), a modern multimedia and exhibition centre that frequently hosts first-class exhibitions ranging from the visual arts to architecture.

CHIOGGIA

Chioggia (see Map p288) marks the southern mainland boundary of the Venetian municipality. Invaded and destroyed by the Republic's maritime rival, Genoa, in the late 14th century, the medieval core of modern Chioggia is a crumbly but not uninteresting counterpoint to its more illustrious patron to the north. In no way cute like Murano or Burano, Chioggia is a firmly practical town, its big sea-fishing fleet everywhere in evidence. For tourist-office details, see p262.

If you arrive by way of the Lido and Pellestrina – easily the most enchanting way to get here – you'll find yourself at the northern end of Main St, Chioggia, (Corso del Popolo) as soon as you set foot on dry land. First, head left down Calle della Santa Croce to the Chiesa di San Domenico, built in 1745 on the site of an earlier Dominican church. The site is a little island unto itself and the church's main claim to fame is the painting *San Paolo* (St Paul), said to be Vittore Carpaccio's last known work. The bell tower, raised in 1200, is the sole remnant of the original structure.

After visiting the church, return to Corso del Popolo. A brisk walk down this cobblestoned and largely pedestrianised thoroughfare takes you to the heart of the old town. Along the way, you reach the cathedral. Rebuilt in the 17th century to a design by Longhena, about all that is left of the earlier structure is the bell tower, raised in 1350.

The historic centre of Chioggia is located on an island, and was transferred here from its original position in what is today Sottomarina, on the coast, after the Genoese siege of 1379–80. The reasoning was simple enough: just as water was Venice's best defence, so it would be for Chioggia. People began to repopulate the Sottomarina area only three centuries later.

Through the middle of the island runs the utterly Venetian Canale della Vena, complete with little bridges. On either side it is protected by the Canale Lombardo and Canale di San Domenico. Beyond the latter (after crossing another narrow islet), the Ponte Translagunare bridges the lagoon to link Chioggia with Sottomarina and thus the Adriatic beaches.

More interesting than the monuments is simply pottering about, ducking down the alleys that branch off like ribs to the east and west from the spine of Corso del Popolo. The **mercato ittico** (fish market; Tue-Sat), alongside Canale di San Domenico where the Ponte Translagunare reaches into Chioggia, is an eye-opener if you can get there at about 6am.

If you want a swim, the beaches at Sottomarina are pretty clean, although the water can be murky. It's a typical seaside scene, with cheap hotels, bouncy castles for kids, snack bars, tat and even the odd tacky disco.

1 *Harry's Dolci (p156), Giudecca*
2 *Waiter, Caffè Florian (p161),
Sestiere di San Marco*
3 *Travellers about to enjoy a ride
on a gondola (p246)* 4 *Market
stall, Padua (p228)*

1 *Reflected Campanile (p55), Sestiere di San Marco* 2 *Vaporetto to Lido di Venezia (p94)* 3 *Traditionally painted house (p87)* 4 *Piazza San Marco (p51), Sestiere di San Marco, at dawn*

1 Vibrant Canale di Cannaregio, Sestiere di Cannaregio (p76)
2 Resting spot by the Grand Canal, Rialto (p74), Sestiere di San Polo 3 Sun-soaked corner house, Giudecca (p89) 4 Gondola poster (p13)

1 *Domes of the Basilica di San Marco (p51), Sestiere di San Marco*
2 *Shoppers throng the arcades surrounding Piazza San Marco (p178), Sestiere di San Marco*
3 *Façade detail, Basilica di San Marco (p52), Sestiere di San Marco*
4 *Corner stone with winged lion, symbol of St Mark (p54)*

1 *Piazza San Marco (p51), Sestiere di San Marco, on a misty day*
2 *Venice is filled with unique accommodation options (p192)*
3 *The Venetian flag once flew as far afield as Cyprus (p129)*
4 *A rare snowy day in Piazzetta San Marco, Sestiere di San Marco (p252)*

1 *Replica bronze horses outside the Basilica di San Marco (p52), Sestiere di San Marco* **2** *View past the Ponte di Rialto (p73) along the Grand Canal, Sestiere di San Polo* **3** *Mosaic detail, Basilica di San Marco (p53), Sestiere di San Marco* **4** *Chiesa del Redentore (p90), Giudecca*

1 *Embossed doors, Basilica di San Marco (p51), Sestiere di San Marco* 2 *Chiesa di Santa Maria della Salute (p65), Sestiere di Dorsoduro* 3 *View below the Ponte di Rialto (p73), Sestiere di San Polo* 4 *Detail of carving, Chiesa di Santa Maria della Visitazione (p64), Sestiere di Dorsoduro*

1 The frescoed exterior of Casa Mazzanti (p223), Verona **2** A visitor gazes at one of the splendid paintings housed in the Gallerie dell'Accademia (p66), Sestiere di Dorsoduro **3** A featured artwork of the Biennale Internazionale d'Arte (p11) **4** Artwork for sale, Sestiere di San Marco (p179)

The
Grand Canal

The Grand Canal

Main St, Venice, is a river, or rather the extension of one. Centuries before people realised that the islets of Rivoalto would be a cosy place to found a city, the River Brenta (it is believed) had been carving a path through the mud flats and shallow waters of the Venetian lagoon towards the Adriatic Sea. After ducking and weaving its way past the islets, it widens into what the Venetians subsequently called the Canale di San Marco or Grand Canal, and then heads on to the sea.

Like any self-respecting central boulevard, the Grand Canal is lined with classy hotels, grand old churches and fine *palazzi* (mansions) dating from the 12th to the 18th century. A mirror-image 'S' 3.8km long, the canal is only 6m deep. Its width ranges from 40m to 100m. In the city's glory days the warehouses along its banks were constantly busy with the transfer of goods from all over the known world. Back in the 15th century the French writer Philippe de Commines declared the Grand Canal 'the finest street in the world, with the finest houses'.

Today the trading may have stopped, but the canal is as busy as ever. Traffic jams are not as much of a problem as in other cities, but the riot of colour and noise as vaporetti (ferries), *traghetti* (commuter gondolas), private runabouts, taxis, ambulances, vessels from the fire department, delivery boats and gondolas churn their way up, down and across it makes the Grand Canal hectic enough.

Prime Venetian real estate has always included canal views. It follows that many of the jewels of centuries of Venetian architecture face the canal. They've been counted up: 185 private buildings of monumental importance, along with 15 religious buildings and a few others of lesser interest.

Often the only way to see them up close is from the water. On the assumption that you don't walk on the stuff and don't wish to shell out a sizable wad of notes for a gondola, the best way to get a look is on vaporetto No 1 – the all-stops Grand Canal 'omnibus'.

The pages in this section briefly detail the notable bridges, churches and *palazzi* along the way, starting at the uninspiring northwestern end, by Stazione di Santa Lucia (just beyond the unfinished and seemingly botched Ponte di Calatrava bridge; see p73), and winding down towards Piazza San Marco. The number refers to the map location in this section. Many of the buildings mentioned are also covered either in some detail in the Sights chapter or in glancing fashion in the Walking Tours chapter. Where this is the case, a cross-reference has been inserted to the relevant point in the book.

All you need to do now is jump on board the No 1 at Ferrovia (the train-station stop) and try to grab a deck seat at the back.

Before you head out onto the canal, you might want to pop into a local bookshop and hunt out a copy of *Venezia. Il Canal Grande*, by local photographer Daniele Resini. This is a rather extraordinary work of photography, lining up in perfect panoramic shape both sides of the canal. You could use it to help identify buildings as you go (although it might get awkward crammed onto the poop of the vaporetto), or simply study it before and after.

A gondola ride (see p246) is a classic way to enjoy Venice

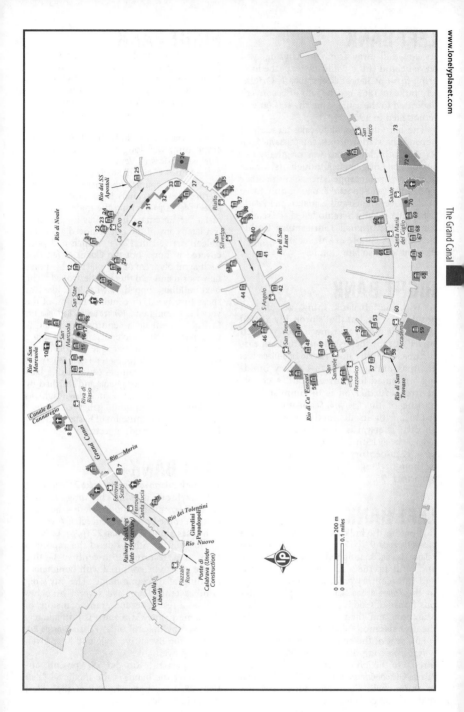

LEFT BANK

As you pull away from the landing, you leave behind (for a while anyway) the lowering form of **Stazione di Santa Lucia 1**. Originally built in 1865 on the site of a convent dedicated to the same saint, the station was remodelled in 1954.

The baroque chocolate-cake façade just beyond the station fronts the **Chiesa dei Scalzi 2** (p76), a building that was originally designed by Longhena, although its façade was done by Giuseppe Sardi. On the other side of the **Ponte dei Scalzi 3**, one of only three bridges over the Grand Canal, is the **Palazzo Calbo-Crotta 4**. Much remodelled, it retains some of the original 15th-century Gothic elements. A couple of smaller buildings to its right are also late Gothic.

RIGHT BANK

As with the left bank, things get off to a desultory start, but that's probably a good thing: it'll give you time to get yourself sorted out for the visual feast that appears further down the line. **Palazzo Emo-Diedo 5** is an unassuming late-17th-century building attributed to Andrea Tirali. A couple of streets further on is the unmistakable outline of the **Chiesa di San Simeon Piccolo 6** (p126), with its distinctive brass dome. Shortly afterwards, the **Palazzo Foscari-Contarini 7** is a 15th-century reconstruction of a 12th-century mansion, in which it is thought Doge Francesco Foscari was born in 1375.

LEFT BANK

Just before the hulking 18th-century **Chiesa di San Geremia 9** (p77) is the four-storeyed **Palazzo Flangini 8**, designed by Giuseppe Sardi and built in 1682. A row of grand 17th- and 18th-century *palazzi* then stretches up to the **Chiesa di San Marcuola 10** (p77). After this house of God, you pass the Rio di San Marcuola and then a house of the devil, the Renaissance **Palazzo Vendramin-Calergi 11** (p80), seat of the city casino and the place where the composer Richard Wagner expired. On the left corner of Rio di Noale is **Palazzo Gussoni-Grimani della Vida 12**, attributed to Sanmicheli. Tintoretto added frescoes that have since faded away.

RIGHT BANK

Shortly after Canale di Cannaregio on the left, the elegant 15th-century **Palazzo Giovanelli 13** emerges on the right. Next follows **Casa Correr 14**, a modest 17th-century house where Teodoro Correr started the collection that would form the basis of Museo Correr (p57).

The **Fondaco dei Turchi 15** (p73), or Turkish emporium, was long the headquarters of Turkish traders in Venice and is now home to the Museo Civico di Storia Naturale, where you can see a couple of prehistoric skeletons. Across the *rio* (canal) is the 15th-century **Deposito del Megio 16**, long the main grain silo of La Serenissima. The serious-looking lion is a later copy of the one removed after Napoleon arrived in 1797. (Venice had been covered in lions, but the Corsican felt that such symbols were out of place in his brave new world and had them all destroyed.) The next building, topped by what look like two spear tips, is a 17th-century creation of the very busy Longhena, **Palazzo Belloni Battaglia 17**. **Ca' Tron 18** went up a century earlier and is now part of the university. Further along you can't miss the baroque façade of the **Chiesa di San Stae 19** (p72). **Ca' Pesaro 20** (p70) is an important example of canalside baroque. Started by Longhena and finished by Gaspari, it is worth a visit in its own right, as it is home to an important gallery of modern art and a curious museum of Eastern (mostly Japanese Edo period) objects.

LEFT BANK

The pink **Palazzo Fontana-Rezzonico 21** was built in the style of Sansovino's buildings. In 1693 Carlo Rezzonico was born here – he went on to become Pope Clement XIII. A couple of houses along is **Ca' d'Oro 22** (p76). **Ca' Pesaro 23**, just on the other side of the vaporetto stop, is a restored 15th-century Gothic house, not to be confused with Longhena's building of the same name. The city's big families tended to have several branches and, as a result, several grand mansions of the same name. Ca' Pesaro is immediately followed by the still older **Palazzo Sagredo 24**, built in the Byzantine style and later given a Gothic overhaul.

Just past the Rio dei SS Apostoli, approaching the bend, is the medieval **Ca' da Mosto 25**, once home to one of the oldest hotels in Venice.

When you've almost reached the **Ponte di Rialto 27** (p73), you'll see the former German trading house and present-day post office, **Fondaco dei Tedeschi 26** (p56).

RIGHT BANK

Begun in 1724, the present version of **Palazzo Corner della Regina 28** appeared centuries after Caterina Corner, short-lived queen of Cyprus, had passed into history. The bijou 14th-century **Ca' Favretto 29** (p199) is now a hotel.

When you chug by the neogothic arches of the **Pescaria 30** (p74) you have reached what was long the commercial heart of Venice – Rialto. The produce markets still do a brisk trade, but the bankers have long since been replaced by tourist-tat stalls. The long buildings are the **Fabbriche Nuove 31** (p74) and the **Fabbriche Vecchie 32** (p74). They are followed by the grand Renaissance **Palazzo dei Camerlenghi 33** (p74), just before the Ponte di Rialto, and the **Palazzo dei Dieci Savi 34** (p74), just beyond it.

LEFT BANK

A couple of blocks south of the Ponte di Rialto are **Palazzo Dolfin-Manin 35** (p120), designed by Jacopo Sansovino, and **Palazzo Bembo 36** (p120). Look for the narrow, early-Gothic **Palazzo Dandolo 37** (p138), four houses along. Just past Calle del Carbon stand two fine Veneto-Byzantine *fondachi* (trading houses), **Palazzo Loredan 38** and **Ca' Farsetti 39**. The grand entrances onto the canal were once opened to goods from all over the world; they now house the city council (p119).

The third building along from here is the imposing Renaissance **Palazzo Grimani 40** (p119), designed by Sanmicheli just before his death in 1559.

On the other side of Rio di San Luca are clustered several Gothic edifices, among them the 15th-century **Palazzo Tron 41**, followed further down by **Palazzo Corner-Spinelli 42**, which was the work of Codussi.

RIGHT BANK

When the vaporetto leaves the San Silvestro stop, **Palazzo Papadopoli 43** (p128) is the mansion after the first canal on the right. More than anything else, it is locally renowned for its lush, but unfortunately private, gardens. Just past the next canal is **Palazzo Bernardo 44**,

Good-luck charms are part of gondola lore (see p13)

a fine Gothic structure whose tracery on the upper main floor is copied from the Palazzo Ducale's loggia. Also worthy of note is **Palazzo Pisani-Moretta 45**, dating from about the same period. Next door, the 16th-century **Palazzo Tiepolo 46** still boasts some original (if faded) frescoes.

LEFT BANK

Shortly before the next bend in the canal, four mansions, the **Palazzi Mocenigo 47**, belonging to the powerful family of the same name, abut one another. The two outside houses were originally Gothic, but all four were substantially made over in the following centuries. Part of the property has been converted into ultraluxury holiday apartments run by the Bauer hotel (p194). The detached **Palazzo Contarini dalle Figure 48** is a fine Renaissance house where Palladio lived for a while.

A couple of Gothic mansions lie between Palazzo Contarini and **Palazzo Moro-Lin 49**, a stout house raised by the Tuscan architect Sebastiano Mazzoni in 1670. Larger still is the **Palazzo Grassi 50** (p118). In a backstreet next to the **Palazzo Malipiero 51**, Giacomo Casanova was born in 1725. **Ca' del Duca 52** (p117) is the next major building down the canal. It is swiftly followed by **Palazzo Giustinian-Lolin 53**, a 14th-century pile reworked by Longhena in 1630.

RIGHT BANK

Down at **Palazzo Balbi 54**, on the northern side of Rio di Ca' Foscari, we can see some tentative early-baroque touches on an essentially Renaissance structure. Across the side canal is **Ca' Foscari 55**, long the central seat of the city's university (which has faculty buildings spread across the length and breadth of Venice).

At the next vaporetto stop is the 17th-century **Ca' Rezzonico 56** (p63), another important building that repays visiting. The fourth mansion along from here, **Palazzo Loredan dell'Ambasciatore 57**, is so called because Habsburg imperial ambassadors lived here in the 18th century.

Just across Rio di San Trovaso, **Palazzo Contarini degli Scrigni 58** is an interesting hybrid composed of a late-Gothic structure with an early-17th-century add-on. The nucleus of the art collection that would later end up in the Gallerie dell'Accademia was housed here. Moving it can't have been too onerous, as the **Gallerie dell'Accademia 59** (p66) are about 100m to the southeast. In front of the Gallerie, the last of the Grand Canal's three bridges, the **Ponte dell'Accademia 60** (p62), links Dorsoduro on the right bank with the Sestiere di San Marco on the left.

LEFT BANK

Past the Ponte dell'Accademia, the next edifice of substance on the left bank is Sansovino's imposing **Palazzo Corner 61** (p117), also known as Ca' Grande. The 15th-century Gothic **Palazzo Pisani-Gritti 62** was altered during the 19th century and is now a luxury hotel. The rather narrow **Palazzo Contarini-Fasan 63** (p117) is an ornate Gothic building raised in the second half of the 15th century. **Palazzo Giustinian 64** was built in 1474 in late-Gothic style. At this point, the No 1 vaporetto calls in at the San Marco stop.

RIGHT BANK

What distinguishes **Palazzo Barbarigo 65** are the mosaics added towards the end of the 19th century. Next up is the Palazzo Venier dei Leoni, which houses the **Peggy Guggenheim Collection 66** (p68), followed a block later by the lopsided **Palazzo Dario 67** (p68). Don't let its early-Renaissance marble façade lull you

into a false sense of artistic security. They say this house is cursed, and many of its owners have come a cropper.

Just on the other side of the next canal, **Palazzo Salviati 68**, with its exuberant mosaic decoration, is hard to miss. The Salviati glass firm added this touch in 1924 – quite recently, by Venetian standards.

Don't be fooled by the seemingly Gothic grandeur of **Palazzo Genovese 69**. It is actually a neogothic whim erected late in the 19th century. Much of the former **Abbazia di San Gregorio 70** was destroyed to make way for it. What is left dates from the 12th century, although it has been so often remodelled that you'd never know. It presents a rather forlorn picture on the canal today, and all the more so because this part of Dorsoduro is completely dominated by the baroque splendour of Longhena's **Chiesa di Santa Maria della Salute 71** (p65).

Next to it are former seminary buildings and then the long, low structure of the **Dogana da Mar 72** (p122), where for centuries traders paid customs duty on seaborne imports. Like the bow of a ship, Dorsoduro ends here in a point known as the **Punta della Dogana 73** (p122).

The Grand Canal widens out here into the Bacino di San Marco, and the No 1 vaporetto continues on its way to San Marco, San Zaccaria and eventually out to the Lido and Venice's beaches.

DID YOU KNOW?

- Over 185 *palazzi* line the banks of the Grand Canal.
- The stripy poles outside the mansions are used to moor boats. The municipality caused an uproar when it replaced traditional oak poles on the Zattere with plastic ones in a bid to save money.
- The contents of the canal drained away completely, leaving an avenue of thick sludge, when Venice was hit by an earthquake in the 14th century. An unusual occurrence of *acqua bassa* (low tide) very nearly replicated the effect in early 2005.
- The canal divides the city neatly in two – with three *sestieri* on either side.
- You can see what the Ponte di Rialto's timber predecessor looked like, in paintings dedicated to the *Miracoli della Vera Croce* (Miracles of the True Cross) in Sala (Room) 20 of the Gallerie dell'Accademia (p66).

Walking Tours

Walking Tours

Perhaps more than any other city, Venice is best discovered on foot. Clearly, you can use the vaporetti to get around some places too, but often it's just as quick (or even quicker) to get from A to B by walking. Where the vaporetti do come into their own (apart from getting out to the islands, of course!) is after a long day's exploration, to take you back to base.

The following walks cover the *sestieri* (municipal divisions) that make up the city: San Marco, Dorsoduro, San Polo, Santa Croce, Cannaregio and Castello. The suggested routes provide possible links from one *sestiere* to the next. If you kept to the order in this chapter (and no-one is suggesting you should!), you would, at the end of several days' exploration, find yourself meandering west along the Riva degli Schiavoni in Castello towards the starting point – Piazzetta San Marco.

The routes should be viewed as suggestions for orientation. The distances given are deceptive – this is not a race, and even a few kilometres can take you a day if you stop to visit sights and take your time. The suggested walking times allow for a leisurely pace but not for visiting sights. Let your imagination do the work and wander off wherever your nose leads you.

SESTIERE DI SAN MARCO

Ever since the rail link with the mainland opened in the 19th century, the magical symbolism of Piazzetta San Marco, the theatrical waterside gateway to the Most Serene Republic, has been largely lost to the city's visitors.

Stand between the two 12th-century red and grey granite **columns 1** bearing the emblems of Venice's patron saints – the winged lion of St Mark and the figure of the demoted St Theodore, whom St Mark replaced. The lion faces east, perhaps to signify Venice's domination of the sea, while St Theodore (placed here in 1329) stands calmly on top of a crocodile-like dragon. The tip of his spear is pointed skywards, so perhaps he has killed his prey (some say the statue represents St George). He also holds a shield, as if to say that Venice defends itself but does not seek to attack.

Imagine yourself on a galley after months at sea, making your way to La Serenissima. To some observers, the lion's and dragon's tails face each other to form the crossbeam of a perennially open gate – suggesting that Venice is open to whoever visits. At any rate, it must have been a reassuring sight to Venetians returning home.

The columns were erected in 1172. In succeeding centuries the area around them was a hive of activity, with shops selling all manner of goods and food. On a more sinister note, public executions took place between the two columns. After the killings, culprits were usually quartered and the various chunks displayed at four points around the city as a warning to others.

One of the lowest parts of the city, the Piazzetta is always the first to be inundated when the *acque alte* (high tides) arrive. Indeed until the 12th century there was nothing but water here. The level has since been raised several times, and since 2003 work has again been carried out to protect the square. Like so much of Venice, this area is the result of landfill. The square is bordered on one side by the **Palazzo Ducale 2** (p58), long the seat of power in the lagoon city, and on the other by the 16th-century **Libreria Nazionale Marciana 3** (p57).

Linked to Piazzetta San Marco is Piazza San Marco, dominated by one of the world's most opulent churches and symbol of the city – the **Basilica di San Marco 4** (p51). Before it rises its proud **Campanile 5** (p55). Back in 1162 the local authorities used Piazza San Marco as the stage for the city's first *caccia al toro* (bull hunt), a mad jape that would have made Pamplona's running of the bulls look orderly. Stretching west away from the basilica on the north and south sides of the square are the elegant arcades of, respectively, the **Procuratie Vecchie 6** and the **Procuratie Nuove 7**. The former, designed by Mauro Codussi, were once the residence and offices of the Procurators of St Mark, who were responsible for the upkeep of the Basilica di San Marco and the administration of sizable properties belonging to the

SAVING VENICE

Floods, neglect, pollution and many other factors have contributed to the degeneration of Venice's monuments and artworks. Since 1969 a group of private international organisations, under the aegis of Unesco, has worked to stem the tide of damage.

The joint Unesco–International Private Committees Programme for the Safeguarding of Venice has raised millions of dollars for restoration work in the city. Since 1969 more than 100 monuments and 1000 works of art have been restored. Major projects down the years have included the Chiesa della Madonna dell'Orto, the façade of the Chiesa di San Zulian, Chiesa di San Francesco della Vigna, Chiesa di Santa Maria Formosa, Chiesa di San Nicolò dei Mendicoli, Basilica di Santa Maria Assunta on Torcello, the Loggetta of the Campanile in Piazza San Marco, the Palazzo Ducale's Porta della Carta, the Antico Cimitero Israelitico (Old Jewish Cemetery) on the Lido and the bronze equestrian statute of Bartolomeo Colleoni in Castello.

Funding comes from 29 private and charitable organisations from Italy and a dozen other countries. Apart from restoration work, the programme also finances specialist courses for trainee restorers in Venice. Among the higher-profile groups involved is the UK's Venice in Peril Fund, whose honorary chairman is Viscount Norwich, one of the best-known historians of Venice in English. For £50 a year you can join **Venice in Peril** (☎ 020-7736 6891; www.veniceinperil .org; Unit 4, Hurlingham Studios, Ranelagh Gardens, London SW6 3PA). The fund is presently helping to restore the Emiliana chapel on San Michele.

Important though the work of these organisations is in keeping Venice's difficulties in the public eye, more than 90% of the finance for restoration and related projects in Venice since 1966 has come from the Italian government.

basilica around the square and beyond. Even today it is considered a mighty honour to be named a Procurator of St Mark, although their financial clout has waned. The Procuratie Nuove were designed by Jacopo Sansovino and completed by Vincenzo Scamozzi and Baldassare Longhena.

The square is closed off by the **Ala Napoleonica 8** (p57). When Napoleon waltzed into Venice in 1797, he was so taken with the square he dubbed it 'the finest drawing room in Europe'. Not content to admire, he proceeded to demolish the church of San Geminiano to make way for a new wing that would connect the Procuratie Nuove (which he had decided to make his Venetian residence) and the Procuratie Vecchie, and house his ballroom. At first glance it seems to blend in perfectly, but the row of statues depicting Roman emperors was a typically Napoleonic touch.

Nowadays, the square plays host to competing flocks of pigeons and tourists. Stand and wait for the bronze Mori (Moors) to strike the bell of the 15th-century **Torre dell'Orologio 9** (p62), which rises above the entrance to Le Marzarie (or Mercerie), the streets that form the thoroughfare from San Marco to the Rialto. Or savour an expensive coffee at **Caffè Florian 10** (p161), **Caffè Quadri 11** (p162) or **Lavena 12** (p162), the 18th-century cafés facing each other on the piazza. On occasion, you may witness a minor military ceremony to hoist or haul in the three flags of Venice, Italy and the EU. The flagpoles have been around a lot longer than the EU, so you might at first wonder what the third flag used to be. You'll find the answer in Gentile Bellini's painting *Processione in Piazza San Marco*, housed in Sala (Room) 21 of the Gallerie dell'Accademia (p66). All three poles carried the ensign of the Republic in the days of La Serenissima.

West of Piazza San Marco

West of the Ala Napoleonica, you find yourself on Salizada San Moisè. Down the first street to your left, Calle Vallaresso, is a gaggle of fashion stores and **Harry's Bar 13** (p162). At No 1332 is the former (and recently restored) **Teatro al Ridotto 14**, part of the Hotel Monaco & Grand Canal complex.

In the 17th century the Ridotto gained a name as the city's premier gaming house. During the twilight years of La Serenissima, Venetian nobles were wiping out their fortunes at the gaming tables. The state took a cut, but this was insufficient compensation for the ruin wrought on an already shaky local economy. In November 1774 the Ridotto was shut *per tutti i tempi ed anni avvenire* (for all time and years to come). 'All time' was a relative term – less than 20 years later it was back in business. It remained so until the more purposeful

Walking Tours

SESTIERE DI SAN MARCO

Austrians shut it for good in the early 19th century. You might be able to get a glimpse of the theatre if you wander into the Hotel Monaco & Grand Canal's first entrance as you wander down Calle Vallaresso from the Frezzaria. A staircase sweeps away to the right towards the richly decorated former theatre, used by the hotel for conferences and banquets.

Retracing your steps back onto Salizada San Moisè, as you approach Campo San Moisè you pass a busy shopping street on your right, **Frezzaria 15**. In medieval days no-one would have dreamt of opening a fashion store here: the product on sale was *frecce* (arrows). All males above a certain age had to do regular archery practice and be ready to sail off to war. Campo San Moisè is dominated by the **church 16** (p55) of the same name.

From here, the street widens into Calle Larga XXII Marzo, which was opened in 1881 and commemorates the surrender of the Austrians to Venetian rebels on 22 March 1848. The victory was short-lived, however, and it would be another 18 years before the Austrians received their definitive marching orders. One Italian guide rather hopefully describes this as 'the City'

WALK FACTS

Start Piazzetta San Marco (vaporetto San Marco)

End Piazza San Marco

Distance 4km

Duration 1½ hours

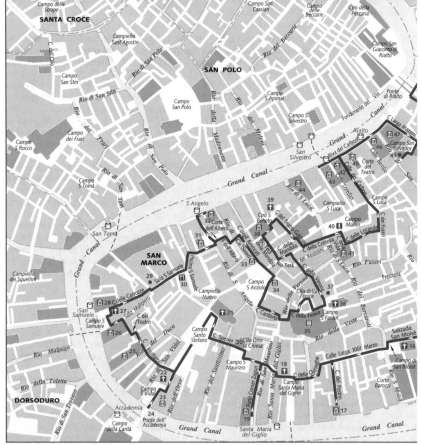

of Venice (an allusion to London's business district), given the presence of the local *borsa* (stock exchange) and several banks. Down Calle del Pestrin, which runs south off Calle Larga XXII Marzo, is the landward entrance to the **Palazzo Contarini-Fasan 17**. It is nothing much to look at, but legend has it that Desdemona, the wife of Othello and victim of his jealousy in Shakespeare's play, lived here.

Calle Larga XXII Marzo then contracts into Calle delle Ostreghe and brings you to Campo Santa Maria del Giglio, where the **church 18** of the same name (p56) will charm you into halting your westward march.

After crossing two bridges in quick succession, you could wander south towards the Grand Canal and sidle up next to **Palazzo Corner 19** (aka Ca' Grande, or Big House), Sansovino's 16th-century masterpiece of residential building. He built it for Jacopo Corner, a nephew of the ill-fated Caterina, the queen of Cyprus (see A Queen Cornered, p129). Claimed to be the biggest mansion in the city, it is also said that the Corner clan managed to prevent the rival Venier family from completing their house (today home to the Peggy Guggenheim Collection) on the other side of the Grand Canal because it would have blocked the Corners' view beyond Dorsoduro to Giudecca. During the latter stages of WWII the building was the German HQ in Venice, and a partisan bomb attack ripped out much of the ground floor. Today it houses Venice's provincial administration.

Back on the westward route, you emerge in Campo San Maurizio, occasional scene

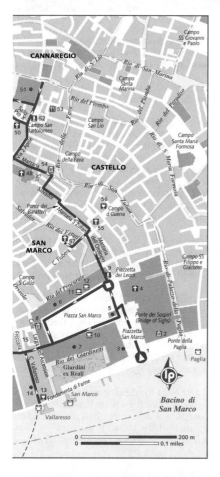

of an antiques market and surrounded by elegant 14th- and 15th-century mansions, along with the church of the same name and its curious **Museo della Musica 20** (p58). Just off this square to the north you can sneak around to Campiello Drio la Chiesa and get a close-up look at just how much the bell tower of the **Chiesa di Santo Stefano 21** (p56) is leaning. Pause, too, when you cross the bridge leading from Campo San Maurizio to Campo Santo Stefano. Looking north, you can see how the same church is in part built over the Rio del Santissimo. You enter the church from Campo Santo Stefano (also known as Campo Francesco Morosini, after the 17th-century doge). From the church it is a brief stroll south across the grand expanse (a rare thing in Venice) of the *campo* (square) past the **Chiesa di San Vidal 22** (p56) and the magnificent **Palazzo Franchetti 23** (p61) to the Grand Canal and the **Ponte dell'Accademia 24** (p62) that spans it.

Santo Stefano to Ponte di Rialto

You could cross the bridge into Dorsoduro (see p121) or instead turn back a little to the southwest end of Campo Santo Stefano, where Calle Fruttarol swings off to the northwest on a twisting and winding route towards the Ponte di Rialto.

You immediately cross a narrow canal and then another, the Rio del Duca. The building on the northwest bank, with a fine façade on the Grand Canal, is the **Ca' del Duca 25**, or Duke's House, so called because the Duke of Milan, Francesco Sforza, bought it

Piazza San Marco (p114), Sestiere di San Marco

from the Corner family in 1461. Apart from the 14th-century ground floor, the mansion was rebuilt in the 19th century. At the next street, Calle del Teatro, turn left. The street name is all that remains of the Teatro San Samuele, where playwright Carlo Goldoni first hit the limelight.

Turn right and follow the rear side of **Palazzo Malipiero 26**, in the wall of which is a plaque just before you enter Salizada Malipiero. It reminds you that in a house along this lane, Giacomo Casanova was born in 1725.

Palazzo Malipiero forms the southern limit of the quiet Campo San Samuele. On the east side is the unobtrusive outline of the former **Chiesa di San Samuele 27**, and to the north the stately **Palazzo Grassi 28**, frequent host to temporary art exhibitions. Massari's 1749 design shows a clear tendency to neoclassicism. Long owned by Fiat, the building was bought from the ailing automobile manufacturer by the city council (through the casino) in early 2005, with a view to renting it out to another private-sector company. Venice's then mayor, Paolo Costa, assured the populace that the building's role as a prime centre for exhibitions would be maintained, although many Venetians could not quite see why taxpayers' money should be used in such a risky operation. In the end, a French investor came to the rescue and all could breathe a sigh of relief.

Wheeling around the church, head more or less east along Calle delle Carrozze and on into Salizada San Samuele. A number of shops, flogging everything from expensive glass to wooden sculptures of unironed shirts, line these streets. You can only wonder what Paolo Veronese, who lived at **No 3337 29**, would have thought of it all. A good lunch stop presents itself here in the form of **Osteria al Bacareto 30** (p143).

Although this itinerary barrels along towards Fondamenta dell'Albero, unhurried strollers might like to wander down any of the several lanes around here that end at the Grand Canal. Just off Calle dell'Albero is a neat little square, the Corte dell'Albero, walled on two sides by the interesting **Casa Nardi 31** at No 3884–87, built in 1913 and incorporating Veneto-Byzantine architectural themes. It has a hint of the Barcelona Modernista style (calling to mind the architect Lluís Domènech i Montaner) in its use of brick and the attempt to recycle a proud and distant design tradition. Facing the Grand Canal at No 3877 is Codussi's **Palazzo Corner-Spinelli 32**, later reworked by Sanmicheli.

From Calle dell'Albero you cross a tiny canal and head southeast down Calle degli Avvocati, which leads into Campo Sant'Anzolo. A good deal of the square is raised. The two wells clue you in that directly below is a large cistern. A 15th-century *palazzo*, **Palazzo Gritti 33**, dominates the northern corner of the square. In 1801 the Italian musician Domenico Cimarosa died in **Palazzo Duodo 34** (No 3584), which in those days was the Albergo Tre Stelle and dates to the same period as Palazzo Gritti.

The *campo* was no stranger to crime, according to city chronicles. In 1476 a launderer by the name of Giacomo was sent to jail after having taken a certain Bernardino degli Orsi under the portico of the Chiesa di Sant'Anzolo Michiel (now disappeared) and raped him. In 1716 the body of a violently murdered woman was discovered in one of the wells. A Florentine was accused of assaulting, robbing and killing the poor wretch. There's more where that came from, but enough. It's time to move on.

Take Calle Caotorta and cross the first bridge you see. Turn immediately left, left again and then right and you end up in Calle della Fenice, on the northern flank of the **Teatro La Fenice 35** (p62), now gloriously back in business. A few steps along this street turn left again. The hotel on the tiny square (Campiello della Fenice) is covered in cannonballs used by the Austrians in their campaign to retake control of the city in 1849. Follow this little arc around and you are again in Calle della Fenice.

You now emerge into Campo San Fantin. Opposite the Teatro La Fenice is the **Chiesa di San Fantin 36**, whose final incarnation was wrought by either Sansovino or Pietro Lombardo.

The other main building on this square is the **Ateneo Veneto 37**, home to a learned society founded in Napoleon's time. Previously it had been the headquarters of the confraternity of San Girolamo and Santa Maria della Giustizia. The main charitable work of confraternity members was to accompany death-row criminals in their last moments prior to execution. The confraternity's building was known as the Scuola di San Fantin or 'dei Picai' (the old Venetian version of 'dead men walking').

To proceed, take Calle della Verona north out of the square. Just before you hit the T-junction with Calle della Mandola, you cross Rio Terà dei Assassini. In medieval times murder was a common nocturnal activity around here. Street crime got so bad that in 1128 the government banned the wearing of certain 'Greek-style' beards that, it was said, were in vogue among wrongdoers to prevent them from being identified. It was at that time too that the first all-night lamps were set burning in dodgier parts of town – the devotional niches you still see around were created specifically for this purpose – and the Signori di Notte (literally 'Night Lords', meaning night watchmen) started patrolling.

At Calle della Mandola, turn left then right into Rio Terà della Mandola. This street bumps right into the side of the splendid **Palazzo Fortuny 38** (p61). The **Chiesa di San Beneto 39**, also in the square, was rebuilt in the early 17th century and is closed.

From Campo San Beneto, drop south along Calle del Teatro Goldoni and turn left at the junction into Calle della Cortesia, which leads over a bridge and into Campo Manin. At the square's centre stands the proud **statue of Daniele Manin 40**, a lion at his feet. He lived in a house just on the other side of Rio di San Luca and is known for leading the anti-Austrian revolt of 1848–49. The square also boasts a remarkably thoughtless 20th-century contribution at its east end, the Cassa di Risparmio di Venezia bank. More interesting than the square itself is what lies off it, via Calle della Vida: the curious **Palazzo Contarini del Bovolo 41** (p58) with its grand Renaissance open spiral staircase.

From the dead end at the Palazzo Contarini del Bovolo, the route proceeds east along Calle delle Locande to Calle dei Fuseri, which, heading north across Campo San Luca, brings you to the Grand Canal along Calle del Carbon (Coal St). Not surprisingly, Coal St leads to Riva del Carbon (Coal Quay), which until well into the 19th century was the main unloading point for the city's coal supply. Calle del Carbon, it is said, was also something of a red-light district.

To the left of Calle del Carbon are **Palazzo Loredan 42** and, one street southwest, **Ca' Farsetti 43**. Both started life in the 12th century as *fondachi* (or *fonteghi*). These were family houses where the ground floor, with a grand entrance on the canal, was used for the loading, unloading and storage of the merchandise upon which the wealth and standing of most of the great patrician families of Venice long depended. In some cases (as in the nearby Fondaco dei Tedeschi), a *fondaco* was more a trading house and hotel for foreign communities.

In 1826 the town hall moved its offices to Ca' Farsetti from the Palazzo Ducale. Forty-two years later it also acquired Palazzo Loredan. You can wander into the foyer of the latter. On the corner of Calle del Carbon is a plaque announcing that Eleonora Lucrezia Corner Piscopia (of the family that once owned Palazzo Corner) was the first woman to receive a university degree – she was awarded a Doctor of Philosophy at the university of Padua in 1678.

Just west of Ca' Farsetti, the Renaissance **Palazzo Grimani 44** was completed by Sanmicheli, although the 2nd floor was done later. It houses law courts.

Walking northeast towards the Ponte di Rialto from Calle del Carbon, you may notice the narrow, Gothic, 14th-century **Palazzo Dandolo 45**. It's just left of Bar Omnibus, a touristy restaurant that started life as a café in the 19th century. The house belonged to blind doge Enrico Dandolo, who led the Fourth Crusade to a famous victory over Constantinople in 1204. Never mind that the Crusaders were actually supposed to be toughing it out against the infidels in the sands of the Middle East rather than bludgeoning their fellow (albeit Orthodox) Christians in Byzantium (see p39)!

Wedged in between Calle Bembo and Rio di San Salvador is the magnificent red façade of **Palazzo Bembo 46**. What you see is the result of 17th-century restoration of a 15th-century late-Venetian-Gothic structure. It is almost certain that Pietro Bembo – cardinal, poet, historian and founding father of the grammar of standard Italian – was born here. On the other side of Rio di San Salvador, **Palazzo Dolfin-Manin 47**, easily identified by its portico, was designed by Sansovino and completed in 1573.

At this point, proceed inland a block along Calle Larga Mazzini. In front of you is the main entrance to the **Chiesa di San Salvador 48** (p56), among the city's oldest churches. Diagonally across from the church to the west is the **Scuola Grande di San Teodoro 49**, one of the many confraternity headquarters in Venice, now used frequently for music recitals and exhibitions.

Heading northeast along Via 2 Aprile, you pass the small and much interfered-with **Chiesa di San Bartolomeo 50** (p55), which at one time served as the parish church for the local German merchant community based at the **Fondaco dei Tedeschi 51** (p56). When the

KNOCKING REBELLION ON THE HEAD

By 1310 Venice was in serious difficulties. Doge Pietro Gradenigo's pursuit of mainland conquest had brought upon the city a papal interdict. The pope was in no way amused by Venice's attempts to seize Ferrara, to which the Holy See had a long-standing claim. The Venetians had been defeated in the field, and many Venetian merchants abroad had been arrested and had their goods confiscated.

Gradenigo was not without his opponents, foremost among them the Querini family. Marco Querini, who had commanded Venetian forces at Ferrara, claimed Venice had not given him the support he needed. Querini convinced General Baiamonte Tiepolo to lead a revolt against Gradenigo. They both lived near the Rialto and so planned to send two armed columns over the bridge. Querini's would proceed down Calle dei Fabbri to Piazza San Marco and Tiepolo's down Le Marzarie. They would join in the piazza and assault the Palazzo Ducale, at which point a third force would arrive across the lagoon from the mainland.

It might have worked, but word of the plan got out. Gradenigo and his allies gathered forces in Piazza San Marco, alerted the workers of the Arsenale, who served as a kind of ducal militia in times of uncertainty, and ordered the *podestà* (mayor) of Chioggia to intercept the invasion fleet.

Things went wrong for the rebels from the start. A storm delayed the fleet, and while Querini marched on Piazza San Marco, Tiepolo's troops hung about looting in Rialto. By the time they went clattering down Le Marzarie, Querini was already battling it out with ducal troopers in Piazza San Marco.

Tiepolo's boys were engaged while still in Le Marzarie. The decisive moment came when a local housewife, who was leaning out her window and bombing the rebels with anything that came to hand, pelted Tiepolo's standard-bearer on the head with a mortar (another version suggests she just leant out the window to see what the fuss was about and accidentally bumped the mortar off her sill). The standard fell and the fight was over. Querini had already died in Piazza San Marco. The leader of the fleet was captured and summarily executed. Tiepolo beat a hasty retreat home, from where he negotiated to keep his life, but in exile.

The woman who had struck the winning blow requested the right to hang the flag of the Republic from her balcony on holidays. This she received, but she was no sentimental dummy – she also asked that the rent on her house never be raised by its owners, the Procurators of St Mark. In 1436 the procurators did raise it while a descendant of the long-deceased woman was away on military service. Thirty-two years later he demanded, and obtained, a return to the original rate.

Today a bas-relief of the woman leaning out of her window marks the spot just above the Sotoportego e Calle del Cappello. A simple stone with the date of the incident in Roman numerals (XV.VI.MCCCX) marks the place on the ground where the standard-bearer fell.

Republic meekly surrendered to Napoleon in 1797, an angry mob set about looting the houses of those they held responsible for such ignominy around Campo San Bartolomeo. The Venetian militia set up cannons on the Ponte di Rialto to control the unrest – the last time the guns of San Marco were fired in anger, they spilled the blood of their own people. The **statue 52** in the middle of the square is of Carlo Goldoni, Venice's greatest playwright. Nearby, **Osteria alla Botte 53** (p144) is perfect for a glass of wine, *cicheti* (bar snack) or a modest meal.

Back to Piazza San Marco

At this point you could head north into Cannaregio, duck across the Ponte di Rialto into San Polo or continue this itinerary back to Piazza San Marco.

Retrace your steps to the Chiesa di San Salvador and follow the narrow shopping street around its northern flank, the Marzaria San Salvador. Where the street runs into a canal, you can see the late-Gothic **Palazzo Giustinian-Faccanon 54**, which for a long time housed the editorial team of the city's main newspaper, the conservative *Il Gazzettino*.

The lanes that lead from San Salvador to the Torre dell'Orologio and into Piazza San Marco are all called *marzaria* (*merceria* in Italian), referring to the merchants who traditionally lined this route. For a millennium this was one of the busiest thoroughfares in the city, directly linking Piazza San Marco with Rialto (in other words, the political with the financial lungs of La Serenissima).

The arrival of the railway in the 19th century and a new axis through Cannaregio did little to change this. The influx of *foresti* (non-Venetians) along this narrow commercial trail remains a constant. Whether you're coming from the train station or from Rialto, Le Marzarie are to this day one of the most direct routes to Piazza San Marco. It was also thus for the conspirators in the 1310 plot to overthrow Doge Pietro Gradenigo, who came a cropper in the Marzaria dell'Orologio just before the Torre dell'Orologio. See Knocking Rebellion on the Head, opposite.

Where Marzaria dell'Orologio begins, you can see off to the left (east) the **Chiesa di San Zulian 55** (☎ 041 523 53 83; ⊙ 9am-6.30pm Mon-Sat, 9am-7.30pm Sun), founded in 829, although its present form, covered in a layer of Istrian stone, was designed by Sansovino. Inside are a few works by Palma il Giovane and Paolo Veronese's *Cristo Morto e I Santi* (The Dead Christ and Saints), on the right as you enter. Mass in English is held here daily at 9.30am. You might slope off to nearby **Cavatappi 56** (p162) for a tipple 'n' nibble.

Heading right (west) from the top of Marzaria dell'Orologio over the bridge, duck right into the first little lane. In the *sotoportego* (street continuing under a building, like an extended archway) just before the T-junction, you will see on your right, at No 956/b, the entrance to the **Chiesa della Santa Croce degli Armeni 57**. On Sundays only, Armenian priests from the Isola di San Lazzaro celebrate a service here. The church has been active since at least the 14th century.

Return to Marzaria dell'Orologio, proceed south towards the Torre dell'Orologio and pass below it. You are back in Piazza San Marco.

SESTIERE DI DORSODURO

The first buildings you bump into on crossing the Ponte dell'Accademia from the Sestiere di San Marco constitute the **Gallerie dell'Accademia 1** (p66), the city's single most important art collection. Indeed, this corner of town is a bit of an art haven. If you follow the signs for the Peggy Guggenheim Collection eastwards from the Gallerie dell'Accademia, you soon arrive at the relatively minor collection of the **Galleria di Palazzo Cini 2** (p65).

Cross the bridge into cute Campo San Vio, one of a handful of squares that back onto the Grand Canal. Its eastern flank is occupied by **Palazzo Barbarigo 3**, whose façade is strikingly decorated with mosaics on a base of gold. They were carried out at the behest of the Compagnia Venezia e Murano, a glass and mosaics manufacturer that moved in here towards the end of the 19th century. You can't really see it from the square, but keep an eye out when you chug up or down the Grand Canal on the vaporetto. Calle della Chiesa and then Fondamenta Venier dai Leoni lead you to Venice's premier excursion into the world of international contemporary art, the **Peggy Guggenheim Collection 4** (p68). You could do worse than have a cuppa at the gallery's coffee shop.

Back on the street, keep moving east. The next bridge brings you into a shady square. The exuberant gardens dripping over the walls, seemingly in an attempt to drop down into Rio delle Toreselle, belong to the cursed **Palazzo Dario 5** (p68).

After the bustle of the art galleries, it is a pleasure to arrive in tranquil Campo San Gregorio. The Gothic façade of the deconsecrated **church 6** of the same name boasts a graceful doorway with a Venetian pointed arch. A straggly garden on the square's northern flank belongs to the **Palazzo Genovese 7**, built over part of what was once the abbey to which the church belonged.

As you wander under the rough-hewn portico of Calle dell'Abbazia, Longhena's dazzling white monolith, the **Chiesa di Santa Maria della Salute 8** (p65), fills your entire field of vision. Beyond, the customs offices that long occupied the low-slung **Dogana da Mar 9** are empty and awaiting a new role.

To stand at dawn on the **Punta della Dogana 10**, which marks the split between the Grand Canal and the Canale della Giudecca, is to feel oneself on the prow of a noble fighting vessel. Waxing lyrical? Not really. Giuseppe Benoni, who designed it in 1677, was hoping for just that effect. On top of the little tower behind you, two bronze Atlases bend beneath the weight of the world. Above them twists and turns capricious Fortune, an elaborate weather vane.

WALK FACTS

Start Ponte dell'Accademia (vaporetto Accademia)

End Campo San Pantalon

Distance 4.8km

Duration 1½ hours

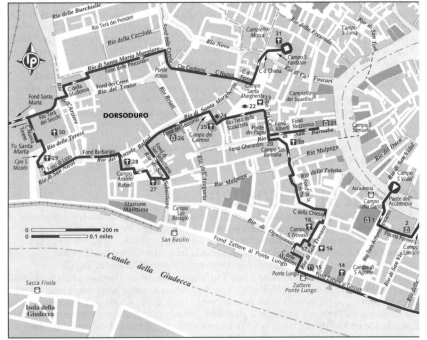

Fondamenta Zattere to Campo Santa Margherita

Fondamenta Zattere runs the length of the south side of Dorsoduro along the Canale della Giudecca, from Punta della Dogana to the Stazione Marittima. It is a popular spot for a lingering *passeggiata* (the afternoon or Sunday stroll that is something of an institution in Italian life) and came to be known as the Zattere because of the giant rafts (*zattere*) that used to deliver timber from the mainland.

The first buildings of note as you walk west are the city's **Saloni Ex-Magazzini del Sale 11** (the one-time salt warehouses). Although the façade (hard to appreciate from the street because you are standing so close) is a neoclassical job from the 1830s, the warehouses were built in the 14th century. A monopoly on the all-important salt trade was one of the foundations of medieval Venice's wealth. Why salt? In the days before fridges and electricity, the only way to preserve meat and other foodstuffs was to bury them in salt. It wasn't a perfect method, but that was all people had. Salt was thus crucial to commerce. The buildings are now used in part by the Bucintoro rowing club (see p174) and as temporary exhibition space.

A few paces further on is the unremarkable Renaissance façade of the small **Chiesa di Santo Spirito 12**. From here a pontoon bridge is thrown across the Canale della Giudecca for the Festa del Redentore in July (see p11). About 100m separate the church from the **Ospedale degli Incurabili 13**. Put up in the 16th century to park incurable syphilis sufferers (the so-called 'French sickness' had taken particular hold across Europe at the time), who had a tendency to end up quite potty, the building was later used as an orphanage. It now houses the Accademia delle Belle Arti (Fine Arts School), which until 2003 lived in the Gallerie dell'Accademia building. At the time of research, a minor museum dedicated to works by the school's teachers since the 1930s was due to open by the end of 2005. After crossing a couple of bridges, you end up in front of the imposing 18th-century **Chiesa dei Gesuati 14** (p63). A few metres further on is a classic gelato stop, **Gelateria Nico 15** (p144). If you're looking for something more grown up, scoot around the corner to **Al Bottegon 16** (p163) for an *ombra* (small glass of wine).

At the next bridge you hit one of the most attractive of Venice's waterways, the Rio di San Trovaso, home to one of the few remaining *squeri* (gondola workshops) – the **Squero di San Trovaso 17**. The leafy square behind the *squero* is backed by the **Chiesa di San Trovaso 18** (☉ 8-11am & 3-6pm Mon-Sat, 3-6pm Sun & holidays), rebuilt in the 16th century on the site of its 9th-century predecessor. The associated *scuola* housed the confraternity of *squerarioli* (gondola-builders). Inside the church are a couple of Tintorettos.

A few hundred metres north, the unprepossessing 18th-century **Chiesa di San Barnaba 19** (☉ 9.30am-12.30pm Mon-Sat) hosts a handful of paintings, including one by Veronese and a couple by Palma il Giovane. Opening times are extended during temporary exhibitions. From Campo San Barnaba wander west along Fondamenta Gherardini and cross the bridge by the permanently moored greengrocer's barge. The bridge is known as **Ponte dei Pugni 20** and is one of several throughout the city where local factions, known as the Nicolotti (who wore black berets) and Castellani (who wore red berets), would regularly encounter each other for a bout of fisticuffs, sometimes good-natured, sometimes less so. The object of these *guerre dei pugni* (fist wars) was to throw opponents into the canal, and the marks showing where to place one's feet are

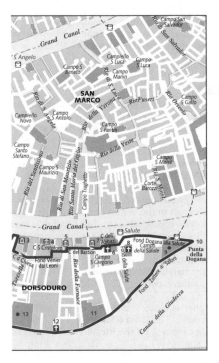

still in evidence. The practice was outlawed in 1705 when one such 'war' turned nasty – knives were drawn and lives lost.

Once over the bridge head east towards the Grand Canal for the magnificent 18th-century residence of Ca' Rezzonico 21 (p63). When you're done admiring how the other half lived in Venice's glory days, turn back towards Rio Terà Canal, which leads you north to Campo Santa Margherita. This is a real people's *platz*. Sure, any number of tourists or foreign students can be heard at the tables of the many restaurants and bars, but in the afternoon, when all the local kids come out to play, it takes on a special, living air. Henry James' words spring to mind, when he speaks of '...that queer air of sociability, of cousinship and family life, which makes up half the expression of Venice. Without streets and vehicles, the uproar of wheels, the brutality of horses, and with its little winding ways where people crowd together, where voices sound as in the corridors of a house...the place has the character of an immense collective apartment' (*The Aspern Papers*, 1888).

The square is headed at its northern end by what little is left of a former church, long ago swallowed up by residential buildings. The squat object at its south end was one of the city's many *scuole*, or religious confraternities, the Scuola Varoteri 22. The square is perfect for taking a weight off over a *spritz* (*prosecco*-based drink) at, say, Margaret Duchamp 23 (p164). The more important Scuola Grande dei Carmini 24 (p69) caps the *campo*'s southwest corner, along with the church 25 (p63) of the same name. Stride across Campo dei Carmini and head southwest along Fondamenta del Soccorso. The dominating mansion on your left is Palazzo Zenobio 26 (p68), the Armenian college. Continuing along and round the corner to the left, cross the second bridge and you stand before the Chiesa di San Sebastian 27, Veronese's parish church (p64).

Santa Marta to Campo San Pantalon

When you leave the Chiesa di San Sebastian, head into the unknown and wander around the back through the interlinked squares that take you to the Chiesa di San Basilio, better known as Chiesa dell'Arcangelo Raffaele 28 (p64). The uneven squares, with clumps of grass pressing up between the flagstones, are intriguingly quiet during the day, and eerily so at night, save for the meek buzz of activity emanating from the sole trattoria here.

As you cross the bridge to the north of Campo Anzolo Rafael and look left (west), you'll espy the bell tower of the Chiesa di San Nicolò dei Mendicoli 29 (p64). Across the Rio delle Terese are the former Chiesa di Santa Teresa 30 and its attached former convent (now used occasionally as theatre space during the Biennale). A stroll up to Fondamenta Santa Marta and west into the quarter of the same name reveals a curious contrast to the Venice of monuments. It's a working-class district with orderly housing blocks and broad walkways. Just beyond, across the Canale Scomenzera, you can watch the desultory activity of Venice's commercial port, now much overshadowed by the monster of Marghera on the mainland.

You could then follow the suggested route back towards Campo Santa Margherita via Fondamenta delle Procuratie. Along here and the parallel Fondamenta dei Cereri, rental housing was built as early as the 16th century by the Procurators of St Mark for the less well off. It has remained largely unchanged since.

A short walk north from Campo Santa Margherita along Calle della Chiesa and over the bridge will bring you into Campo San Pantalon. The Chiesa di San Pantalon 31 (p64) is worth a peek for the remarkable cycle of ceiling canvases on the life and martyrdom of St Pantaleone.

SESTIERI DI SAN POLO & SANTA CROCE (SANTA CROSE)

From Campo San Pantalon, follow Calle San Pantalon around to the right of the church and head north over the next bridge. You will emerge in Campo San Rocco. In front of you rises the brooding Gothic apse of the **Chiesa di Santa Maria Gloriosa dei Frari 1** (p72), which you enter from the side. On your left, the **Scuola Grande di San Rocco 2** (p75) and the church of the same name face each other at an angle. Between them they contain a formidable concentration of Venetian art. A good ice-cream stop is **Gelateria Millefoglie da Tarcisio 3** (p144).

A brief detour towards the Grand Canal from Campo San Rocco along Calle Larga Prima brings you to the charming Campo San Tomà, marked at its western end by the **Scuola dei Calegheri 4**, the shoemakers' confraternity, and closed off at the far end by the **Chiesa di San Tomà 5**, whose façade dates from 1742. Across Rio di San Tomà is Palazzo Centani, better known as the **Casa di Goldoni 6** (p71), the house of Venice's great playwright. From here you could head to Campo San Polo, to the northeast over the Rio di San Polo, but the route outlined here takes you back to the Frari. Next door to the great church spread the buildings and peaceful cloisters of the former Convento dei Frari, suppressed in 1810 by Napoleon. Since 1815 it has housed the **Archivio di Stato 7**, the city's archives and treasure-trove of some 15 million documents covering the breadth of Venice's history from the 9th century on.

Cross the Rio dei Frari, turn left and cross the next bridge. Turn right and then veer left around the block, and you end up in the nondescript Campo San Stin. Take the western exit off the *campo* and turn right. Almost immediately on the left you will be struck by what seems like an iconostasis. Behind it, two impressive façades give onto a courtyard.

On the south side is the **Chiesa di San Giovanni Evangelista 8**. The heavy-pillared building next door was once used as the church cemetery. Opposite is one of the six major Venetian *scuole*, the **Scuola Grande di San Giovanni Evangelista 9** (p75).

Back on Calle dell'Olio, proceed north to the canal and turn left. Cross the first bridge over Rio Marin and head along the bank to Calle della Croce. Head east down this lane, turn right then left into Campo San Nazario Sauro, and keep heading east down Ruga Bella, which takes you into Campo San Giacomo dell'Orio and the **church 10** (p71) of the same name.

Detour from Rio Marin to Piazzale Roma

Before you head northeast of Rio Marin to Campo San Giacomo dell'Orio, a few words on a possible detour and some minor but noteworthy items between Calle della Croce and the western end of the Sestiere di Santa Croce. Just across Rio Marin you are facing the **Palazzo Soranzo-Cappello 11**, a 16th-century mansion graced with what must once have been a beautiful (but is now an unruly) garden. From the same period is the **Palazzo Gradenigo 12**, further northwest, by the last bridge over the canal. Were you to walk up to that bridge and look to your right, you'd see the tiny **Chiesa di San Simeon Grande 13** (8.30am-noon & 5-7pm). Of ancient origins, it was heavily restored in the 18th century. Inside you can see an *Ultima Cena* (Last Supper) by Tintoretto.

Across the bridge, you end up on Calle Bergami. Turn right at its end and head for the high-arched **Ponte dei Scalzi 14**. Built in

FOOD FOR THOUGHT

From Calle della Croce, you can make a detour to one of the rare strips of footpath actually on the Grand Canal. Turn left (north) up Calle Larga dei Bari, right along Lista dei Bari and left (north) along Ramo Zen then Calle Zen to the Riva de Biasio. A couple of the mansions here are interesting enough to behold and the views to the other side of the canal are more impressive still.

But the prize goes to a tale we all hope is taller than true. A sausage maker by the name of Biagio (Biasio) Cargnio had a shop here in the 16th century. They say he was sent to the next world (beheaded and then quartered) on charges of having sausages made of – wait for it – children. The celebrated case was immortalised for all time, with what is claimed to be a sculpted effigy of Biasio's removed head decorating the right flank of the Chiesa di San Giovanni Decollato (p71).

1934, it replaced an iron bridge built by the Austrians in 1858. Crossing over this bridge puts you onto the route through the Sestiere di Cannaregio (see p130).

If you turn left before the Ponte dei Scalzi and follow Fondamenta San Simeon Piccolo southwest, you'll pass the **church 15** of the same name. The present version was completed in 1738, and its outstanding feature is the bronze dome. Just before the next bridge, turn left down Fondamenta dei Tolentini. The modern façade on the bend is the entrance to the **Istituto Universitario di Architettura di Venezia 16**, designed by Carlo Scarpa. The institute is one of the country's most prestigious architecture schools. Beside it, the late-16th-century **Chiesa di San Nicolò dei Tolentini 17** houses works by Palma il Giovane.

The **Giardini Papadopoli 18** (⏰ 8am-dusk) across the canal seems almost an afterthought. The park was a deal more impressive until the Rio Novo was slammed through in 1932. Beyond the park lies Piazzale Roma with its unlovely bus station and car parks. A wander around it and along Rio di Santa Chiara is a sobering reminder

WALK FACTS

Start Campo San Pantalon (vaporetto San Tomà)

End Ponte di Rialto

Distance 5.5km (including detours)

Duration two hours

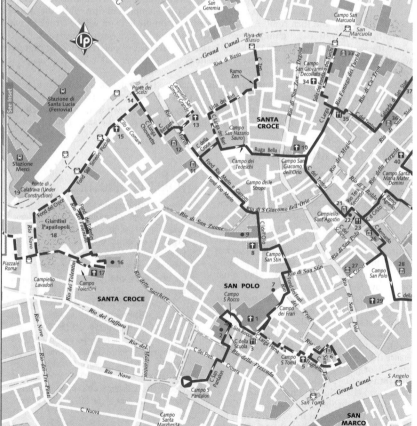

of how even the most beautiful of cities contain pockets of ugliness and neglect. From here you can admire the rather sad concrete points of what was billed as a dazzling new bridge for the city, the problem-plagued **Ponte di Calatrava 19** (p73).

Beyond the canal lies the now little-used merchant-shipping harbour and then the Isola del Tronchetto – a giant car park and host of the **PalaFenice 20** (p172), the big-top theatre originally raised in 1996 to replace the then largely destroyed Teatro La Fenice. The future of the PalaFenice remains uncertain, but it will not be pulled down.

San Giacomo dell'Orio to Rialto via Campo San Polo

From Campo San Giacomo dell'Orio, two separate routes suggest themselves to get you to the Ponte di Rialto. This first one follows a trail largely ignored by tourists. The other, via Campo San Stae (see p129), is busier but still loaded with interest. You can also join them together into a circular route that would bring you right back into this square. From here you could then backtrack to Rio Marin and go on to the Ponte dei Scalzi to pick up the next route through Cannaregio (see p130).

From Campo San Giacomo dell'Orio, follow Calle del Tentor southeast, cross the bridge and continue until you hit a T-junction. As you turn left into Rio Terà Secondo,

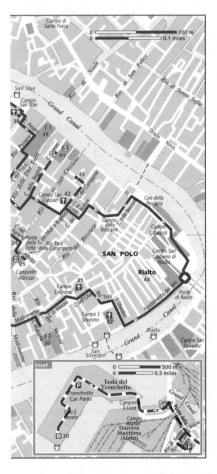

note on the right-hand side, opposite the Gothic **Palazzo Soranzo-Pisani 21**, the building in which Aldo Manuzio got his **Aldine Press 22** started and so revolutionised the world of European letters. His was an address much frequented by learned fellows from across the Continent.

Head northeast and turn right into Calle del Scaleter. At **Da Fiore 23** (p147), Venice's only Michelin-star restaurant, turn left into Calle del Cristo, cross the bridge and take the second right (Ramo Agnello). Follow it straight over the bridge and stop at the second bridge.

It's hard to tell now, but this was long the centre of Venice's main red-light zone. The bridge is known as **Ponte delle Tette 24**, or Tits Bridge, because a city ordinance stipulated that whores who worked here should hang about in windows and doorways bare-breasted to encourage business. Pardon? Back in the 14th century the city fathers had in fact tried to clamp down on prostitution (see The Oldest Profession, p128), but by the late 15th century found it the only hope of reviving the ardour of Venetian men, who were apparently more keen on sodomising each other. La Serenissima took a far dimmer view of this than prostitution, so much so that anyone successfully prosecuted for sodomy under a law of 1482 found themselves executed and incinerated between the columns on Piazzetta San Marco.

Beyond the bridge is Rio Terà delle Carampane. The name originally came from a noble family's house in the area (Ca' Rampani), and at some point the ladies of the

THE OLDEST PROFESSION

Although prostitution in Venice was generally tolerated, and in some periods encouraged, attitudes towards the practice and its practitioners were always ambiguous.

In 1358 local authorities selected an area of Rialto to set aside for prostitution. Prostitutes and their matrons, who took care of the till and paid their workers a monthly wage, soon occupied a group of houses that came to be known as Il Castelletto (Little Castle), which was kept under surveillance by six guardians. Prostitutes were not allowed on the streets after a certain hour and were forbidden to work on religious holidays. The atmosphere must have been oppressive, for prostitutes began to spread out across the city, especially to the nearby area around Rio Terà delle Carampane. At first, attempts were made to force them back into Il Castelletto, but in the end the authorities gave in to the situation and even proclaimed laws obliging the girls to display their wares to attract business.

By the 1640s, however, various regulations were in place to put a brake on prostitution. Prostitutes could not enter churches or potter around in two-oared boats (only 'ladies' could be taken about in such a manner). They were not to adorn themselves with gold or other jewellery. They could not testify in criminal court cases, nor could they prosecute when services rendered were not paid for (which was generally where pimps came in). Your average street whore was made to feel very much like a second-class citizen.

Different strokes for different folks – there was a whole other class of prostitution. In the 16th century the myth of the *cortigiane* (courtesans) began to take shape. These were women of distinction, not simply better-paid, better-looking bimbos. Schooled in the arts, fluent in Latin, handy with a harpsichord, they were women of keen intellect and talent not fortunate enough to have been born into nobility. For such daughters of middle-class families, working for a high-class escort service seemed the only way to acquire independence and wellbeing.

In 1535, when the Venetian populace totalled about 120,000 and some 11,000 prostitutes were registered, a very handy tourist guide was published: *Questo si è il Catalogo de tutte le principal, et più honorate Cortigiane di Venetia* (This is the Catalogue of the main and most honoured Courtesans of Venice). It contained names, rates and useful addresses. No wonder the city had such a lascivious reputation.

night working here came to be known as *carampane*. The word is now a colourful part of standard Italian and denotes the mutton-dressed-as-lamb kind of lady.

From Ponte delle Tette, look south down Rio di San Cassiano and you will notice a high, wrought-iron walkway linking **Palazzo Albrizzi 25** to private gardens. Inside the 16th-century mansion Isabella Teotochi Albrizzi held her literary salon around the end of the 18th century, with sculptor Antonio Canova and writer Ugo Foscolo among her guests.

Backtrack to Da Fiore. From here turn left (southeast) across the bridge and along Calle Bernardo (the fine Gothic **mansion 26** of the same name is best seen from the bridge), which brings you into the leafy expanse of Campo San Polo. Among the several mansions facing the square are **Palazzo Corner 27**, designed by Michele Sanmicheli in the 16th century, and the Gothic **Palazzi Soranzo 28**. Well worth visiting if you are a Tiepolo fan is the **Chiesa di San Polo 29** (p71).

A glance at the map will show that you have almost completed a circuit to the Frari. You could head down that way and beyond into Dorsoduro (see p121), or stroll eastwards towards Rialto and the Grand Canal.

From Campo San Polo, take Calle della Madonnetta and follow it to Campo Sant'Aponal. On the way, duck down Calle Malvasia to peer enviously through the gates at the gardens of the **Palazzo Papadopoli 30**. It seems almost unfair that such luxuriant greenery should be the preserve of the Istituto per lo Studio della Dinamica delle Grandi Masse (Institute for the Study of the Dynamics of Large Masses)!

The former **Chiesa di Sant'Aponal 31** has a simple Gothic façade topped by five statues, and its freestanding bell tower is Romanesque. From here, Calle dell'Olio takes you around the right side of the church. Turn right down Rio Terà San Silvestro and pass the unremarkable early-20th-century façade of the **Chiesa di San Silvestro 32**. Turn onto the former wine docks on the Grand Canal, the Fondamenta del Vin, and you'll see that the Ponte di Rialto is clearly in view ahead. The restaurants along here make a tempting spot for a break, but the food is ordinary and the drinks priced to match the privileged views.

San Giacomo dell'Orio to Rialto via Campo San Stae

Follow the signs north from the *campo* along Calle Larga (turning off at the canal) to reach the **Fondaco dei Turchi 33** (p73), which houses a natural-history museum. From the *fondaco*, backtrack a little and duck into Campo San Giovanni Decollato for a look at the **church 34** (p71) of the same name. Return then to the Rio Fontego dei Turchi, cross it and take Calle del Tentor east. A great lunch stop with vegetarian options is **Osteria La Zucca 35** (p148).

At Salizada di San Stae, turn left (northeast). On the right is the **Palazzo Mocenigo 36** (p73), a patrician mansion containing 18th-century period furnishings. At the end of the street is the tiny canalside Campo San Stae, named after the baroque **church 37** (p72). Next door to the left (No 1980) is the **Scuola dei Tiraoro e Battioro 38**, the former seat of the goldsmith confraternity.

From Campo San Stae, cross the bridge, turn right then left, cross another bridge and you reach the land entrance to **Ca' Pesaro 39** (p70), a fine, restored baroque mansion with important collections of modern art and Japanese Edo-period objects.

Walking southwest away from Ca' Pesaro, you could be forgiven for missing the **Chiesa di Santa Maria Mater Domini 40**. Sansovino supposedly had a hand in it, and inside (if you happen to find it open) is an early work by Tintoretto, the *Invenzione della Croce* (Invention of the Cross).

Campo Santa Maria Mater Domini is an intriguing square, with well-preserved late-Byzantine and Gothic buildings. No 2174 dates from the 13th century. Cross the square and turn left (north) into Calle della Regina (Queen St). At the end of the street, looking onto the Grand Canal, is **Palazzo Corner della Regina 41**. The Corners, a powerful trading family, had mansions all over town. On this site lived Caterina Corner, who ended up on the throne of Venetian-controlled Cyprus in the late 15th century, only to be obliged later by the schemers of San Marco to abdicate and accept a galling if golden exile in Asolo (p239). For more on her unlikely story, see the boxed text, below. The building was remodelled in the early 18th century.

Tintoretto fans may want to stop at the **Chiesa di San Cassian 42** (🕙 9am-noon Tue-Sat) in the *campo* of the same name. The sanctuary is decorated with three of his paintings, the *Crocifissione* (Crucifixion), the *Risurrezione* (Resurrection) and the *Discesa al Limbo* (Descent into Limbo). Make a quick detour towards the Grand Canal along Calle del Campanile and duck into **Corte de Ca' Michiel 43**. This was once known as Calle del Teatro, reputedly the site of one of the city's first theatres in 1580. It didn't last too long, as the Inquisition (not an overly popular institution in Venice) shut it down for what it claimed was lewd goings-on.

A couple of streets east of Chiesa di San Cassian, you arrive at Campo delle Beccarie. Welcome to the nerve centre of Venice – **Rialto 44** (p74).

A QUEEN CORNERED

In 1468, as 14-year-old Caterina Corner was escorted in pomp out of the family mansion in San Polo to the Palazzo Ducale, she must have wondered what was coming next. *'Niente di buono'* ('nothing good') would have been the response of wise onlookers. Betrothed to 28-year-old James, the usurper king of Cyprus, Caterina found herself four years later pregnant, widowed and surrounded by enemies in her new island home.

James' untimely (and suspicious) death convinced Venice that it must act to protect its growing interest in the island. Captain General Pietro Mocenigo was dispatched first to fortify Venetian forts and then later to reverse a coup against the queen. The Cypriots were none too enamoured of de facto Venetian rule on their island, but after the coup attempt, government was effectively in the hands of two Venetian *consiglieri* (councillors), ostensibly in the service of the queen.

After the death of her infant son in 1474, Caterina's problems only increased. Plots against her from Cypriot nobles came thick and fast, and her protectors, the Venetians, virtually held her prisoner. In 1488, Venice decided enough was enough. Cyprus was threatened by Turkish invasion and the latest plots against Caterina were proving insufferable. It was decided to absorb the island into the Venetian Empire. For this, Caterina had to be convinced to abdicate.

This she did with some reluctance, but she had little choice. For her trouble she was compensated with a mainland fief centred on Asolo and a generous life pension. She returned to her Venetian home only in 1509, where she died the following year. She kept her title of queen until the end. Less than a century later, Venice would lose Cyprus to the Turks anyway.

SESTIERE DI CANNAREGIO

Assume you have just stumbled over Ponte dei Scalzi after following the routes around Santa Croce and San Polo. Or you might have arrived at the train station. Either way, you are ready for an exploratory stroll through Cannaregio. The long thoroughfare connecting the train station and Piazza San Marco crawls with tourists heading from one to the other – few venture off it into the peaceful back lanes.

The first sight of any significance you lay eyes on is the Carmelite **Chiesa dei Scalzi** 1 (p76). At the northeastern end of bustling Rio Terà Lista di Spagna is the **Chiesa di San Geremia** 2 (p77), flanked by the **Palazzo Labia** 3 (p78), known for its Tiepolo frescoes.

At **Ponte delle Guglie** 4, or Needles Bridge, so called because of the obelisks at each end, the itinerary splits into two. The first option takes you to the Sestiere di San Marco via the Ghetto. The second is a more meandering stroll through many of the backstreets and canals of Cannaregio that brings you to Campo SS Giovanni e Paolo in Castello.

Ponte delle Guglie to Sestiere di San Marco

Cross Ponte delle Guglie and turn left. Just before you do, you may want to poke around the daily **fish and produce market** 5 on Rio Terà San Leonardo.

Turn off the Fondamenta di Cannaregio at Calle del Ghetto Vecchio. You'll recognise it by the kosher restaurant **Gam Gam** 6 (p151). A few steps down this lane look up at the wall to your left, at house number 1131. Carved in stone is a decree from the Republic dated 20 September 1704, forbidding Jews converted to Christianity entry into the Ghetto or into the private houses of Jews, on pain of punishment that, depending on the gravity of the 'crime', might include 'the rope [hanging], prison, galleys, flogging…and other greater punishments, depending on the judgement of their excellencies (the Executors Against Blasphemy). To enquire into transgressions, Inquisitorial processes will be established, and secret denunciations may be deposited in the usual receptacles. The accusers will be entitled to a bounty of 100 ducats, to be taken from the property of the accused…'

On emerging into the small square, you will see two of the Ghetto's five synagogues, also known as *schole* (schools) because they were used for scripture studies. The existence of five places of worship within the Ghetto reflected in part the density of the Jewish population, and also liturgical variations between the different communities. The **Schola Spagnola** 7 (p78) is at the square's southern end (look for the plaque commemorating Italian Jewish victims of the Holocaust). It and the **Schola Levantina** 8 (p78), opposite, were erected by Jews from the Iberian Peninsula. The interior of the latter betrays a hefty rococo influence, best seen in the décor of the pulpit. The Schola Levantina is used for Saturday prayers in winter (it has heating), while the Schola Spagnola is used in summer.

Calle del Ghetto Vecchio proceeds northeast over a bridge into the heart of Venice's Jewish community, Campo del Ghetto Nuovo, where you will find the **Museo Ebraico** 9 (p78).

Leave the Ghetto by the portico that leads across the canal to Calle Farnese. This was one of the Ghetto gates that used to be locked at midnight. Proceed straight to Rio Terà Farsetti and turn right, then duck down Rio Terà del Cristo to look at the **Chiesa di San Marcuola** 10 (p77). Heading east across Rio di San Marcuola, you will come up against the **Palazzo Vendramin-Calergi** 11 (p80), where Wagner died and gamblers lose fortunes.

From here, return to the main drag (at this point called Rio Terà della Maddalena – you'll know you've hit it when you are sucked up into the crowds again). Proceed a couple of blocks eastwards, then head off to the right (south). In a quiet little *campo* is the unique, circular **Chiesa della Maddalena** 12, the only round building in the city and a rare neoclassical presence. Should you find it open, you will find several Tiepolos inside. The pretty square around the church is flanked by houses with their upper parts poking over heavy timber barbicans. Notice anything yet? Like you are about the only one with sufficient curiosity to get off the strip and have a look here? Try jumping back into the flood of passers-by and then jumping out again. Amazing, isn't it?

You could go around the back of the church and follow Calle del Forno around to a dead end right on the Grand Canal. It's a little mucky but it is always interesting to get another view of the canal. By backtracking and then taking Calle Correr, you end up back on the strip. The bronze statue on the square opposite you is of **Paolo Sarpi 13**, La Serenissima's greatest (some might suggest only) philosopher. You could make a detour at this point and scurry northeast across a couple of bridges to the **Chiesa di San Marziale 14**. If it's open, have a peek inside at the baroque baubles.

Otherwise skip it and head southeast along the main street. It's called Strada Nova here and was bulldozed through the area some years after the rail link was opened in the 19th century. On your right you pass a veritable parade of Venetian mansions, but you'd never know it – they present their photogenic profiles only to the Grand Canal. The second of them after you cross Rio di San Felice (named after

Children splashing in a fountain outside Santa Lucia train station (opposite), Sestiere di Cannaregio

the church you pass on the left just before the bridge) is **Ca' d'Oro 15** (p76). One of Venice's classic eateries, **Osteria dalla Vedova 16** (p151) lurks nearby.

Strada Nova then leads into the pleasing Campo dei SS Apostoli. The **church 17** (⏰ 7.30-11.30am & 5-7pm Mon-Sat, 8.30am-noon & 4-6.30pm Sun) of the same name is worth visiting for the 15th-century Cappella Corner by Mauro Codussi, which features a Tiepolo painting of St Lucy.

Keep following the crowd over the next two bridges; on the left is the curious **Chiesa di San Giovanni Grisostomo 18** (p77). Around the back, Corte Prima del Milion leads into a chain of brief streets, *sotoporteghi* and squares. At No 5845 in Corte Seconda del Milion, you are supposedly looking at **Marco Polo's house 19**. That's one theory. Another suggests the Polo family house disappeared to make way for the **Teatro Malibran 20** (p172) in 1677. During restoration work on the theatre, traces of what might have been the Polo residence were unearthed in 2001.

Return to the Chiesa di San Giovanni Grisostomo and head south along Salizada San Giovanni. The next canal marks the boundary between the *sestieri* of Cannaregio and San Marco. The building you are looking at on the right is the **Fondaco dei Tedeschi 21** (p56).

OF WELLS & RAINWATER PRIESTS

Sooner or later you will probably ask yourself, as you enter one *campo* or another: what are those squat stone cylinders with the metal lids firmly clamped on top? The answer is obvious enough once you think about it: they're wells.

That there are so many reflects every neighbourhood's need to have its own source of drinking water in the good old days. With bridges few and far between throughout much of the history of the city, it was easier to provide each of the many *insulae* (blocks or small districts) that make up the fabric of Venice with its own well than attempt to transport water.

There's a whole lot more to this system than meets the eye. In general, the well is surrounded by up to four depressions around 4m from it. Rainwater drained into these depressions and seeped into a cistern below. Sand and/or gravel inside the cistern acted as a filter. In the middle of the cistern, a brick cylinder (the well proper) extends to the bottom. The cistern itself was sealed off with impenetrable clay to keep salty water out. Engineers also sought out relatively high spots for wells to shield them from the *acque alte*.

The parish priest long held the keys to the local well cover, something that gave rise to a Venetian linguistic oddity. The water collected in the wells was *acqua piovana* (rainwater), and so often a priest was referred to as a *piovan*. Eventually the term stuck and is now one of the Venetian words for priest.

With the introduction of direct running water to all Venice's buildings, the wells have been closed up and are no longer in use. But it is intriguing to think how much the city's survival depended on these ingenious structures.

Walking Tours   SESTIERE DI CANNAREGIO

Ponte delle Guglie to Castello

For this second ramble, you don't cross Ponte delle Guglie, but instead head northwest along Fondamenta Venier, named after the late-18th-century neoclassical **mansion 22** of the same name. Further up, **Palazzo Savorgnan's 23** big draw is its garden, now a **public park** (✪ 8am-5.30pm Oct-Mar, 8am-7.30pm Apr-Sep) with slides and other amusements for the kiddies.

Beyond the palace, the character of the area changes quickly – it's clearly a working-class district. It was perhaps not always thus. Across the canal, just before you reach the last bridge (Ponte di Tre Archi), the 17th-century **Palazzo Surian 24** stands out. During the last century of the Republic, the French moved their embassy in here and Jean Jacques Rousseau managed to blag his way into a job as secretary to the ambassador.

To the left, down along Rio di San Giobbe, the rather ordinary **church 25** of the same name boasts a remarkable ceiling faced with multicoloured glazed terracotta.

Before crossing Ponte di Tre Archi, stroll to the end of Fondamenta di San Giobbe. The enormous complex at the end here was the **Macello Comunale 26**, the city's abattoir. Le Corbusier designed a hospital for the site, but (much to the annoyance of many citizens) it got the thumbs down in 1964. The Università Ca' Foscari now has its economics faculty here.

Across the bridge, towards the end of Fondamenta di Cannaregio, the former **Chiesa di Santa Maria delle Penitenti 27** was one of the seemingly abundant religious institutions set up to take in wayward women anxious to put their wicked past behind them.

WALK FACTS

Start Ponte dei Scalzi/Ferrovia (vaporetto Ferrovia)

End Fondaco dei Tedeschi or Campo SS Giovanni e Paolo

Distance 2.5km to Fondaco dei Tedeschi or 4.8km to Campo SS Giovanni e Paolo

Duration 45 minutes or 1½ hours

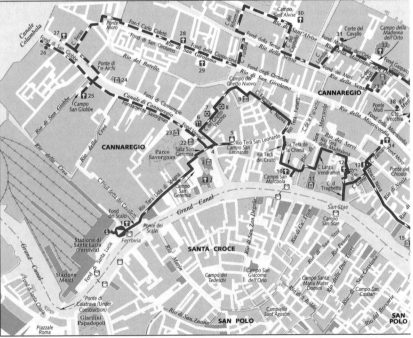

The winding walk along Calle Ferau and through the Sacca di San Girolamo area, an unpretentious residential district, takes you past the barely noticeable **Chiesa delle Cappuccine 28** on the left and the ugly hulk of the **Chiesa di San Girolamo 29** on the right across the canal. Apart from soaking up the peace and quiet, your objective is the **Chiesa di Sant'Alvise 30** (p77).

From here there is no choice but to make a detour across Rio di Sant'Alvise and then a little way east along Fondamenta della Sensa and back up Calle Loredan to Fondamenta Madonna dell'Orto. The long courtyard on the left as you head east is called **Corte del Cavallo 31**, or Horse Court, because here the bronze was melted down for the great equestrian statue to Colleoni in Campo SS Giovanni e Paolo (see p88). A little way along to the east is the striking **Chiesa della Madonna dell'Orto 32** (p76).

If you cross the first bridge to the east of the church and head south, you will end up in Calle dei Mori. Follow it to the next canal and turn left down Fondamenta dei Mori. Almost immediately you will see on your left a plaque noting that **Tintoretto's house 33** was at No 3399. The strange statue of a man with a huge turban that sticks out of the wall next door on **Palazzo Mastelli 34** is one of four spread out along the building's façade. The street names here (dei Mori) mean 'of the Moors' and refer to these statues, traditionally said to represent members of the Mastelli family (the one on the corner is known as Sior Rioba), 12th-century merchants from the Morea, one of La Serenissima's most important Greek possessions. The building on which they appear is also known as Palazzo del Cammello because of the distinctive bas-relief depicting this animal on the façade overlooking Rio della Madonna dell'Orto. The Mastelli family were said to be an unpleasant lot, forever on the lookout for a fast ducat and impoverishing local families. A tall tale says that one day they went too far and were turned to stone, later to be installed in their present positions.

Backtrack to the Chiesa della Madonna dell'Orto and continue east along Fondamenta Gasparo Contarini, named after **Palazzo Contarini del Zaffo 35**, which extends to the end of the street. A narrow **wooden quay 36** protrudes out into the small protected bay off the lagoon. Locals use it for sunbathing and from here you enjoy good views across to the islands of San Michele and Murano. Behind the *palazzo* spread luxuriant private gardens leading to

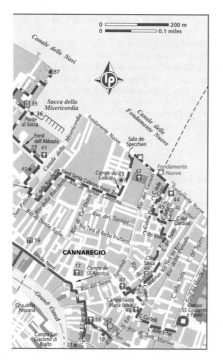

Canale delle Navi

Sacca della Misericordia

Ponte di Sacca

Fond dell'Abbazia

Fondamente Nuove

Saliz dei Specchieri

Canale delle Fondamente Nuove

Fondamente Nuove

Campo dei Gesuiti

San Felice

Fond Santa Caterina

Rio di Santa Caterina

Rio della Racchetta

Rio dei Sartori

Rio Terà di Barba Fruttarol

Rio di Santa Sofia

CANNAREGIO

Strada Nova

Campo dei SS Apostoli

C dei Volti

Calle Larga G Gallina

C dei Botteri

C del Cordoni

Clo Stella

Rio Terà dei Biri

Rio dei Santi

Campo Santa Maria Nova

Campo SS Giovanni e Paolo

Cpo della Pescaria

Grand Canal

Campo San Giacomo di Rialto

C delle Erbe

Rio di San Marina

0 ————— 200 m
0 ————— 0.1 miles

an isolated building on the lagoon, the so-called **Casinò degli Spiriti 37**, where in the 16th century students, literati and glitterati with the right contacts would gather for learned chitchat and a few drinks.

There is little choice here but to cross Rio della Madonna dell'Orto and follow Corte Vecchia southwest to Rio della Sensa. Before turning left to continue southeast, turn around to the right and you'll see what remains of a former **squero 38**, or gondola-building yard, complete with slipways into Rio dei Muti.

The next important stop is I Gesuiti, the massive hulk erected by the Jesuits. To get there, pass down Fondamenta dell'Abbazia under the portico of the **Scuola Vecchia della Misericordia 39**, once the seat of one of the city's grand religious confraternities and now home to a complex of state-run restoration laboratories and workshops. The confraternity later moved into the immense **Scuola Nuova della Misericordia 40**, designed by Sansovino in the 1530s, on the southern side of Rio della Sensa. Next to the Scuola Vecchia, on the *campo* that overlooks Rio della Sensa, is the **Chiesa di Santa Maria della Misericordia 41**, established in the 10th century and altered in the 13th. The dead-end bridge leading to a private

Chiesa di Santa Maria della Visitazione (p84), Sestiere di Castello

house, Ponte del Chiodo, is notable for the absence of any kind of railing; it's about the only one of its kind in Venice now. Once most of the city's bridges were like this – not good for stumbling home tipsy late at night! Indeed, in the early centuries of the life of Venice bridges were often little more than a couple of rough planks.

A series of bridges takes you into Calle della Racchetta. To get to **I Gesuiti 42** (p78), follow this street northeast to Fondamenta Santa Caterina and head east until you reach Campo dei Gesuiti. Virtually across the *campo* from the grand Jesuit church is the tiny **Oratorio dei Crociferi 43** (p78). Right on the Grand Canal, along the Fondamente Nuove, is a fine spot for a drink and long wistful gazing north across the lagoon, **Algiubagiò 44** (p166).

Titian fans can find his **house 45** by walking up to the Fondamente Nuove, heading southeast as far as Calle delle Croci and penetrating the web of lanes in search of Corte della Carità. North of this square, a narrow, dead-end lane is your objective – at the end of it on the right is Titian's place.

From Corte della Carità you can trace a path down along Calle del Fumo, past the 17th-century **Palazzo Widman 46** and down the narrow *calle* of the same name. You emerge on Campo Santa Maria Nova. Off to the right (northwest) is the **Chiesa di San Canciano 47**. Although here since the 9th century, what you see is the result of intervention by Massari and Gaspari. The real stunner is off to the left (southeast), the Renaissance **Chiesa di Santa Maria dei Miracoli 48** (p77). From the church, you can turn left (east) along Calle Castelli (which continues over the canal as Calle delle Erbe). Once over the next bridge, you are obliged to swing left and arrive in Campo SS Giovanni e Paolo. You are now in the city's easternmost *sestiere*, Castello.

SESTIERE DI CASTELLO

Presiding over Campo SS Giovanni e Paolo is the proud figure of the *condottiero* (professional mercenary commander) **Bartolomeo Colleoni 1** (p88).

Around the mercenary commander rise the imposing edifice of the **Chiesa dei SS Giovanni e Paolo 2** (p82) and, next to it, the marble trompe l'oeil frontage of the **Scuola Grande di San Marco 3** (p88), now part of the city hospital. Just east of the church is the extraordinary baroque façade of the **Ospedaletto 4** (p86), with its *Übermensch* statuary bulging out at you in the street. After a quiet stroll east along residential streets, you emerge in Campo San Francesco della Vigna, where the sudden appearance of the massive Palladian façade of the **church 5** of the same name (p83) comes as a shock.

Proceeding east around the south flank of Chiesa di San Francesco della Vigna, you'll end up in Campo della Celestia. Follow the only lane exiting off it across the canal and into Campo San Ternità. Calle Dona veers to the left (east) off this square. After the canal, turn right (southwest) and almost immediately on your left is **Casa Magno 6**, a unique example of Gothic housing. Now head straight down to and across Campo Do Pozzi. You'll end up on Calle degli Scudi, at which point you turn right (northwest) and cross the canal into

Campo de le Gate. A quick dogleg and you will run into Rio di San Lorenzo. Just before the bridge, on the right, is the **Scuola di San Giorgio degli Schiavoni 7** (p88), the Dalmatian community's religious school.

After admiring Carpaccio's contributions to the school, proceed south along the canal and at the **Chiesa di Sant'Antonin 8** follow the main street south into Campo Bandiera e Moro. This quiet square is named after the Venetian brothers Bandiera, who lived in **Palazzo Soderini 9**, at No 3611, and their companion Domenico Moro (who lived nearby), all of whom were executed by troops of the Bourbon Kingdom of the Two Sicilies after a failed pro-unity insurrection in Cosenza (Calabria) in 1844. All three are buried in the Chiesa di SS Giovanni e Paolo. The square is fronted in the southeast corner by the **Chiesa di San Giovanni in Bragora 10** (p83).

From that church follow Calle Crosera east. You will stumble across a good restaurant near here, the **Trattoria Corte Sconta 11** (p154). About the shortest route to what was once the military powerhouse of the Republic takes you up Calle Erizzo past the Renaissance **palazzo 12** of the same name and across the bridge to the **Chiesa di San Martino 13** (p83). Across the canal are the walls of the **Arsenale 14** (p80). To reach its entrance, walk along Fondamenta di Fronte until you reach the Rio dell'Arsenale. Continuing on a seafaring theme, the **Museo Storico Navale 15** (p85) is a short hop south of the Arsenale.

Heading east, you enter very-few-tourists territory. Following the walls of the Arsenale past its entrances on Campo della Tana, cross the bridge and take Fondamenta della Tana, turning right down Calle di San Francesco di Paola – you'll soon hit the broad Via Giuseppe Garibaldi. The **Chiesa di San Francesco di Paola 16** is a fairly uninteresting 18th-century remake of the 16th-century original.

Follow the road east and cross the last bridge northwards across the Rio di Sant'Anna (named after the ruined **church 17**, now encased in restorers' scaffolding, that looks out over the Canale di San Pietro). Proceed north across Campo di Ruga and take the last lane on the right (east). The bridge at the end of it takes you across to the Isola di San Pietro, where you may wish to visit what was long the city's official cathedral, the **Cattedrale di San Pietro di Castello 18** (p82).

There is no need to rush through. An aimless wander through the simple grid pattern of residential streets allows you to immerse yourself in the simple, gritty, everyday world of ordinary Venetians. No sights, just life.

The only other way off the Isola di San Pietro is by the more southerly of the two bridges, which brings you back to the ruins of Sant'Anna. Walk past them (heading west) and duck down Calle Correra. Cross the broad Secco Marina, keep on down Corte del Solda and cross the bridge. A stroll past the **Chiesa di San Giuseppe di Castello 19** will bring you into the somewhat tatty Giardini Pubblici (p85), one of the city's few public parks and location of the Biennale.

From here, wander over Rio dei Giardini to Sant'Elena, the quietest and leafiest residential corner of Venice. Housing construction began in 1925, before which there was little here but an abandoned pilgrims' hospice and the now closed **Chiesa di Sant'Elena 20**, a small Gothic number abandoned in 1806 (a great deal of housing was destroyed further west to make way for the Giardini Pubblici) and reopened for a while from 1928 when people started moving into the new residential district. The arrival of riot police and armies of football supporters occasionally snaps it out of its usual (and not unpleasant) torpor. The crowds make for the **Stadio Penzo 21** to see the home side struggle

THE EXCOMMUNICATION OF VENICE

They say that late in the 16th century Cardinal Camillo Borghese and the Venetian ambassador to Rome, Leonardo Donà, had a verbal skirmish one day in the halls of Roman power. The cardinal hissed that, were he pope, he'd excommunicate the entire Venetian populace. Donà replied with aplomb: 'And I, were I doge, would thumb my nose at the excommunication.'

As luck would have it, cardinal and ambassador were, in 1606, Pope Paul V and doge, respectively. Rome had never liked the fact that the Venetian government reserved for itself a degree of control over church property, the appointment of clerics and the right to try wayward priests in secular courts. Paul V decided to excommunicate Venice. The doge ignored the papal bull, ordered all churches to remain open on Venetian territory and ordered into exile anyone who tried to apply the bull. Paolo Sarpi, a philosopher of some note, became for a year the Republic's orator in a year of quarrelling that ended with a humiliating climb-down for the pope. Venice's obstinacy not only confirmed its position on ecclesiastical matters, it damaged papal credibility in all Catholic territories.

Towards San Marco

At this point the weary could get the No 42 or No 52 circle line vaporetto from the Sant'Elena stop to San Zaccaria to continue this itinerary, or hop on to the No 1 and potter up the Grand Canal to do something else altogether. Otherwise, it's a pleasant and leafy walk from Sant'Elena through the Parco delle Rimembranze and then the Giardini Pubblici along the waterfront.

You will eventually find yourself on the waterfront boardwalk known as Riva degli Schiavoni (p87), just as busy now with tourists as it once was with all sorts. Just at the point where you turn inland is the **Chiesa di Santa Maria della Visitazione 22** (or more simply La Pietà; see p84), associated with Vivaldi.

A short walk north brings you to the rear side of the **Chiesa di San Giorgio dei Greci 23** (p83). Walk around the church to reach the main entrance alongside Rio dei Greci. Virtually next door is the Hellenic Institute's **Museo delle Icone 24** (p85).

WALK FACTS

Start Campo SS Giovanni e Paolo (vaporetto Ospedale)

End Piazzetta San Marco

Distance 9km

Duration three hours

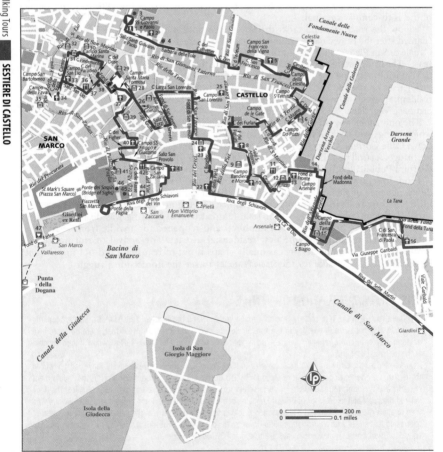

As you leave San Giorgio and cross the bridge to the west, take Fondamenta di San Lorenzo north. At the second bridge east across the canal is Campo San Lorenzo, dominated by the rather shaky-looking brick façade of the **church 25** of the same name. It is an odd structure, divided down the middle to form a section for the general public and another for members of a Benedictine nunnery that has long since ceased to exist. The church is closed for restoration. Also being restored is the massive Renaissance **Palazzo Grimani 26**, at Ramo Grimani 4858, one of whose grand façades dominates the Rio di San Severo. Initially the home of Doge Antonio Grimani (who reigned from 1521 to 1523), the palace is a curious combination of Venetian and Tuscan-Roman grandeur.

From here the objective is Campo Santa Maria Formosa, a winding walk to the northwest. One of the most appealing squares in Venice, it is full of local life, eateries, benches where you can take the weight off your feet and some interesting buildings. There was a time when all sorts of popular festivals were played out here (chasing bulls around the square was one of the less sensible activities). One of Venice's best-remembered courtesans, Veronica Franco, lived in a house on this *campo*. Poet, friend of Tintoretto, and lover, however briefly, of France's King Henry III, Miss Franco was listed in the city's 16th-century guidebook to high-class escorts as 'Vero. Franco a Santa Mar. Formosa. Pieza so mare. Scudi 2'. The last bit is the base price for her services, which ranged from intelligent conversation to horizontal folk dancing.

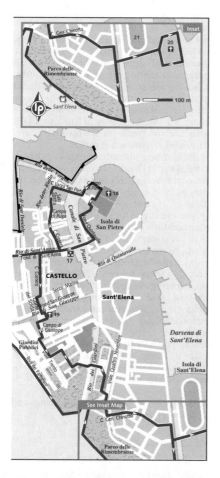

Perhaps there was always a little ribaldry in the air around here: the **Chiesa di Santa Maria Formosa 27** takes its name from a curiously saucy legend (see p84).

Among the ageing mansions facing the square, **Palazzo Vitturi 28** is a good example of the Veneto-Byzantine style, while the buildings making up the **Palazzi Donà 29** are a mix of Gothic and late Gothic. While you're here, a further quick circuit suggests itself. Leave the square and head northwest. Don't cross the canal – veer right (north) instead along Calle del Dose and then left along Calle Pindemonte. You end up in Campo Santa Marina, faced by the 13th-century **Palazzo Dolfin Bollani 30** and the Lombard-style **Palazzo Loredan 31**. A side lane north off the square leads you to the 15th-century **Palazzo Bragadin-Carabba 32**, restored by Sanmicheli.

Coming out of the square to the south, head south along Calle Carminati, which brings you into Campo San Lio. Pop into the **church 33** (p83) of the same name. A brief detour further south down Calle della Fava brings you to the square of the same name and the **Chiesa di Santa Maria della Fava 34** (☎ 041 522 46 01; Campo della Fava 5503; admission free; ☺ 8.30am-noon & 4.30-7.30pm). The church, more properly known as Santa Maria della Consolazione, was begun by Gaspari and finished in 1753 by Massari. Inside, the first painting on your right after you enter is Giambattista Tiepolo's *Educazione della Vergine* (The Virgin's Education). Back outside, you can get a good view across Rio della Fava of the late-Gothic **Palazzo Giustinian-Faccanon 35**, over in the Sestiere di San Marco.

Scurrying back to Campo San Lio, turn right (more or less east) down the busy Salizada San Lio, where you'll encounter a mouth-watering ice-cream outpost, the **Boutique del Gelato 36** (p144). The street retains some intriguing examples of Byzantine housing. More interesting still is **Calle del Paradiso 37**, which branches off it back in the direction of Campo Santa Maria Formosa. It is marked by the Gothic arch beneath which you enter, and gives you a pretty good idea of what a typical Gothic-period street in Venice looked like. On the ground floor were shops of various types. Jutting out above them on barbicans are the upper storeys, which were offices and living quarters. At the end of the street is another more elaborate arch. Known as the **Arco del Paradiso 38**, it depicts the Virgin Mary and bears the standards of the families who financed its construction.

Once back in Campo Santa Maria Formosa, walk around the church. Behind it, a bridge leads you to **Palazzo Querini Stampalia 39** (p86), a private mansion–turned–cultural foundation with a varied collection of period furniture, art, and other odds and ends.

From Palazzo Querini Stampalia, the route winds south past the former **Chiesa di San Giovanni Novo 40** (now used occasionally as exhibition space). A quick detour to the **Museo Diocesano d'Arte Sacra 41** (p85), southwest of Campo SS Filippo e Giacomo, is worthwhile, especially for fans of Romanesque architecture. Back on the main street, instead of turning left (west) for Piazza San Marco, head in the opposite direction down Salizada San Provolo and stop in at **Alla Rivetta 42** (p155) for some tasty snacks. You are heading for the **Chiesa di San Zaccaria 43** (p84), and you'll know you've struck pay dirt when you pass under a Gothic arch depicting the Virgin Mary and Jesus, thought to have been crafted by a Tuscan sculptor around 1430. Beyond, you arrive in Campo San Zaccaria and stand before the Renaissance façade of the church.

Reading the 1620 decree by the Most Illustrious and Excellent Executors for Blasphemy, etched in stone above the souvenir shop at No 4967, is enough to make you think twice about entering the square. The venerable gentlemen solemnly decree that 'all games, tumultuous behaviour, loud talk, uttering obscene language, committing acts of dishonesty, dirtying, putting up boat masts or other such objects, leaving refuse or any other kind of things is strictly forbidden on pain of the most severe penalties…'. So watch yourself. The decree went up at a time when the authorities were at pains to make sure undesirable lay persons kept well clear of convents, such as the one that was here by the Chiesa di San Zaccaria.

When you exit the church, head south off the square and you'll emerge through a *soto-portego* onto Riva degli Schiavoni again, not far from where you left it earlier.

Turn right (west) to cross the Ponte del Vin; the building immediately on the right is Palazzo Dandolo, better known to most as the **Danieli 44** (p211), one of Venice's most prestigious hotels. For a curious tale about the origins of the hideous Danieli extension on the other side of Calle delle Rasse, see A Dogey Death, p215.

Calle delle Rasse takes its name from the word *rascia* or *rassa*, meaning a rough woollen material sold along this street that was made into protective covers for gondolas. The material came from what is now Serbia, known to the Venetians centuries ago as Rascia. The next street, Calle degli Albanesi, was so named because an Albanian community lived on and around it. Interesting choice of address when you consider that prisons line its western side.

Walking past the **prisons 45**, which you may have visited while touring the Palazzo Ducale (see p58), you arrive at the bridge that marks the boundary between the *sestieri* of San Marco and Castello. Look north at the unassuming closed passage linking the Palazzo Ducale with the prisons. Yes folks, this is it, the bridge you've all been waiting for: the **Ponte dei Sospiri 46**, which you are looking at from Ponte della Paglia. Now you can breathe a sigh of relief that you've seen it. Some people walk away inconsolably despondent that the bridge in no way corresponds to all their romantic imaginings.

The pink and white walls of the Palazzo Ducale lead you back to the Piazzetta San Marco, the gateway to Venice, where you finally complete this long and tortuous circuit of the lagoon city that for more than 1000 years was the Most Serene Republic. Perhaps now is an opportune moment to again gaze out over the Bacino di San Marco and let your well-primed imagination do a little wandering.

On the other hand, maybe it's time for a drink. Why not loosen the old purse strings and pop across to **Harry's Bar 47** (p162) for a soothing (if costly) cocktail?

Eating ▪

Eating

If you've enjoyed the cuisines of Tuscany and Emilia-Romagna, the 'down-home' style of a Roman meal or the Sicilians' gift for seasoned fantasies, you might find Venetian fare a trifle disappointing. Indeed, other Italians tend to be rather disparaging about La Serenissima's kitchen attempts, lamenting that *'si spende tanto e si mangia male'* ('you spend a lot and eat badly'), but then they are rather fastidious. For the rest of us, Venice isn't that bad. Even that august collective of self-appointed Italian foodies, Slow Food, has found about 20 places to stick into their annual *Osterie d'Italia* guide.

Search out the little eateries tucked away in the side alleys and squares, since many of the restaurants immediately around San Marco, near the train station and along main thoroughfares are tourist traps. If you don't find enough suggestions to keep you busy here, a fine local guide is Michela Scibilia's *A Guide to the Eateries of Venice*.

Opening Hours

Italians rarely eat a *colazione* (sit-down breakfast). They tend to drink a *cappuccino* and eat a *cornetto* (croissant) or other type of pastry (generically known as *pastine*) at a bar before heading off to work.

For *pranzo* (lunch), restaurants usually open from 12.30pm to 3pm. Few take orders after 2pm. Traditionally, lunch is the main meal of the day, and many shops and businesses close for two or three hours to accommodate it.

A full meal will consist of an *antipasto* (starter), which can vary from fried vegetables to a small seafood offering. Next comes the *primo piatto* (first course), generally a pasta or risotto, followed by the *secondo piatto* (second or main course) of meat or fish. This does not usually come with vegetables, and Italians will order a *contorno* (vegetable dish) to go with it. *Insalate* (salads) have a strange position in the meal. They are usually ordered as separate dishes and, in some cases, serve as a replacement for the *primo piatto* – although there is nothing to stop you ordering a salad as a side order to a *secondo*.

Opening hours for *cena* (dinner) vary, but people start sitting down around 7.30pm. You'll be hard pressed to find a place still serving after 10.30pm. The evening meal follows a similar pattern to that of lunch. It was once a simpler affair, but habits are changing because of the inconvenience of travelling home or going out for lunch every day.

Restaurants and bars are generally closed one day each week; the day varies depending on the establishment. In the reviews in this chapter, operating days are listed, but opening times are mentioned only where they vary substantially from the norm.

Cafés and bars that serve sandwiches and other snacks generally open from 7.30am to 8pm, although some stay open after 8pm and turn into pub-style drinking and meeting places.

How Much?

Venice is among the priciest of Italian cities for eating out. How much dosh you shell out for your nosh depends on what you want. Many bars serve filling snacks with lunchtime and predinner drinks. Most also have a wide range of *panini* (sandwiches or filled bread rolls) with every imaginable filling. *Tramezzini* (sandwich triangles) and huge bread rolls cost from €2 to €3.50 if you eat them standing up or take them away. You'll also find numerous outlets where you can buy pizza *a taglio* (by the slice) for not more than a couple of euros. Another option is to go to an *alimentari* and ask them to make a *panino* with the filling of your choice. This can cost €3 to €4.

For a sit-down meal there are several options. Many restaurants offer a *menú turistico* or *menú a prezzo fisso*, a set-price lunch for €12 to €18. Generally, choice is limited, and the food is breathtakingly unspectacular. Sometimes it's bloody awful. From your taste buds' point of view, you are generally better off settling for a plate of pasta, some salad and some wine at a decent restaurant. That said, a few good restaurants also offer worthy set-lunch menus.

Prices throughout this guide are given for a full meal, by which we mean a *primo*, a *secondo*, a dessert and some house wine. You could also add an *antipasto* at the front end of your meal, but these are generally expensive and will simply stunt your appetite. At modest restaurants a meal is unlikely to cost less than €30 per person. Any place where you have a good chance of paying less than €30 for a full meal, or places where you would mainly eat pizza, *cicheti* (snacks) or sandwiches, have been classified as Cheap Eats. At good midrange places expect to part with €30 to €80 per person. Much depends on your choice of dish and wine. You can easily hit €120 to €150 in top-flight joints, partly depending on your choice of wines.

Many Italians are breaking with the habit of the full meal, preferring instead, say, a *secondo* with a side dish. Clearly, your costs will decrease if you resist the pleasures of total gluttony, although the change in Italian habits is one reason, along with the effect of the introduction of the euro in 2002, cited by restaurateurs for the rise in prices over the past few years.

Read the fine print if you want seafood, as most fish is sold by weight. Note that prices are usually quoted per *etto* (100g).

In many bars and eateries a two-tier system operates – one price for locals and another for all the *foresti* (non-Venetians). This is not something you can do much about. In restaurants locals often get a small discount at least. Just asking for the bill in Venetian *('podemo ghaver el conto?')* is enough to prompt most restaurateurs to chop a few euros off the bill in an attempt to win a regular local customer. It's unlikely to work unless you can really manage to sound like a born-and-bred Castello kid!

Booking Tables

For much of the year Venice heaves with visitors, so you should consider booking a table. You can often get one when you walk in off the street, but you can by no means bank on it.

OSTERIA 'OPPING

Venice's *osterie* (aka *bacari*), long ago the preserve of men (women could wait outside to drag drunken husbands home!), are a cross between bars and trattorie (cheap restaurants). Here you can sample *cicheti* (small finger-food snacks such as stuffed olives, vegetables deep-fried in batter and an endless array of seafood items – basically the local version of Spanish tapas), washed down with an *ombra* (glass of wine). They say the name *ombra*, which means 'shade', comes from the days when people would go to stands set up in the shade of the Campanile di San Marco for an afternoon tipple.

Locals sometimes bar-hop from *osteria* to *osteria*, munching *cicheti* as they go. It's a great way to experience a more down-to-earth side of Venice. Some *osterie* serve full meals, and several are noted in the course of this chapter. The genre is experiencing a slow revival in Venice, although most locals will tell you that the real thing has all but died out. The reinventions, which often go to some lengths to serve carefully prepared meals, are sometimes wonderful, but few ooze the gritty history of Venice past. As with the many old London pubs that have been given the once-over and reconstituted as shiny chrome bars or mock throwbacks, the genuine article has often been lost.

Tipping

Most eating establishments have a cover charge ranging from €1 to €6. You also have to factor in a service charge of 10% to 15%. Since most places include this, further tipping is strictly optional. Most locals don't bother adding any more unless they have been particularly overwhelmed by service and quality. Remember this if you are presented with a credit-card receipt with space to add in the tip. In any case, it is always preferable to leave a tip in cash for the person who has waited on your table.

Self-Catering

Making your own snacks is the cheapest way to keep body and soul together. The best markets are on the San Polo side of the Ponte di Rialto (Map p296).

For salami, cheese and wine, shop in *alimentari* or *salumerie*, which are a cross between grocery stores and delicatessens. Freshly baked bread is available at a *fornaio* or *panetteria*, a bakery that sells bread, pastries and sometimes groceries. You'll find a concentration of these around Campo delle Beccarie in the Rialto, which happens to lie next to the city's main fish market, or *pescaria* (Map p300). See To Market, To Market, p186. Supermarkets are listed in the Cheap Eats sections of the following reviews.

SESTIERE DI SAN MARCO

A handful of classy restaurants and one or two more modestly priced hideaways ply their trade in the heart of Venice, surrounded by the serried ranks of mediocre tourist rip-off joints. Of the six *sestieri*, San Marco is in many respects the worst when looking for dining options.

ACQUA PAZZA Map pp294-5   Neapolitan
☎ 041 277 06 88; Campo Sant'Anzolo 3808; meals €60; ☺ Tue-Sun; ☖ Sant'Angelo
Pull up an outdoor pew for an evening of southern Italian tastes and smells. A full meal can be a pricey experience, so you may want to settle for an excellent (and still rather expensive) pizza (€14 to €16) – after all, Naples is the home of the edible flying saucer.

AI ASSASSINI Map p296   Osteria
☎ 041 528 79 86; Rio Terà dei Assassini 3695; meals €30; ☺ lunch & dinner Mon-Fri, dinner Sat; ☖ Santa Maria del Giglio
This backstreet joint offers a glimpse into a fairly typical Venetian eating scene. Head through the Gothic doorway into a lowlit, cluttered (all those pots and pans hanging from the ceiling) and bustling ambience and pull up a pew at one of the long timber tables for simple Venetian fare. The food is not spectacular but the prices are reasonably under control and, wonder of wonders, even locals eat here.

ANTICO MARTINI Map p296   Venetian
☎ 041 522 41 21; Calle della Veste 1987; meals €100-130; ☺ lunch & dinner Thu-Mon, dinner Wed; ☖ Santa Maria del Giglio
It was the favourite hang-out for artists and theatregoers at the nearby Fenice from the theatre's earliest days. After all, this place has been in business since 1720; it changed its name to Martini in 1863. Sit deep inside on cold winter nights or take up a place on Campo San Fantin in more clement weather. You will be treated to exquisitely presented local and national dishes. Igor Stravinsky, Charlie Chaplin, Harrison Ford and Nicolas Cage can't all be wrong.

GELATERIA PAOLIN
Map pp294-5   Gelateria & Café
☎ 041 522 55 76; Campo Santo Stefano 2962; breakfast dishes €10; ☺ 9am-10pm daily; ☖ Accademia
Not a bad place at all for gelato, it is even better for a relaxing breakfast in the morning sunshine. A limited range of toasted sandwiches is on offer, the orange juice is good, and instead of a straightforward coffee you could opt for the more gluttonous Venetian speciality *bicerin*, a marvellous coffee and chocolate combo topped off with thick cream.

HARRY'S BAR Map p296   Venetian
☎ 041 528 57 77; Calle Vallaresso 1323; meals €90-150; ☺ noon-11pm daily; ☖ Vallaresso/San Marco

Arrigo Cipriani's classic location is better thought of as a bar (see p162). The Cipriani family, who started the place in 1931, claims to have invented many Venetian specialities, including the Bellini cocktail. A meal here is incredibly expensive and, given the fiscal effort involved, lacklustre, but many take comfort from knowing that the likes of Toscanini, Chaplin and Hemingway have preceded them.

OSTERIA AL BACARETO
Map pp294-5   Venetian & Cicheti
☎ 041 528 93 36; Calle Crosera 3447; meals €35-50; ⊗ lunch & dinner Mon-Fri, lunch Sat; 🚊 San Samuele
The search for a good trattoria in this corner of San Marco is over when you reach Osteria al Bacareto. As the place doubles as an *osteria*, you can take the simple option and go for a plateful of *cicheti* with a glass of wine. Some people will tell you that the fried sardines are the best to be had in Venice.

RISTORANTE DA IVO
Map p296   Meat
☎ 041 528 50 04; Calle dei Fuseri 1809; meals €100-120; ⊗ Mon-Sat; 🚊 Rialto
At the quietly elegant da Ivo you can choose from an array of mouthwatering meat dishes, such as *tagliata di manzo* (a juicy beef cut), or a limited selection of seafood, all washed down with a fine range of wines. It's rock solid, if perhaps pricey for what you get.

VINI DA ARTURO Map pp294-5   Meat
☎ 041 528 69 74; Calle dei Assassini 3656; meals €80; ⊗ Mon-Sat; 🚊 Santa Maria del Giglio
There's not the slightest whiff of sole, bream or prawns in this carnivores' club buried in the backstreets of San Marco. Not only that, but the sizzling slabs of meat are accompanied by respectable vegetable garnishings. At the price they command, though, they'd want to be.

Cheap Eats
AI RUSTEGHI Map p296   Cicheti & Panini
☎ 041 523 22 05; Campiello del Tentor 5513; mini-panini from €1.20; ⊗ 8am-9.30pm Mon-Sat; 🚊 Rialto
For a great range of mini-*panini* with all sorts of fillings, pop in to this cosy bar and eatery that is something of an institution around here (although it has changed address once or twice). There's nothing better than an *ombra* or two and a couple of delicious *panini* as a quick lunchtime snack.

ENOTECA IL VOLTO Map p296   Cicheti & Wine
☎ 041 522 89 45; Calle Cavalli 4081; snacks €2-3; ⊗ Mon-Sat; 🚊 Rialto
Near Campiello San Luca, this longtime *osteria* (established 1936) has an excellent wine selection (more than 1000 labels according to one claim). Tipple in hand, proceed to choose from the tempting array of snacks, which no doubt will induce you to hang about for another glass. They will cook up a hot meal if you wish.

THAT ASHEN LOOK
There's nothing quite so irritating when you start in on your delicately flavoured risotto as sucking in a deep draft of Marlboro from the table next door. Smoking in restaurants (and everywhere else) was as deeply entrenched a social habit in Italy as anywhere in the Mediterranean, but no more.

Silvio Berlusconi's government put a sudden stop to it from 10 January 2005. From then on it became illegal to smoke in any enclosed public space, on pain of a fine ranging from €27 to €275 (double if the transgressor is caught puffing away in the presence of pregnant women or children under 12). The first of these fines was issued in a Naples bar at exactly one minute past midnight on the day the law came into force.

The owner of the establishment can be fined up to €2500 for not alerting the local police to the presence of a recalcitrant smoker on his/her premises. Theoretically, restaurants have the option of creating separate, enclosed smoking sections that must be equipped with ventilation equipment. Few have done so.

Nonsmokers, notably led by the Noi Consumatori consumer group, are enchanted by the law. Despite initial protests from unrepentant puffers, it appears the majority have quickly become used to it. And some restaurants are opting for street heating in winter to allow smokers to indulge their habit outdoors, rather than investing in equipment to create smokers' areas inside.

Eating

SESTIERE DI SAN MARCO

TOP FIVE MEAT EATS

In a city where just about everyone seems to 'special-ise' in seafood, finding a place that offers a decent choice of nonseafood dishes is quite a challenge!

- **Ai Gondolieri** (right)
- **Osteria La Pergola** (p158)
- **Ristorante La Bitta** (opposite)
- **Da Marisa** (p150)
- **Al Nuovo Profeta** (right)

OSTERIA ALLA BOTTE
Map p296   Venetian & Cicheti
☎ 041 520 97 75; Calle Bissa 5482; meal €25-30;
🕑 lunch Wed-Mon, dinner Mon-Wed; 🚊 Rialto
Wander into this backstreet *bacaro* (old-style bar) near the Ponte di Rialto for an array of *cicheti* and a glass of *prosecco* (sparkling white wine). Racy music and brisk bar staff suit the crowds of young punters. Sit out the back for no-nonsense Venetian food washed down with some decent reds, and round off your meal with a glass of sweet *fragolino* (strawberry-flavoured wine).

VINO VINO
Map p296   Wine Bar, Cicheti & Venetian
☎ 041 241 76 88; Calle della Veste 2007/a; meals €25; 🕑 Wed-Mon; 🚊 Santa Maria del Giglio
This fine old wine bar (it claims to offer 350 labels) can also be heartily recommended as an old-style cheap eatery. A limited menu might include *sarde in saor* (sardines fried in an onion marinade), but that depends on the day. Or you can accompany your tipple with some tempting bar snacks.

SESTIERE DI DORSODURO
Some excellent restaurants are scattered about Dorsoduro, many not far from the social hub of Campo Santa Margherita.

AI GONDOLIERI Map pp294-5   Meat
☎ 041 528 63 96; Fondamenta Ospedaletto 366; meals €60-70; 🕑 Wed-Mon; 🚊 Accademia
Surrounded by innumerable seafood restaurants, Ai Gondolieri is a welcome change for carnivores. All the mains are constituted from land-going critters, with such options as Angus steak, duck and liver.

AL NUOVO PROFETA
Map pp294-5   Pizza & Italian
☎ 041 523 74 66; Calle Lunga San Barnaba 2669; pizzas €6-10, meals €35; 🕑 lunch Tue-Sun, dinner Mon-Sun; 🚊 San Basilio
With its cool garden out the back, this is a boisterous spot to try a decent pizza (100 varieties, the place claims) before heading into Campo Santa Margherita for the evening's drinks. It also does a limited range of pasta and *secondi*. Most of the latter are of the meaty persuasion, and there's a decent mixed grill.

FUJIYAMA BEATRICE TEAHOUSE
Map pp294-5   Teahouse
☎ 041 724 10 42; Calle Lunga San Barnaba 2727/a; cake & coffee €4; 🕑 8.30am-7pm Thu-Tue; 🚊 Ca' Rezzonico
This vaguely eccentric new teahouse has established itself along what is becoming a busy gourmet street with more and more eateries. Here there's a courtyard out the

TOP FIVE GELATO STOPS

- **Alaska** (Da Pistacchi; Map pp290–1; ☎ 041 71 52 11; Calle Larga dei Bari, Santa Croce 1159; 🕑 8am-1pm & 3-8pm daily; 🚊 Riva de Biasio) This is a great place tucked away in a quiet residential part of Santa Croce.
- **Boutique del Gelato** (Map p296; ☎ 041 522 32 83; Salizada San Lio, Castello 5727; 🕑 10am-8.30pm Sun-Fri, 10am-9.30pm Sat; 🚊 Rialto) Rock up for some dreamy creamy ice cream at Silvio's place in Castello.
- **Gelateria Il Doge** (Map pp294–5; ☎ 041 524 40 49; Campo Santa Margherita, Dorsoduro 2604; 🕑 8am-9pm daily; 🚊 Ca' Rezzonico) In among all the cafés, bars and restaurants in this lively section of Dorsoduro is this strategically placed gelateria. The serves are decent and flavours true.
- **Gelateria Millefoglie da Tarcisio** (Map pp294–5; ☎ 041 524 46 67; Salizada San Rocco, San Polo 3033; 🕑 8am-10pm daily; 🚊 San Tomà) This gelateria, behind the Chiesa di Santa Maria Gloriosa dei Frari, is an excellent ice-cream stop where hordes queue up on hot, sunny days.
- **Gelateria Nico** (Map pp294–5; ☎ 041 522 52 93; Fondamenta Zattere, Dorsoduro 922; 🕑 6.45am-10pm Fri-Wed; 🚊 Zattere) Head here for some of the best ice cream in Venice, or just sit down for a juice or coffee. The locals take their evening stroll along the *fondamenta* while eating their heavily laden cones.

back, and the management rents out a few rooms upstairs. It's a pleasant spot to take a weight off and relax during the day's sightseeing.

OSTERIA AI QUATRO FERI

Map pp294-5   Venetian Seafood

☎ 041 520 69 78; Calle Lunga San Barnaba 2754/b; meals €35; ⏱ Mon-Sat; 🚊 Ca' Rezzonico

Seafood only is the deal here, and it's done well. Tuna is a house speciality, but you can also tuck into some swordfish at your cosy (sometimes a little too cosy) oak table. The *antipasti* are a possible option in place of pasta *primi*; there's also a good mixed grill of vegetables or seafood salad, with plenty of octopus and other tempting sea critters.

RISTORANTE LA BITTA Map pp294-5   Meat

☎ 041 523 05 31; Calle Lunga San Barnaba 2753/a; meals €35-40; ⏱ dinner Mon-Sat;
🚊 Ca' Rezzonico

The short and regularly changing menu is dominated by a few *primi* – try the *gnocchi con zucche ricotta affumicata* (gnocchi with pumpkin and smoked ricotta) – and meat dishes, and not so much as a fin of fish. The bottle-lined dining room leads out to an attractive internal courtyard. Speaking of bottle, an extensive wine list covers the whole Triveneto area (Veneto, Friuli and Trentino). Leave room for dessert! Credit cards are politely declined.

RISTORANTE RIVIERA

Map pp294-5   Italian

☎ 041 522 76 21; Fondamente Zattere 1473; meals €45-50; ⏱ Tue-Sun; 🚊 San Basilio

Balmy nights and sun-drenched lunches on the *fondamenta* are one of the key calling cards of this spot. The menu, an even balancing act between fish and meat at the main-course level, leaves the way open to most tastes, and includes a few Venetian specialities, too.

Cheap Eats

BILLA Map pp294-5   Supermarket

Fondamenta Zattere 1492; ⏱ 8.30am-8pm Mon-Sat, 9am-8pm Sun; 🚊 San Basilio

Near the Stazione Marittima, this is a big supermarket where you could stock up before hitting the high seas for Greece.

CASIN DEI NOBILI

Map pp294-5   Pizza

☎ 041 241 18 41; Calle del Lombardo 2763; pizzas €7-10; ⏱ Tue-Sun; 🚊 Ca' Rezzonico

This is a handy pizza stop (pizzas are only served in the evening from 7pm to 11pm), although you can opt for some less exciting pasta dishes and mains, too (but the quality of these is not so hot). The lighting is low and the atmosphere infectious, except for the sometimes-surly service.

OSTERIA DA TONI

Map pp294-5   Venetian

☎ 041 523 82 72; Fondamenta San Basegio 1642; meals €20-30; ⏱ Tue-Sun; 🚊 San Basilio

For simple workaday lunches, this is a fun, bustling old-style place where you'll get no-nonsense grub with at-times-trying slow service. Sit at one of the handful of tables outside when the weather permits; otherwise fight your way inside for a cramped spot around the back. It's a house wine–sloshing, bang-the-plates-down-on-the-table kind of place.

PUNTO SMA Map pp294-5   Supermarket

Rio Terà della Scoazzera 3113; ⏱ 9am-12.50pm & 4.30-8pm Mon-Sat; 🚊 Ca' Rezzonico

This well-located supermarket is just off the Campo Santa Margherita, itself a good spot to pick up fruit and veg at the market.

TRATTORIA DONA ONESTA

Map pp294-5   Italian
☎ 041 71 05 86; Calle Dona Onesta 3922; meals
€20-25; daily; San Tomà
The Honest Woman hostelry is a straightforward, no-frills eatery that you might
consider if money is tight but you wish to
avoid overt tourist traps. The food is OK but
no culinary dream – the main attraction is
the modesty in price.

ZAPATA Map pp294-5   Italian-Mexican
☎ 041 524 26 91; Fondamenta Barbarigo 2344;
meals €20; daily; San Basilio
A happy haunt for young architecture students at the nearby branches of the Istituto
Universitario di Architettura di Venezia
(IUAV), this place offers burritos, fajitas,
quesadillas and plates of penne with Latin
sauces. All good fun and occasionally accompanied by a DJ. The kitchen stays open
until midnight, and just to top it off there's
a sangria happy hour from 6pm to 8pm.

SESTIERI DI SAN POLO & SANTA CROCE (SANTA CROSE)

Tucked away in all sorts of corners of these
sestieri you'll stumble across cosy Venetian
restaurants, the city's sole Indian redoubt,
some of the oldest and most genuine of *osterie*
and the city's lone Michelin-star splurge!

AL NONO RISORTO

Map pp290-1   Pizza
☎ 041 524 11 69; Sotoportego de Siora Bettina,
Santa Croce 2338; meals €30-40; Thu-Tue;
San Stae
Stop in if only to luxuriate in the leafy,
wisteria-filled canalside garden in summertime. In the cooler months customers head
inside the lofty, timber-lined dining area.
Pizzas (€6.50 to €8.50) are the best bet,
although locals say quality has declined.
Service is friendly if scatty.

ANTICHE CARAMPANE

Map pp290-1   Venetian
☎ 041 524 01 65; Rio Terà delle Carampane, San
Polo 1911; meals €40-45; Tue-Sat; San Stae
If you manage to navigate to this place in
the heart of the one-time red-light district
(the nearest bridge is Ponte delle Tette,
or Tits Bridge), you could be forgiven for

hesitating to enter. The handwritten sign
declaims: 'No lasagne, no pizza, no tourist
menu'. A tad tetchy? Never mind – for good
home-cooked fresh fish and vegetables,
you have come to the right place.

BANCO GIRO Map p300   Italian
☎ 041 523 20 61; Campo San Giacometto, San Polo
122; meals €30-35; Tue-Sun; Rialto
A convivial place that once served simply
as a bar and snack stand for market workers, it buzzes in the evening with a young
set in for an evening of beers and light
meals. In the warmer weather take a seat
outside by the Grand Canal.

CANTINA DO MORI

Map p300   Cicheti & Other Snacks
☎ 041 522 54 01; Sotoportego dei do Mori, San
Polo 429; snacks €3-4; 8am-8.30pm Mon-Sat;
Rialto
Way back in 1462 they started selling wine in
this dark tavern near the Ponte di Rialto. They
haven't stopped since (except for a few years
in the 16th century when fire and plague
wrought havoc in the Rialto). In its present
form the place has operated as an *osteria* –
offering a nice range of snacks, though not
all the seafood items are fresh from the lagoon – since the 1940s. Prices have crept up,
but it remains an enticing place with its copper pots hanging from the ceiling. Oozing
history, it still attracts a lot of local custom.

CHAIN GANG

Those on a tight budget could keep an eye out for
chain eateries. Several Italian firms have taken the
fast-food concept and put a local spin on it. The result
is a cut way above the McDonald's of this world.

Brek (Map pp290–1; ☎ 041 244 01 58; Rio Terà
Lista di Spagna, Cannaregio 124; 1/2 courses about
€4/6; 7.30am-10.30pm daily) If you have to do
cheap fast food, you could do a lot worse than take
a break here. This is light years from hamburgers
and hot dogs! The restaurant area is open normal
hours for lunch and dinner, but you can get snacks
at the bar all day. There is another branch in Mestre
(Map p305; Via Carducci 54).

Spizzico (Map p296; Campo San Luca, San Marco
4475-6; pizza slices €3-4.50; 9am-11pm daily,
sometimes closed Sun) For quick slices of pizza, this
isn't bad – the chain is popular in northern Italy.

DA FIORE

Map pp290-1   Refined Venetian

☎ 041 72 13 08; Calle del Scaleter, San Polo 2202; meals €130-150; ☺ Tue-Sat; ⚓ San Stae

The unprepossessing shopfront appearance here belies an Art Deco interior and traditional dishes, such as *risotto di scampi* (prawn risotto) and *bigoli in salsa* (thick pasta in tomato sauce), prepared with optimum care. They need to be. Once praised by Patricia Wells as one of the finest eateries in Italy and the only one in Venice to have a Michelin star, Da Fiore has cheekily sent prices up steadily, and the view is gaining currency that the place has priced itself out of the market.

IL REFOLO Map pp290-1   Pizza

☎ 041 524 00 16; Campo San Giacomo dell'Orio, Santa Croce 1459; pizzas €7-12, meals €30-35; ☺ lunch & dinner Wed-Sun, dinner Tue; ⚓ Riva de Biasio

This place, hiding behind the mass of the Chiesa di San Giacomo dell'Orio, remains a firm favourite for quality pizza, especially in summer when you can take up a position along the peaceful canal. Run by the son of the owners of **Da Fiore** (above), the restaurant's other big plus is the divine home-made desserts. It does a limited selection of pasta, main courses and salads.

MURO VINO E CUCINA

Map p300   Italian

☎ 041 523 47 40; Campo Cesare Battisti, San Polo 222; meals €45-50; ☺ 4pm-1am Mon-Sat; ⚓ Rialto

Upstairs from the designer bar scene take a seat in a gleaming industrial-style setting. Try for a spot by the grand windows overlooking the market area. There is nothing overly Venetian about what's on offer, which can range from Angus or Florentine steaks to grilled fish of the day with potatoes and herbs.

NARANZARIA Map p300   Fusion

☎ 041 724 10 35; Campo San Giacometto, San Polo 130; meals €30-40; ☺ Tue-Sun; ⚓ Rialto

Step into this corner bistro for a Venice-meets-Tokyo encounter. Opt for a selection of Venetian-style *cicheti*, light summer dishes or sushi, prepared on the spot by a chef from **Mirai** (p151). Perhaps you could do both and compare notes. Swilled down with fine

local and Friuli wines, this microscopically sized locale with cool ambient music adds a nicely understated metro touch to the Rialto market bustle. Grab a table upstairs in winter or a canalside position in summer. (The Naranzaria was long the orange market. Oranges were prized by mariners not for making juice but as a preventive measure against scurvy while at sea.)

OSTERIA AL DIAVOLO E L'ACQUASANTA Map p296   Venetian

☎ 041 277 03 07; Calle della Madonna, San Polo 561/b; meals €30-35; ☺ lunch & dinner Wed-Sun, lunch Mon; ⚓ Rialto

This tiny spot is divided into two dining areas. Punters line up at the bar for a tipple while waiting for a cramped table in front of the bar or out the back. The sometimes gruff owner runs a tight ship but has his stalwart local customers. The place is loaded with atmosphere, the walls covered in all sorts of photos and memorabilia. Beware that the kitchen closes at 9.30pm, although you can wander in as late as midnight for a quick tipple at the bar.

OSTERIA ALLA CIURMA

Map p300   Cicheti

☎ 041 523 95 14; Calle Galeazza, San Polo 406; meals €25-30; ☺ 8am-8pm Mon-Sat; ⚓ Rialto

Locals have quickly cottoned on to this new *cicheteria* in the heart of Rialto market territory. As is typical in this kind of place, space is limited: drinkers and snackers inevitably pile out on to the street as well. Hemingway would have approved of this 'clean, well lighted place'. Aside from the *cicheti* you'll find mini-*panini* and a couple of dishes, such as the classic *sarde in saor*.

OSTERIA ALLA PATATINA

Map pp294-5   Venetian & Cicheti

☎ 041 523 72 38; Calle dei Saoneri, San Polo 2741/a; meals €30; ☺ lunch & dinner Mon-Fri, lunch Sat; ⚓ San Tomà

Pile in around the rough timber tables and benches for *cicheti* (including *sarde in saor* and other classics) or simple pasta dishes, well washed down with a couple of glasses of robust red wine. The Potato Chip Inn – as it is called, named after its scrummy fried potato slices – makes no compromise with fickle trends and retains a traditional air that keeps regulars coming.

OSTERIA LA ZUCCA

Map pp290-1   Italian

☎ 041 524 15 70; Calle del Tentor, Santa Croce 1762; meals €30-35; ⏱ Mon-Sat; 🚤 San Stae
It seems like just another Venetian trattoria, but the menu (which changes daily) is an enticing mix of Mediterranean themes. The vegetable side orders (around €4) alone are inspired, while the mains (€12 to €16) are substantial. You won't need to order pasta as well.

OSTERIA VIVALDI

Map pp294-5   Venetian

☎ 041 523 81 85; Calle della Madonnetta, San Polo 1457; meals €30-40; ⏱ Mon-Sat; 🚤 San Silvestro
You could easily rush past here in the crush of the San Polo shopping district, but if it's a food time of day, drop in to this traditional eatery, with its low timber-beam ceiling and cosy dark-wood tables. Some just like to sip on an *ombra*, but you should accompany the wine with a few *cicheti*. Alternatively, sit down to a full meal and try the *grigliata di pesce* (mixed fish grill).

PANE VINO E SAN DANIELE

Map pp294-5   Italian

☎ 041 523 74 56; Campo Anzolo Rafael 1722; meals €30-35; ⏱ Fri-Wed; 🚤 San Basilio
The owner of this place, sitting out on its own in an eerily quiet part of town, has taken a punt by reviving what was a legendary old-time trattoria, haunt of post-war artists and other bohemians. On offer is a limited range of starters and gnocchi first courses, followed by various meat-based dishes including a fine winter goulash.

RIBÒ Map pp294-5   Venetian

☎ 041 524 24 86; Fondamenta Minotto, Santa Croce 158; meals €35-40; ⏱ Thu-Tue; 🚤 Ferrovia
In a part of town where good dining options do not abound, this is one to watch for. In the extensive rear-garden dining area you will be served meticulously prepared Venetian dishes. Pasta and desserts are made on the premises.

TRATTORIA ALLA MADONNA

Map p296   Venetian

☎ 041 522 38 24; Calle della Madonna, San Polo 594; meals €30-40; ⏱ Thu-Tue; 🚤 Rialto
This is one of those time warps. A long, rowdy series of dining areas, swarms of busy waiters in white jacket and black tie, and a menu that hasn't changed in decades (the place opened as Italy struggled its way out of the post-war doldrums in 1954). Expect lashings of simple food. Try the *pasta e fagioli* (pasta and bean soup) to start and move on to fish or, say, veal done in a butter sauce. All sorts wind up in here, from local market workers on a night out to American tourists in search of an experience. All are welcomed with speedy aplomb.

TRATTORIA DA IGNAZIO

Map pp294-5   Italian

☎ 041 523 48 52; Calle dei Saoneri, San Polo 2749; meals €35; ⏱ Sun-Fri; 🚤 San Tomà
The first thing one appreciates here is the space between the tables – no forced cosiness (and in summer you can sit under the pergola in the rear courtyard). Service is the old-fashioned, white-jacket variety and meals are Veneto-Italian with a marine leaning. A classic *primo* is the *spaghetti al sugo di pesce* (spaghetti with a substantial fish sauce).

VECIO FRITOLIN

Map pp290-1   Inventive Venetian

☎ 041 522 28 81; Calle della Regina, Santa Croce 2262; meals €45-50; ⏱ Tue-Sun; 🚤 San Stae
Traditionally, a *fritolin* was an eatery where diners sat at a common table and dug into fried seafood and polenta, or wrapped it up in paper and took it away, a tradition that goes back to the early 1800s. It was basically a chippie. At lunchtime you can still pick up takeaway *pesse in scartosso* (fried fish), but things have changed. The present owners regale you with fine meals based on local and national cooking. Pasta is home-made (as are the bread and desserts), and all the ingredients are purchased daily at the nearby Rialto markets.

Cheap Eats

AE OCHE Map pp290-1   Pizza

☎ 041 524 11 61; Calle del Tentor 1552/a; pizzas €6.50-9; ⏱ daily; 🚤 San Stae
Students love this place, with its low timber ceiling and old-style travel ads from the US on the walls. Choose from around 90 types of pizza and a good range of salads in a busy, youthful atmosphere.

Rialto Produce Markets (p186), Sestiere di San Polo

AL VECIO POZZO

Map pp290-1   Pizza

☎ 041 524 27 60; Corte Canal, Santa Croce 656;
pizzas €7-10, meals €25; ⏰ noon-3pm & 6pm-2am
Tue-Sun; 🚇 Ferrovia

Better known to locals by its former name
in English (the Old Well), this spot's main
claim to fame is as one of the few places
you can normally get a bite after midnight
(you're best off with the pizza, but you can
tuck into a steak, too). Wash it down with a
beer and hang about as late as 2am (folks
have been known to be served food at this
absurd hour).

ALL'ANFORA Map pp290-1   Pizza

☎ 041 524 03 25; Lista dei Bari, Santa Croce 1223;
pizzas up to €9; ⏰ Tue-Sun; 🚇 Riva de Biasio

Head out the back into the courtyard to
indulge in an enormous choice of generous, tasty pizzas over a beer. Try the pizza
all'Anfora, loaded up with various meats,
artichokes and asparagus.

ALL'ARCO Map p300   Cicheti

☎ 041 520 56 66; Calle dell'Arco, San Polo 436;
cicheti €1.50-3; ⏰ Mon-Sat; 🚇 Rialto

For good-value *cicheti* and a glass or two
of wine, this is one of the most authentic
osterie in San Polo. People gather around
the bar or, on warmer days, cramp together
on stools by tiny tables among the hubbub
of the cramped lanes outside.

BAR AI NOMBOLI

Map pp294-5   Panini & Sandwiches

☎ 041 523 09 95; Calle dei Nomboli, San Polo
2117/c; sandwiches €3-4; ⏰ 8am-8pm Mon-Sat;
🚇 San Tomà

Francesco is the local king of the fresh
tramezzino (sandwich triangle). His corner
bar may not look like much, but all Venice
knows that he makes the best, partly because he actually makes them with freshly
cut bread, rather than having them delivered prefabricated and vacuum packed. He
also offers an enormous selection of *panini*.

GANESH JI Map pp290-1   Indian

☎ 041 71 90 84; Fondamenta Rio Marin, San Polo
2426; meals €20-25, set menus €23; ⏰ lunch &
dinner Fri-Tue, dinner Thu; 🚇 Ferrovia

Fancy a quick curry? Forget it. But a good
slow one can be had on the canalside
terrace of this place. Charmingly chaotic
staff members serve up authentic dishes
at reasonable prices – particularly pleased
guests have scribbled their appreciation on
the walls. The place also offers a vegetarian lunch menu (€12) and a nonvegetarian
lunch option (€13.50).

IN-COOP Map pp290-1   Supermarket

Campo San Giacomo dell' Orio, Santa Croce 1492;
⏰ 9am-1pm & 4-7.30pm Mon-Sat; 🚇 Riva de Biasio

This supermarket is a handy option for self-
caterers. There's another, bigger branch in
Cannaregio (p152).

TRATTORIA DA RENATO
Map pp290-1   Italian

☎ 041 524 19 22; Rio Terà Secondo, San Polo 2245/
a; meals €20-25; ⏱ Fri-Wed; 🚊 San Stae
Affectionately known to local aficion-
ados of reliable down-home cooking as
Da Vittorio (a reference to the owner),
or good-naturedly as Il Lento (the Slow
One – some say service can be tardy, but
this is largely because he prepares the
food when you order it, not the night
before!). You are unlikely to eat as well for
this price in many other Venetian eateries. There is no pretence at gastronomic
adventure, just tasty pasta dishes and
decent second courses.

SESTIERE DI CANNAREGIO
Numerous bars along the main thoroughfare between the train station and San
Marco serve sandwiches and snacks. For
restaurants, it is best to head for the side
streets to look for trattorie and pizzerie.
Fondamenta della Misericordia is something of a foodies' street where locals crowd
into several *osterie* and bars.

AL FONTEGO DEI PESCATORI
Map p300   Venetian

☎ 041 520 05 38; Sotoportego del Tagiapiera 3711;
meals €45-55; ⏱ Tue-Sun; 🚊 Ca' d'Oro
Over the bridge and at the canalside dead-
end is a fine if somewhat overpriced dining

option. The trick here is that occasional
sleight of culinary hand leading to dishes
like *maccheroni con puntarella e mazzan-
colle* (macaroni with chicory hearts and
king prawns). Service can be lethargic,
but the results are good.

ANICE STELLATO
Map pp290-1   Inventive Venetian

☎ 041 72 07 44; Fondamenta della Sensa 3272;
meals €35-40; ⏱ Wed-Sun; 🚊 Madonna dell'Orto
Awaiting you in the guise of doorman is a
huge *damigiana* (glass wine cask) by the
entrance. Inside, the heavy timber tables
and wooden chairs invite you to a chatty,
convivial meal. The pasta dishes are excellent and the mains imaginative, including
the occasional use of curry and other
spices not immediately associated with
local cuisine.

DA MARISA Map pp290-1   Meat
☎ 041 72 02 11; Fondamenta di San Giobbe 652/b;
meals €30; ⏱ lunch daily, dinner Tue & Thu-Sat;
🚊 Tre Archi
They're not especially fond of tourists
here, so you may need to work up some
Italian credentials to squeeze in (it's popular). If you do get in, expect robust, no-
nonsense meat-based cooking (Da Marisa
is near the former abattoir but seems
to have taken no notice of its demise).
Recently, fish and seafood options have
crept into the menu, too.

TOP FIVE FOR DELUXE HOTEL DINING

Often enough, dining in the hotel smacks of a lack of a sense of adventure, or even plain laziness. This is not always the
case. In some of Venice's grand hotels, masters of gastronomy are producing first-rate food for guests and outsiders
alike. Some of the smaller hotels and *pensioni* are also home to good-food havens. **Albergo agli Alboretti** (p196) is a
fine example. Here we list some high-flyers, which require a certain fiscal flexibility.

- **Ristorante de Pisis** (Bauer, Map p296; ☎ 041 520 70 22; Calle dei 13 Martiri, San Marco 1413/d) A combination
  of international cuisine and Mediterranean influences in what has become one of the top restaurants in town. The
  13 martyrs to which the street name refers were people executed here by the Fascists in July 1944.
- **Cipriani & Cip's Club** (Hotel Cipriani, Map pp302–3; ☎ 041 520 77 44; Giudecca 10) Both these restaurants
  offer fine views across the Venetian lagoon, already a highlight. In Cipriani you will be regaled with *haute cuisine*,
  especially seafood, while Cip's Club is more relaxed, offering anything from pizza to bruschetta on the terrace.
- **Terrace** (Hotel Monaco & Grand Canal, Map p296; ☎ 041 520 02 11; Calle Vallaresso, San Marco 1325) Looking
  out over the Grand Canal and recently restored, this is one of the most stunning eating locations in town.
- **Ristorante Met** (Map p298; ☎ 041 520 50 44; Riva degli Schiavoni, Castello 4149) The arrival of a young new
  chef, Corrado Fasolato, has turned the kitchen at the Hotel Metropole into a mine of good food, including the ever-
  present fish and game.
- **Terrazza** (Hotel Danieli, Map p296; ☎ 041 522 64 80; Riva degli Schiavoni, Castello 4196) A meal on the hotel's
  rooftop terrace is a delight for the palate and for the eyes.

FIASCHETTERIA TOSCANA

Map p300   Venetian

☎ 041 528 52 81; Salizada San Giovanni Grisostomo 5719; meals €60-70; ☽ lunch Thu-Mon, dinner Wed-Mon; ⚓ Ca' d'Oro

A classic that has long maintained quality, the Fiaschetteria Toscana is about as Tuscan as a gondola. Here they serve up solid Venetian food, washed down with a choice of wines from an impressive list that includes tipples from around the country. The *frittura della Serenissima*, a mixed fried-seafood platter, is memorable. Almost better still are Mariuccia's home-made desserts, especially the house speciality, the *rovesciata*, a rich upside-down apple-and-caramel concoction. If money is a consideration, drop by for the lunchtime specials.

GAM GAM

Map pp290-1   Mixed Med Kosher

☎ 041 71 52 84; Calle del Ghetto Vecchio 1123; meals €30; ☽ noon-10pm Sun-Thu, lunch Fri; ⚓ Guglie

Gam Gam is great for your taste buds if you like Israeli-style falafels and other Middle Eastern delicacies. This place is fully kosher and presents a diverse menu, from Red Sea spaghetti to couscous (with choice of meat, fish or vegetable sauce) and from hummus to that arch-Venetian side order of *fondi di articiochi* (artichoke hearts).

L'ANGOLO DI TANIT

Map pp290-1   Sicilian

☎ 041 72 05 04; Calle dell'Aseo 1885; meals €35; ☽ Wed-Mon; ⚓ San Marcuola

Locals in search of a little regional spice rave about this modest Sicilian restaurant, lurking unsuspectedly close to the main stream of foot traffic between San Marco and the train station. As the place is run by Sicilians, expect rich sauces (capers, almonds and spices feature high in Sicilian dishes) and generous helpings.

MIRAI Map pp290-1   Japanese

☎ 041 220 65 17; Rio Terà Lista di Spagna 227; meals €40-50; ☽ dinner Tue-Sun; ⚓ Ferrovia

What a surprise – halfway decent Japanese food in Venice. Sure, the Venetians have their own way with fish, but sometimes sushi and sashimi is the way to go. Strange that it should be alone in a city renowned for its Eastern-languages faculty! The ambience is a chilled modern-design affair, itself the exception rather than the rule in this tradition-tied town.

OSTARIA DA RIOBA

Map pp290-1   Venetian

☎ 041 524 43 79; Fondamenta della Misericordia 2553; meals €40; ☽ Tue-Sun; ⚓ Madonna dell'Orto

Named after the Moorish-looking figure that presides over the corner of the Palazzo Mastelli (see p133), Da Rioba offers a crisp, almost Spartan, interior and a carefully prepared if limited menu. Unlike some of the immediately surrounding places, it concentrates largely on typical Venetian cuisine with a briny bent.

OSTERIA ALLA FRASCA

Map p300   Venetian

☎ 041 528 54 33; Corte della Carità 5176; meals €40; ☽ Wed-Mon; ⚓ Fondamente Nuove

The dishes on offer are standard, favouring seafood, and pricey for what you get (locals get especially favoured treatment). However, the setting, with tables spilling out into the charming *campiello* rarely touched by tourist caravans, is a winner. It's best for a quick snack and tipple or two.

OSTERIA DA ALBERTO

Map p300   Seafood

☎ 041 523 81 53; Calle Larga G Gallina 5401; meals €30; ☽ Mon-Sat, kitchen closes 9pm; ⚓ Fondamente Nuove

Another hidden Venetian jewel, this *osteria* is run by Alberto, a well-known figure in the business of serving up traditional food in Venice. The dried cod, a house speciality prepared in various ways, is good. Dark-wood tables are spaced out nicely and surrounded by huge *damigiane* (glass wine casks) and other odds and ends on the walls.

OSTERIA DALLA VEDOVA

Map p300   Venetian & Cicheti

☎ 041 528 53 24; Calle del Pistor 3912; meals €30-35; ☽ lunch & dinner Mon-Wed, dinner Fri, Sat & Sun; ⚓ Ca' d'Oro

The 'Widow's Inn', off Strada Nova, is also called Trattoria Ca' d'Oro and is one of the oldest *osterie* in Venice. It was once a cheese store and was taken over by a

Eating

SESTIERE DI CANNAREGIO

family from Puglia in the 19th century. The food is reasonable, whether you nibble on the *cicheti* or settle in for a full (mostly seafood) meal. The snacks are copious, including battered vegetables and all sorts of weird and wonderful sea creatures.

TRE SPIEDINI DA BES

Map p300   Venetian

☎ 041 520 80 35; Salizada San Canciano 5906/d; meals €25-30; ☽ lunch & dinner Tue-Sat, lunch Sun; ⚓ Rialto

A classic *osteria* where you can crowd in for no-nonsense food. Choose from several broths and pasta for the first course and then dig in to, say, a slab of sole for the main. It's a typically cramped Venetian locale, with ponderous timber ceiling beams and all sorts of paraphernalia hanging on the walls.

UN MONDO DI VINO

Map p300   Cicheti & Wine

☎ 041 521 10 93; Salizada San Canciano 5984/a; meal €25-30; ☽ Tue-Sun; ⚓ Rialto

It's virtually standing room only in this postage stamp–sized place where you can sample from a long list of wines and a barload of snacks. It gets nice and lively

---

WHERE NOT TO EAT

Feeding tourists second-rate meals is a Venetian sport. Places offering a set-price *menú turistico* (tourist menu) are frequently a trap, as are those displaying a menu in multiple languages (although this is not always the case). One fairly clear warning sign is tour groups chomping together on identical meals – usually a sorry-looking plate of pasta with a tomato sauce, a side order of wilting salad and maybe even chips! Anyone who takes up a waiter/tout's invitation to step inside and enjoy their food deserves everything they get.

The worst spots are in Cannaregio – along the route from the train station towards San Marco – and San Marco. This is not to say you can't find good places in either area; it's just that they have more than their fair share of bad 'uns.

There's something else to watch for. A new law allows most bars to serve food, but bear in mind that most bars do not have proper kitchens, so many dishes are pre-prepared and probably microwaved.

---

with the chatter of locals and the clinking of glasses. Try a cheese platter (€8). Wine by the glass goes for €2 to €3 depending on your tipple.

VINI DA GIGIO Map p300   Venetian

☎ 041 528 51 40; Fondamenta della Chiesa 3628/a; meals €50-60; ☽ Wed-Sun; ⚓ Ca' d'Oro

Gigio stocks a fine selection of reds and whites from the Veneto and beyond – come here to taste good wines in the company of excellent cooking. How about the *gnocchetti con scampi e pesto* (little dumplings with prawns and pesto)? Prices have edged up over the years, but there's no denying the quality.

Cheap Eats

BILLA Map pp290-1   Supermarket

Strada Nova 3660; ☽ 8.30am-8pm Mon-Sat, 9am-8pm Sun; ⚓ Ca' d'Oro

You can stock up at this big supermarket to make your own meals if eating out doesn't attract you.

IGUANA Map pp290-1   Latin American

☎ 041 71 35 61; Fondamenta della Misericordia 2515; burritos, tacos & fajitas €6.50-10.50; ☽ 6pm-1am Tue-Sat; ⚓ Madonna dell'Orto

The low, wooden-beamed ceiling makes for a warm atmosphere at this Venetian excursion into South American food. The burritos, tacos, *quesadillas* and other Latin American specialities are OK and moderately priced. Some people just show up for tequila at the bar, especially at happy hour (6.30pm to 8pm), when you get three tipples for the price of two.

IN-COOP Map p300   Supermarket

Rio Terà dei SS Apostoli 4662; ☽ 9am-1pm & 4-7.30pm Mon-Sat; ⚓ Fondamente Nuove

This is a bigger branch of the store in Santa Croce (p149).

OSTARIA AL PONTE Map p300   Cicheti

☎ 041 528 61 57; Calle Larga G Gallina 6378; cicheti €1.50-3 ☽ Mon-Sat; ⚓ Ospedale

On the 'frontier' with Sestiere di Castello is this aptly named and highly recommended snack joint. Enter the bright red doors and sidle up to the bar to nibble on *cicheti* and indulge in good wines. Or you could pull up a pew at one of the couple of tables. Locals hang about in here, chatting vociferously and sipping their *ombre*.

SAHARA Map pp290-1 — Middle Eastern

☎ 041 72 10 77; Fondamenta della Misericordia 2520; meals €20-25; ⏰ 7pm-2am Mon-Fri, 11am-3pm & 7pm-2am Sat & Sun; 🚤 Madonna dell'Orto

At Sahara you can get a reasonable version of Syrian food, with old favourites such as falafel, hummus, kebab meat and other Eastern delights. The food is not bad and certainly makes a change. You may even get a display of belly-dancing thrown in on Saturday night. The place doubles as drinkery, where the beer is cheap at €1.20 a can.

SESTIERE DI CASTELLO

If you've wandered around the Castello area you'll have already realised that this part of the town, the tail of the fish that Venice resembles and the largest of the *sestieri*, is perhaps the most real.

ACIUGHETA ENOTECA

Map p296 — Cicheti & Wine

☎ 041 522 42 92; Campo SS Filippo e Giacomo 4351; meals €30-35; ⏰ daily; 🚤 San Zaccaria

Born as a strange design outgrowth of the classic trattoria Aciugheta next door, this is its antithesis. A spacious bar with sheet-glass frontage, low tables, angular furniture and a chilled feel, it's a great place from which to observe the zoo outside. The servings are fine wine and *cicheti*, notably the anchovy pizzas from which the place takes its name. Or you can opt for a full meal.

AL GIARDINETTO DA SEVERINO

Map p298 — Venetian

☎ 041 528 53 32; Salizada Zorzi 4928; meals €60; ⏰ Fri-Wed; 🚤 San Zaccaria

You will be inspired by the magnificent dining room (or, in summer, the pleasant garden) to tuck into well-prepared Venetian classics (*sarde in saor, bigoli* and so on). The restaurant is housed in a 14th-century building and has been treating guests to good food since the early 1900s.

ALLE TESTIERE Map p296 — Seafood

☎ 041 522 72 20; Calle Mondo Novo 5801; meals €60; ⏰ Tue-Sat; 🚤 Rialto

In a cosy, nay, tiny dining area with B&W photos on the walls the chef may well come up for a chat as you sample the tasty offerings. Fish is the leitmotif. A handful of starters and pasta courses (around €15) are followed by a couple of set main courses or fresh fish (whatever happens to have been caught that day).

Eating

SESTIERE DI CASTELLO

WINE FOR DINING

Vino (wine) is an essential accompaniment to any Italian meal. Italians are justifiably proud of their wines and it would be surprising for dinnertime conversation not to touch on the subject, at least for a moment.

Wine is graded according to three main classifications – *denominazione d'origine controllata e garantita* (DOCG), *denominazione d'origine controllata* (DOC) and *vino da tavola* (table wine) – which are marked on the label. A DOC wine is produced subject to certain specifications, although the label does not certify quality. DOCG is tested by government inspectors for quality.

Your average trattoria will generally stock only a limited range of bottled wines, but quite a few of the better restaurants offer a carefully chosen selection of wines from around the country. Indeed, some places are better known for their wine lists than their grub. Ordering the house wine is generally safe if unexciting.

Although the Veneto is not one of Italy's prime winemaking regions, some good drops are produced around Verona, including Soave whites, Valpolicella reds and Bardolino reds and rosés. Nosiola, another white, is not bad. The Vicenza area is also dotted with wineries. Wines from the Friuli-Venezia Giulia area, Italy's easternmost region and for centuries part of Venice's mainland empire, are often good and readily available. Look out for Pinot Grigio whites and Pinot Nero reds.

A regional curiosity is the sweet *fragolino*. This strawberry-flavoured red isn't strictly wine and cannot be sold as such commercially, although you'll occasionally find it in bars in Venice and elsewhere in the Veneto. You sometimes come across a white version, too. You can be fairly sure you are drinking the real thing if it is served in unlabelled bottles. Many stores have taken to selling a fizzy 'wine' they call *fragolino*. This is a travesty – it is little more than poor wine with strawberry flavouring added.

ENOITECA LA CANEVA & CANTINA CANALETTO

Map p296   Venetian & Wine bar

☎ 041 521 26 61; www.cantinacanaletto.it; Calle de la Malvasia 5490; meals €60; 🕐 restaurant daily, enoiteca 7pm-2am daily; 🚇 Rialto

This place is a combination of restaurant and copiously equipped wine bar. At the former rich *primi* of pasta (most around €16) are followed by such offerings as the mixed fish grill or the *involtino di lattuga con orata al timo e patate rosse* (bream done with thyme rolled up in lettuce and accompanied by little red potatoes). Afterwards (or beforehand), you can lounge around for a little oenological exercise in the wine bar. The Cantina's name is no coincidence. The great painter of Venetian scenes (see p30) lived a few houses away, at No 5485.

ENOITECA MASCARETA

Map p296   Cicheti & Wine

☎ 041 523 07 44; Calle Lunga Santa Maria Formosa 5138; meals of snacks and wine €35; 🕐 7pm-2am Fri-Tue; 🚇 Rialto

A brief stroll off Campo Santa Maria Formosa is the Little Mask, a genial tavern for the sipping of wine accompanied by a limited menu. Mauro Lorenzon, something of a local character, has taken over here and offers a rich *taier misto* (a fat platter of cold meats and cheese chunks), but you can also opt for various first and main courses. The emphasis is the excellent choice of wines.

OSTERIA DI SANTA MARINA

Map p296   Inventive Venetian

☎ 041 528 52 39; Campo Santa Marina 5911; meals €45; 🕐 lunch & dinner Tue-Sat, dinner Mon; 🚇 Rialto

This *osteria* offers a pleasant dining area and tables on the square. The cuisine is largely a refined take on Venetian seafood dishes. The highlights are without doubt the exquisite desserts, such as the artfully presented chocolate mousse.

TRATTORIA CORTE SCONTA

Map p298   Seafood

☎ 041 522 70 24; Calle del Pestrin 3886; meals €50; 🕐 Tue-Sat; 🚇 Arsenale

A cosy eatery with a vine-shaded rear courtyard, the Corte Sconta is hidden well off even the unbeaten tourist track, although good publicity has locals and *foresti* wearing a track to its door. The chefs prepare almost exclusively seafood classics, such as their delicious *risotto ai scampi*. The owners claim to use only the catch of the day. Who can carp at such a policy?

TRATTORIA DA REMIGIO

Map p298   Venetian

☎ 041 523 00 89; Salizada dei Greci 3416; meals €30-35; 🕐 lunch & dinner Wed-Sun, lunch Mon; 🚇 San Zaccaria

It is not often you find a restaurant that in the early evening can post a sign in the window saying *completo* (full), as though it were a hotel, but this place can. It has a mixed menu, featuring Venetian fish dishes and a handful of meat options. Service is fast and the results are reliable. It's clearly busy, and you'll need to book to be sure of a spot.

Cheap Eats
AL PORTEGO

Map p296   Venetian & Cicheti

☎ 041 522 90 38; Calle de la Malvasia 6015; cicheti €1.50-3; 🕐 10.30am-10pm Mon-Sat; 🚇 Rialto

Situated beneath the portico that gives this *osteria* its name, Al Portego is an inviting stop for *cicheti* and wine, along with some more robust meals. It's all timber in here and very cosy. Try the thick spaghetti-like pasta, *bigoli*, whatever sauce it comes with, or perhaps a risotto.

AL VECIO PENASA Map p296 Sandwiches

☎ 041 523 72 02; Calle delle Rasse 4587; panini
& other snacks €3-5; ☺ 6.30am-11.30pm daily;
🕮 San Zaccaria

Between Riva degli Schiavoni and Campo
SS Filippo e Giacomo, this remains a good
spot for its excellent selection of sandwiches and snacks at reasonable prices.

ALLA RIVETTA Map p296 Venetian

☎ 041 528 73 02; Ponte San Provolo 4625;
meals €20-25; ☺ Tue-Sun; 🕮 San Zaccaria

This is one of the few restaurants near
Piazza San Marco that can be recommended. Surrounded by tourist traps, it
has resisted the temptation to abandon
all quality, and even gets a few locals
(including famished gondoliers) in for its
no-nonsense dishes (especially the fried-
seafood options).

OSTERIA ALE DO MARIE

Map p298 Italian

☎ 041 296 04 24; Calle dell'Olio 3129; meals €40;
☺ Tue-Sun; 🕮 Celestia

Hidden deep in the back alleys of Castello
is this simple, welcoming eatery. You can
grab a reasonable set lunch (€20); otherwise, order from the menu – a range of
pastas, and fish and meat mains.

SUVE Map p296 Supermarket

Salizada San Lio 5817; ☺ 8.30am-7.45pm Mon,
Tue & Thu-Sat, 8.30am-1pm Wed; 🕮 Rialto

This handy supermarket is situated between Rialto and San Marco.

TRATTORIA DA PAMPO

Map p299 Venetian & Cicheti

☎ 041 520 84 19; Calle Gen Chinotto 3, Sant'Elena;
meals €25; ☺ Wed-Mon; 🕮 Giardini

They say *'dal pampo non c'é scampo'* (there's
no getting away from Pampo) and why
would you want to? This is a real locals'
place for *ombre* and *cicheti*, but you can sit
down (inside or out) for a full, simple meal.
The place is set opposite a shady park in
the quietest end of the city.

AROUND THE LAGOON

Across the islands you'll find various enticing spots to sit down to eat – you need
not go hungry anywhere in the lagoon!

AL GATTO NERO Map p304 Buranese

☎ 041 73 01 20; Fondamenta della Giudecca 88,
Burano; meals €40; ☺ Tue-Sun; 🕮 Burano

Noisy Venetian families pile into this off-
the-beaten-*calle* trattoria in Burano. Sure,
you could join the crowds in the cheaper
places along the island's main drag, but the
food is generally not the greatest. Here you
pay a premium, but the quality is better.

ALLA MADDALENA

Map p304 Seafood & Game

☎ 041 73 01 51; Mazzorbo 7/c; meals €30;
☺ Fri-Wed; 🕮 Mazzorbo

On this peaceful, leafy island adjacent to
Burano is a lively seafood oasis. Walk over
the bridge from Burano to reach this soothing spot near the vaporetto stop. Relax by

---

DECIDING ON DESSERT

For some, the question of what to have for *dolci* (dessert) poses a primordial prandial dilemma. What about a Venetian
classic: tiramisu, a rich dessert with mascarpone? All sorts of light biscuits have also been dreamed up over the centuries
in Venice – start looking in cake-shop windows. They come with such names as *baicoli*, *ossi da morto* (literally 'dead
man's bones') and *bigarani* and are supposed to be taken with dessert wine.

You may well be offered *sorbetto* (lemon sorbet) at the end of the main course. It is designed to clean your palate
before dessert, but for many it makes a good dessert on its own account. An alcoholic version with vodka and a dash
of milk, called a *sgroppino*, will be more to the liking of some.

Speaking of alcohol, another classic way to round off a meal is with a *digestivo*, some strong liquor to aid digestion.
You could try a shot of grappa, a strong, clear brew made from grapes whose name comes from a Veneto region (see
Bassano del Grappa, p238). Or you could go for an *amaro*, a dark liqueur prepared from herbs. If you prefer a sweeter
liqueur, try an almond-flavoured amaretto or the sweet aniseed *sambuca*.

A death-by-chocolate option you are unlikely to find in restaurants but is a speciality in some gelaterie and cafés is
the *gianduiotto*, a little slab of *gianduia* chocolate ice cream surmounted by a cup of whipped cream.

the canal or in the garden out the back. In the hunting season (autumn) you may encounter various birds on the menu – enough to make you feel a little like Hemingway!

BUSA ALLA TORRE Map p301   Seafood

☎ 041 73 96 62; Campo Santo Stefano 3, Murano; meals €40; ☺ lunch daily; 🚢 Faro

Come here for lunch on your day out in Murano and try the seafood pasta, such as sea-bass ravioli in a *granseola* (crab meat) sauce. On the subject of crabs, the place is also known for its fried *moeche* (little shore crabs).

HARRY'S DOLCI

Map pp302-3   Inventive Venetian

☎ 041 522 48 44; Fondamenta San Biagio 773, Giudecca; meals €80-120; ☺ Wed-Mon Apr-Oct; 🚢 Palanca

This place is run by the Cipriani clan of Harry's Bar fame and has tables by the Canale della Giudecca looking across to Venice. The fantastic desserts and pastries are the main reason for stopping by. Should you want a full meal, they can also accommodate you, at a price.

LA FAVORITA

Map pp302-3   Seafood

☎ 041 526 16 26; Via Francesco Duodo 33, Lido; meals €35-40; ☺ lunch Wed-Sun, dinner Tue-Sun; 🚢 Lido

For lashings of excellent seafood in a pleasing, relaxed setting, this is one of the best spots on this long and gastronomically meagre island. In the warmer months you can sit outside.

LOCANDA CIPRIANI

Map p304   Inventive Venetian

☎ 041 73 01 50; Piazza Santa Fosca 29, Torcello; meals €50-80; ☺ lunch Wed-Mon & dinner Sat, closed Jan; 🚢 Torcello

Giuseppe Cipriani established this exclusive hideaway – also a **boutique hotel** (p214) – in 1946. Ernest Hemingway set down his bags here in 1948 and wrote part of *Across the River and into the Trees*. The food is prepared with care, and the leafy setting is magical. The internal dining areas, with low timber ceilings and exposed brick, are as enticing in cooler weather as the chirrupy garden is in summer.

MISTRÀ

Map pp302-3   Venetian & Ligurian

☎ 041 522 07 43; Giudecca 212/a, Giudecca; meals €40-45; ☺ lunch Wed-Mon, dinner Wed-Sun; 🚢 Redentore

Grab a table at the back for views south over the lagoon. Located among the workshops of a major boatyard, this is a suitably maritime setting for great seafood, with a combination of local dishes and a few Ligurian imports (such as pesto). At lunchtime you can join the shipwrights for a cheaper midday meal. To get here,

---

TOP FIVE FOREIGN EATS

- **Mirai** (p151) Japanese
- **Ganesh Ji** (p149) Indian
- **Gam Gam** (p151) Mixed Med kosher
- **Iguana** (p152) Latin American
- **Sahara** (p153) Middle Eastern

look for No 211 on Fondamenta di San Giacomo and pass down the narrow passage beside it. It opens out as you saunter through the shipyards to the rear end of the island.

RISTORANTE AL TRONO DI ATTILA
Map p304 Venetian
☎ 041 73 00 94; Fondamenta Borgognoni 7/a, Torcello; meals €30-35; ⊙ daily; ⚓ Torcello
Unless you plan to blow your budget at the Locanda Cipriani, try this place, between the vaporetto stop and the cathedral. The atmosphere is suitably bucolic, and you will want to dine in the charming garden with pergola. Try the *gnocchetti con rucola e scampi* (little dumplings with rocket and shrimps). The restaurant generally opens for lunch only, unless you book ahead for dinner.

TRATTORIA DA SCARSO
off Map pp302-3 Venetian
☎ 041 77 08 34; Piazzale Malamocco 4, Lido; meals €25-30; ⊙ lunch Wed-Mon, dinner Wed- Sun; ⚓ Lido, then bus 11
This is a simple trattoria with a pleasant pergola. Set in the tiny old Venetian settlement of Malamocco (which was moved here when the original settlement further south was flooded out centuries ago), it isn't too heavily frequented by *foresti*. Local colour alone makes it an attractive stop.

Cheap Eats
AI TRE SCAINI Map pp302-3 Venetian
☎ 041 522 47 90; Calle Michelangelo 53/c, Giudecca; meals €25; ⊙ lunch Fri-Wed, dinner Tue, Wed & Fri-Sun; ⚓ Zitelle
In this rambunctious and chaotic trattoria you can settle down with ebullient local families for copious pasta and seafood dishes (there are one or two meat options, too). Throaty wine comes from a couple of small barrels set up inside. You can eat in the garden as well.

THE MAINLAND
The mainland half of Venice, Mestre is by far the bigger and uglier brother. It's unlikely to attract your attention for long, but if you happen to be here there are some good eating options to consider. Chioggia, on the south shore of the lagoon, is a bustling fishing port and well worth a visit.

AL CALICE Map p305 Cicheti & wine
☎ 041 98 61 00; Piazza Ferretto 70/b, Mestre; meals €25; ⊙ Tue-Sun; train
Set just off the square at the heart of historic Mestre is this good-natured wine bar cum eatery. You can snack, have a light meal or just tipple away at the long list of wines.

TOP FIVE PASTRY SHOPS
- **Antica Pasticceria Tonolo** (Map pp294–5; ☎ 041 523 72 09; Calle dei Preti, Dorsoduro 3764; ⊙ 7.45am-1pm & 3-8.30pm Tue-Sat, 7.45am-1pm Sun; ⚓ San Tomà) This place has been turning out delicious pastries since 1886. Stop by for a coffee or perhaps a midday *prosecco* and bar snacks.
- **Bucintoro** (Map pp290–1; ☎ 041 72 15 03; Calle del Scaleter, San Polo 2229; ⊙ 7.15am-8pm Tue-Sun; ⚓ San Stae) The Venetian word for pastry maker is *scaleter*, which comes from the step-shaped sign (the Italian word for stairs is *scale*) they once etched onto their sweets, which were known as *scalete*. Gino Zanin carries on antique Venetian traditions with his sweets and pastries, which come with such wonderful names as *bacingondola* (kiss in the gondola), a little meringue-and-chocolate number.
- **Gobbetti** (Map pp294–5; ☎ 041 528 90 14; Rio Terà Canal, Dorsoduro 3108/b; ⊙ 8am-1pm & 3.30-8pm Wed-Mon; ⚓ Ca' Rezzonico) This is another good place for sweet things, just off Campo Santa Margherita.
- **Pasticceria da Bonifacio** (Map p296; ☎ 041 522 75 07; Calle degli Albanesi, Castello 4237; ⊙ 7.30am-8.30pm daily; ⚓ San Zaccaria) This classic Venetian pastry shop has remained unspoiled by its proximity to Piazza San Marco. Alongside traditional local sweets and pastries you will occasionally encounter others sneaked in from surrounding provinces.
- **Pasticceria Puppa** (Map p300; ☎ 041 523 79 47; Calle Spezier, Cannaregio 4800; ⊙ 7am-1.30pm & 3-7.30pm Tue-Sun; ⚓ Fondamente Nuove) Sweeties for the kids, traditional pastries and cakes, and a range of good national items like Christmas panettone are on offer at this pastry shop that doubles as a café-bar along an otherwise quiet street in the north of town.

FROM BELLINIS TO MANHATTAN

Giuseppe Cipriani was a young survivor of WWI when in 1918 he applied for a chef's job in a fancy hotel in the town of Madonna di Campiglio. He had no idea about cooking or waiting tables but in the following years he learned everything there was to learn. He wound up in Venice and in 1931, in partnership with a moneyed American, Harry Pickering, launched what became one of the world's most celebrated bars (and restaurants), Harry's.

Three years later he bought a small wine and oil store on Torcello and in the 1940s converted it into a simple, rustic hostelry, the Locanda Cipriani (now in the hands of Bonifacio Brass, son of Giuseppe's daughter Carla). Giuseppe's next big thing was a hotel. He put together partners and in the 1950s set up the Hotel Cipriani in a former noble family's mansion on Giudecca. It went on to become one of the world's greatest (and still is, although it left Cipriani family control in the 1970s). Another Cipriani stroke of genius was the Villa Cipriani hotel in Asolo (see p239), in a splendid 16th-century villa. In the meantime, the Cipriani opened a gourmet dessert locale on Giudecca, Harry's Dolci.

Everyone who was anyone, from the Aga Khan to the Queen of England, sooner or later wound up in Venice and one or more of the Cipriani joints. Giuseppe had an especially soft spot for Ernest Hemingway, with whom he (perhaps inevitably) had some memorable drinking bouts. Giuseppe not only invented the Bellini (see The Cocktail Circuit, p160) but also came up with *carpaccio* (see p16).

When Giuseppe died in 1980 the business passed on to his son, Arrigo. The Cipriani name had been attracting a celebrity who's who to Venice for decades, but now Arrigo decided to take Cipriani to the celebrities. He opened the first of their international eateries in New York in 1985 and he and his son, Giuseppe, have since gone from strength to strength in the Big Apple. They own several top-flight restaurants and banqueting places, including Cipriani 42nd Street, in the landmark 1921 Bowery Savings Bank building. With a presence now stretching to London, Hong Kong and Sardinia's Costa Smeralda, and activities ranging from catering to the production of brand-name food items, the immortality of the Cipriani clan seems assured.

OSTERIA LA PERGOLA

Map p305   Meat

☎ 041 97 49 32; Via Fiume 42, Mestre; meals €25-30; ☽ lunch & dinner Mon-Fri, dinner Sat; train
As the name suggests, here you can sit under a pergola (or inside beneath a fine timber ceiling) and enjoy some of the best-value food in Mestre. For a first course consider the chunky, homemade *spaghetti alla chitarra* (thick spaghetti made with a tool known as the *chitarra*, or guitar). Venetians swear by this place, which, by the way, serves no seafood.

OSTERIA PENZO

     Seafood

☎ 041 40 09 92; Calle Larga Bersaglio 526, Chioggia; meals €35-40; ☽ lunch Wed-Mon, dinner Wed-Sun; ⛴ Lido, then bus 11

Once, all you would get here was wine and basic snacks, but nowadays staff prepare good local dishes based entirely on the fleet's catch. The setting remains homy and simple, a little *osteria* with photos of Chioggia as it once was on the walls. The cooking is equally down-home, featuring local dishes.

RISTORANTE EL FONTEGO

     Pizza

☎ 041 550 09 53; Piazzetta XX Settembre 497, Chioggia; meals €25; ☽ Tue-Sun; ⛴ Lido, then bus 11
The setting here is a little brassy, but it's a popular place. The restaurant offers a broad range of vegetarian dishes and 'cream pizzas' with a Brie base – they're not bad. Vegetarian pizzas cost around €7.

Entertainment

Entertainment

When you consider that there are fewer than 65,000 permanent residents in Venice, the offerings for nocturnal diversion are quite broad. You can take in some theatre or an opera, go to the movies, prop up a bar or even lose a few euros at the roulette wheel. But this is not the big city, and Venice is a rather staid sort of place – not at all the licentious, hedonistic whirl it was in its twilight years before Napoleon and then the Austrians arrived to stamp out all the decadence.

A number of musical ensembles perform the music of Vivaldi and other baroque composers for visitors, often in period costume and in some of the otherwise largely disused monuments of the city. Although these performances can be a little cheesy, the musical quality is often not bad and it can make for a pleasant night out.

Venice is by no means a teetotal town. People like a drink and plenty of bars will oblige you on this front. Just don't expect long, crazy nights out.

Of course, Venice puts on various one-off parties. Carnevale in February is perhaps the best known, with masked balls in Piazza San Marco, parades, street theatre and all manner of diversions. Other big festivals (see City Calendar, p10) also serve as an excuse for locals to let their hair down.

Information

For general listings on upcoming events and shows, see *Leo* and *Un Ospite di Venezia*. They are available from tourist offices, which also have brochures listing events for the entire year. Keep your eyes on the monthly *VeNews*, available at newsstands, as well as the freebie distributed in many bars and restaurants, *VDV (Venezia da Vivere)*.

DRINKING

Venetians have something of a reputation in Italy for being inveterate tipplers. Locals can often be seen propping up bars in the morning for a heart starter, and the ever-popular *prosecco*, the Veneto's lightly bubbly white wine, pours freely throughout the day. Just as Brits might pop down to the local for a pint, Venetians will nip down to the nearest bar or *osteria* for a quick *ombra* (small glass of wine) or *prosecco* and maybe a snack.

The colour of one's drink changes as the day progresses, and the early-evening *aperitivo* (apéritif) favourite is the *spritz*. This is one part sparkling white wine, one part soda

---

THE COCKTAIL CIRCUIT

Back in the 1950s, behind the bar at Harry's, a new sensation was born. It was deceptively simple: mix *prosecco* with peach nectar, and you have a Bellini. Of course, they will tell you there is more to it than that – the quality of the ingredients and, more importantly, the proportions. Whatever – it is good.

You don't have to shell out the €12 for one at Harry's Bar, as Bellinis and other cocktails are popular at *aperitivo* time (that loose early-evening, predinner period) all over town. Still, if you can afford a drink or two at Harry's, it's worth it. Apart from the Bellini they do some other mean mixes. These guys have been practising the art of the martini for as long as the place has been open.

Truman Capote called a good martini a Silver Bullet. What's in it? Good gin and a drop of Martini Dry. But of course the amount of the latter varies according to taste. For a strong, dry martini, 'rinse' the glass with Martini and then pour in freezing-cold gin. Hemingway, who set part of his book *Across the River and into the Trees* at Harry's, had his own recipe – pour freezing-cold gin into a glass dipped in ice and sit it next to a bottle of Martini for a moment before drinking!

water and one part bitter (Campari Bitter, Amaro, Aperol or Select), topped with a slice of lemon and, if you wish, an olive. It's said this drink dates from the days of the Austrian occupation in the 19th century. In warm weather the bright red and orange versions of this tipple decorate the tables of outdoor terraces.

While it may be true that Venetians like a drink, it can't be said that Venice rocks. There are two poles of interest. Campo Santa Margherita in Dorsoduro is a lively and bar-fronted square that attracts a mix of the young, the hip and the wannabes of town. Further away from the centre of things is the area around Fondamenta della Misericordia in Cannaregio, which has a vaguely bohemian studenty feel.

A range of bars is scattered across the Sestiere di San Marco, and a handful of other good ones are strung across Dorsoduro and San Polo.

About the latest you can hope for these places to remain open is 2am. You could then put on your dancing shoes but, as you will very quickly discover, the options for late nights out in Venice can be counted on the fingers of one hand!

Opportunities for a nice cup of coffee and a pastry abound. Piazza San Marco alone hosts some of the grandest old cafés in Europe.

SESTIERE DI SAN MARCO

The San Marco area offers a disparate set of drinking options, from fine old taverns to UK-style pubs, and from trendy wine bars to slightly out-of-time piano bars. And, of course, there's Harry's.

B BAR Map p296
☎ 041 240 68 42; Campo di San Moisè 1455;
🕒 6.30pm-1am Wed-Sun, happy hr 6-9pm Tue-Thu; 🚢 Vallaresso/San Marco

Can't afford a night in the Bauer? Not to worry. Why not just nip into its hip, plush ground-floor bar for a cocktail, with a little luck in a spot overlooking the Grand Canal.

BACARO JAZZ Map p296
☎ 041 528 52 49; Salizada del Fontego dei Tedeschi 5546; 🕒 4pm-3am Thu-Tue, happy hr 2-8pm; 🚢 Rialto

The dark red interior and unabashedly brash feel, not to mention the location right on the main tourist thoroughfare, may not make it your favourite, but a drink's a drink in a town where bars aren't exactly in surplus.

BACARO LOUNGE Map p296
☎ 041 296 06 87; Salizada San Moisè 1348;
🕒 10am-2am; 🚢 Vallaresso/San Marco

You feel like you've been tele-transported to New York in this cool cocktail bar behind the Mondadori bookstore. It's best to sidle up to the red-tiled oval bar, as the rear seating area lacks in atmosphere. Or head up the glass stairway, lined with wine bottles waiting to be opened at the bar (you'll see waiters dashing off to grab a couple every now and then) to the restaurant above.

CAFFÈ FLORIAN Map p296
☎ 041 520 56 41; Piazza San Marco 56/59;
🕒 10am-midnight Thu-Tue Apr-Oct, 10am-11pm Thu-Tue Nov-Mar; 🚢 Vallaresso/San Marco

The plush interior of this, the city's best-known café, has seen the likes of Lord Byron and Henry James taking breakfast (separately!) before they crossed the piazza to Caffè Quadri for lunch. Venetians started paying exorbitant sums for the pleasure of drinking here in 1720.

CONFUSED OVER COFFEE

Coffee in Italy is complex. An espresso is a small cup of strong black coffee. A *doppio espresso* is a double. A *caffè lungo* is more watery, and an approximation of bland filter coffee is a *caffè americano*.

Enter the milk. A *caffè latte* is coffee with milk. *Cappuccino* is a frothy version. Both are breakfast drinks to Italians. *Caffè macchiato* is an espresso with a dash of frothy milk. The Venetians have discovered that sometimes a *macchiato* is too little and a *cappuccino* too much, and so they have invented the *macchiatone* (big *macchiato*), which is halfway between the two. In summer you can opt for a *caffè freddo*, a long glass of cold coffee with ice cubes. Good on winter afternoons is a *corretto* – an espresso 'corrected' with grappa or other hard liquor.

CAFFÈ QUADRI Map p296

☎ 041 522 21 05; Piazza San Marco 120; meals €80-100; ☯ 9am-midnight Tue-Sun; ⛴ Vallaresso/San Marco

Quadri is in much the same league as Florian, and it's equally steeped in history. Indeed, it opened its doors well before its better-known competitor, in 1683. The 1st-floor dining area is a luxury trip, all dripping chandeliers, baroque mirrors and heavy wall-hangings.

CAVATAPPI Map p296

☎ 041 296 02 52; Campo della Guerra 525; ☯ 9am-midnight Tue-Sat; ⛴ Vallaresso/San Marco

This is a modern creamy-white bar with halogen lighting and wines from all over Italy. In a rather daring departure for what is in many ways a small, tradition-bound town, this place will appeal to all who miss a slightly metropolitan touch. Try cheeses from around the country, with a few French and Swiss additions. Light meals are also available.

CENTRALE Map p296

☎ 041 296 06 64; www.centrale-lounge.com; Piscina Frezzaria 1659/b; cocktails €9-12; ☯ 6.30pm-2am Mon-Sat; ⛴ Vallaresso/San Marco

Translucent, emerald-green lighting contrasts with dark swaths of black in this chilled-out lounge bar for nocturnal types in search of a late-night tipple. Take a high table for two or head deeper inside for a low lounge in what is a slice of Soho in San Marco. You can eat here, too, although the nosh is nothing to write home about.

DEVIL'S FOREST Map p296

☎ 041 520 00 23; Calle dei Stagneri 5185; ☯ 10am-1pm & 5pm-12.30am Mon-Sat; ⛴ Rialto

This is a reasonable imitation of a UK pub, complete with old red telephone box, sports TV and Irish beers on tap (Kilkenny and Harp). It sometimes closes early if business is slow.

HARRY'S BAR Map p296

☎ 041 528 57 77; Calle Vallaresso 1323; cocktails €10-12; ☯ noon-11pm; ⛴ Vallaresso/San Marco

Although it's also a place to eat (see p142), Harry's is, of course, first and foremost a bar. Everyone who is anyone passing through Venice usually ends up in Harry's sooner or later. The Aga Khan lounged around here, and other characters as diverse as Orson Welles, Ernest Hemingway and Truman Capote have all sipped a cocktail or two at Harry's.

LAVENA Map p296

☎ 041 522 40 70; Piazza San Marco 133; ☯ 9am-10pm daily Apr-Sep, Wed-Mon Oct-Mar; ⛴ Vallaresso/San Marco

Founded in 1750 and less renowned than its big brothers Florian and Quadri, Lavena is in the same vein. Wagner was among its more visible customers, but historically gondoliers and *codegas* (stout fellows who lighted the way home for people returning at night) also hung out here.

MARTINI SCALA Map p296

☎ 041 522 41 21; Corte San Gaetano 1980; ☯ 10pm-3.30am Wed-Mon; ⛴ Santa Maria del Giglio

If you like the piano-bar scene, maybe this place is for you. It's a little cheesy and somewhat pricey, but then the options aren't bountiful (especially this late at night), are they? And it is rather a classic of the Venetian scene. Look for the intriguing entrance underneath an external stone staircase opposite the southern flank of the Teatro La Fenice.

TORINO@NOTTE Map p296

☎ 041 522 39 14; Campo San Luca 4592; ☯ 8pm-1am Tue-Sat; ⛴ Rialto

This unlikely-looking spot (during the day) livens up at nighttime as a young student set, combined with carefree and relaxed holidaying visitors, settles in for mixed

THE BIG STING

People keep doing it and keep complaining about it: that outrageously expensive cup of coffee taken at one of the big pavement cafés on Piazza San Marco is for some visitors the single most unforgettable (and unpleasant) Venetian experience. So, before you sit down for a cuppa (or any other drink or food) at the terraces, consider the following facts.

An espresso at a regular bar costs 80c to €1. It costs €5 at Caffè Florian and more still if you sit outside. At Caffè Quadri prices are similar. In addition, you pay for the privilege of listening to the quartets playing outside these cafés (except in the colder months) – a €5 surcharge! Thus the infamous US$10 (more like US$15 nowadays) cup of coffee on Piazza San Marco. An Irish coffee can cost €13 (plus music surcharge). Of the big three on Piazza San Marco, only Lavena offers standard prices for your espresso at the bar.

If you can cope with these sorts of prices, spend an hour or so sitting at an outdoor table at Florian, Quadri or Lavena, soaking up the atmosphere in Piazza San Marco. But don't say we didn't warn you! The aforementioned quartets compete with one another for attention, one striking up some stirring Vivaldi and the other countering with a little jazz. Usually they have the courtesy to play in turns, but if you stand in the middle of the square when they aren't being so gentlemanly, the effect is more cacophonous than melodious.

drinks, music and the occasional live performance (jam sessions often take place on Wednesday).

VITAE (IL MURO) Map p296
☎ 041 520 52 05; Calle Sant'Antonio 4118;
🕙 9am-1am Mon-Fri, 9am-2am Sat; 🚇 Rialto
When things around here start to look grim, people converge on this place. On a Friday or Saturday night it's a lively joint for a convivial drink – and one of the few seriously decent options in the San Marco area for a fun-loving, unpretentious crowd. Vitae is also busy by day – it's a popular brunch spot for local office workers – and it's packed for after-work drinks, too.

SESTIERE DI DORSODURO
Campo Santa Margherita is without doubt one of nocturnal Venice's major entertainment magnets. The extensive square is fronted on three sides by restaurants and bars, and it attracts a fun, eclectic crowd of students, hipsters, Biennale bods, local residents (at least those of them who aren't complaining about the noise) and, while the sun's still out, groups of children playing.

AI DO DRAGHI Map pp294-5
☎ 041 528 97 31; Calle della Chiesa 3665;
🕙 7.30am-2am Fri-Wed; 🚇 Ca' Rezzonico
This tiny but historic bacaro (old-style bar) is an obligatory stop for an ombra or spritz. The place consists of three distinct spaces. First is the tiny cubicle of a bar itself, all aged timber and a perfect retreat in winter if you can get in. Out the back there's some seating for

the colder months, while the tables set out on the campo (square) are ideal in summer. Finally, there's the street.

AL BOTTEGON (CANTINA DI VINI GIÀ SCHIAVI) Map pp294-5
☎ 041 523 00 34; Fondamenta Maravegie 992;
🕙 8.30am-8.30pm Mon-Sat; 🚇 Zattere
Wander into this fusty wine bar across from the Chiesa di San Trovaso for a prosecco beneath the bar's low rafters and in the light provided by dodgy bulbs. Alternatively, buy a bottle of whatever takes your fancy and take it away. The place has been known to stay open longer than the advertised times, and the panini (sandwiches) are great if your tummy's rumbling.

AL CHIOSCHETTO Map pp294-5
☎ 338 117 40 77; Fondamente Zattere al Ponte Lungo 1406/a; 🕙 7.30am-5pm Oct-Apr, 7.30am-1am May-Sep; 🚇 San Basilio
Live music is no longer allowed here, so the place occasionally hires a boat with musicians – come aboard and groove around the Canale della Giudecca. It's a strictly summertime scene, with tables sprawled out around a tiny bar in the kind of kiosk where you'd normally expect to buy the paper.

CAFÉ NOIR Map pp294-5
☎ 041 71 09 25; Calle dei Preti 3805; 🕙 7am-2am Mon-Sat; 🚇 San Tomà
You can start the day with breakfast or hang out into the night with a mixed crowd of Italian students and foreigners. The place has a laid-back, underground feel about it. A cocktail costs around €5.

Entertainment

DRINKING

Entertainment

DRINKING

CAFFÈ Map pp294-5
☎ 041 528 79 98; Campo Santa Margherita 2693; ☽ 7am-1am Mon-Sat; 🚊 Ca' Rezzonico
A lively student bar with snacks, this place is known to locals affectionately as the *caffè rosso* because of the red sign. It is something of a classic, and on warmer nights the animated bustle at the outside tables is hard to pass up.

CAFFÈ BLUE Map pp294-5
☎ 041 71 02 27; Calle dei Preti 3778; ☽ 8am-2pm & 5pm-2am Mon-Sat; 🚊 San Tomà
At this coolish student bar you may encounter live music, but it's more likely to be a DJ, as the residents have been complaining. If the DJ is good, the place packs to the rafters and punters spill out onto the street. It can be quiet on mid-week evenings. As an added incentive, the management has installed a computer with free Internet for customers – handy on a quiet afternoon.

CHET BAR Map pp294-5
☎ 041 523 87 27; Calle della Chiesa 3684; ☽ 9am-1am Mon-Sat; 🚊 Ca' Rezzonico
Venetians who prefer old-time bars frown on this cheerful splash of modernity with a black-and-white chessboard floor, plastic retro stools and bright lighting. On Friday and Saturday there's usually a DJ (God knows how s/he squeezes in).

CORNER PUB Map pp294-5
☎ 329 917 65 61; Calle della Chiesa 684; ☽ 10am-12.30am Wed-Mon; 🚊 Accademia
As the name suggests, this cosy alehouse sits on a corner. Cram inside for a McEwan's or Bulldog Red, or in summer order at the hatch that gives onto the street.

IMAGINA Map pp294-5
☎ 041 241 06 25; Rio Terà Canal 3126; ☽ 8am-2am Mon-Sat; 🚊 Ca' Rezzonico
A one-time art gallery that briefly flirted with the idea of being a combined bar and gallery has now settled for the former alone. True, the art on the walls gave the place a cultural sheen, but it is still a comfortable drinking stop. Sit on fat white lounges around timber-top tables over a wine or head outside for a table on the street.

LINEA D'OMBRA Map p296
☎ 041 241 18 81; Ponte dell'Umiltà 19; meals €35-40; ☽ Thu-Tue; 🚊 Salute
Although this is a restaurant, we include it as a bar because the food is nothing special but the location is. Some of the tables are set aside for drinking only, and a summertime spot over the water, perhaps indulging in just a snack to accompany your glass, is a grand idea.

MARGARET DUCHAMP Map pp294-5
☎ 041 528 62 55; Campo Santa Margherita 3019; ☽ 10am-2am Wed-Mon; 🚊 Ca' Rezzonico
Across the square from Caffè, this is a highly popular spot for a *spritz* and chat until the early hours. It attracts a hip mix of young wannabes and Biennale types with shades – you can't blame them, as you get the afternoon sun shining straight through your cocktail glass.

ORANGE Map pp294-5
☎ 041 523 47 40; Campo Santa Margherita 3054/a; ☽ 8am-2am; 🚊 Ca' Rezzonico
Huge sheet-glass windows now dominate the southern end of the *campo*. The colour of an Aperol *spritz* inside, the bar appeals to fashionistas and other narcissists. Skip the lurid bar and head out the back to the pleasant garden or the ringside terrace upstairs. And since the all-out smoking ban came in, this has become possibly the first bar in Venice to have a legal smokers' section.

OSTERIA DA CODROMA Map pp294-5
☎ 041 524 67 89; Fondamenta Briati 2540; ☽ 8am-midnight; 🚊 San Basilio
Popular with students, Codroma has been a favoured meeting place of workers, artists, musicians and just about everyone else in this part of town for more than 100 years. It's a knockabout spot, where people crowd in at timber benches and tables for an *ombra* and snacks.

SUZIECAFÉ Map pp294-5
☎ 041 522 75 02; Campo San Basegio 1527/a; ☽ 7am-7pm Mon-Thu, 7am-1am Fri & concerts; 🚊 San Basilio
This happy student bar picks up in buzz in the summer months as punters crowd the outdoor tables and live music is staged. Together with the nearby **Al Chioschetto**

(p163), it creates a lively summertime corner in Dorsoduro. From May to June it organises occasional concerts of anything from blues to ska.

TAVERNA DA BAFFO Map pp290-1
☎ 041 520 88 62; Campiello Sant'Agostin 2346;
🕓 7.30am-2am Mon-Sat; 🚊 San Tomà
Named after Casanova's licentious poet pal Giorgio Baffo and lined with his rhymes in praise of 'the round arse' and other parts of the female body, this bar has a young, chirpy feel. In summer the tables outside are an especially pleasant spot to sip a *spritz* or two, and the imported beers are good as well. Shame the residents are leaning so hard on the owners over street noise.

VINUS VENEZIA Map pp294-5
☎ 041 71 50 04; Calle del Scaleter 3961;
🕓 10am-midnight Mon-Sat; 🚊 San Tomà
This is a classy spot for tasting wines in an area better known for its more ebullient student bars. The clean, crisp lines of the cherrywood-bedecked bar create a pleasing atmosphere for wine-hopping across Italy and beyond. On Wednesday it presents a little live jazz.

SESTIERI DI SAN POLO & SANTA CROCE (SANTA CROSE)
The options around these parts are limited, but a couple are worth seeking out.

AI POSTALI Map pp290-1
☎ 041 71 51 76; Fondamenta Rio Marin, San Polo 821; 🕓 6pm-2am Mon-Sat; 🚊 Ferrovia
This is a buzzy locals' bar along the Rio Marin. Roberto gave up flying for Alitalia to pilot this place, which in years gone by served as an early opener for dawn posties. On warmer nights a seat by the canal is ideal for a *spritz* or two (according to some, they are among the best in town).

AL PROSECCO Map pp290-1
☎ 041 524 02 22; Campo San Giacomo dell'Orio, Santa Croce 1503; 🕓 8am-10pm; 🚊 Ferrovia
Pop into this pleasant little watering hole to taste a few wines from around the world, accompanied by a few bar snacks, in particular an aromatic selection of cheeses.

ANTICA OSTERIA RUGA RIALTO
Map p300
☎ 041 521 12 43; Ruga Rialto, San Polo 692;
🕓 11am-3pm & 6pm-midnight; 🚊 Riva di Biasio
Although *cicheti* and light meals are served here, we have included this osteria as a drinking establishment. Revellers often spill out into the street.

BAGOLO Map pp290-1
☎ 041 71 75 84; Campo San Giacomo dell'Orio, Santa Croce 1584; 🕓 7am-midnight Sep-Apr, 7am-2am May-Aug; 🚊 Riva de Biasio
This place, with its timber floors and low lighting inside and candlelit tables outside on the *campo*, has added a little nocturnal adrenalin to this pretty square, aided and abetted by a couple of busy spots round the corner on Calle del Tentor.

TOP FIVE CAFÉS
- Caffè Florian (p161)
- Caffè Quadri (p162)
- Lavena (p162)
- Caffè del Doge (p166)
- Algiubagiò (p166)

165

CAFFÈ DEI FRARI O TOPPO Map pp294-5
☎ 041 524 18 77; Fondamenta dei Frari, San Polo 2564; ⏰ 8am-9pm; 🚊 San Tomà
With more than a century of history, this is a leap back in time. On a cold winter's day especially, there's nothing better than sinking into a cushioned bench behind a tiny round table and hugging a hot cuppa, an afternoon *spritz* or wine and the paper.

CAFFÈ DEL DOGE Map p296
☎ 041 522 77 87; www.caffedeldoge.com, in Italian; Calle dei Cinque, San Polo 608; ⏰ 8.30am-8pm Mon-Sat, 9am-1pm Sun; 🚊 San Silvestro
Long a coffee-roasting workshop, this is now a gourmet coffee-tasting spot. The creamy décor and sometimes-loud music might not appeal, but the brew is sublime. Italian coffee is good but here it goes one better. Have a Guatemala Huehuetenango espresso (€1.70) and taste the difference.

MURO VINO E CUCINA Map p300
☎ 041 523 47 40; Campo Cesare Battisti, San Polo 222; ⏰ 4pm-1am Mon-Sat; 🚊 Rialto
Another attempt to lend a metropolitan touch to Venice's bar scene, this place has made a splash. Spread over two storeys and looking down over the Rialto markets, the downstairs level is a bustling designer bar, while upstairs you can eat well (see p147).

NOVECENTO Map pp290-1
☎ 041 522 65 65; Campiello Sansoni, San Polo 900; ⏰ 7pm-2am Tue-Sun; 🚊 Rialto
Generally a quiet spot for pizza and a drink, it winds up a little more energy on those occasional evenings when live jazz is staged.

TOP FIVE DRINKING ESTABLISHMENTS

- Al Bottegon (p163) Classic old wine cellar.
- Taverna da Baffo (p165) Rambling old tavern inside, pretty summertime terrace outside.
- Centrale (p162) A chilled touch of Soho in San Marco.
- Harry's Bar (p162) Ready for *the* Bellini?
- Margaret Duchamp (p164) A hip place to hang out on *the* square.

SESTIERE DI CANNAREGIO
There are some noisy bar-restaurants on the main drag leading away from the train station that fill with day-trippers tanking up on beakers of amber fluid after a hard day's sightseeing. You may well be inclined to leave this lot to the fast-drinking, unsteady newbies and proceed instead to a more pleasant local scene around Fondamenta della Misericordia.

ALGIUBAGIÒ Map p300
☎ 041 523 60 84; Fondamente Nuove 5039; ⏰ 7am-midnight; 🚊 Fondamente Nuove
There's nowhere better for a coffee on the way to or from Murano and the northern lagoon islands. Join the vaporetto staff at the bar or take a lagoonside seat. Late in the day, you may be tempted to skip the caffeine hit and switch to a generous goblet of a *spritz*, a fine sunset option.

FIDDLER'S ELBOW Map p300
☎ 041 523 99 30; Corte dei Pali 3847; ⏰ 5pm-1am Thu-Tue; 🚊 Ca' d'Oro
This place is representative of the Venetian Irish-pub genre. It's warm and cosy, and in summer tables are set up on the street.

OSTERIA AGLI ORMESINI Map pp290-1
☎ 041 71 58 34; Fondamenta degli Ormesini 2710; ⏰ 7.30pm-2am Mon-Sat; 🚊 Madonna dell'Orto
Oodles of wine and 120 types of bottled beer in one knockabout little place? Perhaps you should get along to this *osteria*. It's something of a student haunt, and tipplers spill out onto the *fondamenta* to enjoy their grog.

PARADISO PERDUTO Map pp290-1
☎ 041 72 05 81; Fondamenta della Misericordia 2640; ⏰ 7pm-2am Thu-Mon; 🚊 Madonna dell'Orto
The management has changed and the place has a less conspiratorial feel now that the nationwide smoking ban is in place, but Paradise Lost is still a relaxed place to hang out for a beer at the long benches and a little live music to boot. The food is so-so.

PUB TORTUGA Map p300
☎ 041 277 01 30; Calle delle Cadene 4888; ⏰ 9am-2am; 🚊 Fondamente Nuove
During the day it's a fairly standard café-bar, where you can pop by for a coffee, a beer and perhaps a bruschetta. Various imported

beers on tap and, on Friday nights, some live music warm up the atmosphere considerably in this lonely Cannaregio corner.

SESTIERE DI CASTELLO

Not a helluva lot goes on in Castello at night, but there are a couple of watering holes.

BIRRERIA BARBANERA Map p296

☎ 041 521 07 17; Calle Casselleria 5356;
🕑 noon-11.30pm; 🚇 Rialto

This place could be in the States. A happy-go-lucky sort of drinking and pizza dive, it makes no pretence to be anything but what it is, a place for young folk to grab a beer or five and perhaps line the tummy with some cheapish pizza or pasta.

INISHARK Map p296

☎ 041 523 53 00; Calle Mondo Novo 5787;
🕑 6pm-1.30am Tue-Sun; 🚇 Rialto

This is a good, old, slightly gloomy Anglo-style pub in the heart of Castello, fine for pints of Guinness (and a selection of hearty ales) and football (on Sunday). A few bar snacks and *panini* are available, too.

L'OLANDESE VOLANTE Map p296

☎ 041 528 93 49; Campo San Lio 5658; 🕑 11am-12.30am Mon-Sat, 5pm-12.30am Sun; 🚇 Rialto

The Flying Dutchman is basically a UK-style pub that attracts a curious mix of local students out for a beery night and tourists feeling a little nostalgic for…a beery night. The terrace gets vaguely rowdy on summer evenings.

ZANZIBAR Map p296

☎ 339 200 6831; Fondamenta Santa Maria Formosa 5840; 🕑 9am-1am; 🚇 Rialto

This crooked kiosk that looks set to crumble into the canal provides some great life-theatre entertainment. Pull up a seat on the square, settle in for a few people-watching drinks to the thumping music emanating from the bar, and enjoy.

CLUBBING

The club and dancing scene (locals call a club a *discoteca*) in Venice is virtually zero. One or two possibilities are available, but if you are looking for serious clubbing action you are in the wrong town.

Things look up a little in summer, when a handful of places open on the Lido, but the real action then is out at Jesolo (p242), about an hour's drive northeast of Venice, where there are more than half a dozen places to chose from. Azienda Trasporti Veneto Orientale (ATVO) bus No 10a from Piazzale Roma takes about 70 minutes and costs €3.60 (€6.40 return). The problem is getting back – buses don't run particularly late. If you find a taxi, you are looking at €80 or more, depending on traffic.

Mestre and a couple of small towns on the mainland have a handful of clubs, a few of them gay, and host basically a local crowd of mainlanders (who far outnumber those living in Venice itself). If you have your own transport they are all accessible. If you have the patience for night buses from Mestre, a couple are also possible. Otherwise it's a taxi.

As elsewhere in Italy, you need to be right up to date with what's in and what's out. Get hold of *VeNews* for some specific ideas. Expect to pay anything from €5 to €20 to get into a club. This may include the first drink.

AREA CLUB Off Map p305

☎ 041 95 80 00; www.areacity.it, in Italian; Via Don Federico Tosatto 9, Mestre; 🕑 11.30pm-4am Fri-Sun; taxi

This is one of the most popular nightspots in Mestre, where a long line-up of local and national DJs keeps people in the groove. If you want to come along earlier and partake

---

LAPPING IT UP

For a city that in its twilight years was considered by many a European to be one great pleasure dome of the senses, modern Venice is remarkably conservative. The few attempts to set up sex shops have failed miserably, and the city's red-light district (except for the streets around the mainland Mestre train station) can be summed up in one address. A dim red light indeed indicates you have arrived at the coyly named **Piccolo Teatro delle Melodie Veneziane** (Map p298; ☎ 041 523 14 03; Campo San Lorenzo, Castello 5063; 🕑 11pm-4am Wed-Sun). There's nothing very Venetian about the melodies, and the entertainment consists of half-hearted striptease and a little louche lap-dancing. Casanova and Byron would have been mortified!

of a truly Italian phenomenon, book a table for dinner from 9pm and stick around. It attracts a mostly 20s crowd.

BLV ROOMS Off Map p305

☎ 349 660 03 47; www.blunotte.it, in Italian; Via delle Industrie 29, Marghera; admission free; ⊙ Fri & Sat; train, then taxi

In one shape or another this former factory has been used as a dance hall for decades. In its latest guise there are two spaces, one red and the other white, where different types of music reign. Rock up here for house sessions on Friday and classic mainstream pop, both homegrown and international, on Saturday. Or perhaps the occasional tango sessions will incite you to penetrate this rather desolate industrial corner of the world.

Entertainment
CLUBBING

GAY & LESBIAN OPTIONS

Virtually nothing is done to cater specifically for gays and lesbians in Venice, and the only thing for it is to head for a handful of places in Mestre and Padua. The big news is the gay sauna club in Mestre, Metrò Venezia (see right), with several sauna and massage rooms. In Padua half a dozen bars cater to the gay scene, including the four-storey **Flexo Video Bar** (Off Map p226; ☎ 049 807 47 07; www.flexoclub.it; Via Tommaseo 96a; ⊙ 10pm-2am Wed-Thu, 10pm-5am Fri-Sun), with dark room, glory holes and porn. There is also one fairly basic gay club, **Black & White** (Off Map p226; ☎ 340-646 5696; www.black-disco.com, in Italian; Viale della Navigazione Interna 49b; ⊙ 11pm-5am Fri & Sat, 5am-10am Sun) in the industrial outskirts of town, along with a couple out in satellite towns. The Sunday session goes by the name of New Babol (after the Italians' favourite bubble gum).

CASANOVA Map pp290-1

☎ 041 524 06 64; Rio Terà Lista di Spagna, Cannaregio 158/a; admission free; ⊙ 10pm-4am Tue & Thu-Sat; ⊕ Ferrovia

A quick stumble from the train station, this is it: about the only place in Venice that can vaguely call itself a disco (and it really is more disco than club). Each night has its own musical theme, from rock revival on Thursday to Latin on Friday and thumping techno on Saturday.

CLUB MALVASIA VECCHIA Map pp294-5

☎ 041 522 58 83; Corte Malatin, San Marco 2586; admission free; ⊙ 11pm-4am Fri & Sat; ⊕ Santa Maria del Giglio

You pay a small fee to become a member of this social club that functions as a late-night bar and dance spot. Beloved of students and a hip, artsy type of crowd, it takes a bit of finding.

IL MURETTO

☎ 393 410 11 20; www.ilmuretto.net, in Italian; Via Roma Destra 120/d, Lido di Jesolo; admission up to €25; ⊙ 10pm-5am Sat; bus 10a, taxi

An army of DJs spins mostly house in this, one of the hippest dance locales. Flyers can be seen floating around as far away as bars in Padua. A couple of other spots are located on the same road.

KRYSTAL KLUB Off Map p305

☎ 041 541 51 00; Via Ca' Zorzi 2, Tessera; admission up to €20; ⊙ 9pm-4am Fri & Sat; bus 5 & 55, taxi

The best club offering in the Mestre area is this venue, near Marco Polo airport. In four dance spaces you can weave from house to Latin rhythms or mainstream pop.

MAGIC BUS

☎ 041 595 21 51; www.magicbus.it; Via delle Industrie 118, Marcon; ⊙ 11pm-5am Fri & Sat; taxi

Here you can expect the unexpected – anything from live rock nights to more experimental electronic stuff. A second dance floor was added in 2002, meaning that on any given evening you could run into a clash of different sounds depending on which bit of the club you wind up in.

METRÒ VENEZIA Map p305

☎ 041 538 42 99; Via Cappuccina 82/b, Mestre; admission €14; ⊙ 2pm-2am; train, night bus N2

This is basically a gay sauna, with various sauna and massage rooms but also a bar. Rather than a dark room it has a dark labyrinth!

PACHUKA Off Map pp302-3
☎ 041 242 00 20; Spiagga San Nicolò, Lido; admission free; ☼ 8.30am-4am Wed-Mon Oct-May, 8.30am-4am daily Jun-Sep; ⚓ Lido, then taxi
The most reliable of the Lido's summertime dance spots, this place right on the beach works year-round as a snack bar and pizzeria, but summer weekend nights it cranks up as a bit of a beachside dance club, too.

PICCOLO MONDO Map pp294-5
☎ 041 520 03 71; Calle Corfu, Dorsoduro 1506/a; admission free; ☼ 10.30pm-4am Tue-Sun; ⚓ Accademia
This teensy disco and bar is a bit on the slimy side but perfectly all right in its own wide-lapel fashion. It pulls a 30-plus crowd, and the uncared-for retro décor (can we call it that?) harks back to the 1970s.

ROUND MIDNIGHT Map pp294-5
☎ 041 523 20 56; Fondamenta dello Squero, Dorsoduro 3102; admission free; ☼ 10.30pm-4am Mon-Sat Sep-May; ⚓ Ca' Rezzonico
After you're through hanging out on Campo Santa Margherita, head around to this drink-and-dance cove on a nearby back canal. You can sip all sorts of cocktails and even get a snack. The music tends towards acid jazz and Latin. Although it's open quite early, you'll be lucky to see a soul in here before, well, midnight.

SOUND GARDEN
☎ 338 875 28 23; www.soundgardencafe.com, in Italian; Via Aleardi 18 (Piazza Mazzini), Lido di Jesolo; admission free, after midnight Sat €8; ☼ 10pm-4am Fri & Sat Dec-Sep; bus 10a, taxi
Sound Garden concentrates on rock (sometimes of the hard variety) and features live bands on Friday. It is one of the stalwarts of Jesolo. Inhouse DJs Max and Marco Marini keep tunes running when the live stuff stops.

TAG CLUB Off Map p305
☎ 338 429 95 98; Via Giustizia 19, Mestre; admission free; ☼ 10pm-5am Wed, Fri & Sat; train, night bus N1

A mix of local live bands followed by DJs pumping out a predictable but enjoyable mix of house and rock keeps this small club busy. Although the official finishing time is 5am, don't be surprised to stumble out the door later still.

TERRAZZAMARE
☎ 041 37 00 12; www.terrazzamare.com, in Italian; Vicolo Faro 1, Lido di Jesolo; ☼ 10pm-4am Tue-Sat; bus 10a, taxi
Sitting on a beach at the southern end of Lido di Jesolo is this classic self-described 'theatre-bar'. Music thumps into the night, and punters often groove in the sand. Theme nights dot the summer calendar.

LIVE MUSIC
Tickets & Reservations
Tickets for the classical and baroque music performances staged by several groups in various churches and *scuole* (religious confraternities) around Venice can generally be purchased on the spot from touts around town (they're hard to miss, as they generally dress in 18th-century kit) or from travel agents such as **Agenzia Kele & Teo** (Map p296; ☎ 041 520 87 22; www.keleteo.com; Ponte dei Baratteri, San Marco 4930). For jazz and other live-music gigs you generally pay at the door. Bigger concerts tend to be held at the PalaGalileo concert hall (Map pp302–3) behind the Palazzo della Mostra del Cinema on the Lido.

CLASSICAL & BAROQUE
Musical ensembles dressed in billowing 18th-century costume regularly perform concerts of baroque and light classical music (especially from about Easter to September). These shows are clearly aimed at tourists and can be cheesy, but the musical quality is not necessarily bad. On the whole, serious music lovers should abstain, as they are likely to be disappointed. The ensembles listed here and others change venues, so check when purchasing tickets. In addition to what is listed below, more serious concert programmes are sometimes staged in churches, including on occasion the Basilica di San Marco. Keep your eye on the listings publications noted at the start of this chapter.

COLLEGIUM DUCALE Map p296

☎ 041 98 42 52; www.collegiumducale.com, in Italian; Palazzo delle Prigioni, San Marco, & Chiesa di Santa Maria Formosa, Castello; adult/student & senior €25/20; 🕙 Wed, Thu, Sat & Sun; 🚇 San Zaccaria

The first thing you will notice about this ensemble, which plays alternately in the Palazzo delle Prigioni and the Chiesa di Santa Maria Formosa, is the absence of period costume. It carries out a series of concerts, covering old chocolate-box favourites from Vivaldi, Albinoni and a few rank outsiders like Mozart and Mendelssohn. As this sort of thing goes, the quality is not bad.

CONCERTI DELLA VENEZIA MUSICA
Map p298

☎ 041 520 87 67; www.vivaldi.it; Chiesa di Santa Maria della Visitazione, Castello 4149; adult/student €25/15; 🚇 San Zaccaria

Divided into several different ensembles, such as the five-member Putte di Vivaldi (Vivaldi's Girls) and the grander I Virtuosi dell'Ensemble, this gang performs a range of Venetian baroque music, usually at the church where Vivaldi himself often worked. From 2004 the concerts were temporarily transferred to Palazzo Ca' Papafava (Map p300; Calle della Racchetta, Cannaregio 3764).

INTERPRETI VENEZIANI Map pp294-5

☎ 041 277 05 61; www.interpretiveneziani.com; Chiesa di San Vidal, San Marco 2862/b; adult/student €22/17; 🚇 Accademia

Since the mid-1980s this group has been presenting concerts of, above all, Venetian music, in the Chiesa di San Vidal. Vivaldi, of course, heads the list, but the musicians handle other Italian masters and the occasional interloper such as Bach. They have performed as far away as the Bayreuth festival in Germany and Melbourne, Australia. Other than when the group is away on tour, the concert season lasts year-round. Performances generally start at around 8.30pm.

JAZZ, ROCK & CONTEMPORARY

A handful of eateries and bars such as **Para-diso Perduto** (p166), **Caffè Blue** (p164), **Novecento** (p166), **Al Chioschetto** (p163), **SuzieCafé** (p164), **Torino@notte** (p162), **Vinus Venezia** (p165), **Pub Tortuga** (p166) and **Osteria da Codroma** (p164)

intermittently put on live music, usually jazz, blues and mild pop. It is all a bit problematic as the local constabulary frequently comes down hard on bars that burst through a fairly low decibel ceiling. Bands playing rock with, heaven forbid, an amplifier, can attract a swift response from the noise police. As this was being written, for instance, all concerts at Pub Tortuga were suspended for a month precisely for this reason.

In summer occasional concerts are organised in Jesolo – watch the local press. A big rock event is Jesolo Beach Bum (the Italian rendering of the English 'boom'), usually held over a weekend at the beginning of July. In Mestre's Forte Marghera area the big annual event is Marghera Estate Village (www.villagestate .it, in Italian), a programme of nightly live music, from rock to ethnic, that runs from mid-June right through the summer.

AL VAPORE Map p305

☎ 041 93 07 96; www.alvapore.it, in Italian; Via Fratelli Bandiera 8, Marghera; admission varies; 🕙 7pm-2am Tue-Sun; train, bus 6, 6B, 66 & N2

The best place for a consistent programme of jazz, blues and other music is this spot in the rather dispiriting Marghera, on the mainland. Concerts start at 9.30pm and finish at midnight, on Friday and Saturday.

COLLEGIUM DUCALE Map p296

☎ 041 98 42 52; www.collegiumducale.com, in Italian; Palazzo delle Prigioni, San Marco; adult/student & senior €25/20; 🕙 9pm Fri; 🚇 San Zaccaria

Better known for its baroque concerts, the Collegium also presents a jazz quartet, which performs on Friday in the Palazzo delle Prigioni. It rolls out a selection of mainstream favourites, including pieces by Gershwin, John Coltrane and Italy's '70s doll, Mina.

FILM

Venice doesn't have an English-language cinema. The time to see foreign cinema in the original language is during the Mostra del Cinema di Venezia (Venice International Film Festival; p11) in September, which is when local residents go screen-happy, subjecting themselves to days on end of cinema happenings and so squeezing a year's viewing into a few weeks. Otherwise, while it is possible to see good movies at a handful of cinemas, the foreign ones are almost inevitably dubbed into Italian.

CINEMA DANTE D'ESSAI Map p305

☎ 041 538 16 55; Via Sernaglia 12, Mestre; adult/student €7/4.50; train, bus 1

This is the best bet in Mestre for good flicks, a balanced mix of mainstream cinema and some quirkier stuff from the non-Hollywood circuits.

CINEMA GIORGIONE MOVIE D'ESSAI

Map p300

☎ 041 522 62 98; Rio Terà di Franceschi, Cannaregio 4612; adult/student €7/4.50; 🚋 Fondamente Nuove

This modern cinema frequently presents quality movies, not just the big-name Hollywood schlock. There are two screens and as many as three screenings a day (roughly 5pm, 7.30pm and 10pm).

MULTISALA ASTRA Map pp302-3

☎ 041 526 57 36; Via Corfu 9; adult/student €7/4.50; 🚋 Lido

This cinema shows a broad range of art-house movies and mainstream releases, much along the lines of the programme at the Giorgione. Screening times are similar.

SUMMER ARENA Map pp294-5

Campo San Polo; 🕙 Jul-Aug; 🚋 San Silvestro

Set up under the stars in Campo San Polo in the hot months of summer, this outdoor cinema allows residents to see the movie from their windows! Again, it's all dubbed, and sound quality is poor.

VIDEOTECA PASINETTI Map pp290-1

☎ 041 524 13 20; Palazzo Carminati, Santa Croce 1882; 6-month member's pass €13; 🚋 San Stae

This film archive and research centre occasionally puts on film nights featuring classics. By way of example, in January 2005 it ran a series of films in a cycle dedicated to the work of Wong Kar-Wai. No *Star Wars* here.

THEATRE, OPERA & DANCE

Fine opera comes to Venice, but dramatic theatre and ballet are more limited. Local theatre-lovers dream of liberation from what seems to them an endless diet of Shakespeare and Goldoni, although the scene is not as restricted as that. A smattering of fringe stuff surfaces from time to time.

Tickets & Reservations

Tickets are available directly from the theatre concerned, usually one hour before the show. To book you can call or go online as indicated under individual entries.

You can purchase tickets for the majority of events in Venice at **Vela outlets** (Map p296 & pp290–1; ☎ 041 24 24; www.hello venezia.it, www.velaspa.com), which are part of the Azienda Consorzio Trasporti Veneziano (ACTV). Vela has kiosks out the front of the train station, on Piazzale Roma and at the Venice Pavilion Infopoint.

A handy website for checking what's on in which theatre is www.culturaspetta colovenezia.it, in Italian.

KAIRÓS Map pp294-5

☎ 041 241 35 30; Calle delle Botteghe, Dorsoduro 3170; 🚋 Ca' Rezzonico

This association stages intimate performances of local theatre, sometimes in Venetian dialect, and usually followed by a drop of wine and snacks. The centre runs courses in everything from theatre for kids to shiatsu.

TEATRINO GROGGIA Map p289

☎ 041 524 46 65; Parco Villa Groggia, Cannaregio 3161; 🚋 Sant'Alvise

In this tiny space, performances ranging from contemporary theatre to classical-music recitals dot the calendar, generally on Friday and Saturday nights only.

TEATRO A L'AVOGARIA Map pp294-5

☎ 041 520 92 70; Corte de l'Avogaria, Dorsoduro 1617; 🚋 San Basilio

A tiny brass plate on the door of what looks like just another shuttered house tells you that you've reached this modest avant-garde theatre, which has been experimenting with unknown and new playwrights since the late 1960s.

TEATRO AI FRARI Map pp294-5

☎ 041 71 04 87; Calle Drio l'Archivio, San Polo 2464; 🚋 Ferrovia

You may have a hard time locating this backstreet theatre, where local companies put on anything from a Carlo Goldoni classic to contemporary pieces.

TEATRO FONDAMENTA NUOVE Map p300

☎ 041 522 44 98; Fondamente Nuove 5013;
🚶 Fondamente Nuove

Expect the unexpected. Here you might see a modern adaptation of a classic by Carlo Goldoni (see also Teatro Goldoni, below), Sardinian folk dancing or world-music performances. A €20 season pass gives discounts on all performances.

TEATRO GOLDONI Map p296

☎ 041 240 20 11; Calle Teatro Goldoni, San Marco 4650/b; tickets €6-42; 🚶 Rialto

Named after Venice's greatest playwright (see p34), this is the city's main drama theatre. It's not unusual for Goldoni's plays to be performed here – after all, what better location? You might see anything from Shaw's *Pygmalion* done by a Calabrian theatre company to contemporary Italian drama. All sorts of other events, including concerts, also take place. Prices vary greatly depending on the show, session and seats.

TEATRO JUNGHANS Map pp302-3

☎ 041 277 04 07; Giudecca 494/a; tickets €5-20;
🚶 Palanca

Locals call it the Teatro Formaggino (Little Cheese Theatre) because it looks like a wedge of cheese. With seating for 150 and a unique three-sided stage, it was inaugurated in early 2005 and is part of an urban-regeneration project in the formerly rundown factory zone of the island.

TEATRO LA FENICE Map pp294-5

☎ 041 78 65 75; www.teatrolafenice.it; Campo San Fantin, San Marco 1977; tickets €20-1000; 🚶 Santa Maria del Giglio

The grand opera theatre of Venice is back in action, providing an experience music lovers will not want to miss. First-night spots can cost several thousand euros. Some of the operas are staged at the **Teatro Malibran** (below) instead. The **PalaFenice** (Map p289), the big top–style space created in just three weeks on Isola del Tronchetto to temporarily replace La Fenice after the 1996 fire, is still in use for occasional performances of anything from classical music to boxing (!).

TEATRO MALIBRAN Map p300

☎ 041 78 65 11; www.teatrolafenice.it; Calle del Teatro, Cannaregio 5870; tickets €10-95; 🚶 Rialto

This charming 17th-century theatre (a good hundred years older than La Fenice) was restored to its former glory in 2001. With a capacity of 900, it has become an important aide to La Fenice, taking on some of the overspill in demand.

TEATRO PICCOLO ARSENALE Map p298

☎ 041 522 17 40; Arsenale, Castello; tickets up to €20; 🚶 Arsenale

Since the early 2000s La Biennale organisers have run several small theatre spaces in disused parts of the once mighty Venetian shipyards. They include the **Teatro alle Tese** (Map p299) and the Teatro Piccolo

---

BACK FROM THE ASHES

Self-appointed pace-making arbiter of architectural taste *Wallpaper* magazine declared in its 2004 annual design awards the Teatro La Fenice re-creation the restoration of the year. And so one of the more lamentable chapters in Venetian theatrical history finished on a high note.

What had started as a tragedy – with the fire that destroyed the 18th-century theatre on 29 January 1996 – quickly descended into tragicomedy in the worst possible taste. To many, it seems miraculous that all ended well.

The then-mayor, Massimo Cacciari, vowed to have the theatre back in action by 2000. But the mysterious circumstances of the fire and subsequent irregularities in the awarding of contracts brought things to a halt in a mire of judicial and extrajudicial bickering. Cacciari's successor, Paolo Costa, sacked the building companies and started again, awarding the contract to a local firm that would work 16 hours a day to have the theatre virtually ready for an inaugural concert by Riccardo Muti in December 2003. Accustomed to cock-ups, even the most sceptical of Venetians was pleasantly surprised that Muti was indeed able to give the concert. The theatre is now a mirror image of its former self, with 250 more seats and the latest in technology.

First built in 1792, La Fenice remains a tangible link with the final days of the Republic. The horseshoe-shaped auditorium created exquisite acoustics. Before a fire in 1836 (after which it was rebuilt in commendably speedy fashion in 1837) various opera greats, including Rossini, Bellini and Donizetti, had made their mark here. The theatre's halcyon days came with the years of close association with Giuseppe Verdi. As the 20th century dawned, a more international flavour dominated, with works by composers such as Britten and Prokofiev. All the greats have graced its stage, from Callas to Pavarotti.

Arsenale (once a cinema), and are used for experimental theatre and as conference space. The Piccolo Arsenale has become a fixture on the city's theatre scene.

TEATRO TONIOLO Map p305

☎ 041 97 16 66; Piazza Battisti 1, Mestre; admission €15-30; train, bus 1

This busy forum in Mestre, in business since 1912, runs programmes ranging from Shakespeare to local drama, occasionally in dialect. Concert cycles are also a feature. The theatre was renovated in 2004.

CASINOS

People under 18 are not allowed into the following gambling dens.

CASINÒ DI VENEZIA Map pp290-1

☎ 041 529 71 11; www.casinovenezia.it; Palazzo Vendramin-Calergi, Cannaregio 2040; admission €5 (or €10 incl €10 gambling token & use of shuttle boat to/from Piazzale Roma); 🕑 3.30pm-2.30am; 🚊 San Marcuola

It feels quite distinguished to step off a water taxi at the Grand Canal entrance to this mansion and go in for a night on the tables. This is old-world class – the jacket-and-tie dress code is no surprise.

VENICE CASINO Map p288

☎ 041 529 71 11; www.casinovenezia.it; Ca' Noghera, Via Triestina 222, Tessera; admission €5 (or €10 incl €10 gambling token & use of shuttle to/from Piazzale Roma); 🕑 11am-4.30am Sun-Fri, 11am-6am Sat

If you feel that quantity is more important than ambience, then this might be the casino for you. It's Italy's premier mainland gambling house and is near the airport. The dress code is casual.

ACTIVITIES
HEALTH & FITNESS
Gyms

Tucked away in hidden corners of Venice is a handful of gyms where you can get a workout if walking around from one end of the city to the other is not enough.

Bronze doors, Teatro Goldoni (opposite)

PALESTRA BODY WORLD Map pp290-1

☎ 041 71 56 36; Calle del Ravano, Santa Croce 2196/a; 🕑 9am-10pm Mon-Fri, 10am-1pm Sat Sep-May, 9am-10pm Mon-Fri Jun-Aug; 🚊 San Stae

Here in a tiny lane is a decent gym with the usual options for cardiovascular exercise and body building. The emphasis is on the latter. Ten entries (valid for 60 days) cost €65. Alternatively, you can join for €26, after which 10 entries at a time cost €50, or take out membership for three, six or 12 months.

PALESTRA INTERNATIONAL CLUB
Map p296

☎ 041 528 98 30; Sotoportego dei Amai, San Marco 4249; 🕑 9am-10pm Mon-Fri, 9am-12.30pm Sat; 🚊 Rialto

This handily placed gym near Rialto is hidden down a blind alley. Friendly staff members run a weights section and cardiovascular exercise machines section. You can wander in any time and use all the equipment for €10. If you are thinking about hanging about for a while, it may pay to sign up for €30 and then opt for a subscription, which start at €45 a month (single entries are €7).

PALESTRA OASI Map pp294-5

☎ 041 296 05 05; Fondamenta dello Squero, Dorsoduro 3076; 🕑 9am-10pm Mon-Fri, 9am-12.30pm Sat; 🚊 San Basilio

The most extroverted fitness club in Venice with its enormous glass panes, this place proudly occupies the ground floor of a grand *palazzo* and looks onto the canal. In winter the floors are heated, and there's air-con in summer. You pay a sign-up fee of €25, after which you can get a block of 10 entries (valid for 10 weeks) for €70 or opt for a membership. One month is €70, two €110.

Swimming Pools

Opening hours are limited and complicated at both of the following pools – go along and pick up a copy of the latest timetable.

PISCINA COMUNALE A CHIMISSO
Map p289

☎ 041 528 54 30; Sacca S Biagio, Giudecca; swims €5, 10 tickets €43; ☉ Sep-Jun; ⛴ Sacca Fisola
This pool is often crowded, but some semblance of lane discipline is maintained.

PISCINA COMUNALE DI SANT'ALVISE
Map p289

☎ 041 71 35 67; Campo Sant'Alvise, Cannaregio 3161; swims €5, 10 tickets €43; ☉ mid-Sep–mid-Jul; ⛴ Sant'Alvise
A slightly more modern pool, this one gets just as full and can be a little chaotic.

OUTDOOR ACTIVITIES

It comes as little surprise that Venetians are keen rowers. Venice and the lagoon count nine rowing clubs, all of which usually line up to participate in the many regattas held during the year.

ASSOCIAZIONE CANOTTIERI
GIUDECCA Map pp302-3

☎ 041 528 74 09; www.canottierigiudecca.com, in Italian; Fondamenta del Ponte Lungo, Giudecca 259; ☉ office 4-6pm Tue & Thu; ⛴ Redentore
Established in 1981 by a mixed group of rowers living on Giudecca, the club has become one of the most active and competitive in Venice. When expert rowers are available, outsiders can sign up for lessons in voga alla veneta (Venetian-style rowing, done standing up) for €6 an hour.

REALE SOCIETÀ CANOTTIERI
BUCINTORO Map p296

☎ 041 520 56 30; www.bucintoro.org; Punta della Dogana, Dorsoduro 15; ⛴ Salute

The oldest rowing club in Venice was established in 1882. Inspired by the Oxbridge rowing clubs, it went on to furnish Italy with Olympic champions (the entire gold medal team at the 1952 Olympics consisted of Bucintoro members). Nowadays the club boasts about 300 members. Outsiders are welcome to join. You can sign up for lessons in voga alla veneta; eight lessons cost €100 and can be organised at any time. It's also possible to join courses in vela al terzo (lugsailing) with traditional lagoon vessels. These tend to take place late in spring or in September and require a minimum of five people.

REMIERA CANOTAGGIO
CANNAREGIO Map p289

☎ 041 71 68 08; Calle del Capitelo, Cannaregio 3160; ☉ office 9am-6pm Tue-Sun; ⛴ Sant'Alvise
Around 2002 several rowing clubs, including this one, were transferred here. If you pay the monthly membership fee of €10, you can get a few hours of rowing lessons.

WATCHING SPORT

As with residents elsewhere in the country, il calcio (football) reigns supreme in the hearts of many Venetians. Venezia, or the arancioneroverde (orange, black and greens), is a middling team that for years has hovered at the bottom of Serie B (2 division). Since it was founded in 1907 it has all too rarely played in the top division.

The team plays at the Stadio Penzo (Map p289), on Isola di Sant'Elena, at the far eastern end of the lagoon city. Venice's uniqueness makes for some interesting logistics when the side plays at home. Special ferry services are laid on between the Tronchetto car parks and Sant'Elena. All buses arriving in Venice on a match day are diverted first to Tronchetto to disgorge their loads of fans before reaching Piazzale Roma.

Tickets to see the local football side, AC Venezia (☎ 041 238 07 11; www.venezia calcio.it, in Italian), are available at Stadio Penzo and from Vela outlets (see p171). They can cost around €15 to €20 depending on the seat. Getting a ticket on the day is rarely a problem.

Shopping

Shopping

A city best seen on foot, Venice is a honeytrap for shopaholics. You will find it hard to resist wandering into an endless array of stores purveying everything from Italian high fashion to exquisite Carnevale masks, from model gondolas to Murano glass, from antiques to old lace.

Shopping Areas

The greatest concentration of Italian name fashion brands is west of Piazza San Marco on and around Calle Larga XXII Marzo, Calle Vallaresso and Frezzaria, and on Calle dei Fabbri, north of the piazza (Map p296). If you can't make it to Milan, you'll find a good selection right here, with everything from Armani to Valentino. We haven't mentioned individual stores in this chapter because they are all bunched together in the same area.

For less high-flying clothes, shoes, accessories and jewellery, hunt around the narrow streets between San Marco and Rialto, particularly La Marzarie (or Mercerie in Italian) and around Campo San Luca (Map p296).

There is no shortage of workshops and showrooms full of Murano glass, particularly between San Marco and Castello (Map p298) and, of course, on Murano itself – on the island you can also see glass-blowing. Shop around, as quality and prices vary dramatically. Similarly, you can find Burano lace on the island and in stores scattered across the city centre.

Art lovers should make for Dorsoduro. The city's single biggest concentration of galleries, containing all kinds of stuff, is on the streets between the Gallerie dell'Accademia and the Peggy Guggenheim Collection (Map pp294–5). A few stragglers line Calle del Bastion on the approach to the former Chiesa di San Gregorio just east of the Guggenheim. The area around Campo San Fantin in San Marco is also replete, of galleries, and another area to look is Calle delle Carrozze, close to Palazzo Grassi in San Marco (Map pp294–5). Anyone looking for innovative, cutting-edge, contemporary art will be sorely disappointed in Venice, as most galleries peddle safer goods likely to appeal to a broad, passing trade (tourists or otherwise). Some galleries are one-person shows, where the artist has their own work for sale.

For arts and crafts, including Carnevale masks and costumes, ceramics and model gondolas, San Polo (Map pp294–5) is the place to look. You'll encounter some mouth-watering delicatessens and speciality food shops in the area, too.

Opening Hours

In general, shops are open 9am to 1pm and 3.30pm to 7.30pm (or 4pm to 8pm) Monday to Saturday. They may remain closed on Monday morning or Wednesday and/or Saturday afternoon. Laws on opening hours are fairly flexible, so shopkeepers have a large degree of discretion. Many shops whose customers are mostly tourists will also open on Sunday. On the other hand, some shops close for the holidays for all or part of August. Department stores such as Coin and most supermarkets are open 9.30am to 7.30pm Monday to Saturday. Some even open 11am to 7pm on Sunday.

In the following reviews, opening hours are given only if they differ considerably from these general opening hours.

If you time your visit to coincide with the sales you could pick up some great bargains. Winter sales run from early January to mid-February and the summer sales from July to early September. Look for the *saldi* signs.

> **TOP FIVE SHOPPING AREAS**
>
> - **High fashion** West of Piazza San Marco (Map p296)
> - **Carnevale masks & other crafts** Sestiere di San Polo (Map pp294–5)
> - **Art galleries** Between Gallerie dell'Accademia and Peggy Guggenheim Collection in Dorsoduro (Map pp294–5) & San Marco (Map p296)
> - **Books** Sestiere di San Marco (Map p296)
> - **Glass** Murano (Map p301)

Stationery at Il Papiro (p79), Sestiere di San Marco

How to Shop

Venice bulges with shops and stands hoping to sell you anything they can, from extreme kitsch to serious art. Traps abound. One basic rule applies to all purchases – shop around.

Some of us (more perhaps than care to admit it!) can't resist cheap, kitsch souvenirs (pencil sharpeners in the shape of the Campanile di San Marco, gondoliers' hats, cheap masks and so on). That's fine and you'll find plenty of this all over the more frequented parts of town (like along Rio Terà Lista di Spagna on the way from the train station to Piazza San Marco, Map pp290–1). Know that it's basically rubbish and try to haggle the price down.

Haggling is not an option in most straightforward stores (supermarkets, clothing stores and the like) but can be a useful skill in certain shops retailing higher-quality souvenirs. Murano glass is a good example. Shop around carefully, and when you find something you like, see if you can get the price down.

As a rule, heavy, cumbersome and fragile items (this especially means glass, ceramics and some antiques) need to be shipped home. Many stores will take care of this for you and include the costs of shipping in the price. Ask before you buy, as shipping it yourself can be a pain. If you do find yourself with something that you need to ship, head for the main post office (Map p296).

What to Buy

Carnevale masks make beautiful souvenirs, but quality and price are uneven. You can find people selling masks on just about every canal corner, but for serious craftsmanship you have to look a little closer. The cheap, touristy rubbish is manufactured industrially in Padua, for instance, and worthless. The genuine articles are carefully crafted objects in *cartapesta* (papier-mâché) or leather (although you can find some nice decorative porcelain versions). Several fine stores are listed here. Some of them double as costume purveyors – these are the places to pick up your 18th-century clobber, powdered wig and tricorn hat to join in the grand masked balls of Carnevale.

The other two obvious objects of your retail desire will be Murano glass and Burano lace. The latter is clearly easier to take home but often just as pricey. Glass comes in all conceivable shapes and sizes, from elegant tableware to the most outlandish glass statuary – the sky is the limit in terms of price, size, imagination and…taste. In an effort to protect the name of real Murano glass-makers, the **Consorzio Promovetro** (www.promovetro.com) has since the mid-1990s been campaigning to increase customer awareness to distinguish between the genuine article and cheap imitations. This does not protect you from rip-offs by the Murano guys, but at least it helps set you on the right path. Also check out www .muranoglass.com.

Shopping

Occasionally you'll see ceramics shops. Although ceramics can't really be said to be at the forefront of traditional Venetian crafts (Gubbio, in Umbria, and several towns in Sicily are Italy's most renowned pottery producers), some pieces are particularly arresting.

One much less cumbersome way to remember a visit to Venice is by taking home images of the city. Several shops produce high-quality prints and etchings, and plenty of street stalls churn out cheap material. These can be a good, lightweight souvenir or gift. The serious art collector can also wallow in the splendours of a range of galleries.

Venice is noted for its *carta marmorizzata* (marbled paper), often made to traditional and evocatively named designs. It has become something of a hit with visitors and is used for all sorts of things, from expensive gift wrap to book covers.

Needless to say, Italian fashion is always a winner. Aside from the big names, you'll find plenty of small boutiques and artisans producing fine-quality fashion, shoes and accessories.

SESTIERE DI SAN MARCO

This the core of old Venice, its most venerable face and predictably where the highest class of city shopping is concentrated. Prices are high, and there's loads of tourist tat, too.

ANTICA MODISTERIA GIULIANA

LONGO Map p296   Hats
☎ 041 522 64 54; Calle del Lovo 4813; 🚢 Rialto
Want some fancy headgear? This is *the* millinery stop in central Venezia. From gondoliers caps to the most extravagant ladies hats and a range of imported fashion for the scalp, you'll find it all here. If hats ever really come back, this place will be taken by storm.

ANTIQUUS Map pp294-5   Antiques
☎ 041 520 63 95; Calle Crosera 3131;
🚢 San Samuele
This inviting shop along the continuation of Calle delle Botteghe, where several antiques stores reside, boasts a solid collection of old masters, silver and antique jewellery. In among the few items of furniture sit grand tea sets and other aristocratic bric-a-brac.

TAX REFUNDS

A value-added tax of around 19%, known as IVA, is slapped onto just about everything in Italy. If you are resident outside the EU and spend more than €155 in the same shop on the same day, you can claim a refund on this tax when you leave the EU. The refund only applies to purchases from affiliated retail outlets that display a 'Tax-Free for Tourists' (or similar) sign. You have to complete a form at the point of sale, then get it stamped by Italian customs as you leave. At major airports you can get an immediate cash refund.

BEVILACQUA Map p296   Fabrics
☎ 041 528 75 81; www.bevilacquatessuti.com; Fondamenta Canonica 337/b; 🕙 10am-7pm Mon-Sat, 10am-5pm Sun; 🚢 San Zaccaria
Since the mid-19th century the Bevilacqua clan has produced top-quality brocades, tapestries and high-grade materials for home decoration. Not just any old home, mind you. If you think of your lounge room as worthy of a little noble treatment, if your sofa has distinction, this could be the place to order your cushions. The work is still done locally.

BUGNO ART GALLERY

Map p296   Art Gallery
☎ 041 523 13 05; Campo San Fantin 1996/a;
🚢 Vallaresso/San Marco
This gallery has some works by contemporary artists on permanent display, although money is the object. While you might not be able to afford a Miró or De Chirico, there's plenty of other material for the modern-art collector. Needless to say, this is not a hobby for anybody short of Rockefeller status.

CODOGNATO Map p296   Jewellery
☎ 041 522 50 42; Calle Seconda dell'Ascensione 1295; 🚢 Vallaresso/San Marco
Possibly the city's best-known jeweller, Codognato sells classic, antique and new pieces that attracted the likes of Jackie Onassis in their time.

DISNEY STORE Map p296   Toys
☎ 041 522 39 80; Campo San Bartolomeo 5257;
🚢 Rialto
All right, perhaps you'll think it's as bad as mentioning McDonald's. Fact is, kids love Disney toys, and this place may well save a failing parental relationship with loved little ones.

FIORELLA GALLERY

Map pp294–5   Fashion

☎ 041 520 92 28; Campo Santo Stefano 2806; 🔝 Accademia

All sorts of odd, billowing and fantastical clothing items adorn the transsexual doge mannequins scattered about the inside and in the windows of this unique store. High fashion it ain't, but it's definitely a spur to curiosity.

LA GALLERIA VAN DER KOELEN

Map pp294–5   Art Gallery

☎ 041 520 74 15; www.galerie.vanderkoelen. de, in German; Ramo Primo dei Calegheri 2566; 🔝 Santa Maria del Giglio

Long established in Germany, this branch of the Van Der Koelen gallery brings a note of contemporary vigour to the somewhat staid Venetian art scene. The gallery frequently stages fine exhibitions of internationally known artists, well worth seeing whether you're a buyer or not.

GALLERIA MARINA BAROVIER

Map pp294–5   Glass

☎ 041 522 61 02; Calle delle Carrozze 3216; 🔝 San Samuele

Marina Barovier is one of the key names in quality Murano glass, and this store is a handy outlet for assessing just how expensively exquisite pieces can be.

GALLERIA TRAGHETTO

Map pp294–5   Art Gallery

☎ 041 522 11 88; Calle di Piovan 2543; 🔝 Santa Maria del Giglio

A stalwart on the Venetian art scene, this is one of the most respected of the few Venetian galleries dealing in contemporary art, most of it Italian but open to international flavours.

IL PAPIRO

Map pp294–5   Marbled Paper & Stationery

☎ 041 522 30 55; Calle del Piovan 2764; 🕙 Mon-Sun; 🔝 Santa Maria del Giglio

A bright, spacious stationer's, Il Papiro doesn't pretend to compete with the handful of traditional marbled-paper shops around town. Among a modest selection of such items you will also find anything from elegant envelopes to letter openers and quills.

LEGATORIA PIAZZESI

Map pp294–5   Marbled Paper

☎ 041 522 12 02; Campiello della Feltrina 2551/c; 🔝 Santa Maria del Giglio

At the Legatoria Piazzesi, the oldest purveyor of quality paper products in Venice, time-honoured methods are employed to turn out high-class items. The store is a dark but tempting treasure trove.

LIBRERIA AL PONTE

Map p296   Books

☎ 041 522 40 30; Calle Cortesia 3717/d; 🔝 Rialto

This small but useful shop offers a solid range of guides and other books on Venice, as well as children's books, many in English. It stocks a good assortment of Donna Leon's detective yarns.

L'ISOLA Map p296   Glass

☎ 041 523 19 73; Salizada San Moisè 1468; 🔝 Vallaresso/San Marco

L'Isola stocks glass objects designed by Carlo Moretti, which are much appreciated for their elegance and finesse. The prices aren't exactly low, but then Moretti is one of the leading names in high-end glassware.

LIVIO DE MARCHI

Map pp294–5   Crafts

☎ 041 528 56 94; www.liviodemarchi.com; Salizada San Samuele 3157/a; 🔝 San Samuele

This place, featuring wooden sculptures of underpants, socks and shirts, is rather strange but somewhat endearing all the same. Just how you might incorporate a fine carving of an unironed shirt into your living room's décor is another question. You might find some of the glass sculptures more interesting (or more accessible); among them are life-size balloons and a sweeping lick of paint complete with brush!

MARTINUZZI Map p296   Lace

☎ 041 522 50 68; Piazza San Marco 67/a; 🔝 Vallaresso/San Marco

This is one of the city's most venerable sellers of exquisite Burano lace products. The work is of a high standard, and wares include everything from doilies to tablecloths.

Shopping

SESTIERE DI SAN MARCO

MONDADORI Map p296   Books
☎ 041 522 50 68; Salizada San Moisè 1346;
🚇 Vallaresso/San Marco
Spread over a couple of floors and planted
in the heart of chic San Marco shopping.
After browsing, have a drink in the hip **Bacaro
Lounge** (p161), separated from the books by
just a pane of glass.

RONALDO SEGALIN Map p296   Shoes
☎ 041 522 21 15; Calle dei Fuseri 4365; 🚇 Rialto
'Now this is class,' a group of admiring
French tourists sighed as they peered in
the shop window. One of several old-style
shoemakers dotted about town, Segalin
has hand-fashioned, classic men's shoes,
more imaginative styles for women, and a
host of costume options if you'd like to visit
the 18th century for an evening.

SAN MARCO STUDIUM Map p296   Books
☎ 041 522 23 82; Calle Canonica 337/a; 🚇 San
Zaccaria
Here the books occupy every square
centimetre of space. The broad offering
includes English-language guides and
books on Venice.

SCHOLA SAN ZACCARIA
Map pp294–5   Prints & Posters
☎ 041 523 43 43; Campo San Maurizio 2664;
🚇 Santa Maria del Giglio

In this intriguing place you will find only
works depicting characters of the commedia dell'arte, such as Arlecchino (Harlequin). The colour in some of the paintings
and prints makes them stand out from
much of the standard Venetian fare.

VALESE Map p296   Metalwork Crafts
☎ 041 522 72 82; Calle Fiubera 793;
🚇 Vallaresso/San Marco
Since 1918 the Valese family has cast
figures in bronze, copper and other metals
here. Its reputation is unequalled in the
city. Some items, such as the ornamental
horses that adorn the flanks of the city's
gondolas, suggest themselves more readily
as souvenirs than others.

VENINI Map p296   Glass
☎ 041 522 40 45; www.venini.it; Piazzetta dei
Leoni 314; 🚇 Vallaresso/San Marco
One of the big names in serious artistic
glass production from Murano, this is a
handy branch of the main **island store** (p190).

VIVALDI STORE Map p296   CDs
☎ 041 522 13 43; Salizada del Fontego dei
Tedeschi 5537; ⏱ 9.30am-7.30pm Mon-Sat, 11am-
7pm Sun; 🚇 Rialto
Can't get the sounds of Vivaldi out of your
mind? If you need a CD of music related to
Venice, pop by here. Cristiano Nalesso

specialises in all things Venetian, ranging from the Renaissance through to baroque and including recordings by some of the better baroque groups that perform in Venice, notably Rondó Veneziano.

SESTIERE DI DORSODURO

Art is the word to sum up shopping here. You can inspect the many galleries on and near the short route separating Peggy Guggenheim's modern collection from the classics of the Gallerie dell'Accademia. Can't afford the real thing? You'll find some good print shops too.

BAC ART STUDIO

Map pp294-5   Prints & Posters
☎ 041 522 81 71; Piscina Forner 862; 🚢 Accademia
This studio has paintings, aquatints and engravings signed by two local artists, Cadore and Paolo Baruffaldi, that make fine gifts. Cadore concentrates his commercial efforts on Venetian scenes, while Baruffaldi depicts masked people. The store is a good place for quality postcards, too.

CA' MACANA

Map pp294-5   Carnevale Masks & Costumes
☎ 041 522 97 49; Calle delle Botteghe 3172;
🕐 10am-6.30pm Sun-Fri, 10am-8pm Sat;
🚢 Ca' Rezzonico
Wander in and watch the artists at work on the raw papier-mâché of future masks. Apparently Stanley Kubrick was impressed –

TOP FIVE CRAFT SHOPS

- Ca' Macana (left) Carnevale masks
- Venini (p190) High-class glass
- Atelier Pietro Longhi (p184) Gala costumes
- Arca (p184) Ceramics
- El Fero Novo (p188) Curious ironwork sculptures

he placed a rather large order for his last picture, *Eyes Wide Shut*. Among those used were the mask of the sect leader, and others that featured prominently were the long-nosed Dottore della Peste (Plague Doctor) and Luna (Moon). Along black walls the finished products gaze down at you, beckoning to be donned. It offers short courses for groups on mask-making and decorating (see p253).

CERAMICA CAMILLA Map pp294-5   Pottery
☎ 041 523 52 77; Fondamenta del Soccorso 2609;
🚢 San Basilio
You'll find some lovely decorative ceramics in here, mostly in muted aqua-greens and faded blues. Coffee-table dishes with leaf motifs and imitation Gothic façades in blue could make distinctive souvenirs.

GALLERIA FERRUZZI

Map pp294-5   Prints & Posters
☎ 041 520 59 96; Fondamenta Ospedaleto 523;
🚢 Accademia
Ferruzzi's images of Venice are an engaging, almost naive version of what we see. With fat brushstrokes and primary colours,

Shopping

SESTIERE DI DORSODURO

SAVED BY LACE

Perhaps it helped stave off boredom when their men were out fishing. Burano's business of lace-making goes back at least to the 14th century, when Duchess Morosina Morosini, wife of Doge Morosini, set up a lace workshop on the island employing 130 people. The workshop closed at her death, but a habit had been formed and Venetian lace was already winning a name for itself.

By the 16th century it was in big demand throughout the courts of Europe and produced in various locations around the lagoon, including Burano and Pellestrina. They say the Sun King of France, Louis XIV, wore a black collar of Burano lace that had taken two years to make! The French eventually enticed some Burano lace-workers to Paris, and by the end of the 17th century France was producing it on an industrial scale. It was, however, Napoleon's march into Venice and the collapse of the Republic in 1797 that finally killed off the industry.

The rebirth of lace-making on Burano came, it appears, when the Countess Adriana Marcello opened a lace-making school there in 1872. Several conflicting stories on who resuscitated the island's lace-making tradition compete for our attention, but all seem to agree that the idea of reviving the industry came in part as a response to the extreme hardship Burano's fishing families were experiencing. By the end of the 19th century Burano lace had again attained its worldwide reputation. The school was closed in 1970, and today the number of island women who still practise this delicate but painstaking art is dwindling fast.

the artist creates a kind of children's gingerbread Venice. On sale are screen prints, paintings and postcards.

GUALTI Map pp294-5   Jewellery & Shoes
☎ 041 520 17 31; Campo Santa Margherita 3111; 🚇 San Tomà

The searing white interior of this fashion oddity houses two quite unrelated collections. On the one hand there's a set of daring ladies' satin shoes in a range of colours. On the other there are strangely luminous brooches, pins and similar accessories that look like something in between a burst of fireworks and those 1970s table lamps that resemble clumps of unkempt hair with luminous split ends. Intriguing.

IL BAULE BLU Map pp294-5   Toys
☎ 041 71 94 48; Campo San Tomà 2916/a; 🚇 San Tomà

Cuddly teddy bears, old dolls, ancient toys – this is the place to come for a nostalgic

look around. The owners actively seek out old items, so what's on display and for sale continually changes.

IL GRIFONE Map pp294-5   Leather
☎ 041 522 94 52; Fondamenta del Gaffaro 3516; 🚇 Ferrovia

A virtually décor-free shopfront disguises this one-man leather workshop where you can get to grips with quality handmade bags, belts, wallets and other leather objects for quite reasonable prices.

IL PAVONE Map pp294-5   Marbled Paper
☎ 041 523 45 17; Fondamenta Venier dai Leoni 721; 🚇 Accademia

The dominant colours (blues, reds and yellows) and motifs (floral shapes, cherubs and others) at Il Pavone change from one day to another. The templates are applied to hand-printed paper as well as ties and other objects. You can have T-shirts made here, too.

FILL 'ER UP

Yes, it's all very fine sitting about posturing in fine restaurants, but sometimes you just want some plonk to have at home. And there's the question of cost – not everyone can afford to go out and invest in great-name labels.

Fortunately, apart from the wonderful option of sipping wines in a local *osteria* or *bacaro* (restaurant-bar), a fine take-home tradition persists in Venice. Every now and then you will stumble across a wine shop. You'll know you've hit one if you find it crammed with huge glass containers (the kind of 'bottle' even Hercules would have trouble slugging from) known as *damigiane*. From these monsters, each containing a sea of simple and quite acceptable Veneto table wine, you make a choice and have it poured into whatever you bring – used wine or mineral-water bottles, it's up to you. You will be charged, on average, €2 per litre.

A chain called Nave de Oro has at least five branches in Venice (listed below) and one each on the Lido and Murano. A handful of other places along the same lines can also be found. None opens on Sunday.

Al Canton del Vin (Map p298; ☎ 041 277 04 49; Ramo San Francesco, Castello 3156; ⏲ 8.30am-1pm & 4.30-7.30pm Mon-Sat)

Cantina del Canton (Map p290–1; Fondamenta degli Ormesini, Cannaregio 2678; ⏲ 8.30am-1pm & 4.30-7.30pm Mon, Tue, Thu-Sat, afternoon only Wed)

Nave de Oro (Map pp290–1; Rio Terà San Leonardo, Cannaregio 1370; ⏲ 8am-1pm & 4.30-7.30pm Mon, Tue, Thu-Sat, afternoon only Wed)

Nave de Oro (Map p300; Rio Terà dei SS Apostoli, Cannaregio 4657; ⏲ 9am-1pm & 4-7.45pm Mon, Tue, Thu-Sat, morning only Wed)

Nave de Oro (Map p296; Calle Mondo Novo, Castello 5786/b; ⏲ 9am-1pm & 5-7.45pm Mon, Tue, Thu-Sat, morning only Wed)

Nave de Oro (Map pp294–5; Campo Santa Margherita, Dorsoduro 3664; ⏲ 9am-1pm & 5-7.30pm Mon, Tue, Thu-Sat, morning only Wed)

Nave de Oro (Map p298; Calle Santa Maria Formosa, Castello 5179; ⏲ 9am-1pm & 5-7.45pm Mon, Tue, Thu-Sat, morning only Wed)

Wine Shop (Nameless; Map pp290–1; Fondamenta di Cannaregio, Cannaregio 1116; ⏲ 8.30am-12.30pm & 4.30-7.30pm Mon, Tue, Thu-Sat, morning only Wed)

L'ANGOLO DEL PASSATO

Map pp294-5   Glass

☎ 041 528 78 96; Campiello Squellini 3276;
🛳 San Tomà

Giordana Naccari has a talent for doing her own characteristic work in glass. In particular she does a very curious and attractive range of cups (€38 per piece). But you'll discover all sorts of one-offs, from towering emerald lamps to kitchenware with an Art Deco design look.

LE FORCOLE DI SAVERIO PASTOR

Map pp294-5   Forcole & Oars

☎ 041 522 56 99; Fondamenta Soranzo detta Fornace 341; 🛳 Salute

In need of an oar or, more importantly, a *forcola* (wooden support for gondolier's oar) to sit it on? These unique timber contraptions could make a quirky decorative item, or you might want one of the handful of souvenir items Saverio makes on the side.

LEGNO E DINTORNI

Map pp294-5   Crafts

☎ 041 522 63 67; Fondamenta Gherardini 2840;
🛳 Ca' Rezzonico

Wonderful little wooden models of various monuments and façades, akin to simple three-D puzzles, are sold here. They make rather refined gifts for kids but wouldn't go amiss with many an adult.

LORIS MARAZZI Map pp294-5   Crafts

☎ 041 523 90 01; Campo Santa Margherita 2903;
🛳 Ca' Rezzonico

Like **Livio de Marchi** (see p179), Loris Marazzi presents sculptures on a weird wooden theme. The ideas are remarkably similar, suggesting there must be a customer base for this kind of thing!

MONDONOVO MASCHERE

Map pp294-5   Masks

☎ 041 528 73 44; www.mondonovomaschere.it, in Italian; Rio Terà Canal 3063; 🛳 Ca' Rezzonico

One of Venice's master mask-makers, Guerrino Lovato, runs this higgledy-piggledy store, producing fine facial disguises for all and sundry, including, as he is not too bashful to point out, some of the models used by the late Stanley Kubrick for his last movie, *Eyes Wide Shut*.

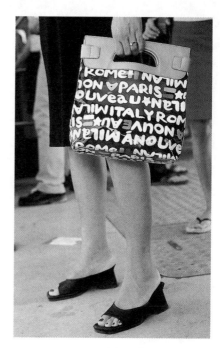

VETRO & ARTE Map pp294-5   Glass

☎ 041 522 85 25; www.venicewebgallery.com; Calle Cappeller 3212; 🛳 Ca' Rezzonico

For a browse of fine artistic pieces that still have some utility, such as elaborate vases, dessert plates and more, this is an understated showroom for quality glass.

SESTIERI DI SAN POLO & SANTA CROCE (SANTA CROSE)

These *sestieri* seem somehow more labyrinthine than the rest. In many of their almost maddening nooks and crannies lurk all sorts of surprises, from speciality food stores to a series of quality mask and costume workshops.

A MANO Map pp294-5   Crafts

☎ 041 71 57 42; Rio Terà, San Polo 2616;
🛳 San Tomà

This shop is full of all sorts of decorative items, all handmade. Quirky lampshades, mirrors and a host of other gewgaws certainly make it an interesting stop for some window-shopping.

ALIANI Map p300 — Food & Drink

☎ 041 522 49 13; Ruga Vecchia San Giovanni, San Polo 654; 🚇 San Silvestro
For its outstanding collection of cheeses and other delicatessen products, Aliani has long been a favoured gastronomic stop in the Rialto area.

ARCA Map pp290-1 — Ceramics

☎ 041 71 04 27; Calle del Tentor, Santa Croce 1811; 🚇 San Stae
The designs in this eye-catching shop are powerful and, for some, the colours are possibly a little strong. Teresa della Valentina paints her tiles and other ceramic objects in bold, bright, deep colours.

ARTEMISIA Map pp294-5 — Art Supplies

☎ 041 244 02 90; Campiello Zen, San Polo 972; 🚇 San Tomà
This well-stocked shop has just about everything imaginable for painting, restoration, sculpture and so on – perfect for the artist inspired by the lagoon city. Students get a 20% discount.

ARTISTICA FERRO

Map pp290-1 — Wrought Iron
☎ 041 520 04 90; Calle Lunga, Santa Croce 2137; 🚇 San Stae
Want a perfect replica *fero de prova* (the iron piece that graces the prow of the gondola and represents the six *sestieri* of Venice)? This is your place. The same shop (which has its forges on the mainland) can also produce just about anything in wrought iron or stainless steel, from staircases to artwork.

ATELIER PIETRO LONGHI

Map pp294-5 — Carnevale Masks & Costumes
☎ 041 71 44 78; Rio Terà, San Polo 2604/b; 🚇 San Tomà
This is the place to come if you've ever fancied buying a helmet and sword to go with your tailor-made Carnevale costume. Or indeed, just about any kind of costume item, from a Harlequin outfit through to 18th-century gala wear.

ATTOMBRI Map p296 — Jewellery

☎ 041 521 25 24; www.attombri.com; Sotoportego Oresi, San Polo 74; 🚇 Rialto
The long gallery that runs along the Palazzo dei Dieci Savi in Rialto has for years served as a quiet fast lane for hurried Venetians anxious not to be caught up in the tidal wave of tourists hovering around the adjacent produce and tourist-tat markets. For centuries it glistened with the wares of the Oresi (goldsmiths), but nowadays about half a dozen gold and jewellery shops eke out a living here. Attombri is the exception. The inventive Byzantine-style jewellery constitutes a captivating and original collection, and not just in gold.

BEATRICE PERINI

Map pp294-5 — Old Toys & Dolls
☎ 041 520 75 02; www.rialto.com/beatrice; Calle della Madonnetta, San Polo 1462; 🚇 San Silvestro
A delightful world of old-fashioned toys and handmade dolls of all descriptions awaits you here. If you can't convince the kids of the merits of these items over PlayStations, perhaps you'll be captivated and pick something up as decorative nostalgia.

THE BOAT MAN

Long before there were palaces in Venice, there were boats. Gilberto Penzo doesn't tire of telling anyone who will listen that Venice began on the water. Nowadays he is known to many Venetians for his painstaking replicas of boats. But he doesn't just make nice models. A Chioggia man, his life's passion has been to painstakingly gather all the material he can on Venetian vessels past and present. His research has led him to write several books on the many kinds of traditional Venetian and lagoon vessels, many now extinct. It has also allowed him to construct detailed replicas. An engineer, Penzo comes from a shipbuilding family. His grandfather and earlier forebears built the classic Chioggia vessel, the *bragozzo*. Penzo found that one way to pay for his almost obsessive studies was to make models – which he does with equal love and attention. His best efforts wind up in museums; although they're scale models, he tries to get the details of construction as close to the real thing as he can. As the last of the great gondola-builders disappear (the death of master Nedis Tramontin in 2005, three years after Giovanni Giuponi's death in 2002, caused quite a commotion in Venice), Penzo is fast becoming the last living repository of information on Venice's maritime history and traditions.

CENERENTOLA Map pp294-5 — Lampshades

☎ 041 527 44 55; Calle dei Saoneri, San Polo 2718; 🚇 San Tomà

Every conceivable kind of lampshade is on display here, but the tendency is towards classic pieces, often made of old embroidered cloth with a 19th-century feel – nothing slick and modern. It also sells antique lace.

DROGHERIA MASCARI

Map p300 — Food & Drink

☎ 041 522 97 62; Ruga degli Spezieri, San Polo 381; 🚇 San Silvestro

Not far from **Aliani** (opposite), this is another foodies' classic. All sorts of goods in jars are accompanied by a mouth-watering range of sweets, including slabs of chocolate and nougat (especially around Christmas).

FANNY Map pp294-5 — Gloves & Accessories

☎ 041 522 82 66; Calle dei Saoneri, San Polo 2723; 🚇 San Tomà

Decided on an off-season trip to Venice in the quiet depths of winter? Find that your hands are freezing off? Drop by here for an extensive range of his and hers gloves, with some slinky models for her and classic cashmere-lined leather jobs for him.

GILBERTO PENZO

Map pp294-5 — Crafts

☎ 041 71 93 72; Calle 2 dei Saoneri, San Polo 2681; 🚇 San Tomà

Here you can buy exquisite, hand-built wooden models of various Venetian vessels. Mr Penzo also takes in old ones for restoration. For the kids, you can fork out €25 for gondola model kits or buy them ready-made and painted. Round the corner you can have a peek at his workshop. See the boxed text, opposite.

HIBISCUS

Map pp294-5 — Women's Fashion

☎ 041 520 89 89; Ruga Ravano, San Polo 1061; 🚇 San Silvestro

Anything but a classic women's fashion store, Hibiscus presents an imaginative array of stylish threads for the lady about town, but with a vaguely alternative, even ethnic bent. It also has some nice chunky jewellery in unabashedly primary colours.

KIRIKÙ Map pp294-5 — Children's Clothes

☎ 041 296 06 19; Calle della Madonnetta, San Polo 1463; 🚇 San Silvestro

It is easy to feel badly dressed in Venice (or just about anywhere else in Italy). Maybe your kids are feeling the same way! If so, this is the place to stock up on some stylish threads for small people, from fresh-born babies to pimply adolescents.

L'ARLECCHINO

Map p296 — Carnevale Masks & Costumes

☎ 041 520 82 20; Ruga Ravano, San Polo 789; 🚇 San Silvestro

The folks at L'Arlecchino claim the masks are made only with papier-mâché to their own designs. To prove it you can inspect the workshop and see production from the earliest phases to the final touches. The quality of masks is evident and reflected in the price tags.

LEGATORIA POLLIERO

Map pp294-5 — Marbled Paper

☎ 041 528 51 30; Campo dei Frari, San Polo 2995; 🚇 San Tomà

Here is a traditional exponent of the art of Venetian bookbinding with (and without) marbled paper. You barely have room to stand when you penetrate this den, with piles of leather-bound books, paper-bound folders and all sorts of other stationery piled haphazardly to the rafters.

MANUELA CALZATURE

Map pp294-5 — Shoes

☎ 041 522 66 52; Calle del Galizzi, San Polo 1046; 🚇 San Silvestro

This is a small family business with a nice range of shoes, including more expensive footwear that the family makes under its own name. Don't judge it by the cheap junk outside.

MAZZON LE BORSE

Map pp294-5 — Leather

☎ 041 520 34 21; Campiello San Tomà, San Polo 2807; 🚇 San Tomà

A modest store and workshop, Mazzon le Borse is a good place to shop for hand-made leather bags and accessories. The goods are top class and often better than many of the big names (with their commensurately bigger prices).

TOP FIVE SHOPS FOR KIDS

- **Gilberto Penzo** (p185) Model gondolas
- **Il Baule Blu** (p182) Teddy bears
- **Legno e Dintorni** (p183) All sorts of gewgaws and toys in wood
- **Molin Giocattoli** (opposite) Toys and models
- **Disney Store** (p178) An old favourite

MILLE E UNA NOTA

Map pp294-5   Musical Instruments

☎ 041 523 18 22; Calle di Mezzo, San Polo 1235;
🚊 San Silvestro

If during your stay in Venice you require strings for your guitar, or would like to acquire some new panpipes, a shiny new mouth organ or perhaps even a harp, this is the place.

PETER PAN Map pp290-1   Masks

☎ 041 71 64 20; Campo Santa Maria Mater Domini, Santa Croce 2118; 🚊 San Stae

Valentina Franceschini runs this delightful little mask shop, producing some nice stuff in both papier-mâché and porcelain.

SABBIE E NEBBIE

Map pp294-5   Ceramics

☎ 041 71 90 73; Calle Nomboli, San Polo 2768/a;
🚊 San Tomà

Time for tea at this ceramics boutique, where the goodies include a range of hand-crafted tea and coffee pots and sets. On the other side is an elegant set of Japanese imports, from tea sets to sushi platters.

TRAGICOMICA

Map pp294-5   Carnevale Masks & Costumes

☎ 041 72 11 02; Calle Nomboli, San Polo 2800;
🚊 San Tomà

This is one of the city's bigger mask and costume merchants, and is quite over-whelming at first sight. It also organises costume parties during Carnevale.

VALERIA BELLINASO Map pp294-5   Fashion

☎ 041 522 33 51; www.valeriabellinaso.com;
Campo Sant'Aponal, San Polo 1226;
🚊 San Silvestro

With her experience in the Milan fashion circuits, Valeria has brought an inimitable touch of class to her pert little Venice

TO MARKET, TO MARKET

Hanging about Venice's handful of markets is in many ways more interesting than browsing through shops. Here Venetians are out in force, searching for the perfect artichoke or halibut. Every now and then the local citizenry gets the chance to potter about antique markets, too.

Cannaregio Produce Market (Map pp290–1; Rio Terà San Leonardo, Cannaregio; ⊗ Mon-Sat) This bustling market, stretched out along the main route from the train station to San Marco, makes a handy stop for picking up some fruit and veg.

Dorsoduro Produce Market (Map pp294–5; Campo Santa Margherita, Dorsoduro; ⊗ daily) In the mornings you can stock up at this limited farm-produce market, held in one of the city's most likable squares.

Mercatino Dei Miracoli (Map p300 & p299; ☎ 041 274 73 15; Cannaregio/Castello) On the second or third weekend of each month a bric-a-brac fair is held either in the Campo San Canciano and the adjacent Campo Santa Maria Nova or along Via Giuseppe Garibaldi. You can turn up all sorts of odds and ends at this market and the atmosphere is always fun.

Mercatino dell'Antiquariato (Map pp294–5; ☎ 041 45 41 76; Campo San Maurizio, San Marco) Three times a year this antiques market sets up, to the delight of collectors far and wide. It's a little hard to plan a visit around the market since it happens so infrequently (generally in April, September and December).

Pescaria (Fish Market; Map p300; Rialto, San Polo; ⊗ Mon-Sat) Underneath the neo-Gothic roof built at the beginning of the 20th century, the fish market gets a mixed clientele of housewives and restaurateurs in search of ingredients for the day's menu. They have been selling fish here for 700 years.

Rialto Produce Markets (Map p300; Rialto, San Polo; ⊗ Mon-Sat) The raucous cries of vendors rise above the general hubbub of canny shoppers rubbing shoulders with unsuspecting tourists wandering into the area for the first time. A prized culinary item is the humble artichoke.

Glass fruit, Murano (p189)

boutique. Velours and silks, many of them in subtle denominations of carmine, burgundy and vermilion, are used to produce anything from scarfs to hats and gloves. It's a delicious stop for the feminine fashion victim with class.

SESTIERE DI CANNAREGIO

For the great majority of first arrivals in Venice, the train station is point A and one inevitably marches down the Rio Terà Lista di Spagna and its prolongation towards Piazza San Marco. The shopping around here is nothing to get the blood rushing, but a few interesting exceptions stand out.

CAFFÈ COSTARICA

Map pp290-1   Food & Drink

☎ 041 71 63 71; Rio Terà San Leonardo 1337; 🚇 San Marcuola

Since 1930 the Marchi family has been importing coffee from Costa Rica and other coffee-producing countries, and toasting it up daily for your delectation. If you don't want to take any away, sip on your favourite mix at the bar.

COIN Map p300   Department Store

☎ 041 520 35 81; Salizada San Giovanni Grisostomo 5790; 🕑 9.30am-7.30 Mon-Sat, 11am-7.30pm Sun; 🚇 Rialto

This is a rarity in Venice. Although not gargantuan, the store brings a bit of department-store action to canalside shoppers, with this branch specialising in affordable men's and women's clothes and accessories. Another branch on **Campo San Luca** (Map p296) specialises in beauty products and accessories.

GIUNTI AL PUNTO

Map pp290-1   Books

☎ 041 275 01 52; Campo San Geremia 282; 🕑 9am-8pm Mon & Tue, 9am-9pm Wed & Thu, 9am-10pm Fri & Sun, 9am-midnight Sat; 🚇 Guglie

A limited range of paperbacks in several languages and some material on Venice, ranging from maps to cuisine guides, are sold in this handy store, a kind of book supermarket that keeps uncommonly long hours.

LABORATORIO BLU Map pp290-1   Books

☎ 041 71 58 19; Campo del Ghetto Vecchio 1224; 🚇 Guglie

This handy little children's bookshop has a good selection in English as well as Italian for a range of ages.

MOLIN GIOCATTOLI Map p300   Toys

☎ 041 523 52 85; Salizada San Canciano 5899; 🚇 Rialto

Nestled up along the bridge (locally known as Ponte dei Giocattoli – Toys Bridge), this shop will attract kids with a yearning for something more titillating than Tintoretto. Want a model Ferrari, or for that matter a model vaporetto?

SESTIERE DI CASTELLO

Castello backs onto the Sestiere di San Marco and so takes some of its overflow, whether you understand that to be grand monuments or the tourists who visit them. But as you head east things quickly quieten down into about the closest one comes to Venetian suburbia – fascinating to wander around in but a little short on retail stimulation.

CA' DEL SOLE

Map p298   Carnevale Masks & Costumes
☎ 041 528 55 49; Fondamenta dell'Osmarin 4964;
🚩 San Zaccaria
Although much of what is on sale here is aimed at the theatre business, anyone can purchase a fantasy in this House of the Sun. The masks are of a high standard.

EDITORE FILIPPI Map p296   Books
☎ 041 523 56 35; Calle Casselleria 5763;
🚩 San Zaccaria

Don't let the unremarkable appearance fool you. This is a den of books on all manner of subjects related to Venice, many published and on sale only here. The Filippis have been in the book business for nearly a century, and scholars search them out for their tomes and encyclopaedic knowledge.

EL FERO NOVO

Map p296   Wrought-Iron Sculpture
☎ 041 528 94 22; Calle della Fava 5567; 🚩 Rialto
A highly original enterprise is this workshop run by Primo Bollani, who churns out all sorts of fanciful sculptures in iron, from dreamlike monuments such as bridges and towers to odd-looking gondolas and more.

GIOVANNA ZANELLA Map p296   Shoes
☎ 041 523 55 00; Calle Carminati 5641; 🚩 Rialto
Freaky shoes are the business in this singular little boutique. It's not just the sometimes-surprising colours or the

THE NOBLE ART OF GLASS-BLOWING

Sparks fly off the glowing orange ball of flame inside the furnace. Twisted and twirled on the end of a long iron pole, the glob of glass is heated and shaped, heated and shaped. Sweat drains off the glowing brow of the taciturn Murano glass-worker, repository of centuries of tradition. That articles of such delicacy can emerge from such toil-toughened hands is a source of wonder.

It was the ancient Phoenicians who first discovered that exposing sand to extreme temperatures caused it to melt and form a glassy paste, a useful and malleable substance for making durable household items. The blowpipe used for glass-blowing came into use in Palestine in the 1st century BC.

As the Roman Empire rose to power, imports of glass objects from the East increased. Unequalled imitators, the Romans were soon producing their own material. One of the first centres of glass production in Roman Italy seems to have been Aquileia, northeast of Venice. In later centuries Venetian glass-makers learned the art from Aquileian refugees and colleagues in the East.

By 1291 all Venetian glass-making kilns had been obliged to move to Murano for safety reasons (fires were common), but possibly also to better preserve the secrets of the glass-makers. Their work had achieved Europe-wide renown and was a valuable export product. It was long considered treason for a glass-worker to leave Venice. Most didn't try, and some of the great glass dynasties that began in the Middle Ages are still at work today.

As Islamic glass production faded, Venetian artisans moved away from strictly utilitarian wares to more artistic objects in the course of the 15th century. Enamels were increasingly used to decorate the glass. Venetian crystal, obtained by using soda ash in the melting stage, became increasingly popular. The following century saw the development of diamond-edge engraving of clear glass. Floral motifs dominated. Only towards the end of that century did enamel decoration, by now more sophisticated, come back into vogue.

Things started to go downhill in the 17th century. Competition from France and later Bohemia made itself felt, and tough conditions imposed by the Republic on its Murano glass-workers pushed many of them to seek a living elsewhere. They left the lagoon and sought a better life in capitals across Europe. Some even ended up in the Americas. With Bohemian crystal dominating the European markets in the 1700s, Murano glass-makers began to imitate their products, with uneven success. One hit, however, were the heavy framed Murano glass mirrors.

The 20th century has breathed new life into the glass business, with production ranging from the practical to the strictly fanciful, with all tastes (good and bad) catered for. At the top end, contemporary artists from around the world create designs that master craftspeople then execute in glass. At the bottom end, kitsch is the name of the game.

beyond-fashion approach. Some of the footwear is just plain wacky. Try the gold-coloured feet-shaped shoes for size, or the ones that look like gondolas.

LABORATORIO DEL GERVASUTI

Map p298 Antiques
☎ 041 523 67 77; Campo Bandiera e Moro 3725; ⚲ Arsenale

In this cheerfully chaotic workshop enough goods are stacked to whet the appetite of any antiques collector. If you are a serious purchaser, ask about the warehouse, which you can arrange to see by appointment. Michele Gervasuti is continuing the work of his father, Eugenio, a master craftsman who opened the shop here in 1959.

LIBRAIRIE FRANÇAISE Map p298 Books
☎ 041 522 96 59; Barbaria delle Tole 6358; ⚲ Ospedale

Voulez-vous vos livres en français? Here you will find everything from the latest best-sellers of Gallic literature to tomes on most subjects Venetian – all of it in French.

AROUND THE LAGOON

There's not an awful lot to buy on most of the islands, but two stand out for their specialities. Murano has for centuries been the centre of Venetian glass production. Further away, the lace-making art is associated with the pastel-hued islet of Burano. You can of course shop for glass and lace in Venice itself, but there is something more 'real' about coming to the source. With a little luck, you'll see people making the stuff, too.

On Murano the bulk of the glass-sellers are congregated, as they should be, along and near Fondamenta dei Vetrai. Ever since the *vetrai*, or glass-makers, were transferred to the island at the close of the 13th century, this is where they have practised their art. You can see glass being blown in work-rooms attached to some of the glass shops: look for the sign *'fornace'* (furnace).

Over on Burano, local ladies can occasionally be seen hunched on the front step or sitting in the shade near the vaporetto stop, busily plucking away at some new lace creation. The island's main drag, Via Galuppi, is, well, laced with lace shops. Inspect the wares closely – the stuff on sale is sometimes of uneven quality and/or imported

from Asia. The reason? It's a lot cheaper to import imitations than to make the real thing, and most tourists aren't prepared to spend money on the genuine article.

BERENGO Map p301 Glass
☎ 041 527 63 64; www.berengo.com; Fondamenta dei Vetrai 109/a, Murano; ⚲ Colonna

Here is a purveyor of glass that has long abandoned any pretence of functionality in its products. This is glass for art's sake.

MARCO POLO Map p301 Glass
☎ 041 73 99 04; www.marcopologlass.it; Fondamenta Manin 1, Murano; ☯ 9am-6pm Mon-Sat; ⚲ Colonna

One of the handful of larger reliable glass merchants in Murano, Marco Polo offers you the opportunity to see the masters at work, a large display of traditional glass-ware, the possibility of having objects tailor-made and sent to your country and, upstairs, a quasi-museum of contemporary

CLOTHING SIZES

Measurements approximate only, try before you buy

Women's Clothing

Aus/UK	8	10	12	14	16	18
Europe	36	38	40	42	44	46
Japan	5	7	9	11	13	15
USA	6	8	10	12	14	16

Women's Shoes

Aus/USA	5	6	7	8	9	10
Europe	35	36	37	38	39	40
France only	35	36	38	39	40	42
Japan	22	23	24	25	26	27
UK	3½	4½	5½	6½	7½	8½

Men's Clothing

Aus	92	96	100	104	108	112
Europe	46	48	50	52	54	56
Japan	S		M	M		L
UK/USA	35	36	37	38	39	40

Men's Shirts (Collar Sizes)

Aus/Japan	38	39	40	41	42	43
Europe	38	39	40	41	42	43
UK/USA	15	15½	16	16½	17	17½

Men's Shoes

Aus/UK	7	8	9	10	11	12
Europe	41	42	43	44½	46	47
Japan	26	27	27½	28	29	30
USA	7½	8½	9½	10½	11½	12½

art in glass by local master Andres Pagnes and international names such as Tony Cragg and Costas Varotsos.

VENINI Map p301   Glass

☎ 041 273 72 11; www.venini.it; Fondamenta dei Vetrai 47-50, Murano; 🚉 Colonna

Venini is yet another location for browsing the top-shelf stuff before wandering off to poke your nose into less exalted glass factories and shops. The company was born in the 1920s of an unusual alliance between a Venetian antiquities dealer and a Milanese lawyer by the name of Venini. From the outset they worked with artists to create avant-garde pieces, which were already on show at the Biennale in 1922. Independent wealth comes in handy if you want to take some items home.

SHOPPING IN THE GHETTO

The Ghetto's tiny Jewish community is still busy, and you'll discover a few curious shops around Ghetto Nuovo and along Calle del Ghetto Vecchio. They generally sell an odd mixture of Jewish art, souvenirs, books on Venice's ghetto and religious stuff. One such place is **Arte Ebraica** (Map pp290–1; ☎ 041 72 00 92; www.shalomvenice.com; Calle del Ghetto Vecchio 1218-1219), which purveys all sorts of handmade objects in bronze, filigree silver, pewter, crystal and ceramics (such as mezuzahs, or parchment cases). It also deals in rare books and manuscripts. Another spot worth looking at is the **Studio in Old Jaffa** (Map pp290–1; ☎ 041 520 89 97; http://thestudioinoldjaffa.com). Alon Baker, who divides his time between Venice and Jaffa (in Israel) produces all sorts of bright hand-done artwork, from parts of the Torah to imaginative paintings, all taking their inspiration from Jewish tradition. Ghetto shops are, as a rule, closed on Saturday.

THE MAINLAND

About the only reason for coming across to the mainland is if you have shopping cabin fever and feel the need for major department stores.

LE BARCHE

Map p305   Shopping Centre

☎ 041 97 78 82; www.lebarche.com, in Italian; Piazza XXVII Ottobre 1; ☽ 9am-8pm Tue-Sat, 2-8pm Mon; train

There are no serious department stores in Venice itself. For this kind of thing you will need to head to this shopping complex, just off Piazza XXII Marzo in the centre of Mestre. The complex is home to several of the country's leading stores, including Feltrinelli, the bookshop chain, Ricordi Mediastore, for CDs and music, Coin, a leading budget department store, and PAM, particularly noted for its value-for-money food department. Fashion stores include Timberland, Esprit, Il Pellicano and V&V.

Sleeping ■

Sleeping

There is nothing quite like sleeping in Venice. Instead of wheeled-traffic noise, the more muted sounds of water lapping along canals and people walking and talking waft up into your room, which might easily be centuries old and oozing history or a modern designer gem. Venice fairly swarms with accommodation choices.

Accommodation Styles

The Azienda di Promozione Turistica (APT) office has a list of houses and apartments offering B&B accommodation – this is an option rapidly growing in popularity, with more places opening up all the time. In general they offer only a few rooms but can be great value. Try **Bed & Breakfast Italia** (www.bbitalia.it), a nationwide network that has more than 20 listings for Venice. Prices range from €42 for a single to €126 for a double. The more traditional version is the *affittacamere* (room rental), basically the same deal in private houses but without the breakfast.

Hotels go by various names. An *albergo* is a hotel. A *pensione* or *locanda* is generally a smaller, family-run establishment; frequently, there's little to distinguish them from lower-end hotels. Indeed, the word *locanda* has become one of the most popular in the Venetian dictionary, as new places, great and small, with this epithet have popped up everywhere in the past few years.

Most of these establishments are in buildings dating back several centuries and often have no more than a dozen rooms. Many hotels offer rooms with 'typical Venetian' furnishings and décor (sometimes genuine antiques, often modern remakes), evoking images of the Most Serene Republic.

Serious budget travellers have the choice of the youth hostel on Giudecca or a handful of other dormitory-style residences, some of them religious institutions and most of them home to students. Most open to tourists in summer only.

A good swath of the top hotels is in or near the San Marco area and along the Grand Canal, but it is also possible to find 'bargains' (the concept is, of course, relative) tucked away in tiny streets and on side canals in the heart of the city. A battalion of hotels, especially in the budget to midrange bracket, is marshalled near the train station, but most of them are fairly uninspiring. The Dorsoduro area is tranquil and offers a smattering of interesting options. A growing crop of enticing spots in ancient *palazzi* (mansions) are popping up in San Polo. Further choices are sprinkled further afield in Castello and the islands.

Price Ranges

Sleeping in Venice can be expensive. When business is slow many hotels will offer more competitive deals – always ask. In recent years there has been an accommodation boom in Venice, with many small hotels opening up and the B&B phenomenon taking hold. This has taken some of the strain off and added to your chances of beating down prices. It is always worth bargaining, especially in the low season.

Even in the depths of the low season, however, you are unlikely to pay less than €45/70 for a single/double. In the high season, only a handful of cheapies offer such prices. Expect to pay €80 to €120 for a good budget double, sometimes with bathroom (which often means shower, washbasin and toilet). For attractive midrange places you can be looking at anything from €80/120 to €150/250 for singles/doubles. From there on, more luxurious options open up – how luxurious depends largely on taste, season and purse.

We have included some 'cheap sleeps' in this chapter, by which we mean places where you can pay for a single/double around €80/120 or less in high season.

Travellers on their own are penalised. Most hotels have few, if any, single rooms. When they do, they are often poky. Either way, you generally pay two-thirds to three-quarters of the price two people would pay for a double.

Many hoteliers pad out the bill by including a compulsory breakfast. The (in)famous continental breakfast in these cases generally consists of a lavishly laid-out stale bread roll, accompanied by little packets of butter and jam and a pot of weak instant coffee.

Hotel rates vary wildly for a range of reasons, although the year-on-year tendency is up. That said, since 2001 the hotel-building boom in Venice has kept a lid on prices. A little free market–economy action!

Some hotels have the same prices year round, while others drop them when things are slow. 'Low season' for the average Venetian hotelier means November, early December, and January to Easter (except for the New Year and Carnevale rushes). Lowish season for some hotels comes in the hot July–August period.

La Residenza (p211), Sestiere di Castello

The prices that follow should be regarded as a high-season guide. Rooms come with private bathroom (which often means a shower and not a full bathtub) unless otherwise stated.

Check-in & Checkout Times

Hotels do not hold rooms indefinitely. Always confirm your arrival, especially if it's going to be late in the afternoon or evening. Generally there is no problem if you have paid a deposit or left a credit-card number. While you can check in at any time of the morning, you may not get access to your room until after noon, when it has been vacated and cleaned. Most of the time you will be able to leave your luggage with reception and go for a wander until the room is ready.

Checkout time is generally 11am or noon. Technically, if you overstay you can be charged for another night.

An important point to note in Venice: turning up at night (anything from 10pm on) and searching for your hotel can be daunting, especially if your lodgings are up some small, ill-lit *calle* (street). The city is dark and mostly quiet at night and the streets deadly confusing to the newcomer. Depending on where you are staying, you may find no-one to ask for directions. The first suggestion is try not to arrive at night. If you have no choice, get hold of good directions and a detailed map before you leave for Venice.

Reservations

It is advisable to book, particularly for Christmas, Easter and Carnevale, in May, June and September, and at weekends.

The **Associazione Veneziana Albergatori** (Venice Hoteliers' Association; Map pp294–5 & pp290–1; ☎ freephone in Italy 800 843 006, from abroad ☎ 39 041 522 22 64; www.veneziasi.it; ☯ 8am-10pm Easter-Oct, 8am-9pm Nov-Easter) has offices at the train station, in Piazzale Roma and at the Tronchetto car parks. Staff will book you a room, but you must leave a small deposit and pay a minimal booking fee.

The **Consorzio Alberghi della Terraferma Veneziana** (Hotels' Association of Venice Mainland; Map p305; ☎ 041 93 01 33; www.venicemainland.com; ☯ 8am-7.30pm Mon-Sat, sometimes 10am-6pm Sun) is a separate organisation based in Mestre train station (platform 1). If you arrive in Mestre and are worried Venice may be full, these people can put you up in a hotel in Mestre – be warned, though, that they have been known to be less than frank about the situation in Venice.

Sleeping

Web accommodation-booking sites abound. One of the best Venice-specific ones is **Venice By** (www.veniceby.com). It is worth comparing such sites' rates with those of the hotels themselves, as usually the commission hotels pay such sites is passed onto the guest.

Longer-Term Rentals

Few of us can afford to hang around even the cheapest hotel indefinitely. You could try cutting a deal for more affordable long-term accommodation in a B&B or *affittacamere*.

A cheaper option, but not an easy one to set up, is to share an apartment. In Italy, it is mostly students and young folk who do this, so start by heading to the Università Ca' Foscari notice boards at Calle Larga Foscari in San Polo (Map pp294–5). You can put up your own ad here. You could also try for an apartment to rent alone. It's possible to get a room in a shared place for about €300 to €400 a month. To rent even a studio for yourself, you are looking at €1000 to €1500 for short-term lets. Another approach is to ask small-hotel owners if they know of anything – sometimes they can quickly find a place for you to rent.

Venetian Apartments (☎ 020-8878 1130; www.venice-rentals.com; 403 Parkway House, Sheen Lane, London SW14 8LS), a UK-based organisation, arranges accommodation in flats, often of a luxurious nature. It has more than 100 places on the books. Two- to four-person apartments start at around UK£1000 per week. **Dimora Veneziana** (☎ 041 241 16 97; www.dimoraveneziana .com) has more than 20 apartments of various sizes and quality, starting at €107 a day.

Similar dealers abound on the Web. **Wotspot** (www.wotspot.com) has a series of apartments in Venice that go for around US$900 to US$1500 per week, sleeping two to four people. **Euroflats** (www.ccrsrl.com) has flats sleeping up to six from €650 to €1800 per week. **Guest in Italy** (www.guestinitaly.com) has apartments ranging from €100 to €320 a night. It also has B&Bs. **Interhome** (www.interhome.co.uk) has a selection of flats – small ones about 50 sq m sleeping four (a little cramped) cost around €700 to €800 a week. **Carefree Italy** (www .carefree-italy.com) has a handful of properties in Venice.

With all of these you must add booking and cleaning fees. People with pets in tow should make sure they are allowed before committing.

SESTIERE DI SAN MARCO

The San Marco area, especially along the Grand Canal, is home to some of the city's plush hotels. It is, however, not so hot for good-value midrange or budget deals. A few exceptions prove the rule. Given the tourist throngs in the area, there is a case to be made for opting for something of better quality in a less congested part of town anyway.

BAUER Map p296 — Hotel

☎ 041 520 70 22; www.bauervenezia.it; Campo di San Moisè 1459; d from €495;

🚇 Vallaresso/San Marco

Don't mind the 1949 Soviet-style entrance – the canalside neo-Gothic frontage of the *palazzo* is sufficiently elegant. From some rooms you have views across the Grand Canal to the Chiesa di Santa Maria della Salute. Rooms on the 2nd floor drip Carrara marble and Murano glass. Nonsmoking rooms are available. A few steps away is the boutique branch, the Bauer Il Palazzo, with spectacular suites at equally eye-popping prices. The management also has huge luxury apartments for rent in the Palazzi Mocenigo. Contact the hotel or check out **Living as a Venetian** (www.livingasavenetian.com).

CA' DEL CAMPO Map p296 — Boutique Hotel

☎ 041 241 16 60; www.cadelcampo.it; Campo della Guerra 511; s/d €200/250;

🚇 Vallaresso/San Marco

Located on a busy *campo* (square) 100m north of Piazza San Marco, this refurbished mansion offers tastefully presented and generous rooms. They come in a variety of shapes and sizes, are mostly sunny and look onto the square or a small courtyard. Don't bump your head on the beams in the attic rooms! Breakfast is served in a delightful mansard room.

CASA SUL MOLO Map p296 — Boutique Hotel

☎ 041 528 11 77; www.casasulmolo.com; Marzaria San Zulian 744; s/d €140/160;

🚇 Vallaresso/San Marco

Just seven warm rooms look out over Campo San Zulian in the heart of La Marzarie (or Mercerie in Italian). They are attractively furnished in typical Venetian style, with parquet floors and Murano glass fittings. Breakfast is served in the rooms. The entrance is tucked away inconspicuously on Marzaria San Zulian – look for the Luisa Spagnoli shop.

GRITTI PALACE Map pp294-5   Hotel
☎ 041 79 46 11; www.starwood.com/grittipalace; Campo Traghetto 2467; d €500-2500; 🚇 Santa Maria del Giglio

A luxury property fronting the Grand Canal, the Gritti is one of the most famous hotels in Venice. If you can afford it, you'll mix with celebs and royalty. Of the 90 rooms, the most enticing look out over the Grand Canal. All are stuffed with antique furnishings, although styles vary. You may have a large marble bathroom or Oriental carpets. A good portion of Hemingway's *Across the River and into the Trees* is set here. Hotel guests have access to a range of sporting options on the Lido, including golf, tennis and horse riding.

HOTEL FLORA Map p296   Hotel
☎ 041 520 58 44; www.alberghi-venezia.hotelflora.it; Calle Bergamaschi 2283/a; s/d €180/230; 🚇 San Marco/Vallaresso

A gem tucked away in the warren of San Marco, the Flora boasts more than 40 rooms with 19th-century furnishings and giddy 17th-century décor. All are different and, it has to be said, some are more spacious and attractive than others. The leafy garden out the back is a peaceful nook to while away some down time.

HOTEL GRASPO DE UA Map p296   Hotel
☎ 041 520 56 44; www.graspodeua.com; Calle dei Bombaseri 5094; s/d €190/270; 🚇 Rialto

The position couldn't be more central, right by the hustle and bustle of the Ponte di Rialto. You could feel a little hemmed in by all the tight lanes, but the hotel is good value, especially when it puts on midweek offers. The attached restaurant is a posh affair especially popular with office workers from the nearby town hall in Ca' Farsetti.

HOTEL LOCANDA FIORITA
Map pp294-5   Boutique Hotel
☎ 041 523 47 54; www.locandafiorita.com; Campiello Novo 3457/a; s/d €80/130; 🚇 Accademia

Set on a quiet square near the broad Campo Santo Stefano, the Locanda Fiorita offers simple rooms with nice touches such as the dressing tables, wall tapestries and reproduction artwork. With its greenery, timber beams and friendly service, it feels like home. A few breakfast tables are set up outside. In the same building is atmospheric annexe **Ca' Morosini** (www.camorosini.com; s/d €130/180), which has elegant rooms spread out over several floors.

HOTEL MONACO & GRAND CANAL
Map p296   Hotel
☎ 041 520 02 11; www.summithotels.com; Calle Vallaresso 1325; s/d from €248/420; 🚇 San Marco & Vallaresso

The Benetton family owns this 17th-century *palazzo* on the Grand Canal, a brisk stroll from Piazza San Marco. The rooms looking over the canal are the most sought after, and the canalside terrace is magnificent. A major overhaul was completed in 2004.

LOCANDA ANTICO FIORE
Map pp294-5   Boutique Hotel
☎ 041 522 79 41; www.anticofiore.com; Corte Lucatello 3486; s/d €125/145; 🚇 Sant'Angelo

Located in an 18th-century *palazzo*, this hotel is a charmer. The front door is on a narrow canal just in from the Grand Canal, so you can arrive in style by water taxi. Inside you will find cosy lodgings over a couple of floors. All rooms are tastefully decorated (tapestries and timber furniture), each with a different colour scheme.

LOCANDA ART DECO
Map pp294-5   Boutique Hotel
☎ 041 277 05 58; www.locandaartdeco.com; Calle delle Botteghe 2966; d €160; 🚇 Accademia

Bright, whitewashed rooms with timber-beam ceilings in this cheerful and immaculately kept hotel are especially enticing.

TOP FIVE SMALL HOTELS WITH CHARM

- Ca' Angeli (p199)
- Oltre il Giardino (p199)
- Locanda Leon Bianco (p201)
- Pensione Guerrato (p200)
- Locanda Antico Fiore (right)

Sleeping

SESTIERE DI SAN MARCO

Gritti Palace (p195), Sestiere di San Marco

Iron bedsteads are attached to particularly comfy beds with orthopaedic mattresses – no chance of backache here!

LOCANDA BARBARIGO

Map pp294-5   Boutique Hotel

☎ 041 241 36 39; www.locandabarbarigo.com; Fondamenta Barbarigo 2503/a; d €165; 🚤 Santa Maria del Giglio

Housed in the Palazzo Barbarigo, a grand Venetian noble family's house, this hotel has a handful of doubles – nicely decorated with typical Venetian 18th-century-style painted furnishings – which can be taken as singles for slight reductions. Some have exposed timber beams and views over a side canal, and a couple have a full bathroom; others have showers.

LOCANDA ORSEOLO

Map p296   Boutique Hotel

☎ 041 520 48 77; www.locandaorseolo.com; Corte Zorzi 1083; s/d €170/240; 🚤 San Marco/Vallaresso

Tucked away in a closed courtyard and with views from nine of its 15 rooms (over three floors) to the Bacino Orseolo – a kind of gondola terminal behind Piazza San Marco – this popular location is a beautiful, nonsmoking gem. Jovial young staff members go out of their way to make your stay in the painstakingly decorated rooms a joy. Breakfast is way better

than your average continental job. To find the place, go through the gate off Calle San Gallo and proceed into the courtyard (over which six of the rooms look).

Cheap Sleeps

HOTEL AI DO MORI Map p296   Hotel

☎ 041 520 48 17; www.hotelaidomori.com; Calle Larga San Marco 658; d without/with bathroom €90/135; 🚤 San Zaccaria

Just off Piazza San Marco, this higgledy-piggledy nonsmoking hotel has pleasant rooms, some of which offer close-up views of the basilica. The pick of the crop is the cosy double at the top that comes with a private terrace.

LOCANDA CASA PETRARCA

Map p296   Pensione

☎ /fax 041 520 04 30; Calle delle Schiavine 4386; s/d €65/110; 🚤 Rialto

A family-run place with simple but sparkling rooms in an ancient apartment building, this is one of the nicest budget places in the San Marco area. The cheerful owner speaks English. To get here, find Campo San Luca, follow Calle dei Fuseri, take the second left and then turn right into Calle delle Schiavine.

SESTIERE DI DORSODURO

Dorsoduro offers lots of interesting choices, often a good deal quieter than in San Marco and frequently better quality. Some wonderful deals could have you in a room overlooking either the Grand Canal or the Canale della Giudecca. Perhaps you'd like something along a tranquil side canal or near the bustling Campo Santa Margherita? And if you're looking for a slice of design dash not generally associated with classic Venetian digs, this is the place to look, too.

ALBERGO AGLI ALBORETTI

Map pp294-5   Hotel

☎ 041 523 00 58; www.aglialboretti.com; Rio Terà Antonio Foscarini 884; s/d €105/180; 🚤 Accademia

This charming family hotel almost feels like an inviting mountain chalet when you step inside. The management is friendly, and the bright, white-painted rooms are tastefully if simply arranged and mostly of a good size. There are three suites that can sleep up to four. The restaurant is of a high standard and you can eat in the courtyard on warmer evenings.

CA' MARIA ADELE Map p296   Boutique Hotel
☎ 041 520 30 78; www.camariaadele.it; Rio Terà Catecumeni 111; s/d €400/500, themed r or ste €700; 🚇 Salute

Lying virtually in the shadow of the majestic bulk of the Chiesa di Santa Maria della Salute is this veiled 16th-century pleasure dome of 14 rooms over four floors. Five are themed (ranging from the Doges room to the Oriental room, complete with little Buddha), while the rest are a carefully presented version of the Venetian theme, with splendid tapestries, dark chocolate timber ceilings, traditional Venetian floors and a host of other touches. Booking on the website can bring considerable savings.

CA' PISANI HOTEL Map pp294-5   Design Hotel
☎ 041 240 14 11; www.capisanihotel.it; Rio Terà Antonio Foscarini 979/a; d €260-354; 🚇 Accademia

Named after the hero of the 1380 siege of Chioggia, this centuries-old façade betrays little of the snazzy design hotel inside, filled with 1930s and 1940s furnishings and specially made items. The sleek modern rooms, some with exposed beams, are elegant, well equipped and full of pleasing decorative touches – nothing is left to chance. There are great views from the small roof terrace.

CA' SAN TROVASO Map pp294-5   Pensione
☎ 041 277 11 46; www.locandasantrovaso.com; Fondamenta delle Eremite 1350; s/d €90/130; 🚇 Zattere

With its traditional *terrazzo alla Veneziana* floors (see Of Floors & Walls, p87) and Venetian décor, this lodge is a pleasant surprise package set just a few steps from the Canale della Giudecca. The rooms are spacious and decorated with tapestries. Try for those with views and, in summer, sun yourself on the hotel's *altana*.

CASA REZZONICO
Map pp294-5   Boutique Hotel
☎ 041 277 06 53; www.casarezzonico.it; Fondamenta Gherardini 2813; d €150; 🚇 Ca' Rezzonico

This comfortable spot is well placed and offers attractive rooms with parquet floors and stylish timber furniture. Some look over a quiet canal. You can relax over a drink in the garden and, in summer, take your breakfast there, too.

DD.724 Map pp294-5   Design Hotel
☎ 041 277 02 62; www.dd724.it; Ramo de Mula 724; d €240-300, ste €340; 🚇 Accademia

Dorsoduro is leading the way in a hotel-design departure. At DD.724 the owners have taken a centuries-old shell and lathered it with an ultramodern look and contemporary-art touches. The seven rooms and suites are individually tailored, with features such as LCD TV and home cinema. The hotel looks onto the gardens of the Peggy Guggenheim Collection and a narrow *rio*.

HOTEL ALLA SALUTE DA CICI
Map pp294-5   Hotel
☎ 041 523 54 04; www.hotelsalute.com; Fondamenta di Ca' Balà 222; s/d €115/140; 🚇 Salute

This is a comfortable old-style hotel in a well-kept 16th-century Venetian house on a quiet canal near the Chiesa di Santa Maria della Salute. Some rooms look onto the canal, and all are nicely decorated with rugs and timber furnishings. The owners also have some larger family options sleeping up to five.

HOTEL PAUSANIA Map pp294-5   Hotel
☎ 041 522 20 83; www.hotelpausania.it; Fondamenta Gherardini 2824; s/d €160/250; 🚇 Ca' Rezzonico

A Gothic residence preceded by a courtyard with an internal staircase creates a romantic setting here. Close to Campo Santa Margherita but nice and quiet, the hotel boasts comfortable if smallish rooms, a grand salon and a verdant rear garden where you can take breakfast. Some rooms have ceiling frescoes, others exposed timber beams.

LA CALCINA Map pp294-5   Hotel
☎ 041 520 64 66; www.lacalcina.com; Fondamenta Zattere ai Gesuati 780; s/d €106/186; 🚇 Zattere

John Ruskin wrote *The Stones of Venice* here in 1876. The hotel has a smidgen of garden and looks across to Giudecca. Its immaculate rooms, with parquet floors and timber furnishings, are sober but charming. Some have small terraces and others views over the Canale della Giudecca. One has both views *and* a terrace.

LOCANDA SAN BARNABA

Map pp294-5   Boutique Hotel

☎ 041 241 12 33; www.locanda-sanbarnaba.com; Calle del Traghetto 2785-6; s/d €110/170; 🚊 Ca' Rezzonico

This 13-room hotel has been elegantly carved out of a fine mansion. Rooms are well equipped and some face onto the canal. There is only one single, on the ground floor, and one of the doubles (€180) has a ceiling fresco. A small terrace graces the top of the building, and there's a canalside garden for breakfast or evening drinks.

PENSIONE ACCADEMIA VILLA

MARAVEGE Map pp294-5   Pensione

☎ 041 521 01 88; www.pensioneaccademia .it; Fondamenta Bollani 1058; s/d €125/183-275; 🚊 Accademia

Set in its own lovely gardens right by the Grand Canal and close to the Gallerie dell'Accademia, this 17th-century villa is understandably popular. Grand sitting and dining rooms, capped by splendid timber ceilings and oozing a past grandeur, will tempt you to just stay inside. Rooms are simple but elegant, some with four-poster beds and timber floors. Most look onto the gardens and some have canal glimpses.

PENSIONE SEGUSO

Map pp294-5   Pensione

☎ 041 528 68 58; www.pensioneseguso.it; Fondamenta Zattere ai Gesuati 779; s/d €145/178; ☽ Mar-Nov; 🚊 Zattere

This russet red, typically Venetian, family-run *pensione* is in a lovely, quiet position facing the Canale della Giudecca. It has been in business since WWI. Rooms are nicely furnished with timber pieces, and many enjoy canal views. You can dine here or relax in the reading room.

Cheap Sleeps
ALBERGO ANTICO CAPON

Map pp294-5   Pensione

☎ 041 528 52 92; www.anticocapon.com; Campo Santa Margherita 3004/b; d €90; 🚊 Ca' Rezzonico

This place is right on the liveliest square in Dorsoduro and has seven quite varied rooms. The beds are wide and firm, the rooms in which they stand bright and airy. Bear in mind that the square can be pretty noisy at night.

ANTICA LOCANDA MONTIN

Map pp294-5   Pensione

☎ 041 522 71 51; www.locandamontin.com; Fondamenta di Borgo 1147; s/d without bathroom €70/110, d with bathroom €140; 🚊 Accademia

Ezra Pound and Modigliani favoured this small, comfortable place, located on a quiet back canal a few minutes' walk from the Gallerie dell'Accademia and Campo Santa Margherita. It's been in business since the 1800s, and the cosy rooms look onto either the canal or the rear garden. Some have parquet floors and others the typical Venetian *terrazzo*. The better doubles are surprisingly spacious. The rear pergola-covered garden dining area has attracted everyone from Italian nationalist poet Gabriele d'Annunzio to US President Carter, but the kitchen is dining on past glories.

HOTEL GALLERIA Map pp294-5   Pensione

☎ 041 523 24 89; www.hotelgalleria.it; Campo della Carità 878/a; s/d without bathroom €75/105, d with bathroom up to €150; 🚊 Accademia

The Hotel Galleria is the only one-star digs right on the Grand Canal, near the Ponte dell'Accademia. Space is a little tight in this 17th-century mansion, but the 18th-century décor in the bright rooms is welcoming. If you snag one on the canal, how could you possibly complain?

SESTIERI DI SAN POLO & SANTA CROCE (SANTA CROSE)

A few hotels cluster at the train-station end of the Sestiere di Santa Croce. Further away the pickings thin out, but a few modestly priced lodgings are scattered about, along with some Grand Canal classics, and stunning refurbished private houses and apartments, especially in San Polo.

ALLOGGI AL MERCANTE

Map pp290-1   Locanda

☎ 041 275 01 58; www.alloggialmercante.com; Calle del Campaniel, San Polo 1770; s/d €90/140; 🚊 San Stae

On a quiet lane around the corner from the one-time oil docks and close to the Rialto fish markets lurks this unassuming but spruce guesthouse. Set out over three levels, rooms have parquet floors and functional furniture.

ANTICA LOCANDA STURION

Map p296   Hotel
☎ 041 523 62 43; www.locandasturion.com; Calle Sturion, San Polo 679; s/d €170/240-300; 🚊 San Silvestro

This ancient lodge is two minutes from the Ponte di Rialto and has been a hotel on and off since the 13th century (when it was the Hospitium Sturionis). The best of its 11 rooms are the two generous suites overlooking the canal. All come with mod cons and are a deep wine-red colour harking back to the 18th century. One downside is the long stairway up to the hotel.

CA' ANGELI Map pp294-5   Boutique Hotel
☎ 041 523 24 80; www.caangeli.it; Calle del Traghetto della Madonnetta, San Polo 1434; s/d €180/290; 🚊 San Silvestro

Well might angels opt to stay here. A variety of rooms, from a smallish double with its own roof terrace to a generous suite overlooking the Grand Canal, makes this meticulously run establishment a top choice. Antique furniture and genuine Murano lamps are to be found throughout, and you might never want to leave the sun-filled reading room that looks onto the Grand Canal. Credit cards are not accepted.

CA' SAN GIORGIO

Map pp290-1   Boutique Hotel
☎ 041 275 91 77; www.casangiorgio.com; Salizada del Fontego dei Turchi, Santa Croce 1725; r €110-200; 🚊 San Stae

Even the owners of this restored medieval house aren't sure how old it is, but elements from the 14th century stand out. Half a dozen rooms have been beautifully carved out of the Gothic framework; the nicest is easily the top-floor suite with sloping timber ceiling and *altana* (traditional Venetian roof terrace) to sit out on of a sunny morn.

HOTEL SAN CASSIANO Map pp290-1   Hotel
☎ 041 524 17 68; www.sancassiano.it; Calle della Rosa, Santa Croce 2232; s/d €200/360; 🚊 San Stae

The 14th-century Ca' Favretto has a mixed selection of rooms (and an incredibly mixed range of prices), the better ones doubles with high ceilings overlooking the Grand Canal. The building is a wonderful old pile with stone-framed doorways along the staircases. Try to grab a breakfast table on the balcony overlooking the Grand Canal.

Antica Locanda Sturion (left), Sestiere di San Polo

LOCANDA ARCO ANTICO

Map pp294-5   Hotel
☎ 041 241 12 27; www.arcoanticovenice.com; Corte Petriana, San Polo 1451; d €160; 🚊 San Silvestro

The best rooms are those on the higher floors of this 16th-century *palazzo*, especially the one looking over the medieval courtyard. Many features of the building, such as the mottled *terrazzo alla veneziana* floors, have been retained.

LOCANDA SANT'AGOSTIN

Map pp290-1   Hotel
☎ 041 275 94 14; www.locandasantagostin.it; Campo Sant'Agostin, San Polo 2344; s/d €198/220; 🚊 San Stae

In this cosy residence you'll find a variety of rooms, the best of them a couple of spacious doubles overlooking the square of the same name. All are decorated with taste, from the antique furniture, picked up in various stores around the city, to the deep blue bedding and curtains and the Murano glass lamps.

OLTRE IL GIARDINO

Map pp294-5   Boutique Hotel
☎ 041 275 00 15; www.oltreilgiardino-venezia .com; Fondamenta Contarini, San Polo 2542; d €220-380; 🚊 San Tomà

Back in 1922, Alma Mahler (the composer Gustav's wife), who was then living with writer Franz Werfel, bought this magical house and garden for 100,000 lire. Today's owners have turned it into a beautifully relaxed home away from home, with timber floors, exquisitely chosen furniture and just six rooms, all different. One on the ground floor has a private corner of the garden. Sun streams into those on the top floor. The garden creates a sense of having a private piece of heaven.

Cheap Sleeps
ALBERGO CASA PERON
Map pp294-5   Pensione

☎ 041 71 00 21; www.casaperon.com; Salizada San Pantalon, Santa Croce 84; s/d €85/95; 🚊 San Tomà

This is a small but characterful place, family run and with immaculately maintained rooms tucked around corners and up stairs. It's well placed, not too far from the train station and close to the Frari church. You will be greeted by the resident parrot on the way in.

HOTEL DALLA MORA
Map pp294-5   Pensione

☎ 041 71 07 03; www.hoteldallamora.it; Salizada San Pantalon, Santa Croce 42/a; s/d €60/90; 🚊 Ferrovia

Located on a small canal just off Salizada San Pantalon, this hotel has clean, airy rooms, some with lovely canal views, and a terrace. Some rooms are equipped with shower and sink. It's a popular choice, and prices come down by about 15% in the low season.

PENSIONE GUERRATO Map p300   Pensione
☎ 041 528 59 27; web.tiscali.it/pensioneguerrato; Ruga due Mori, San Polo 240/a; d without/with bathroom €95/125; 🚊 Rialto

Amid the Rialto markets, this *pensione* is a one-star place that has spacious, light rooms (some with glimpses of the Grand Canal) and market views. In some rooms parts of wall and ceiling frescoes have been preserved. It is housed in a former convent, which before (so they say) had served as a hostel for knights heading off on the Third Crusade. The friendly managers run a tight

---

TOP FIVE HOTEL GARDENS
- Hotel Cipriani (p213)
- Il Lato Azzurro (p214)
- Locanda Cipriani (p214)
- Hotel Villa Cipro (p213)
- Pensione Accademia Villa Maravege (p198)

---

ship, so book early. Up on the 4th floor they also run Guerratino, where some of the five rooms (which cost a smidgin more than those downstairs) look out onto the Rialto markets.

SESTIERE DI CANNAREGIO
This is the world of cheap and sometimes cheerful accommodation just a few steps from the train station. Few of these places have anything remarkable to recommend them, but they are handy for quick getaways. You'll find more enticing choices in the side *calli* and further away from the station.

BOSCOLO GRAND HOTEL DEI DOGI
Map pp290-1   Hotel

☎ 041 220 81 11; www.boscolohotels.it; Fondamenta Madonna dell'Orto 3500; d from €330, ste up to €1045; 🚊 Madonna dell'Orto

Once an embassy, this haughty hotel stands in splendid isolation in the northwest of the city. The airy rooms are well appointed in 18th-century style, and the presidential suite enjoys magnificent views of Murano. Others look onto tranquil private gardens. Private hotel boats shuttle you to Piazza San Marco.

CA' POZZO Map pp290-1   Design Hotel
☎ 041 524 05 04; www.capozzovenice.com; Sotoportego Ca' Pozzo 1279; s/d €160/210; 🚊 Guglie

A small-scale haunt of designer touches you'd expect of grander hotels (such as flat-screen TVs and safes in which you can store a laptop), this modern guesthouse is buried deep down a blind alley, not too far from the station. Fear not, and plunge to the end to find this welcoming haven. It offers tastefully designed rooms, each with modern artworks but quite individual. In some you'll find exposed ceiling beams, in others tiled floors. Colour schemes are fresh and varied, and the public areas have a clean, sleek feel that is rare in a city where most hotels go in for a fustier, centuries-old atmosphere.

HOTEL ABBAZIA Map pp290-1   Hotel
☎ 041 71 73 33; www.alberghi-venezia.abbazia hotel.com; Calle Priuli detta dei Cavalletti 68; s/d €225/250; 🚊 Ferrovia

In a restored former abbey just a few minutes' walk from the train station, 50 lovely rooms are spread across this seemingly

Sleeping

SESTIERI DI CANNAREGIO

endless, rambling hotel. Some face onto a blooming central garden where you can take breakfast. The better ones all have a different primary-colour scheme, with yellows, reds and blues dominating.

HOTEL AI MORI D'ORIENTE
Map pp290-1   Boutique Hotel

☎ 041 71 10 01; www.hotelaimoridoriente.it; Fondamenta della Sensa 3319; d €200-400, ste €250-450; 🚤 Madonna dell'Orto

One of the few luxury hotels in this part of the city, this two-storey, freestanding brick residence is a stone's throw from the Ghetto. Richly coloured fabrics adorn all rooms, from the smallish standard doubles to the spacious suites, and lend them a vaguely Eastern flavour. Try for a cosy attic room.

HOTEL GIORGIONE Map p300   Hotel

☎ 041 522 58 10; www.alberghi-venezia.hotel giorgione.com; Calle Larga dei Proverbi 4587; s/d €173/265, ste €400; 🚤 Ca' d'Oro

In this welcoming hotel you will find comfortable, if in some cases rather small, rooms mostly in a 15th-century mansion (part of the building is modern). At the centre of the hotel is a peaceful courtyard. You can take breakfast outside and sip drinks on the 1st-floor terrace. Some of the best top-floor rooms have small terraces, and the entire 3rd floor is nonsmoking.

HOTEL TRE ARCHI Map pp290-1   Hotel

☎ 041 524 43 56; www.hoteltrearchi.com; Fondamenta di Cannaregio 923; s/d €210/240; 🚤 Tre Archi

Set away from the tourist rush, this attractive hotel of 24 rooms is in a bit of the 'real Venice'. The place is furnished and decorated in classical Venetian style. Some rooms (a couple with small terraces) look over the Canale di Cannaregio, while others are set around the internal garden, where you can take breakfast in summer.

LOCANDA LEON BIANCO
Map p300   Boutique Hotel

☎ 041 523 35 72; www.leonbianco.it; Corte Leon Bianco 5629; d with Grand Canal view €200; 🚤 Ca' d'Oro

To find this old *locanda*, cross Rio dei SS Apostoli (heading towards San Marco) and turn right. Pass the high staircase on your left and head straight into the dead-end courtyard.

Go up two flights of stairs in which medieval-style flaming torches would be at home and you are there. The best three rooms (of eight) look onto the Grand Canal (the others are cheaper). The undulating *terrazzo alla Veneziana* floors and heavy timber doors with their original locks lend the rooms medieval charm. Breakfast is served in the rooms. The house next door is the 12th-century Ca' da Mosto, which from the 16th to the 18th century housed Venice's first and most famed hotel, Del Leon Bianco.

Cheap Sleeps
ALLOGGI GEROTTO CALDERAN
Map pp290-1   Pensione

☎ 041 71 53 61; Campo San Geremia 283; s/d/tr/q €42/88/108/125; 🚤 Ferrovia

For a simple, budget deal this place has several advantages. It offers a whole range of rooms with a commensurately bewildering battery of prices depending on size, views and whether there is a private bathroom. Most rooms have pleasing views over the square. Readers seem to be divided on this place. Some sing its praises, while others loathe it. Seems OK to us.

HOTEL ROSSI Map pp290-1   Hotel

☎ 041 71 51 64; www.hotelrossi.net; Calle delle Procuratie 262; s/d €69/92; 🚤 Ferrovia

Set in a tiny lane off the Rio Terà Lista di Spagna, this hotel's rooms are pleasant enough, some with wood panelling and others whitewashed. The location is quiet and handy for the train station, and staff members are chirpy.

HOTEL VILLA ROSA Map pp290-1   Hotel

☎ 041 71 89 76; www.villarosahotel.com; Calle della Misericordia 389; s/d €82/113; 🚤 Ferrovia

This hotel has 33 comfortable rooms, varying considerably in style and recently renovated; some on the top floor (of three) have pleasant terraces. Out the back is a quiet courtyard where you can take your breakfast.

RESIDENZA CA' RICCIO
Map p300   Boutique Hotel

☎ 041 528 23 34; www.cariccio.com; Rio Terà dei Birri 5394/a; s/d €83/99; 🚤 Fondamente Nuove

This 14th-century residence (identified only by the doorbell) has been lovingly restored, with exposed brick and stonework, timber

Hotel Danieli (p211), Sestiere di Castello

ceiling beams and burnt red, polished floor tiles. There is a pleasing simplicity about the rooms, with their graceful metal bedsteads and side tables, white linen and nice touches such as fresh flowers. Most rooms look out onto a garden or courtyard. It is exceptional value.

SESTIERE DI CASTELLO

This area to the east of San Marco, although close to the piazza, is less touristy. From the train station, catch a vaporetto and get off at San Zaccaria. Castello offers a broad palette on the accommodation front, with a couple of gems and some worthy runners-up.

ALBERGO PAGANELLI Map p298   Hotel
☎ 041 522 43 24; www.hotelpaganelli.com; Riva degli Schiavoni 4687; s/d €160/220; 🚢 San Zaccaria
Guests have been staying here since the mid-19th century. Aim for one of the three spacious waterfront rooms with sweeping views across the lagoon through grand

---

picture windows. Other rooms, which look onto Campo San Zaccaria or a small garden, can be almost half the price and are quieter.

ALLOGGI BARBARIA Map p298   Pensione
☎ 041 522 27 50; www.alloggibarbaria.it; Calle delle Cappuccine 6573; s/d €120/150; 🚢 Ospedale
The six rooms in this cheerful *pensione* are white, bright and roomy, with tiled floors and attractive, functional furniture. It's a little out of the way up near the Fondamente Nuove, but that is part of its charm – you don't feel any of the mass tourist pressure around here. Take breakfast on the little balcony.

CA' LA CORTE Map p300   Boutique hotel
☎ 041 241 13 30; www.locandalacorte.it; Calle Bressana 6317; s/d €142/181;
🚢 Fondamente Nuove
This 16th-century house gathers around a pleasant inner *corte* (courtyard, hence the name) with its own private well. Inside, spacious rooms (some featuring *terrazzo alla veneziana* floors) with exposed ceiling beams are decorated in luxurious Venetian style. One door from the breakfast room leads right onto the Rio di San Marina… perhaps you could hail a passing gondola. Ask reception about the owners' nearby property on the corner of two canals, the **Casa Santa Maria Formosa** (Map p296; ☎ 041 241 13 00; www.casaformosa.com;

> ## TOP FIVE FOR SHEER BLOODY LUXURY
> - **Hotel Cipriani** (p213)
> - **Gritti Palace** (p195)
> - **Hotel Danieli** (p211)
> - **San Clemente Palace** (p214)
> - **Excelsior** (p213)

(Continued on page 211)

1 *Masks for sale at a street stall (p177)* 2 *Window display at one of the many dedicated mask shops in the city (p184)* 3 *Take a course in mask-making at Ca' Macana (p253)* 4 *A reveller welcomes Carnevale (p10)*

1 *Old-fashioned service at Caffè Florian (p161), Sestiere di San Marco* 2 *Doors to Harry's Bar (p162), Sestiere di San Marco* 3 *Exterior of Caffè Florian, one of the legendary cafés gracing Piazza San Marco (p163), Sestiere di San Marco* 4 *Menu board, Sestiere di San Marco (p142)*

1 *Markets are a haven for self-caterers (p142)* **2** *Tomatoes on the vine at the Rialto market (p186), San Polo* **3** *Tempting scallops at the Pescaria (p186), San Polo* **4** *Classic seafood is a feature of Venetian cuisine (p14)*

1 *Glamorous shopping options abound in Venice (p175)*
2 *Souvenirs are available to suit all budgets (p177)* 3 *Marbled-paper shop Legatoria Piazzesi (p179), Sestiere di San Marco*
4 *Lace makes an exquisite memento (p177)*

1 *Antique Burano lace (p181)*
2 *Bookstores' wares provide another angle on the city (p31)*
3 *Lace shop, Sestiere di San Marco (p179)* 4 *Glass cherries from Murano (p92)*

1 *Fishing lines hanging up to dry,
Isola di San Pietro (p135)*
2 *A visitor relaxes on a deck chair,
Lido di Venezia (p94)*
3 *View of Torcello (p93)*
4 *Mosaic detail, Cimitero (p92),
Isola di San Michele*

1 *Locals chat by the waterfront, Burano (p93)* 2 *Excelsior hotel (p213), Lido di Venezia* 3 *The cheerful colours of Burano (p93)* 4 *Grave statue, Cimitero (p92), Isola di San Michele*

1 *Doors of the Basilica del Santo (p228), Padua* 2 *Colourful house, Caorle (p242)* 3 *Graffiti-covered exterior, Casa di Giulietta (Juliet's House; p221), Verona* 4 *Roman Arena (p221), Verona*

(Continued from page 202)

Fondamenta dei Preti 5841; d €180-200; 🕭 Rialto). Skip the free Murano tours offered at the latter hotel.

HOTEL DA BRUNO Map p296   Hotel
☎ 041 523 04 52; www.hoteldabruno.it; Salizada San Lio 5726/a; s/d €160/215; 🕭 Rialto
This hotel is just west of Campo Santa Maria Formosa. The rooms are a reasonable size, bright, and decorated in standard Venetian style with painted headboards and matching furniture. The heavy drapes are a nice touch, as are furnishings such as occasional tables and writing desks.

HOTEL DANIELI Map p296   Hotel
☎ 041 522 64 80; www.starwood.com/luxury; Riva degli Schiavoni 4196; s/d from €434/690, ste €825-2648; 🕭 San Zaccaria
Most of the rooms in this Venetian classic look across the water towards the Chiesa di Santa Maria della Salute and the Chiesa di San Giorgio Maggiore. The establishment opened as a hotel in 1822 in the 14th-century Palazzo Dandolo. Just wandering into the grand foyer – all arches, sweeping staircases and balconies – is a trip through centuries of splendour. Dining in the Terrazza Danieli rooftop restaurant is a feast for the eyes and palate.

LA RESIDENZA Map p298   Hotel
☎ 041 528 53 15; www.venicelaresidenza.com; Campo Bandiera e Moro 3608; s/d €100/160; 🕭 Arsenale
If you can live without watery views, head inland to this delightful 15th-century mansion. It is also known as Palazzo Gritti-Badoer, after two of the families who have owned it. The main hall upstairs makes an impression with its candelabras, elaborate decoration and distinguished furniture. The rooms are more restrained, but fine value. The narrow street that wraps around the *palazzo* from the left side, Calle de la Morte (Street of Death), is so named because the Consiglio dei Dieci regularly had people considered a nuisance to the Republic executed here.

LOCANDA CA' DEL CONSOLE
Map p296   Boutique Hotel
☎ 041 523 31 64; www.locandacadelconsole.com; Calle Trevisana 6217; s/d €110/160; 🕭 Rialto

Ambling down this narrow side lane you would never guess that the Austrian consul lived here in the early 19th century. The front door of the building tells you little of what lies inside: eight tastefully restored rooms with period furniture from the consul's days, exposed beams, stuccowork and frescoes. All the rooms (there's only one teeny single) are quite different, and two look onto a canal. The managers also have apartments for rent.

LOCANDA REMEDIO Map p296   Hotel
☎ 041 277 05 25; www.hotelcolombina.com/remedio; Calle del Rimedio 4412; s/d €195/295; 🕭 San Zaccaria
This is indeed a remedy after the streaming masses thronging nearby Piazza San Marco. It's hard to imagine them so close to the tranquil courtyard in which this inn, now run by a nearby four-star, hides. The building belonged to the Rimedio family. In the same courtyard was a *malvasia*, a tavern where wine of the same name (ie malmsey), imported from the Venetian-controlled Greek islands, could be had. In a nice play on words, the building came to be known as *remedio* (remedy) towards the end of the 16th century – the medicinal qualities of *malvasia* were thought to ward off the plague. Try for the front double, the ceiling of which is graced with a mid-16th-century fresco.

LIASSIDI PALACE Map p298   Hotel
☎ 041 520 56 58; www.liassidipalacehotel.com; Ponte dei Greci 3405; s/d €420/490; 🕭 San Zaccaria
A fine converted Gothic palace that backs on to the Rio di San Lorenzo, this hotel is a typical Venetian mansion with a grand 1st-floor hall. The standard rooms are elegantly furnished, but the best are the suites (up to €1200). They eschew much of the typical Venetian décor, opting for more classic, modern pieces in the bedrooms, many of which are graced with dark timber beams. Two suites are adapted for the disabled.

LONDRA PALACE Map p298   Hotel
☎ 041 520 05 33; www.hotelondra.it; Riva degli Schiavoni 4171; s/d €380/585; 🕭 San Zaccaria
Most rooms in this four-star property have views over the water. They feature 19th-century period furniture, spa baths

Sleeping   **SESTIERE DI CASTELLO**

and marble bathrooms. The colour of the brocades and other decorative touches varies from one room to the next. The most expensive double is a spacious junior suite. Less expensive rooms have views over the city rather than the lagoon.

PALAZZO PRIULI Map p298   Hotel

☎ 041 277 08 34; www.hotelpriuli.com; Fondamenta dell'Osmarin 4979; d €315-335, ste €370-385; 🚇 San Zaccaria

Built in the 14th century and long the seat of the powerful Priuli family (which gave the city three Doges), Palazzo Priuli, located just over Ponte del Diavolo (the Devil's Bridge), occupies a privileged position and still oozes much of its past glory. Smallish standard rooms are elegantly decorated and have high ceilings. The best look over the canal.

PENSIONE BUCINTORO Map p298   Pensione

☎ 041 522 32 40; www.hotelbucintoro.com; Riva San Biagio 2135; s/d €94/168; 🚇 Arsenale

The big advantage of this *pensione* is that all the good-sized rooms look onto the lagoon and are well kept. It's especially handy for the Biennale and, speaking of art, was for a while home to Whistler. Some larger family rooms are available, and breakfast is served in the ground-floor dining area – snaffle a table with a view.

Cheap Sleeps

FORESTERIA VALDESE

Map p298   Religious Institution

☎ 041 528 67 97; www.diaconiavaldese.org/venezia; Palazzo Cavagnis 5170; dm €22, d €58-75; 🚇 Ospedale

This is in a rambling old mansion near Campo Santa Maria Formosa. Head east from the square on Calle Lunga Santa Maria Formosa, cross the small bridge and the Foresteria is in front of you. Double rates depend on the room and whether or not it has a bathroom. Breakfast is included. A handful of apartments for up to four people are also available. Book well ahead.

LOCANDA SANT'ANNA Map p299   Pensione

☎ 041 528 64 66; www.locandasantanna.com; Corte del Bianco 269; s/d without bathroom €60/80; d with bathroom €120; 🚇 San Pietro

Hidden away right in the east of Castello, you can't get much further from the heart of Venice and still be there! This is a real residential quarter and may appeal to some for that reason alone. Rooms are modest but comfortable, with dark timber furnishings and parquet floors. The house has a pleasant garden.

LOCANDA SILVA Map p296   Pensione

☎ 041 522 76 43; www.locandasilva.it; Fondamenta del Rimedio 4423; s/d €70/110; 🚇 San Zaccaria

A few of the rooms here, south of Campo Santa Maria Formosa, look onto a narrow canal. They are modest but well maintained and a reasonable deal in the price range. Those without bathroom come in cheaper.

AROUND THE LAGOON

From the luxury villas of the Lido and Giudecca's Cipriani to a Burano *pensione* and a rural hideaway on the little-visited island of Sant'Erasmo, there are plenty of options outside Venice that will give you a different take on the city and its lagoon setting. NOte that most Lido hotels close from December to April.

ALBERGO BELVEDERE Map pp302-3   Hotel

☎ 041 526 01 15; www.belvedere-venezia.com; Piazzale Santa Maria Elisabetta 4, Lido; s/d €168/241; 🚇 Lido

People have been staying here since 1857. Rooms are comfortable, if a little standard, but most have views across the lagoon to Venice, and you couldn't be closer to the vaporetto stop. The hotel has a private stretch of beach and offers a baby-sitting service.

ALBERGO QUATTRO FONTANE

Map pp302-3   Hotel

☎ 041 526 02 27; www.quattrofontane.com; Via Quattro Fontane 16, Lido; s/d €270/400; 📅 Apr-Nov; 🚇 Lido

With some of the feel of an Alpine chalet, this grand country house set in luxuriant gardens is a wonderful place to call home. Rooms of varying types and sizes are graced with iron bedsteads and in some cases balconies. You can dine indoors or in the gardens, which also house a tennis court.

Hotel des Bains (below), Lido di Venezia

EXCELSIOR Map pp302-3   Hotel

☎ 041 526 02 01; www.starwood.com/westin;
Lungomare Guglielmo Marconi 41, Lido; s/d from
€340/445; ☒ May-Oct; 🛉 Lido

A fanciful Moorish-style property, the
Excelsior has long been the top address
on the Lido. The Eastern theme continues
in its luxurious rooms, many of which
look out to sea or across the lagoon to
Venice. Lounge about the outdoor and
heated pools if the beach seems too far
away. The hotel boasts a range of spacious suites, too. The best rooms can cost
around €1500.

HOTEL CIPRIANI Map pp302-3   Hotel

☎ 041 520 77 44; www.hotelcipriani.it; Giudecca 10;
s €335-825, d €625-815, ste €1090-4750; 🛉 Zitelle

Occupying virtually the whole eastern
chunk of the island, this deluxe place is
set in the one-time villa of the Mocenigo
family. It's surrounded by lavish grounds
and pools, and has unbeatable lagoon
views. Rooms and suites are spread out
across several grand *palazzi*, some with
gardens, others directly on the Canale
della Giudecca. You might like to try for
a junior suite by the Olympic pool. Also
available are some self-contained apartments. Exercise fans will appreciate the
fitness centre and tennis court.

HOTEL DES BAINS Map pp302-3   Hotel

☎ 041 526 59 21; www.starwood.com/sheraton;
Lungomare Guglielmo Marconi 17, Lido; s/d
€249/299; ☒ May-Sep; 🛉 Lido

This is the top address for Thomas Mann
fans. Take a room at the tail end of the
season to enjoy the full melancholic effect.
The hotel is graced with Palladian terraces
and a turn-of-the-19th-century feel. Rooms
look out to sea or over private parkland.
Mann's character Aschenbach probably
wasn't into the sporty activities on offer
here, which range from tennis to horse
riding. If you aren't into them either, you
can choose to relax by the tree-lined pool.
Prices rise steeply if you select anything but
a standard room.

HOTEL VILLA CIPRO Map pp302-3   Hotel

☎ 041 73 15 38; www.hotelvillacipro.com; Via Zara
2, Lido; s/d €160/180; 🛉 Lido

A charming villa set in lush gardens only
a short walk from the vaporetto stop,
the Villa Cipro offers spacious, elegantly
decorated rooms, some with balconies
that overlook the charming grounds. A
highlight is taking breakfast in the leafy
courtyard. Like many of the better Lido
hotels, the Villa Cipro offers a baby-sitting
service.

GENTLY DOWN THE STREAM

Venice is surrounded by water, and yet virtually all the city's visitors remain firmly attached to dry land during their stay. There is another way. The UK company **Connoisseur Holidays Afloat** (☎ 0870 160 56 48; www.connoisseur afloat.com; The Port House, Port Solent, Portsmouth PO6 4TH) operates a fleet of cruise motorboats out of two mainland locations not far from Venice. You can hire these for a week of cruising along the River Sile (see Treviso, p236), the lagoon and the Po delta to the south of Venice. There's no need for hotels if you don't want to stay in them, and boating provides a quite different way of getting to know the city and its environs. You need to have some boating experience and can choose from a range of craft for around UK£800 to UK£2000 a week, depending on the craft and time of year. Mooring costs and the like are extra.

LOCANDA CIPRIANI

Map p304   Boutique Hotel

☎ 041 73 01 50; www.locandacipriani.com; Piazza Santa Fosca 29, Torcello; r per person €120, ½ board per person €170; ☽ closed January; 🚊 Torcello
Feel like following in Papa's footsteps? You too can stay over for a night or two in one of the six spacious, tranquil rooms at this country-lagoon getaway that found favour with Hemingway. The food is excellent, so half board is a recommended way to go. The rooms have high ceilings and feel more like studio apartments. Booking is essential.

SAN CLEMENTE PALACE Map p288   Hotel

☎ 041 244 50 01; www.sanclemente.thi.it; Isola di San Clemente; s/d €370/410, ste 600/1900
The rose-coloured buildings of the restored one-time monastery and madhouse of San Clemente make a unique setting. The hotel has 205 rooms and suites, two swimming pools, tennis courts, a golf course, conference space and wonderful gardens. The views out over the lagoon towards southern Venice and the Lido are truly romantic. A private shuttle boat runs to the hotel from the Alilaguna airport boat stop at San Zaccaria (Map p296).

VILLA MABAPA Map pp302-3   Hotel

☎ 041 526 05 90; www.villamabapa.com; Riviera San Nicolò 16, Lido; s/d €159/223-272, ste €418; 🚊 Lido
A grand old residence dating from the 1930s with a couple of annexes, the villa is well worth making an effort for. You will need to book months in advance in summer and for the cinema festival in September. Rooms are elegantly appointed in period furniture and look back across the lagoon to Venice. You can dine well in the garden.

Cheap Sleeps

HOTEL AL SOFFIADOR Map p301   Hotel

☎ 041 73 94 30; www.venicehotel.it; Calle Bressagio 10, Murano; s/d €62/105; 🚊 Faro
A simple hotel connected to a bar, this spot offers straightforward rooms a breath away from several glass factories in the busier part of the island. There's a little garden out the back.

IL LATO AZZURRO Map p288   Hotel

☎ 041 244 49 00; www.latoazzurro.it; Via Forti 13, Sant'Erasmo; s/d €50/70; 🚊 Sant'Erasmo Capannone
This is a unique and rather un-Venetian experience: sleep on the island that was traditionally Venice's market garden, Sant'Erasmo. Pleasant, spacious rooms give onto a veranda. The island still lives mostly from small-scale agriculture and if you choose to eat here you will be presented with a largely vegetarian menu of home-grown products. Staff will also make you a packed lunch for your excursions on the island or into Venice. The place has a very alternative bent and organises everything from bike rides to gay and lesbian holidays in August. Bring your mosquito repellent.

LOCANDA AL RASPO DE UA

Map p304   Locanda

☎ 041 73 00 95; Via Galuppi 560, Burano; s/d €45/80; 🚊 Burano
This modest *locanda* on Burano's main drag is the only hotel on the island and could make your Venetian visit a quite different experience. After the last of the tourists head back to Venice at night, it's just you and the locals on this pretty pastel islet.

LOCANDA CONTERIE Map p301   Locanda
☎ 041 527 50 03; www.locandaconterie.com;
Calle Conterie 12, Murano; s/d €75/100; 🚇 Museo
A bright, renovated two-storey house in a
narrow lane running inland from Campo
San Donato could make the perfect hideaway if you crave the peace of a lagoon
island that pretty much empties of tourists
at night. The intermittent night-vaporetto
service means you're not completely cut
off. Rose and white Venetian décor dominates the crisp, pleasant rooms.

OSTELLO VENEZIA Map pp302-3   Hostel
☎ 041 523 82 11; fax 041 523 56 89; Fondamenta
della Croce 86, Giudecca; dm incl breakfast €18.50;
🕑 check-in 1.30-11.30pm; 🚇 Zitelle
This Hostelling International (HI) property is
open to members only, but you can buy a
card there. Evening meals are available for
€9, and there are family rooms. The hostel,
which is a reasonable example of the genre
and a good place to meet other budget
travellers, is on HI's computerised International Booking Network (www.hostelbooking
.com), so you can book online.

PENSIONE LA PERGOLA
Map pp302-3   Pensione
☎ 041 526 07 84; Via Cipro 15, Lido; s/d without
bathroom €40/65, d with bathroom €85; 🚇 Lido
This homy *pensione*, just off Gran Viale
Santa Maria Elisabetta, is an excellent
budget deal if you want to base yourself
near the beach and make the trip into
Venice when it suits you. The rooms are
simple but pleasant.

RESIDENZA JUNGHANS
Map pp302-3   Hostel
☎ 041 521 08 01; www.residenzajunghans.com,
in Italian; Terzo Ramo della Palada 394, Giudecca;
s/d €35/60; 🚇 Palanca
A Spartan but spotless student-style residence with room for more than 90 people
in singles and doubles, the Junghans is
nicely located midway along the island of
Giudecca. The site was once occupied by
factories and warehouses, and part of the
brand-new residence is used by university
students.

THE MAINLAND
Only 10 to 15 minutes away on city bus Nos
2 and 7 (the former passes Mestre train station) or by train, Mestre is a drab, if sometimes necessary, alternative to staying in
Venice. There are a number of good hotels,
as well as plenty of cafés and places to eat
around the main square.

HOTEL TRITONE Map p305   Hotel
☎ 041 538 31 25; www.httritone.com; Viale
Stazione 16; s/d €160/180; train
This is comfortable in a could-be-anywhere
style and has the obvious advantage
of being right by the station – ideal for

A DOGEY DEATH

When Doge Vitale Michiel returned to Venice with the sorry remains of his fleet in May 1172, he must have known things
weren't going to go well for him. He had set off in the previous September with a war fleet of 120 vessels to avenge
assaults on Venetians carried out in Constantinople. Unfortunately, he decided to agree to talks.

While his negotiators got bogged down in ultimately fruitless chitchat, his idle fleet at the Greek island of Chios
collapsed as plague broke out. By the time it had become clear that Constantinople had no intention of continuing
serious negotiations, the fleet was in no condition to fight. And so Michiel had little alternative but to go home –
taking the plague with him.

Sensing the mounting anger as he gave his sorry report in the Palazzo Ducale, he realised he would have to flee. He
didn't get far. Scampering east along the Riva degli Schiavoni, he was met by the mob and killed. (A conflicting version
of events says Michiel was on his way to the Chiesa di San Zaccaria for Mass when he was struck down.)

When things had settled, the city's leaders searched for, tried and executed the assassin. If anyone was going
to do the killing around here, it was the State. The man's house was found to be at Calle delle Rasse, virtually
next to the spot where Michiel met his end, and was flattened. It was decreed that no building of stone should
be raised on the site.

The decree was respected until 1948. When it was finally repealed, the silent vacuum of reproach was filled with the
rather Mussolini-esque expansion of the Hotel Danieli, an ugly sister that sits uncomfortably beside Palazzo Dandolo,
the hotel's magnificent main home.

quick getaways to the lagoon. Rooms are frequently sold for considerably less than the advertised high-season prices. Several similarly anonymous three- and four-stars line this train-station street.

HOTEL VIVIT Map p305   Hotel

☎ 041 95 13 85; www.hotelvivit.com; Piazza Ferretto 75; s/d €76.50/102.50; bus 2 & 7
In the heart of Mestre's central, lively pedestrianised square, this hotel is housed in a cumbersome-looking *palazzo* dating to the early 1900s. Comfortable rooms with parquet floors and crisp, clean bathrooms are pleasant enough, and the buffet breakfast isn't bad. If you have to be in Mestre, this is about as atmospheric a spot as you will find.

Cheap Sleeps

HOTEL MONTE PIANA Map p305   Hotel

☎ 041 92 62 42; www.hotelmontepiana.it, in Italian; Via Monte San Michele 17; d €90; train
This is a quiet, family-run hotel in a residential street only a few hundred metres from the station. For what you pay, the 20 rooms are surprisingly sparkling and spacious. Breakfast is extra.

Excursions ■

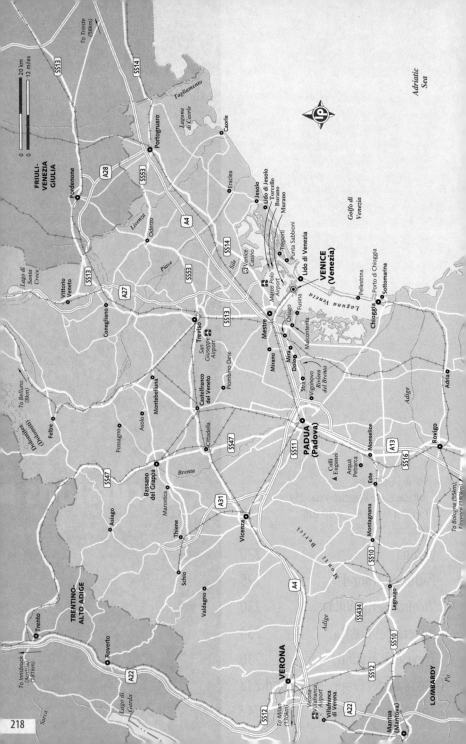

Excursions

For centuries the proud flag of the lion of St Mark fluttered over the cities and towns of most of northeast Italy. At its core is the region today known as the Veneto – a land of plains country in the south, and mountains (great walking territory) on its northern boundary.

Water, as always in the story of Venice, also plays its part. The western extremity of the region is shut off by one of Italy's great northern lakes, Lago di Garda, while to the north and south of La Serenissima stretch the beaches of the Adriatic. The region's southern boundary is marked by the country's mightiest river, the Po, which empties into the Adriatic here after its long passage across northern Italy.

Long before Venice swallowed up the territory in the early 15th century, it was divided into a series of competing city-states, the most important of which were Padua, Vicenza and Verona. The mark of the lion is unmistakable in all, but each has retained its own distinct character.

An abundance of other towns, rarely more than a couple of hours away from Venice, will also draw the curious traveller, from the riverside medieval core of Treviso to the heart of grappa country, Bassano, and the hilltop eyrie of Asolo.

In between the towns rise the proud mansions and villas of Venice's once-wealthy noble families, particularly along the River Brenta and around Vicenza.

THE BIG CITIES

The most striking attractions beyond Venice lie conveniently strung out along the main east–west railway line. First stop is Padua (p225), a busy university town 37km away and still partly protected by its old city walls. Known to some as the city of St Anthony and to others as a fine-arts shrine because of Giotto's remarkable frescoes, it is a dynamic place with a surprisingly extensive medieval core.

Next up on the trail is Vicenza (p230), a quieter town 32km northwest of Padua. Its compact old centre is a palette of Palladian wonders, ranging from the grand Basilica Palladiana through numerous private mansions (including the much-aped La Rotonda) to the delightful Teatro Olimpico.

Another 51km brings you to Verona (p220), the prettiest of the trio. The star attraction is the grand Roman arena, but romantics also come on a Shakespearean quest to seek out reminders of his heart-breaking heroes, Romeo and Juliet. Beautifully sited on the River Adige, the city has much to offer and, although only about two hours out of Venice by train, might tempt you to stay longer than a day.

PALLADIO & THE VENETIAN VILLAS

As wealthy Venetian families turned their sights away from the sea and towards the land, so by the age of Palladio they had come to invest in fine country residences. These Venetian villas, in particular those clustered along the River Brenta (p234) and around Vicenza (p230), provide a remarkable insight into the lives of the lagoon city's aristocrats in a bygone era. Many remain private property but throw open their doors to the masses at certain times. Some are more worth your while than others. While you could spend a day or two touring the villas of the Brenta, you can also be choosy. Keep an eye out for Palladio's Villa Foscari (p234) and the sprawling gardens of the magnificent Villa Pisani (p235).

Part Two of the Venetian Villa escapade takes you to Vicenza (p230). The city itself boasts several mansions by Palladio and others, but those with a passion for villas and a set of wheels can tour the surrounding countryside in search of still more.

FORTIFIED TOWNS &...WINE

In between the grand medieval cities are scattered all sorts of minor gems that are perfect for a day or two's exploration. Several possible circuits suggest themselves, and you can reach many of these places without your own transport.

Just 30km northwest of Venice is a gem often overlooked even by those whose Ryanair flights take them to within a whisker of the place – Treviso (p236). The 'City of Water', as locals like to think of the place, is a surprisingly charming stop whose old centre nestles in between the River Sile and Canal Cagnan, featuring old water mills and leafy corners. To the north and northeast of Treviso is a trio of delightful little towns: Oderzo (a miniature version of Treviso, p237), Conegliano (the wine capital of the Veneto, p237) and Vittorio Veneto (p237). You could pop into the last two on your way north to Belluno (see p239).

West of Treviso, a railway line proceeds to the curious walled town of Castelfranco del Veneto (p240) and on to its more impressive neighbour, Cittadella (p240), before heading to pretty Bassano (p238). Every attempt should be made to reach the nearby hill town of Asolo (p239).

South of Padua is another string of engaging fortified towns: Monselice, Este and the most striking of all, Montagnana (p228).

BEACHES

Although the Adriatic is not the most splendid of Mediterranean coastlines, it does provide a viable summertime escape from the humidity of the Venetian lagoon. Of course, you could always head for the beaches of the Lido di Venezia, but for better beaches you need to head further out of town. One option is Sottomarina, at Chioggia, to the south (see p98). To the northeast of Venice lie the beaches of Lido di Jesolo (p242). You can reach their southern strips by taking the ferry to Punta Sabbioni, or drive around to Lido di Jesolo itself. This is the most popular of the Veneto's sunshine spots, with sandy beaches, reasonably clear water and a fairly busy summer clubbing scene. Further to the northeast, Caorle (p242) is a pleasant seaside fishing town with a good deal more history than its brasher neighbour.

VERONA

Stroll arm in arm with your loved one along the quiet streets of Verona (population 256,000) on a winter's night and you could be forgiven for believing the tragic love story of Romeo and Juliet to be true. Well it ain't, but not to worry – Verona is one of Italy's most beautiful cities (the whole place is a Unesco World Heritage site) and hardly in need of Shakespearean hyperbole.

TRANSPORT

Distance from Venice 120km

Direction West

Air The **Verona-Villafranca airport** (☎ 045 809 56 66) is 12km outside town and accessible by bus from the train station (€4.50, 15 minutes, departures every 20 minutes from 6am to 11pm). Flights arrive here from all over Italy and some European cities, including Amsterdam, Barcelona, Berlin, Brussels, London and Paris. Ryanair flies in from several cities to Brescia, to the west. Airport buses connect the train station with Brescia airport (one way/return €11/16, one hour).

Bus The main intercity bus station is in front of the train station, in an area known as Porta Nuova. Buses are generally useful only for provincial localities not served by train. The AMT city transport company's bus Nos 11, 12, 13 and 14 (bus No 91 or 92 on Sunday and holidays) connect the train station with Piazza Brà. Tickets (on sale at tobacco stores and newsstands) cost €1.

Car Verona is at the intersection of the Serenissima A4 (Milan–Venice) and Brennero A22 autostrade. From Venice you can be there in not much more than an hour.

Train The trip from Venice is easiest by train (€6.10 to €12.65; 1¼ to 2¼ hours).

Casa di Giulietta (Juliet's House; below), Verona

Known as *piccola Roma* (little Rome) for its importance in the days of the Roman Empire, its golden era came during the 13th and 14th centuries under the colourful, roller-coaster reign of the Della Scala family (aka the Scaligeri). The period was indeed noted for the savage family feuding to which ol' Will alluded in his play.

On Monday a lot of sights are closed, or open in the afternoon only. The **Verona Card** (adult for 1/3 days €8/12), available from the sights, tobacco outlets, the train-station tourist office and the Western Union office at the airport, gains you admission to all the main monuments and churches, and reduced admission to a few places of lesser importance. The card also gives you unlimited use of the town's local buses.

For many, the heart of Verona is its pink-marble 1st-century **Roman Arena** in the bustling Piazza Brà. Once the scene of gladiatorial spectacles, it now stages a rather less blood-curdling annual open-air opera season. The third-largest Roman amphitheatre in existence, it could seat around 20,000 people. It is remarkably well preserved, despite a 12th-century earthquake that destroyed most of its outer wall.

Just off Via Giuseppe Mazzini, central Verona's main shopping street, is the **Casa di Giulietta** (Juliet's House). Romeo and Juliet may have been fictional, but here you can swoon beneath what popular myth says was her balcony or, if in need of a new lover, approach a bronze statue of Juliet and rub her right breast for good luck. Others have made their

Excursions

VERONA

MUCH ADO ABOUT NOTHING...

Over the decades lovers, star-crossed and otherwise, have indulged in the custom of scribbling their amorous declarations on to the walls of Juliet's supposed medieval residence and, since 2003, using chewing gum to post messages on paper (the result is seriously nauseating). Sick of the mess, Verona's town council declared an end to these mucky customs in late 2004, promising that the amorous graffiti artists would one day be able to post their messages, via the Internet and SMS, on an electronic bulletin board. In the meantime, space for writing messages has been set aside in the short tunnel giving access to the courtyard. None of this seems to have restrained the romantic gum-chewers' ardour, however.

It was not the first time the town fathers had taken a hand in the fate of the building. As far back as the early 19th century, curious travellers were turning up in Verona to see the house of a person who had never existed. Charles Dickens was one of a line-up of European writers to set eyes on what was long a rundown inn and, later, stables. In 1905 it was put up for sale and, under a wave of media pressure, the Verona town council bought it. Thirty years later the council did the house up, giving an essentially 17th-century structure its rather forced Gothic flavour. It is thought the famous balcony was assembled, of all things, of the sides of a medieval sarcophagus. So much for the romanticism!

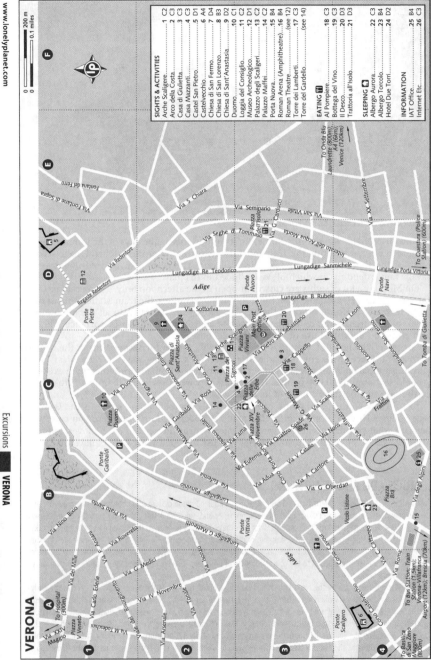

VERONA

0   200 m
0   0.1 miles

To Orda Blu
Laundrette (800m);
A4 (6km);
Venice (120km)

eternal mark by adding to the slew of scribbled love graffiti on the courtyard walls (see Much Ado About Nothing, p221). It is, by the way, doubtful there ever was a feud between the Cappello and Montecchi families, on whom Shakespeare based the play. If the theme excites you sufficiently, you could also search out the **Tomba di Giulietta** (Juliet's Tomb), whose museum contains frescoes transferred from sites across Verona and a collection of 1st-century Roman amphorae.

On the site of the Roman forum, Piazza delle Erbe remains the lively heart of the city. The permanent market stalls in its centre lend the square an agreeable bustling air, although they detract a little from its beauty – it's lined with some of Verona's most sumptuous buildings, including the baroque **Palazzo Maffei**, at the northern end, with the adjoining 14th-century **Torre del Gardello**. On the eastern side the fresco-adorned façade of **Casa Mazzanti**, a former Della Scala family residence, stands out.

Separating Piazza delle Erbe from Piazza dei Signori is the **Arco della Costa**, beneath which is suspended what is said to be a whale's rib. One legend (there are several) says it will fall on the first 'just' person to walk beneath it. In several centuries it has never fallen, not even on the various popes who have paraded beneath it. Ascend the nearby 12th-century **Torre dei Lamberti** for a great view of the city. The building of which the tower is a part, Palazzo della Ragione, is destined to become a major exhibition centre.

Occupying the north side of Piazza dei Signori is the 15th-century **Loggia del Consiglio**, the former city council building and Verona's finest Renaissance structure. It is attached to the **Palazzo degli Scaligeri**, once the main residence of the Della Scala clan. Through the archway at the far end of the piazza are the **Arche Scaligere**, the elaborate family tombs of what was Verona's most illustrious, although often bloodthirsty, ruling family, prior to Verona's submission to Venice's less flamboyant (and more peaceful) rule. You can see the tombs quite well from the outside, but a combined ticket for these and the Torre dei Lamberti allows you to wander in.

North from the Arche Scaligere stands the Gothic **Chiesa di Sant'Anastasia**, started in 1290 but not completed until the late 15th century. A long parade of fine canvases is capped by a Pisanello fresco, in the sacristy, of *San Giorgio che Parte per Liberare la Donzella dal Drago* (St George Setting out to Free the Princess from the Dragon).

The 12th-century **Duomo** (Cathedral) combines Romanesque (lower half) and Gothic (upper half) styles and has some intriguing features. Look for the sculpture of Jonah and the whale on the south porch and the statues of two of Charlemagne's paladins, Roland and Oliver, on the west porch. In the first chapel of the left aisle is an *Assunta* (Assumption) by Titian.

At the river end of Via Leoni, **Chiesa di San Fermo** is actually two churches in one. The Gothic church was built in the 13th century over the original 11th-century Romanesque structure. Southwest from Piazza delle Erbe towards the Ponte Scaligero is the **Chiesa di San Lorenzo**, a Romanesque church raised in the early 12th century but much altered with Gothic and Renaissance additions.

On the banks of the Adige, the 14th-century **Castelvecchio** fortress was raised by Cangrande II (of the Scaligeri family), little loved by the townspeople and anxious to protect himself against threats from home and abroad. Having gone to all that trouble, he was stabbed to death by his charming brother Canfrancesco inside the fortress walls. The restored fortress houses a museum with a diverse collection of paintings, frescoes, jewellery and medieval artefacts. Among the paintings are works by Pisanello, Giovanni Bellini, Tiepolo, Carpaccio and Veronese. Also of note is a 14th-century equestrian statue of Cangrande I, the fortress-builder's ancestor and most illustrious of the Della Scala clan. The **Ponte Scaligero** spanning the Adige was also rebuilt after being destroyed by WWII bombing.

A masterpiece of Romanesque architecture, the **Basilica di San Zeno Maggiore** (named in honour of the city's patron saint) was built mainly in the 12th century, although its apse was rebuilt in the 14th century and its bell tower, a relic of an earlier structure on the site, was started in 1045. The basilica's magnificent rose window depicts the wheel of fortune, which had a habit of turning good and bad for Verona's rulers with dizzying rapidity. On either side of the main doors are sculpted scenes from the two Testaments.

Inside you pass by the graceful cloister into the church proper. It is a feast for the eyes, with an array of striking frescoes still in place – they range from the 12th to the 15th century. Approach those on the right after the steps that lead past the crypt and have a close look.

They are festooned with graffiti, some dating as far back as 1390 and one to…1998! Down in the crypt the robed remains of St Zeno are eerily lit up in his transparent sarcophagus. Artistically, the highlight is Mantegna's *Maestà della Vergine* (The Majesty of the Virgin Mary), above the high altar.

Across Ponte Pietra, north of the city centre, is a **Roman theatre**, built in the 1st century. Take the lift at the back of the theatre to the convent above, which houses an interesting collection of Greek and Roman pieces in the **Museo Archeologico**. On a hill high behind the theatre and museum is the **Castel San Pietro**, built by the Austrians on the site of an earlier castle.

Information

Guardia Medica (☎ 045 807 56 27; ◷ 8pm-8am) A locum doctor service – they usually come to you.

IAT Aeroporto office (☎ 045 861 91 63; Verona-Villafranca airport; ◷ 9am-6pm Mon-Sat May-Aug, 11am-5pm Mon-Sat Sep-Apr)

IAT Ferrovia office (☎ 045 800 08 61; train station; ◷ 9am-6pm Mon-Sat, 9am-3pm Sun)

IAT Verona office (☎ 045 806 86 80; www.tourism.verona .it; Via degli Alpini 9; ◷ 9am-7pm Mon-Sat, 9am-3pm Sun)

Internet Etc (☎ 045 800 02 22; Via Quattro Spade 3/b; per hr €5.50; ◷ 2.30-8pm Mon, 10.30am-8pm Tue-Sat)

Main post office (Piazza Viviani 7; ◷ 8.30am-6.30pm Mon-Sat)

Onda Blu laundrette (Via XX Settembre 62/a; ◷ 8am-10pm)

Ospedale Civile Maggiore (Hospital; ☎ 045 807 11 11; Piazza A Stefani 1)

Questura (Police Station; ☎ 045 809 04 11; Lungadige Galtarossa 11)

Sights

Arche Scaligere (Via Arche Scaligere; combined admission with Torre dei Lamberti by lift/on foot €4/3; ◷ 9.30am-7.30pm Tue-Sun, 1.45pm-7.30pm Mon Jun-Sep)

Basilica di San Zeno Maggiore (Piazza San Zeno; admission €2, or combined ticket for all churches €5; ◷ 8.30am-6pm Mon-Sat, 9am-12.30pm & 1.30-6pm Sun Mar-Oct, 8.30am-1pm & 1.30-5pm Tue-Sat, 9am-12.30pm & 1.40-5pm Sun, 8.30am-midnight & 3-5pm Mon Nov-Feb)

Casa di Giulietta (Juliet's House; ☎ 045 803 43 03; Via Cappello 23; adult/student/child €4/3/1; ◷ 8.30am-7.30pm Tue-Sun, 1.45-7.30pm Mon)

Castelvecchio (☎ 045 806 26 11; Corso Castelvecchio 2; adult/student/child €4/3/1; ◷ 8.30am-7.30pm Tue-Sun)

Chiesa di San Fermo (Stradone San Fermo; admission €2, or combined ticket for all churches €5; ◷ 10am-6pm Mon-Sat, 1-6pm Sun)

Chiesa di San Lorenzo (Corso Cavour; admission €2, or combined ticket for all churches €5; ◷ 10am-6pm Mon-Sat, 1-6pm Sun)

Chiesa di Sant'Anastasia (Piazza di Sant'Anastasia; admission €2, or combined ticket for all churches €5; ◷ 9am-6pm Mon-Sat, 1-6pm Sun)

Duomo (Cathedral; Piazza Duomo; admission €2, or combined ticket for all churches €5; ◷ 10am-5.30pm Mon-Sat, 1.30-5.30pm Sun)

Museo Archeologico (☎ 045 800 03 60; Regaste Redentore 2; adult/child €2.60/1.50; ◷ 8.30am-7.30pm Tue-Sun, 1.45-7.30pm Mon)

Roman Arena (☎ 045 800 32 04, opera bookings ☎ 045 800 51 11; www.arena.it; Piazza Brà; adult/child €3.10/2.10; ◷ 9am-7pm Tue-Sun, 1.45-7.30pm Mon Oct-Jun, 8am-3.30pm opera season Jul-Sep) This is not just an ancient site but also the magnificent setting for Verona's summer open-air opera season.

Tomba di Giulietta (Juliet's Tomb; ☎ 045 800 03 61; Via del Pontiere 35; adult/child €2.60/1.50; ◷ 8.30am-7.30pm Tue-Sun, 1.45-7.30pm Mon)

Torre dei Lamberti (☎ 045 803 27 26; Piazza dei Signori; admission by lift/on foot €3/2, combined admission with Arche Scaligere €4/3; ◷ 9am-7.30pm Tue-Sun, 1.30-7.30pm Mon)

Eating

Al Pompiere (☎ 045 803 05 37; Vicolo Regina d'Ungheria 5; meals €35; ◷ lunch Tue-Sat, dinner Mon-Sat) The fireman's (*pompiere*) hat is still on the wall, along with a host of B&W photos from down the years. On display is a rich assortment of cheeses that you can try before tucking into, say, a plate of *bigoli con le sarde* (chunky spaghetti with sardines) followed by some hearty *pastissada de caval*, a horsemeat dish typical of Verona.

Bottega del Vino (☎ 045 800 45 35; Vicolo Scudo di Francia 3/a; meals €50; ◷ lunch & dinner Wed-Mon) At least wander into this age-old wine cellar for the frescoes and atmosphere. Better still, sit down to fine food, an endless wine list and exquisite service.

Il Desco (☎ 045 801 00 15; Via Dietro San Sebastiano 7; meals €120-150; ◷ lunch Tue-Sun, dinner Tue-Sat) Rated one of the best restaurants in Italy and a Michelin star winner, this is a quietly elegant stop for high-class local cuisine.

Trattoria all'Isolo (☎ 045 59 42 91; Piazza dell'Isolo 5/a; meals €25-30; ☯ lunch & dinner Thu-Tue) Scoot across the river to find yourself in what feels like a more genuine Verona. Much the same can be said of this tiny eatery. Mostly chunky meat dishes dominate the menu, after a raft of pasta options (*bigoli* is big here, too).

Sleeping

Albergo Aurora (☎ 045 59 47 17; www.hotelaurora.biz; Piazza XIV Novembre 2; s/d up to €116/158) The better rooms in this sprawling, central hotel are spacious and comfortable, and many have been given a bit of sprucing up. The terrace is a pleasant spot for a drink and a little sun.

Albergo Torcolo (☎ 045 800 38 71; www.hoteltorcolo.it; Vicolo Listone 3; s/d €75/108) A quiet little building barely 50m off Piazza Brà, this spot has a variety of rooms. Some of the most attractive feature wrought-iron bed heads and timber ceiling beams.

Hotel Due Torri (☎ 045 59 50 44; www.baglionihotels .com; Piazza di Sant'Anastasia 4; s/d up to €420/550) The Hotel Due Torri is Verona's top address: a grand old mansion where the ambience takes you back to a long-abandoned era of slightly stuffy, studied elegance.

PADUA & AROUND

To the pious Catholic faithful, the student city of Padua (known as Padova to the locals, population 206,000) is a place of pilgrimage, the city of the heavenly lost-and-found agent, St Anthony. Art-lovers also take the pilgrim path, anxious to behold the exquisite and precocious frescoes of master Giotto. Pilgrims to the latter are rather more numerous than those to the former, and Giotto's creations alone are worth the effort to get here. But the old city core, with its arcaded streets and grand squares, is replete with jewels awaiting exploration.

As long ago as the 6th century BC the Veneti tribe had an important centre here, later known as Patavium under the Romans. The Lombards made short work of the place in 602, virtually razing it. The comeback was slow, but by the 13th century, when it was controlled by the querulous counts of Carrara, Padua was a burgeoning independent city-state. The Carrara counts encouraged cultural and artistic pursuits (when they weren't busy warring with all and sundry), and established the Studium, the forerunner of the university, in 1222. The foundation of the Basilica del Santo, dedicated to St Anthony, followed 10 years later. Venice put an end to the Carrara counts' passion for conquest when the Republic incorporated Padua into its growing land empire in 1405.

A five-minute walk south along Corso del Popolo (which later becomes Corso di Garibaldi and leads into the city centre) from the train station brings you to the **Cappella degli Scrovegni** in the Giardini dell'Arena. Enrico Scrovegni commissioned its construction in 1303 as a resting place for his father. Giotto's fresco cycle, probably completed by 1306, illustrates the lives of Mary and Christ and is arranged in three bands. Among the most celebrated scenes in the cycle is the *Bacio di Giuda* (Kiss of Judas). The series ends with the *Ultima Cena* (Last Supper) on the entrance wall, and the Vices and Virtues are depicted around the lower parts of the walls.

TRANSPORT

Distance from Venice Padua 37km; Arquà Petrarca 59km; Monselice 59km; Este 68km; Montagnana 83.5km **Direction** West

Bus Regular **SITA** buses (☎ 049 820 68 44) from Venice (€2.90, 45 to 60 minutes) arrive at Padua's Piazzale Boschetti, 400m south of the train station. Local ACAP bus No 10 will get you to Piazza Cavour from the train station, while No 12 goes to Prato della Valle, south of the city centre. Buy tickets (85c) at tobacconists and stamp them in the machines on the bus. To get to Arquà Petrarca you can take one of up to three daily buses (€2.35, 55 minutes) that run through here between Padua and Este. Tickets purchased on the bus itself cost about 30% extra.

Car The A4 connects Venice and Padua. The A13, which connects Padua with Bologna, starts at the southern edge of Padua. The two autostrade are connected by a ring road. Follow the SS16 south of Padua for Monselice and Arquà Petrarca, then branch west on the SS10 for Este and Montagnana.

Train The easiest way to Padua from Venice is by train (€2.50 to €8.95, 30 to 40 minutes). There's little to be gained from catching faster, more expensive trains on this short stretch. Trains run from Padua to Montagnana (€3, 50 to 60 minutes) via Monselice and Este. The trip takes longer if you have to change in Monselice.

PADUA (PADOVA)

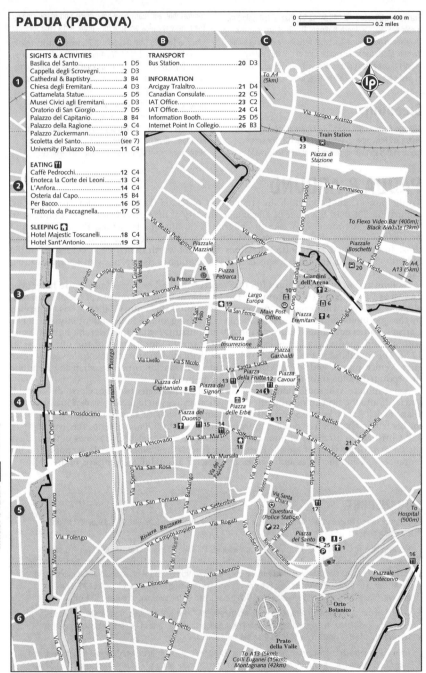

Gattamelata equestrian statue outside the Basilica del Santo (Basilica di Sant'Antonio; p228), Padua

Keep in mind when the frescoes were painted – Giotto was moving well away from the two-dimensional figures of his medieval contemporaries. Giotto effectively was on the cusp between Gothic art and the remarkable explosion of new creativity that was still decades away – the Renaissance.

You will be rushed through the chapel, but a new multimedia attraction on the site, allowing visitors to plunge into Giotto's era and learn more about his art, goes some way towards making up for this. Booking is obligatory.

The admission ticket is also valid for the adjacent **Musei Civici agli Eremitani**, whose broad collection of 14th- to 18th-century Veneto art and largely forgettable archaeological artefacts includes a remarkable crucifix by Giotto. On the same ticket you can visit the nearby early-20th-century **Palazzo Zuckermann**, home to the **Museo d'Arti Applicate e Decorative** on the ground and 1st floors and the **Museo Bottacin** on the 2nd. The former is a rich and varied collection with everything from fine antique furniture to 17th-century clothes, from ceramics to silverware, all spanning the Middle Ages to the late 19th century. The Museo Bottacin holds a private collection of art and coins donated to the city in 1865.

A few steps from the Cappella degli Scrovegni stands the early-14th-century **Chiesa degli Eremitani**, an Augustinian church painstakingly rebuilt after being almost totally demolished by bombing in WWII. The remains of frescoes done by Andrea Mantegna during his 20s are displayed in a chapel to the left of the apse. Most were wiped out in the bombing, the greatest single loss to Italian art during the war. The *Martirio di San Jacopo* (Martyrdom of St James), on the left, was pieced together from fragments found in the rubble, while the *Martirio di San Cristoforo* (Martyrdom of St Christopher), opposite, had been removed before the war.

Corso di Garibaldi spills into the like-named piazza, the first of a series of interlocking squares in the heart of Padua. You might want to stop for a coffee in **Caffè Pedrocchi**, just off Via VIII Febbraio on a little square adjoining Piazza Cavour. It has long been *the* central café in Padua. During the day you can visit the **Museo del Risorgimento e dell'Età Contemporanea** on the grand 1st floor. The succession of rooms created in the first half of the 19th century sweeps in style from ancient Egyptian to Imperial. The museum recounts local and national history in documents, images and mementos, from the fall of Venice in 1797 until the republican constitution of 1848.

About 100m down Via VIII Febbraio is the **university**, the main part of which is housed in **Palazzo Bò** ('ox' in Veneto dialect – it's named after an inn that previously occupied the site). Established in 1222, the university is Italy's oldest after the one in Bologna. Europe's first anatomy theatre opened here in 1594, and Galileo Galilei taught at the university from 1592 to 1610. The main courtyard and its halls are plastered with coats of arms of the great and learned from across Europe.

Excursions

PADUA & AROUND

227

Turn back about 100m to the west and you wander into the contiguous Piazza delle Erbe and Piazza della Frutta. These 'herbs' and 'fruit' squares still live up to their names, with boisterous produce markets setting up daily. The squares are also lined by a cornucopia of shops selling all sorts of delicacies, interrupted by the occasional bar where shoppers and market workers can take a liquid break from the buying and selling.

The two squares are separated by the majestic hulk of the **Palazzo della Ragione**, also known as the Salone for the grand hall that occupies its upper floor. Built in the 13th and 14th centuries, the building features frescoes by Giusto de' Menabuoi and Nicolò Mireto depicting the astrological theories of Pietro d'Abano. It is frequently the scene of temporary exhibitions.

West from here is the Piazza dei Signori, dominated by the 14th-century **Palazzo del Capitanio**, the former residence of the city's Venetian ruler. South is the **cathedral**, built from a much-altered design by Michelangelo. Its 13th-century Romanesque **baptistry** features a series of frescoes of Old and New Testament scenes by Giusto de' Menabuoi, influenced by Giotto.

From Piazza del Duomo return to Piazza delle Erbe and head east along Via San Francesco. When you hit Via del Santo, turn south (right) and you will soon emerge in the grand square of the same name, dominated by the city's most celebrated monument, the **Basilica del Santo** (or Basilica di Sant'Antonio), which houses the corpse of the town's patron saint and is an important place of pilgrimage. Construction of what is known to the people of Padua as Il Santo began in 1232. The saint's tomb, bedecked by requests for his intercession to cure illness or thanks for his having done so, is in the Cappella del Santo, in the left transept.

Florentine Donatello was responsible for the **Gattamelata equestrian statue** that presides over the centre of Piazza del Santo. This magnificent representation of the 15th-century Venetian *condottiero* (mercenary leader) Erasmos da Narni was done in 1453 and is considered the first great bronze of the Italian Renaissance. Erasmos' nickname, Gattamelata, translates as Honeyed Cat, apparently because he was as smooth as honey and as crafty as a cat.

On the southern side of the piazza is the **Oratorio di San Giorgio**, the burial chapel of the Lupi di Soranga family, with 14th-century frescoes. Next door is the **Scoletta del Santo**, with works believed to be by Titian.

Just south of Piazza del Santo is the **Orto Botanico**, a Unesco World Heritage site. Purportedly the oldest botanical garden in Europe, it was first laid out in 1545.

Southwest of Padua, along the A13 or the SS16, the **Colli Euganei** (Euganean Hills) are dotted with vineyards, good walking trails and the popular spa towns of Abano Terme and Montegrotto Terme – ask at a Padua IAT office for information.

The quiet, hilly, medieval village of **Arquà Petrarca** in the southern Colli Euganei was where Italy's great poet Petrarch (Petrarca, 1304–74) chose to spend the last five years of his life. You can visit his **house**, which is set in cheerful gardens and contains various bits and bobs that purportedly had something to do with the scribe.

Monselice, on the train line south from Padua, was once wrapped in five protective layers of fortifications. Only bits of the old walls remain, along with the tower of the Rocca, or hilltop fort. The main point of interest here is the 11th-century **castle**, actually a complex collection of buildings raised over several centuries. The oldest part of the site, the Castelletto, is what remains of the original fort. The grand Torre di Ezzelino is a 13th-century tower. By the time the 15th-century Palazzo Marcello was built, the castle had lost its defensive character.

West of Monselice along the road to Mantua (Mantova), **Este** is another in the chain of fortified strongholds in the area. Padua's Carrara clan members were assiduous fortress builders – it seems they had a

FROM PORTUGAL TO PADUA

St Anthony of Padua (1193–1232) was actually St Anthony of Portugal, where he was born (in Lisbon) and spent most of his life. His wanderings began at the age of 25, when he joined the Franciscans and headed for Morocco to preach among the Muslims. This could easily have proven little more than a suicide mission, but before he had the chance to become a martyr, poor health brought him back to Europe, where he spent the ensuing years travelling and teaching in the less hostile environment of France and northern Italy. He earned great respect for his erudition and capacity to preach to the learned as convincingly as to more simple folk. St Anthony died in Padua, and the shrine built to him became a prime centre of pilgrimage. To this day countless miracles are attributed to him, as well as a knack for being the finder of lost articles.

good number of enemies to keep at bay. Although the walls of their castle are in reasonable condition, the inside is pretty much a ruin. On the bumpy lane that climbs northwards behind the castle is the **Villa Kunkler**, where Byron and Shelley spent time.

About 12km west of Este rise the magnificent defensive perimeter walls, dating to the 13th and 14th centuries, of the fortified plains town of **Montagnana**. Its 2km of impressive crenellated walls are studded by 24 defensive towers and four gates.

Information

Complesso Clinico Ospedaliero (Hospital; ☎ 049 821 11 11; Via Giustiniani 1, Padua)

IAT office (☎ 049 875 20 77; www.turismopadova.it; train station, Padua; ⏰ 9am-7pm Mon-Sat, 9am-noon Sun)

IAT office (☎ 049 876 79 27; Vicolo Pedrocchi, Padua; ⏰ 9am-1.30pm & 3-7pm Mon-Sat)

Information booth (☎ 049 875 30 87; Piazza del Santo, Padua; ⏰ variable Mar-Oct)

Internet Point In Collegio (☎ 049 65 84 84; Via Petrarca 9, Padua; membership €2, first hr €6, subsequent hr €3; ⏰ 10am-2am Mon-Fri, 4-8pm Sat, 2-8pm Sun) Take along ID to acquire the membership card.

Main post office (Corso Garibaldi 25, Padua; ⏰ 8.30am-6.30pm Mon-Sat)

Padova Card (€14; valid 48 hr) A pass that allows you to visit the Cappella degli Scrovegni (plus €1 booking fee), the Musei Civici agli Eremitani, the Palazzo della Ragione, the Museo del Risorgimento e dell'Età Contemporanea at Caffè Pedrocchi, the cathedral baptistry, the Orto Botanico, a couple of minor chapels and Petrarch's house in Arquà Petrarca. It's available from tourist offices and the sights concerned. A family museum card valid for 15 days for two adults and two children for all the above except the Orto Botanico costs €25.

Questura (Police Station; ☎ 049 83 31 11; Riviera Ruzzante 11, Padua)

Sights

Baptistry (☎ 049 65 69 14; Piazza del Duomo, Padua; adult/child €2.50/1; ⏰ 10am-6pm)

Basilica del Santo (☎ 049 824 28 11; Piazza del Santo, Padua; ⏰ 6.30am-7pm Nov-Feb, 6.30am-7.45pm Mar-Oct)

Cappella degli Scrovegni (☎ 049 201 00 20; www .cappelladegliscrovegni.it; Giardini dell'Arena, Padua; adult/child €12/8, Mon €8/5; ⏰ 9am-7pm, at times extended to 10pm) The higher admission price includes admission to the Musei Civici agli Eremitani and Palazzo Zuckermann (both closed on Monday). Booking by phone or online at least 24 hours before your visit is obligatory, and you are given a maximum of 15 minutes inside the chapel. The night session (7pm to 10pm) costs €8/5 or €12/5 if you get a *doppio turno* (double session) ticket that allows a 30-minute stay in the chapel.

Cathedral (☎ 049 66 28 14; Piazza del Duomo, Padua; ⏰ 7.30am-noon & 3.30-7.30pm Nov-Feb, 7.45am-1pm & 3.45-8.30pm Mar-Oct)

Chiesa degli Eremitani (☎ 049 875 64 10; Giardini dell'Arena, Padua; ⏰ 8.15am-6.45pm Mon-Sat, 10am-noon & 4-7pm Sun & holidays Mar-Oct, 8.15am-6.15pm Mon-Sat, 10am-1pm & 4.15-7pm Sun & holidays Nov-Feb)

Monselice Castle (☎ 0429 7 29 31; Monselice; 1hr tours adult/child €5.50/3; ⏰ 9am-noon & 3-6pm Tue-Sun Apr-Nov) Admission by tour only.

Musei Civici agli Eremitani (☎ 049 820 45 50; Piazza Eremitani 8, Padua; adult/child €10/5, incl Cappella degli Scrovegni €12/5; ⏰ 9am-7pm Tue-Sun) The ticket includes admission to Palazzo Zuckermann, which has the same opening hours.

Museo del Risorgimento e dell'Età Contemporanea – Caffè Pedrocchi (☎ 049 878 12 31; Galleria Pedrocchi 11, Padua; adult/child €3/2; ⏰ 9.30am-12.30pm & 3.30-6pm)

Oratorio di San Giorgio (☎ 049 875 52 35; Piazza del Santo 11, Padua; admission €2 with Scoletta del Santo; ⏰ 9am-12.30pm & 2.30-7pm Apr-Sep, 9am-12.30pm & 2.30-5pm Oct-Mar)

Orto Botanico (☎ 049 827 21 19; Padua; adult/child €4/3; ⏰ 9am-1pm & 3-6pm Apr-Oct, 9am-1pm Mon-Sat Nov-Mar)

Palazzo della Ragione (☎ 049 820 50 06; Piazza delle Erbe, Padua; adult/child €8/4, more during exhibitions; ⏰ 9am-7pm Tue-Sun)

Petrarch's House (☎ 0429 71 82 94; Via Valleselle 4, Arquà Petrarca; adult €3; ⏰ 9am-noon & 3-6.30pm Tue-Sun Mar-Oct, 9am-noon & 2.30-5pm Tue-Sun Nov-Feb)

Scoletta del Santo (☎ 049 875 52 35; Piazza del Santo 11, Padua; admission €2 with Oratorio di San Giorgio; ⏰ 9am-12.30pm & 2.30-7pm Apr-Sep, 9am-12.30pm & 2.30-5pm Oct-Mar)

University (Palazzo Bò; ☎ 049 827 30 47; Via VIII Febbraio, Padua; adult/student & child €3/1.50; ⏰ tours 9.15am-12.15pm Tue, Thu & Sat, 3.15-6.15pm Mon, Wed & Fri). Buy tickets from Up shop on the premises.

Eating

Caffè Pedrocchi (☎ 049 878 12 31; www.caffepedrocchi .it, in Italian; Via VIII Febbraio 15, Padua; ⏰ 9am-10pm Sun-Wed, 9am-1am Thu-Sat) A spruced-up neoclassical façade fronts this classic café, which has been in business since the 19th century. It was one of Stendhal's favourite haunts in a town that left him otherwise indifferent.

Basilica Palladiana (opposite), Vicenza

This carefully maintained *osteria* is known throughout town as the perfect spot for quality traditional Veneto cooking. Try the *bavette ai frutti di mare* (a seafood pasta dish).

Per Bacco (☎ 049 875 46 64; Piazzale Pontecorvo 10, Padua; meals €30-35; 🕑 lunch & dinner Tue-Sun) Try the *tagliatelle alla norcina con tartufo nero* (pasta with black truffles), a classic of Umbrian cuisine and a long-standing favourite here.

Trattoria da Paccagnella (☎ 049 875 05 49; Via del Santo 113, Padua; meals €30; 🕑 lunch & dinner Mon-Sat) This trattoria is a comfortably elegant setting for fine Veneto cuisine – try the *arrosto di coniglio disossato alle erbe* (boneless roast rabbit in herbs).

Sleeping

Hotel Majestic Toscanelli (☎ 049 66 32 44; www .goldgate.it/hoteltoscanelli; Via dell'Arco 2, Padua; s/d up to €115/172) Hidden away in a leafy corner of one of the lanes that twist away from Piazza delle Erbe, this hotel boasts classy rooms in various styles (ranging from Imperial to what the owners call '19th-century English'). One floor is completely nonsmoking.

Hotel Sant'Antonio (☎ 049 875 13 93; www.hotel santantonio.it; Via San Fermo 118; s/d €62/82) Here there are comfortable, airy rooms, and some cheaper ones with shared bathroom in the corridor.

Koko Nor Association (☎ 049 864 33 94; www.band b-veneto.it/kokonor) This association can help you to find B&B-style accommodation in family homes as well as furnished apartments (it has 15 places on the books in Padua and four in the surrounding area) for around €60 to €70 for two people. The tourist office has a list of about 30 B&Bs.

Ostello Rocca degli Alberi (☎ 0429 8 10 76; ostello@palio10comuni.it; Castello degli Alberi, Montagnana; per person €11.50; 🕑 Apr–mid-Oct) This unique HI youth hostel is in a former watchtower atop Montagnana's extraordinary walls.

Enoteca la Corte dei Leoni (☎ 049 875 00 83; Via Pietro d'Abano 1, Padua; meals €45; 🕑 lunch & dinner Tue-Sat, lunch Sun) This modern temple of wine (you can taste from a broad by-the-glass list at the bar) in the heart of old Padua is also the site of a fine dining experience. In summer especially, book a table in the courtyard, where jazz concerts are occasionally staged. The food is good if a little *nouvelle* in terms of portions.

L'Anfora (☎ 049 65 66 29; Via dei Sconcin 13; meals €25-30; 🕑 lunch & dinner Mon-Sat) A good-natured place where locals crowd the bar for a wine or two and perhaps a few snacks. Or you can sit down for a hearty meal. Fancy some tripe?

Osteria dal Capo (☎ 049 66 31 05; Via degli Obizzi 2; meals €30; 🕑 lunch Tue-Sat, dinner Mon-Sat)

VICENZA & THE VILLAS

Caught between Padua and Verona, Vicenza (population 110,000) somehow seems to come off as a runner-up. Well, the good people of Unesco don't see why, and so they include the city holus-bolus (along with several villas in the appealing countryside surrounding Vicenza) in the Unesco World Heritage list. What's the big deal? It can be summed up in one word: Palladio. The genius architect left his mark all over town and the province around it.

Typical in many ways of the average northern Italian provincial town – a little prissy and a little chilly but with an undeniably easy charm in its old centre – Vicenza was already a prosperous centre as Roman Vicentia. Down through the centuries it has retained a self-satisfied air, and as a busy textile and computer-parts centre is today one of the country's wealthiest cities. It was swallowed up by the Venetian Republic in 1404, and it appears that many locals rather liked being part of the Venetian mini-empire, reflected in their predilection for Venetian-style Gothic mansions. But it is for the Renaissance and Palladio that the city is now prized by architecture buffs.

From the train station, in the gardens of Campo Marzo, walk along Via Roma into Piazzale de Gasperi. From here Corso Andrea Palladio leads through the city gates into Piazza Castello. The square is lined with several grand edifices, including the oddly truncated **Palazzo Porto-Breganze** on the south side, designed by Palladio and built by Scamozzi (one of the city's leading 16th-century architects). Its couple of outsize columns look strange now, but had the building been completed it would have been one of the city's most imposing structures. Corso Andrea Palladio continues northeast from the square and is the old town's central artery.

The Church has its main square in Piazza del Duomo, but the **cathedral**, rebuilt after WWII, is of comparatively little interest. Allied bombs destroyed the original and only a few of the artworks could be saved.

In nearby Piazza dei Signori rises the immense **Basilica Palladiana**, which Palladio began in 1549 on top of an earlier Gothic building – the slender 12th-century bell tower is all that remains of the original. Palladio's **Loggia del Capitaniato**, at the western side of the piazza on the corner of Via del Monte, was left unfinished at his death.

Contrà Porti, northwest off Corso Andrea Palladio, is one of the city's finest streets. **Palazzo Thiene** (No 12), by Lorenzo da Bologna, was originally intended to occupy the entire block. Palladio's **Palazzo Barbaran da Porto** (No 11) features an elegant double row of columns and is the richly decorated home to a museum and study centre devoted to Palladio (which frequently hosts architecture exhibitions). Palladio also designed **Palazzo Isoppo da Porto** (No 21), which remains unfinished. **Palazzo Valmarana** (Corso Antonio Fogazzaro 18) is considered one of his more eccentric creations, with the combination of two orders of pilasters in the main façade.

Heading north along Corso Andrea Palladio and left into Contrà di Santa Corona, you reach the **Chiesa di Santa Corona**, established in 1261 by the Dominicans to house a relic from Christ's crown of thorns. Inside are the *Battesimo di Gesù* (Baptism of Christ) by Giovanni Bellini and *Adorazione dei Magi* (Adoration of the Magi) by Veronese.

Corso Andrea Palladio ends at the **Teatro Olimpico**, started by Palladio in 1580 and completed by Scamozzi after the former's death. Considered one of the purest creations of Renaissance architecture, the theatre design was based on Palladio's studies of Roman structures. Scamozzi's remarkable street scene, stretching back from the main façade of the stage, is modelled on the ancient Greek city of Thebes. He created an impressive illusion of depth and perspective by slanting the street up towards the rear of the set. The theatre was inaugurated in 1585 with a performance of *Oedipus Rex* but soon fell into disuse – the ceiling caved in and the theatre remained abandoned for centuries until 1934, when it was restored and reopened.

The nearby **Museo Civico**, in the Palladian Palazzo Chiericati, contains works by local artists as well as by the Tiepolos and Veronese. The **Museo Naturalistico e Archeologico** has a modest collection of local ancient artefacts.

The sober baroque façades of the **Gallerie di Palazzo Leoni Montanari** belie a more extravagant interior. Long a private mansion and seat of a bank, the building now contains a collection of more than 400 Russian icons (top floor) and mostly 18th-century Venetian paintings (1st floor). Among the outstanding works on show are some by Canaletto and Pietro Longhi. There are frequent temporary exhibitions, too.

South of the city, the **Basilica di Monte Berico** is set atop a hill that offers magnificent views of the city below. The basilica was built in the 18th century to replace a Gothic structure, itself raised on the supposed site of two appearances by the Virgin Mary in 1426. An impressive 18th-century colonnade runs uphill to the church, roughly parallel to Viale X Giugno. Bus No 18 (€1) runs here from Via Roma.

TRANSPORT

Distance from Venice 69km

Direction West

Bus Regular **FTV** buses (☎ 0444 22 31 15) leave from the bus station, just near the train station, for Thiene, Asiago (in the hilly north of the province), Bassano and towns throughout the nearby Monti Berici (Berici Hills).

Car Vicenza is on the A4 tollway connecting Venice with Milan. The slower (but cheaper!) SS11 also connects Vicenza with Venice (via Padua) and Verona. There is a large car park near Piazza Castello and the train station.

Train Regular trains arrive from Venice (€3.85 to €8.93, 45 minutes to 1½ hours) and Padua (€2.50 to €8.26, 15 to 25 minutes). You can reduce the cost by getting slower *regionali* or *interregionali* trains. Other trains connect Vicenza with Milan, Verona, Treviso and smaller towns in the north.

VICENZA

0 _____ 400 m
0 _____ 0.2 miles

SIGHTS & ACTIVITIES
Basilica di Monte Berico	1 C6
Basilica Palladiana	2 B4
Chiesa di Santa Corona	3 B4
Duomo	4 B4
Gallerie di Palazzo Leoni Montanari	5 B4
Loggia del Capitaniato	6 B4
Museo Civico	7 C4
Museo Naturalistico e Archeologico	8 B4

Palazzo Barbaran da Porto	9 B4
Palazzo Isoppo da Porto	10 B4
Palazzo Porto-Breganze	11 B5
Palazzo Thiene	12 B4
Palazzo Valmarana	13 B4
Teatro Olimpico	14 C4
Villa Valmarana 'ai Nani'	15 D6

EATING 🍴
Al Bersagliere	16 B4
Antica Casa della Malvasia	17 B4
Il Cursore	18 C5

SLEEPING 🏠
Albergo Due Mori	19 B4
Casa San Raffaele	20 C6

TRANSPORT
Bus No 8 for La Rotonda	21 B5
Bus Station	22 A5

INFORMATION
APT Office	23 C4
APT Office	24 B4
Hospital	25 B2

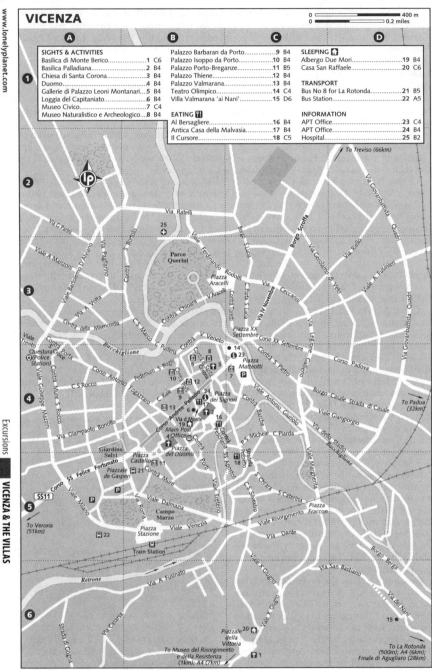

A 20-minute walk down Viale X Giugno and east along Via San Bastiano will take you to the **Villa Valmarana 'ai Nani'**. The villa features brilliant frescoes by Giambattista and Giandomenico Tiepolo. The 'ai Nani' (dwarves) refers to the statues perched on top of the gates surrounding the property.

A path leads on about 500m to Palladio's Villa Capra, better known as **La Rotonda**. It is one of the architect's most admired – and most copied – creations, having served as a model for buildings across Europe and the USA. The name comes from the low dome that caps this square-based structure, each side fronted by the columns of a classical façade. Bus No 8 for Debba or Lumignano (€1.50) from Via Roma stops nearby.

Villa hunters don't need to stop here. As Venetian patricians studded the Riviera del Brenta with their sumptuous summer palaces (see p234), so the rural areas around Vicenza began to mushroom with country residences as early as the 15th century. One reason for this is that the Venetian Senate forbade the high and mighty of Vicenza, or any other of the mainland cities under Venetian control, from building castles. Venice feared a landscape dotted with stout forts occupied by potentially independent-minded individuals. And so Vicenza's great and good cottoned on to the villa-construction fad. Many of the thousands that were built still remain, although most are inaccessible to the public. The Azienda di Promozione Turistica (APT) in Vicenza can provide reams of information about the villas most worth visiting.

Drivers should have little trouble planning an itinerary. One route would see you taking the SS11 south of Vicenza to Montecchio Maggiore and then on to Lonigo and Pojana Maggiore. From there head north for Longare and back to Vicenza. A round trip of 100km, the journey takes in about a dozen villas.

If you don't have a car, take the FTV bus north from Vicenza to Thiene, passing through Caldogno and Villaverla, and then continue on to Lugo. The Villa Godi-Valmarana, now known as the **Malinverni**, at Lonedo di Lugo, was Palladio's first villa.

Information

APT office (☎ 0444 54 41 22; www.vicenzae.org; Piazza dei Signori 8, Vicenza; ☼ 10am-2pm & 2.30-6.30pm)

APT office (☎ 0444 32 08 54; Piazza Matteotti 12, Vicenza; ☼ 9am-1pm & 2-6pm)

Combined-sights ticket Several combined ticket options are available. The Card Musei costs €7 and gives you entry to the Teatro Olimpico, Museo Civico (Palazzo Chiericati) and the Museo Naturalistico e Archeologico. For €8 you can also visit the obscure Museo del Risorgimento e della Resistenza, dedicated to Italian reunification and the Resistance in the latter stages of WWII. It's located southeast of the train station at Viale X Giugno 115. The Card Musei e Palazzi (€11) gets you entry to all of these, plus the Gallerie di Palazzo Leoni Montanari and Palazzo Barbaran da Porto. There is a family card for the museums and Teatro Olimpico (€3) for three family members and up. All are valid for three days.

Main post office (Contrà Garibaldi 1, Vicenza; ☼ 8.30am-6.30pm Mon-Sat)

Ospedale Civile (Hospital; ☎ 0444 99 31 11; Viale Ferdinando Rodolfi 37, Vicenza)

Palladio website (www.cisapalladio.org) A site dedicated to all things Palladian.

Questura (Police Station; ☎ 0444 33 75 11; Viale Giuseppe Mazzini 213, Vicenza)

Sights

Basilica di Monte Berico (☎ 0444 32 09 98; Piazzale della Vittoria, Vicenza; ☼ 6.15am-12.30pm & 2.30-7.30pm Mon-Sat, 6.15am-8pm Sun & holidays)

Basilica Palladiana (☎ 0444 32 36 81; Piazza dei Signori, Vicenza; ☼ 9am-5pm Tue-Sun)

Chiesa di Santa Corona (Contrà di Santa Corona, Vicenza; ☼ 8.30am-noon & 3-6pm Tue-Sun, 4-6pm Mon)

Gallerie di Palazzo Leoni Montanari (☎ 800 57 88 75; www.palazzomontanari.com; Contrà di Santa Corona 25, Vicenza; adult/student €3.50/2.50, or combined-sights ticket; ☼ 10am-6pm Fri-Sun, extended hours during temporary exhibitions)

La Rotonda (☎ 0444 32 17 93; Via Rotonda 29, Vicenza; gardens €3, villa €6, or combined-sights ticket; ☼ gardens 10am-noon & 3-6pm Tue-Sun Mar-Nov, villa 10am-noon & 3-6pm Wed-Nov) Groups can book to visit outside the normal opening hours; the price is hiked up to €8 per person in this case.

Museo Civico (☎ 0444 32 13 48; Palazzo Chiericati, Piazza Matteotti 37/39, Vicenza; admission by combined-sights ticket; ☼ 9am-5pm Tue-Sun Sep-Jun, 9am-7pm Tue-Sun Jul-Aug)

Museo Naturalistico e Archeologico (☎ 0444 32 04 40; Contrà di Santa Corona 4, Vicenza; admission by combined-sights ticket; ☼ 9am-5pm Tue-Sun Sep-Jun, 9am-7pm Tue-Sun Jul-Aug)

Palazzo Barbaran da Porto (☎ 0444 32 30 14; Contrà Porti 11, Vicenza; adult/student €5.50/3.50, or combined-sights ticket; ☾ 10am-6pm Tue-Sun)

Palazzo Thiene (☎ 0444 54 21 31; Contrà San Gaetano Thiene, Vicenza; admission free; ☾ 9am-noon & 3-6pm Tue-Wed Oct-Apr; 9am-noon & 3-6pm Wed & Fri, 9am-noon Sat May-Sep) Bookings are required.

Teatro Olimpico (☎ 0444 22 28 00; Corso Andrea Palladio, Vicenza; admission by combined-sights ticket; ☾ 9am-5pm Tue-Sun Sep-Jun, 9am-7pm Tue-Sun Jul-Aug)

Villa Valmarana 'ai Nani' (☎ 0444 54 39 76; Via dei Nani 2/8, Vicenza; admission €6, or combined-sights ticket; ☾ 10am-noon & 3-6pm Wed-Thu, Sat & Sun, 3-6pm Tue & Fri mid-Mar–early Nov)

Eating

Al Bersagliere (☎ 0444 32 35 07; Contrà Pescheria 11, Vicenza; meals €35; ☾ lunch & dinner Mon-Sat) This is a traditional *osteria* (restaurant-bar) where you can eat *cicheti* (snacks) at the bar or proceed to the cosy little tables for seasonal cooking (watch for the mushrooms in autumn).

Antica Casa della Malvasia (☎ 0444 54 37 04; Contrà delle Morette 5, Vicenza; meals €25; ☾ lunch & dinner Tue-Sun) This den has been around since 1200. Drinking is still a primary occupation in a locale that has changed little in all those centuries – on offer is an array of 80 types of wine (especially Malvasia varieties) and around 100 types of grappa!

Il Cursore (☎ 0444 32 35 04; Stradella Pozzetto 10, Vicenza; meals €25-30; ☾ lunch & dinner Wed-Mon & dinner Sun) They've been serving up food in here to an appreciative audience since the 19th century. Il Cursore is a great little spot to enjoy some local specialities – try the *spaghetti col baccalà mantecato* (spaghetti with cod prepared in parsley and garlic).

Sleeping

Albergo Due Mori (☎ 0444 32 18 86; www.hotel duemori.com; Contrà do Rode 26, Vicenza; s/d up to €48/87) The rooms at this central cheapy are basic, but it's clean and reliable and there's disabled access.

Casa San Raffaele (☎ 0444 54 57 67; www.albergo sanraffaele.it, in Italian; Viale X Giugno 10, Vicenza; d up to €65) Located in a former convent behind the colonnade leading to the Basilica di Monte Berico, this is a charming spot to spend the night.

Villa Saraceno (☎ 0444 89 13 71, Landmark Trust in UK ☎ 01628-825925; www.landmarktrust.org.uk; Via Finale 8, Finale di Agugliaro; building per night UK£295-795) In a magnificent setting, this restored 16th-century Palladian country villa is a noble choice of lodgings. Up to 16 people can stay, and there's a pool. From April to October parts of the building can be visited by the public between 2pm and 4pm on Wednesday. Buses run to Finale di Agugliaro from Vicenza bus station.

RIVIERA DEL BRENTA

As wealthy Venetians turned from seafaring merchants into landlubbers they flashed around their wealth in the hinterland, building fine villas, mostly as summer estates. More than 100 are scattered along the River Brenta, which passes through Padua and spills into the Venetian lagoon.

Many villas are dilapidated and closed, a sorry reflection of the fall from grace of many a Venetian grandee in the Republic's twilight years. Mind you, some prospered, and a number of the villas date only to the 19th century, by which time Venice was under Austrian control (until 1866). Today, mere mortals may snoop around a handful of the most outstanding of these magnificent mansions, among them Villa Foscari (1571), built by Palladio at Malcontenta, and Villa Pisani, also known as Villa Nazionale, at Strà.

No sooner do you roll out of the nightmare industry-scape of Marghera than you find yourself heading for Malcontenta, a Palladian trademark. The riverside façade, with its ionic columns and classical tympanum, echoes the ancients that inspired him. The Villa Foscari is also known as La Malcontenta (the Malcontent), supposedly because a female family member was exiled here for fooling around with people other than hubby. Its interior is remarkable only for the frescoes with which it is covered. They mostly depict scenes from classical literature.

Next up is an early-18th-century rococo caprice lying just west of Oriago, the Villa Widmann Foscari. Built by a trading family, the Serriman (of Persian origin), it was later taken over by the Widmann clan and given the French-rococo flavour it exudes today. Inside, the most impressive element is the grand Sala delle Feste (Ballroom), sumptuously decorated and ringed halfway up by an ornate gallery. The garden is littered with 18th-century statuettes of nymphs and cherubs.

Across the Brenta from Villa Widmann Foscari is the Villa Barchessa Valmarana, which was built a century later and is noteworthy mainly for its frescoes. Similarly alluring are the frescoes in the Villa Barchessa Alessandri, further along in Mira.

View along the Brenta from Ponte degli Alpini (p239), Bassano del Grappa

Villa Pisani is by far the grandest. It is set in extensive gardens just short of **Strà** and was completed in 1760 for Doge Alvise Pisani. It was later used by Napoleon as a temporary residence and in more recent times hosted Hitler's first meeting with Mussolini. It is quite an exercise in family trumpet-blowing. From the outsize statues at the entrance to Tiepolo's ceiling fresco (a pictorial eulogy to the Pisani clan), it is a flashy display of wealth.

In Strà itself is the imposing 17th-century **Villa Foscarini Rossi**, constructed for one of Venice's senior families. Among the many architects involved was Vincenzo Scamozzi (who worked from designs by Palladio), although the present look results partly from a later neoclassical reworking. The restored mansion, surrounded by carefully manicured grounds, hosts a couple of permanent displays, one dedicated to Rossimoda, which for decades has produced footwear for the biggest names in fashion (from Yves Saint Laurent to Fendi), and the other a private art collection of Luigino Rossi, who happens to be behind the shoes and now owns the villa. A separate and more modest building, the **Foresteria** (which once hosted distinguished guests), is used for high-flying conventions.

Other noteworthy villas are **Villa Sagredo** in Vigonovo and **Villa Gradenigo** in Oriago. The former is a romantic spot for weddings and is also used for conventions.

On Sunday and holidays in June, September and October, guided visits are sometimes organised to further villas in the area as part of the Ville Aperte (Open Villas) initiative.

TRANSPORT

Distance from Venice Villa Foscari 12km; Villa Widmann Foscari 16km; Villa Barchessa Valmarana 16km; Villa Pisani 26km; Oriago 14km; Mira 18.5km; Strà 28.7km

Direction West

Boat The luxurious *Burchiello* barge plied the River Brenta from Venice to Padua in the 17th and 18th centuries. Today's modern **Burchiello** (☎ 049 820 69 10; www.ilburchiello.it; adult/12-18yr/6-12yr/under 6yr one way €62/44/31/free; ☼ Mar-Oct) cruises up and down the river between Venice and Strà (the price includes optional tours of Villa Foscari and Villa Barchessa Valmarana; lunch is extra). Departures from Venice (Riva degli Schiavoni) are on Tuesday, Thursday and Saturday; those from Strà are on Wednesday, Friday and Sunday. Shuttle buses connect Strà with Padua's main bus station. Call for information, or try travel agents in Venice. **I Batelli del Brenta** (☎ 049 876 02 33; www.battellidelbrenta.it; half- & full-day tours per person €33-53) offers a range of similar trips. Its main daylong excursion offers stops at more villas, but admission to these is not included in the price.

Bus Regular Azienda Consorzio Trasporti Veneziano (ACTV) buses running between Venice and Padua (via Mestre, Marghera, Oriago, Mira, Dolo and Strà) stop at or near the villas. Take the No 53 (€3.50, less to intermediate stops) bus from Mestre headed for Padua via Malcontenta to visit the Villa Foscari and then proceed west. You'll need some patience if you intend to do this excursion by bus.

Car From Venice follow the signs out of Mestre through Marghera to Malcontenta. From there follow the SS11 for Strà.

Excursions

RIVIERA DEL BRENTA

Information

APT main office (Map p296; ☎ information 041 529 87 11; www.turismovenezia.it; Piazza San Marco 71/f, Venice; ⏰ 9am-3.30pm Mon-Sat)

IAT office (☎ 049 875 20 77; www.turismopadova.it; train station, Padua; ⏰ 9am-7pm Mon-Sat, 9am-noon Sun)

IAT office (☎ 041 42 49 73; Villa Widmann Foscari, Via Nazionale 420, Mira Porte; ⏰ 10am-5pm Tue-Sun Apr, 10am-6pm Tue-Sun May-Sep, 10am-5pm Sat, Sun & holidays Nov-Mar)

Infopoint (Map p296; Venice Pavilion, Venice; ⏰ 10am-6pm)

Sights

Villa Barchessa Alessandri (☎ 041 41 57 29; Via Nazionale 64, Mira; admission €10 incl Villa Barchessa Valmarana & Foresteria in Villa Foscarini Rossi; ⏰ 10.30am-noon & 2.30-5pm Tue-Sun Apr-Oct)

Villa Barchessa Valmarana (☎ 041 426 63 87; adult/child €6/4.50; ⏰ 9.30am-6pm Tue-Sun, Mar-Oct)

Villa Foscari (Map p288; ☎ 041 520 39 66; www.la malcontenta.com; Via dei Turisti 9; admission €7; ⏰ 9am-noon Tue & Sat May-Oct) Groups of 12 or more can book for other times at €8 per person.

Villa Foscarini Rossi (☎ 049 980 10 91; www.villa foscarini.it; Via Doge Pisani 1/2, Strà; adult/12-18yr/

under 12yr €5/2.50/free; ⏰ 9am-12.30pm & 2.30-6pm Mon-Fri, 9.30am-12.30pm & 2-6pm Sat, 10am-6.45pm Sun & holidays, closed Sat & Sun Nov-Jan & 2 weeks mid-Aug)

Villa Gradenigo (☎ 049 876 02 33; Oriago di Mira; admission €3; ⏰ groups by appointment)

Villa Pisani (☎ 049 50 20 74; Via Alvise Pisani 7, Strà; adult/EU citizens 18-25yr/under 18yr €5/2.50/free, grounds only €2.50/1.20/free; ⏰ 8.30am-7pm Tue-Sun Apr-Sep, 9am-4pm Tue-Sun Oct-Mar)

Villa Sagredo (☎ 049 50 31 74; www.villasagredo .it, in Italian; Via Sagredo 3/a, Vigonovo; admission free; ⏰ 5-9.30pm Tue-Fri)

Villa Widmann Foscari (☎ 041 42 49 73; Via Nazionale 420, Mira Porte; admission €5; ⏰ 10am-5pm Tue-Sun Apr, 10am-6pm Tue-Sun May-Sep, 10am-5pm Sat, Sun & holidays Nov-Mar)

Sleeping

Villa Rizzi-Albarea (☎ 041 510 09 33; www.villa-albarea .com; Via Albarea 53; d €200-280) One of the oldest of the Brenta villas, this former monastery (the church is still intact) is now a luxury inn near Dolo (it's 3km north of the Dolo exit from the A4 autostrada). Set in 2 hectares of parkland, the mansion offers plush rooms with antique furnishings. Facilities include a pool, a sauna and a massage service. There's a shuttle to and from Venice airport.

TREVISO & AROUND

For fashion-lovers around the world, the best thing to come out of Treviso (population 80,700) is the United Colors of Benetton (yes, there's a huge store in the heart of town). A distant second is radicchio, the local bitter red lettuce. For locals the best thing coming in is probably Ryanair (see p245), hauling in loads of tourists to discover this delightful riverside town before making for the glories of Venice. Those who skip Treviso, an easy train ride from Venice, are missing a treat.

The Città d'Acqua (City of Water), as local tourist bods would have it, is a miniature version of Venice. Such comparisons are more touching than realistic, but that doesn't make Treviso, through which the River Sile meanders, any less worth visiting.

From the train station, head north along Via Roma (over the canal), past the bus station and across the bridge (the nicely placed McDonald's on the river is an unmistakable landmark), and keep straight along Corso del Popolo. At Piazza della Borsa, veer left down Via XX Settembre and you arrive in the heart of the city, **Piazza dei Signori**.

TRANSPORT

Distance from Venice Treviso 30km; Oderzo 55km; Conegliano 58km; Vittorio Veneto 73.5km

Direction North

Bus The Treviso bus station is on Lungosile Mattei, near the train station in Piazzale Duca d'Aosta. ACTV buses connect Venice with Treviso, and La Marca buses link Treviso with other towns in the province. Buses travel to Oderzo (€2.80, 30 to 35 minutes) Conegliano (€2.80, 45 minutes) and Vittorio Veneto (€3.40, one hour five minutes).

Car Take the SS13 from Venice (Mestre) to Treviso and on to Conegliano and Vittorio Veneto. The A27 autostrada is faster but bypasses all three. For Oderzo, take the SS53 northeast from Treviso.

Train Trains from Venice to Treviso (€2.05, 25 to 30 minutes) make better sense than the bus. Other trains link the town with Belluno (via Conegliano and Vittorio Veneto), Padua and major cities to the south and west.

Piazza dei Signori is dominated by the fine brick **Palazzo dei Trecento**, the one-time seat of city government. Beneath the vaults you can stop for coffee and wistfully contemplate the worn 16th-century **Fontana delle Tette** (Tits Fountain), from whose breasts red and white wine flowed for three days each year on the appointment of a new town governor. The practice ended with the fall of Venice in 1797, itself enough reason for the locals to regret the passing of La Serenissima. The medieval main street is the colonnaded Via Calmaggiore, which leads to the **cathedral**, a massive structure whose main source of interest lies in the frescoes inside by Il Pordenone (1484–1539).

Backtrack to Piazza dei Signori and head east (around and behind the Palazzo dei Trecento), and you will soon find yourself in a tight warren of lanes that leads to five delightful bridges across the Canal Cagnan, which runs roughly north–south and spills into the River Sile. Treviso is a comparatively leafy town, and this is particularly the case at some points along the canal. You can also see the occasional mill wheel (the one by Vicolo Molinetto still turns). Try to catch the bustling atmosphere of the morning fish market, or *pescheria*, which occupies a small island here.

While on the right bank of the canal make for the **Museo Civico di Santa Caterina**. The church and its attached convent and cloisters house many of the city's art treasures. In the church itself are remarkable frescoes attributed to Gentile da Fabriano (who worked in the early 15th century). The beautiful Cappella degli Innocenti contains remarkably fresh and vivid frescoes by two contemporary artists, depicting the lives of Christ and the Virgin Mary. To these have been added the extraordinary fresco cycle by Tomaso da Modena (1326–79) on the life and martyrdom of Santa Orsola (St Ursula), recovered late in the 19th century from another already partly demolished church.

Over two floors of the former convent is part of the eclectic collection of Luigi Bailo, a 19th-century friar who made it his life's work to collect ancient artefacts and artworks to preserve the memory of Treviso's past. The collection starts with an archaeological section, proceeds with Romanesque statuary, and continues with a series of single paintings by Lotto, Titian, Tintoretto, Guardi, Rosalba Carriera and others.

Tomaso also left frescoes in the imposing **Chiesa di San Nicolò** on the other side of town. The star attraction is the **Sala del Capitolo Domenicano** in the seminary alongside the church. Enter and follow the directions across a cloister to the room, which is adorned with the portraits of 40 Dominican friars by Tomaso da Modena, all intent on copying illuminated manuscripts. One of them, on the right as you enter, has a magnifying glass in his hand. This 14th-century painting is thought to be the first-ever pictorial record of a reading glass.

Where the Canal Cagnan empties into the Sile is a particularly pleasant corner, with part of the city walls intact. In summer you can take a **boat cruise** on the *Silis* or *Altino* down the Sile to the Venetian lagoon and back. The tours are by reservation only – call or ask at a tourist office.

Oderzo, 25km northeast of Treviso, is a microcosm of its grander neighbour. The central Piazza Grande is flanked by the 15th-century cathedral and a fine clock tower, and is frequently the scene of classical-music recitals in summer. The town's handful of peaceful canals, crisscrossed by little bridges bearing pretty flower boxes, is inevitably reminiscent of Treviso.

North of Treviso, on the road to Belluno, call in at **Conegliano**, dominated by a castle (which you can reach on foot or by car). The centre of town, a few minutes' walk straight ahead down Via Carducci from the train station, is notable for the long Scuola dei Battuti on Via XX Settembre, decorated inside and out with frescoes. The cathedral, which you enter from the Scuola, is noteworthy for an altarpiece painted by local painter Cima da Conegliano in 1492–93. Treviso province provides rivers of the region's *prosecco*, a light white that comes in three general types, *spumante* (bubbly), *frizzante* (sparkling) and still.

The train from Venice via Treviso stops at Conegliano and then proceeds to the strange animal that is **Vittorio Veneto**. Actually a composite of two towns (Ceneda and Serravalle), Vittorio Veneto is most comfortably visited with your own transport. As you arrive from the south, do *not* follow signs for the *centro*. These take you to the modern part of the conglomerate, which lacks any real interest. Instead, follow signs for **Ceneda**, whose main attractions are the sweeping Piazza Giovanni Paolo I and **Castello di San Martino**, about a 1km hike up into the leafy hills. To reach the picturesque huddle of houses that is **Serravalle**, you need to follow signs for Belluno. These apparently lead you out of Vittorio Veneto, but just as you get that leaving feeling you stumble on this northernmost, and prettiest, part of the sprawling municipality.

Information

APT office (☎ 0422 54 76 32; http://turismo.provincia
.treviso.it, in Italian; Piazzetta Monte di Pietà 8, Treviso;
🕑 9am-12.30pm & 2-6pm Tue-Fri, 9.30am-12.30pm &
3-6pm Sat & Sun, 9am-12.30pm Mon) In a square adjacent
to Piazza dei Signori.

APT office (☎ 0422 81 52 51; Calle Opitergium 5, Oderzo;
🕑 9am-12.30pm Mon-Fri, 3-6pm Tue, Thu & Fri, 9.30am-
12.30pm & 3-6pm Sat & Sun)

APT office (☎ 0438 2 12 30; Via XX Settembre 61,
Conegliano; 🕑 9am-12.30pm Mon-Fri, 3-6pm Tue, Thu &
Fri, 9.30am-12.30pm & 3-6pm Sat & Sun)

APT office (☎ 0438 5 72 43; Viale della Vittoria 110,
Vittorio Veneto; 🕑 9.30am-12.30pm Mon-Wed,
9.30am-12.30pm & 3-6pm Thu-Sun)

Boat Cruises (☎ 0422 78 86 63, 0422 78 86 71) For
cruises along the River Sile.

Sights

Cathedral (Piazza del Duomo, Treviso; 🕑 7.30am-noon &
3.30-7pm Mon-Fri, 7.30am-1pm & 3.30-8pm Sat & Sun)

Chiesa di San Nicolò (Via San Nicolò, Treviso;
🕑 7am-noon & 3.30-7pm)

Museo Civico di Santa Caterina (☎ 0422 54 48 64; Via
di Santa Caterina, Treviso; admission €3; 🕑 9am-12.30pm
& 2.30-6pm Tue-Sun)

Sala del Capitolo dei Domenicani (☎ 0422 32 47;
Piazzetta Benedetto XI 2, admission by donation;
🕑 8am-6pm)

Eating

Piola (☎ 0422 54 02 87; www.piola.it, in Italian; Via
Carlo Alberto 11, Treviso; pizzas from €5-7;
🕑 noon-2.30pm & 7pm-1am Mon-Fri, 7pm-2am Sat,
6.30pm-1am Sun) This is a hip bar-cum-pizzeria where you
can sit outside or bury yourself in the dimly lit innards of
the bar with Treviso's night crowd.

BENETTON'S BURGEONING BUSINESS

Back in 1965 a Treviso lad by the name of Luciano
Benetton and his younger siblings, Giuliana, Gilberto
and Carlo, got into the rag trade. They could not have
known that 40 years later they would have more
than 5000 stores in 120 countries, an average €150
million in annual profit and a brand name that sticks in
the mind. Concentrating on attractive, young fashion
(with lines in children's gear, underwear, perfumes
and home wares thrown in) their two main brands, the
United Colors of Benetton and Sisley, have established
themselves worldwide. This is in part due to the daring
advertising campaigns cooked up at Fabrica, a modern
complex not far from the Benetton headquarters north
of Treviso. The business is emblematic of the Veneto's
economic miracle, which has seen a largely poor,
agricultural economy transform itself into a small
business—oriented dynamo since the 1960s.

Ristorante al Dante (☎ 0422 59 18 97; Piazza Garibaldi
6, Treviso; meals €20-25; 🕑 lunch & dinner Mon-Sat)
An excellent budget option where you can sidle up to the
bar for *cicheti* or dine at one of the teeny tables. In the
summer months you can sit outside, and gaze across to the
river while you enjoy your meal.

Ristorante Alle Becchiere (☎ 0422 54 08 71; Piazza
Ancilotto 10, Treviso; meals €20-25; 🕑 lunch & dinner
Tue-Sat, lunch Sun) This historic central eatery offers a mostly
local menu. The products are fresh and the end results are
pleasing. The owners claim that tiramisù was invented here!

Sleeping

Albergo Campeol (☎ 0422 5 66 01; www.albergo
campeol.it; Piazza Ancilotto 4, Treviso; s/d €52/85) A nicely
maintained place in a restored building just off Piazza dei
Signori, it's about the only decent central choice. Three of the
doubles have canal views.

BASSANO DEL GRAPPA & AROUND

Known above all for its firewater, grappa, and to a lesser degree for its ceramics, Bassano
del Grappa (population 41,000) sits astride the River Brenta south of the first line of hills
that are a prelude to the Dolomites. To art-lovers, the name will ring another bell. The Da
Ponte family of Renaissance painters, known to us now as the Bassano, came from here.
The appealing old centre of town and a chance to get inside the grappa story are enough
of an incentive to come here (a journey easily made by train from Venice), but around
Bassano radiate half a dozen intriguing objectives, from the charming hill village of Asolo
to the fortified plains towns of Cittadella and Castelfranco del Veneto.

From Bassano train station it's about a five-minute walk west to the edge of the old town
and the APT office. Buses halt a couple of hundred metres south of the tourist office at
Piazzale Trento; from there another five-minute walk west takes you to the heart of the old
centre. The River Brenta, crossed by the Ponte degli Alpini, flows to the west.

The centre of Bassano is composed of two sloping, interlinking squares, Piazza Garibaldi and Piazza Libertà. In the latter, the winged lion of St Mark stands guard on a pedestal to remind you of who was long in charge here.

In the **Museo Civico**, attached to the Chiesa di San Francesco on Piazza Garibaldi, you can see an assortment of items, including paintings by members of the Bassano clan and archaeological finds such as ancient Greek ceramics and bronze figurines. Among the Bassano collection, which takes up a floor, are 17 canvases by Jacopo. Also on display is a section devoted to the sculptor Canova, with his letters, books, drawings and plaster casts. A separate ceramics collection with more than 1000 porcelain pieces, the **Museo della Ceramica**, is housed in Palazzo Sturm on the banks of the Brenta and can be visited on the same ticket.

Follow Via Matteotti north off Piazza Libertà towards the remains of **Castello Ezzelini**, the stronghold that belonged to the medieval warlords of the same name.

Via Gamba slithers downhill from Via Matteotti to the River Brenta and the covered bridge designed by Palladio and known as the **Ponte degli Alpini**, after the mountain troops who rebuilt it in 1948. (Retreating German soldiers had seriously damaged the bridge at the tail end of WWII.) Via Gamba and the bridge are lined with ceramics shops and a few grappa outlets. Throw in some bars and snack joints and it makes a pleasant stroll. The views across to old Bassano from the far riverbank alone justify the walk.

While by the bridge, pop into the Poli grappa shop with its **Poli Museo della Grappa**, which outlines the drink's history. You'll have trouble resisting the chance to buy an elegant bottle or two of the clear, high-octane liquid (which comes in a surprising array of styles). Although grappa is made all over Italy and indeed inferior versions are distilled well beyond the peninsula, the people of the Veneto have been doing it since at least the 16th century. In 1601 an institute of grappa distillers was even created in Venice!

A short walk south along Via Ferracina brings you to the above-mentioned Museo della Ceramica.

East of Bassano, **Asolo's** (population 7860) position high in the hills, surrounded by fields, farms and woods, makes it an enchanting village. Caterina Corner, the ill-fated Venetian queen of Cyprus, was given the town and surrounding county towards the end of the 15th century in exchange for her abdication (see A Queen Cornered, p129). The writer Pietro Bembo attended Caterina's salons and, perhaps in search of a hint of that same atmosphere, Robert Browning also spent time in Asolo.

Piazza Garibaldi forms the town centre, from where streets wind up in all directions between the tight ranks of golden-hued houses that lend this place so much of its charm. The **cathedral** lies below and just to the south of the square. It contains a few paintings by Jacopo Bassano and Lorenzo Lotto. Caterina Corner lived in the **castle**, now used as a theatre.

DETOUR: BELLUNO & THE DOLOMITES

Those with a roving heart and a yen for grand mountain scenes will be sorely tempted to scoot up the motorway to Belluno, an attractive town (population 35,000) at the foot of the mighty Dolomites. A long day trip via Treviso is technically feasible (it's about two hours' drive north of Venice along the A27 tollway) but you are better off taking a couple of days and using Belluno as a base to explore the mountains. They offer a feast of summer hiking and winter skiing.

The heart of the old town is formed by Piazza del Duomo, dominated on one side by the 16th-century Renaissance Cattedrale di San Martino, the Palazzo Rosso, from about the same period, and the Palazzo dei Vescovi.

Stretching away to the northwest is the Parco Nazionale Dolomiti Bellunesi, a beautiful national park laden with outdoors opportunities. Six Alte Vie delle Dolomiti (high-altitude walking trails) pass through the territory surrounding Belluno, and along them you will find *rifugi* (mountain huts), on Rte No 1 in particular, where you can stay at the end of a day's hiking. Rte No 1 stretches between Belluno and Lago di Braies in the neighbouring Trentino-Alto Adige region. The huts are generally open from late June to late September.

About 50km north of Belluno and connected by bus is the chic ski resort of Cortina d'Ampezzo, for wintertime visitors to Venice with an urge to rip down a few fashionable Italian slopes. A direct winter bus runs from Venice's Piazzale Roma (3½ hours).

The **IAT office** (☎ 0437 94 00 83; www.infodolomiti.it; Piazza del Duomo 2, Belluno; 9am-12.30pm & 3.30-6.30pm) has further information.

TRANSPORT

Distance from Venice Bassano del Grappa 77km; Asolo 64.5km; Possagno 74.7km; Cittadella 54.5km; Castelfranco del Veneto 42km

Direction Northwest

Bus Regular **SITA buses** (☎ 049 820 68 44) to Padua (€3, one hour) from Bassano train station call in at Cittadella (€1.50, 20 minutes). **La Marca buses** (☎ 0422 57 73 11, up to 11 a day) between Bassano and Montebelluna stop below Asolo. Get off at Ca' Vescovo, (€2.25, 20 minutes). You need to get the little orange shuttle bus from there to reach the centre, otherwise it's a long walk. Up to 12 **CTM** (www.ctmspa.com, in Italian) buses a day run from Bassano to Possagno (€2.80, one hour). Get tickets for all except SITA buses from the newspaper stand at the Bassano bus station. SITA bus tickets can be purchased on the bus. As this is largely a train-replacement service, train tickets are valid on the Bassano–Padua run.

Car The most direct route from Venice is the Castelfranco del Veneto road leading northwest from Mestre. You could also combine tours and head first to Treviso, then arc northwest towards Montebelluna to make for Asolo (and maybe Possagno) before proceeding further west to Bassano del Grappa and returning to Venice via Cittadella and Castelfranco. It's a slightly exhausting itinerary but possible.

Train The easiest way to Bassano from Venice is by train on the Venice–Trento line (€3.85, 1¼ to 1½ hours). A train from Padua (€3, one hour to 1¼ hours) is another option. Castelfranco is on the Venice–Bassano line (€3, 50 minutes to 1¼ hours from Venice).

An arduous climb up Via Collegio from Piazza Brugnoli will get you to the rocca, the town's medieval fortress. The walk north out of town to the Cimitero di Sant'Anna is rewarding for the views over the lush, green countryside. Eleonora Duse (1858–1924), a whirlwind actress romantically involved with the dashing nationalist poet Gabriele d'Annunzio, was buried here. Indeed, the town is linked to more than its fair share of illustrious women. The remarkable British traveller and writer Freya Stark (1893–1993), in between her daring Middle Eastern wanderings, always came home to Asolo. Her tomb lies just a few along from that of Duse. In the town's Museo Civico you can see a section devoted to her life and travels.

Birth and resting place of Antonio Canova, Italy's master of neoclassical sculpture, Possagno (population 2070) is a good place to get an idea of how Canova worked. The Gipsoteca is home to a long series of clay models and other preparatory pieces for his finished work (you can see some statues and reliefs by Canova in Venice's Museo Correr, p57).

Before you reach the Gipsoteca, you'll have been astonished by the rather outsize Tempio, to all intents and purposes the parish church, that Canova was considerate enough to leave to his town. Finished in 1832, it could be described as neo-mongrel-classical, as it is an amalgam of Greek and Roman models.

Southeast of Bassano lie a couple of fortified plains towns worth a quick stop. Cittadella (population 19,000), a 12km bus ride south of Bassano on the busy SS47 to Padua, is enclosed by 1.5km of towering red-brick walls and a moat. Of the four gates, the northern Porta Bassano are the most elaborate. Padua raised the fort in the 13th century to face off the one built by Treviso at Castelfranco del Veneto (population 32,000), 10km east, towards the end of the 12th century.

Castelfranco (Free Fort) could not have been an overly sought-after address, as the then rulers of Treviso exempted from all taxes anyone prepared to move in. From its construction until 1339, when it was absorbed into Venice's mainland empire, Castelfranco del Veneto remained a hotly contested site and frequently changed hands. Padua laid siege to it barely 10 years after its construction. More than 60 years after Venice took control of Castelfranco, the lion of St Mark was finally raised over Cittadella in 1405.

The square-based walls of Castelfranco are less impressive than the circular version at Cittadella, but the town has an extra claim to fame as the birthplace of the mysterious painter Giorgione. Little is known about his life, and only half a dozen works can be definitely attributed to him. One of them, the *Madonna col Bambino in Trono e Santi Francesco e Liberale* (Madonna and Child Enthroned with Saints Francis and Liberale), is in the cathedral.

Information

APT office (☎ 0424 52 43 51; Largo Corona d'Italia 35, Bassano; ◷ 9am-1pm & 2-6pm)

IAT office (☎ 0423 52 90 46; Piazza Garibaldi 73, Asolo; ◷ 9am-12.30pm Mon-Fri, 3-6pm Tue, Thu & Fri, 9.30am-12.30pm & 3-6pm Sat & Sun)

IAT office (☎ 0423 49 14 16; Via F M Preti 66, Castelfranco del Veneto; ◷ 9am-12.30pm Mon-Fri, 3-6pm Tue, Thu & Fri, 9.30am-12.30pm & 3-6pm Sat & Sun)

Sights

Cathedral (Castelfranco del Veneto; ◷ 8am-noon & 3.30-6pm)

Gipsoteca (☎ 0423 54 43 23; Possagno; adult/student €4/3; ◷ 9am-noon & 3-6pm Tue-Sun)

Museo Civico (☎ 0423 95 23 13; Via Regina Cornaro 74, Asolo; adult/senior & under 26yr/under 6yr €4/3/free; ◷ 10am-noon & 3-7pm Sat & Sun)

Museo Civico (☎ 0424 52 22 35; Via del Museo 12, Bassano; adult/student incl Museo della Ceramica €4.50/3; ◷ 9am-6.30pm Tue-Sat, 3.30-6.30pm Sun)

Museo della Ceramica (☎ 0424 52 49 33; Palazzo Sturm, Via Schiavonetti, Bassano; adult/student incl Museo Civico €4.50/3; ◷ 9am-12.30pm & 3.30-6.30pm Tue-Sat, 3.30-6.30pm Sun Apr-Oct, 9am-12.30pm Fri, 3.30-6.30pm Sat & Sun Nov-Mar)

Poli Museo della Grappa (☎ 0424 52 44 26; www.poligrappa.com; Ponte Vecchio, Bassano; admission free; ◷ 9am-1pm & 2.30-7.30pm)

Tempio (Possagno; admission free; ◷ 9am-noon & 3-6pm)

Grappa, namesake speciality of Bassano del Grappa (p238)

Eating

Ca' Derton (☎ 0423 52 96 48; Piazza d' Annunzio 11, Asolo; meals €40; ◷ lunch & dinner Tue-Sat) It does a tempting *capretto alle erbe aromatiche* (kid meat in herbs), and it has a fine wine list and dessert menu.

Nardini (☎ 0424 2 77 41; Ponte degli Alpini, Bassano; ◷ 9am-8pm) Sit down among the venerable wine barrels and sip grappa at this wonderful bar right on the old-city-centre side of the bridge.

DETOUR: MAROSTICA'S LIFE-SIZE CHESS MATCH

For the most colourful game of chess you are ever likely to see, you need to be in the quiet medieval town of Marostica (population 13,000) on the second weekend of September in even-numbered years (2006, 2008 and so on). You know you have almost arrived (if coming from nearby Bassano) when you see the jagged line of battlements that climbs the hill from Marostica's town centre to the upper castle.

Pretty enough to warrant a brief stop in its own right, Marostica comes into its own for the biennial Partita a Scacchi (Chess Match). Back in 1454, they say, two knights challenged each other to a duel for the hand of the fair Lionora, elder daughter of the town's ruler, Taddeo Parisio. The latter, not wanting to lose either warrior, banned the duel and ordered them to 'fight' it out in a grand game of chess using real people on a 'board' at the gates of the lower castle. The two knights ordered the moves and the winner got Lionora. The loser didn't come off too badly, since he wed Parisio's equally radiant younger daughter.

The carefully choreographed event today is as colourful as the original must have been, with an assembly of players and other characters in period costume. If you can't be here for the match, you can admire the costumes in the lower castle, or **Castello da Basso** (Piazza Castello; admission €1; ◷ 10am-noon & 2.30-6pm except holidays). Marostica is a 15-minute bus ride from Bassano.

More information can be found at the **tourist office** (☎ 0424 7 21 27; www.marosticascacchi.it; Piazza Castello 1, Marostica).

Ristorante Ottone (☎ 0424 52 22 06; Via Matteotti 50, Bassano; meals €25-30; ⏲ lunch & dinner Wed-Sun & lunch Mon) For a leap back in time, this characterful spot (in business since 1870) just off Piazza della Libertà is good for a hearty Hungarian goulash or grilled horse meat.

Sleeping

Hotel Castello (☎ /fax 0424 22 86 65; Via Bonamigo 19, Bassano; s/d up to €52/82) In the shadow of the old castle walls, this is the only hotel within the old town. It's a fairly small and simple affair but perfectly acceptable.

Hotel Duse (☎ 0423 5 52 41; www.hotelduse.com; Via Browning 190, Asolo; s/d €60/120) The hotel has lovely rooms – and they would certainly want to be at this price. Bear in mind that the Duse is the cheapest option in town.

Hotel Villa Cipriani (☎ 0423 52 34 11; www.sheraton .com; Via Canova 298, Asolo; d €200-360) Dating from the 18th century, this villa overlooking Asolo is one of Italy's great luxury retreats. The views are splendid, as is the villa.

Villa Ca' Sette (☎ 0424 38 33 50; www.ca-sette.it; Via Cunizza da Romano 4, Bassano; s/d €130/210) Home to a renowned restaurant since the 1950s, this 18th-century mansion and its dependencies, 1km north of central Bassano, form a marvellous retreat set in tranquil grounds.

THE ADRIATIC COAST

The Adriatic coast, spreading east and gradually north away from Venice, is lined with a selection of popular local beach resorts. They tend to be crowded on summer weekends but not so bad during the week. Quite a few foreigners flock to them too, using the resorts as the core of their summer holiday and chucking in the odd excursion to Venice. These places are pleasant enough, but the northern Adriatic is not the place to plan a classic Mediterranean beach holiday.

Lido di Jesolo, the strand a couple of kilometres away from the main town of Jesolo, is far and away the Venetians' preferred beach. The sand is fine and clean, the water is OK, and the place hops in summer with several dance clubs grooving through the night.

Jesolo (population 23,000) marks the northern end of a long peninsula that becomes Litorale del Cavallino as you head south and culminates in Punta Sabbioni, which together with the northern end of the Lido di Venezia forms the first of the three Adriatic entrances into the Venetian lagoon.

The beaches tend to be covered in umbrellas, recliners and the people using them. The area also has camping grounds and plenty of hotels. The whole is predictably short on character but can make a fun diversion from heavy-duty Venetian sightseeing – sort of a sunny Blackpool-near-Venice.

Nothing is left to remind you of the ancient roots of **Eraclea**, now a small agricultural town on the way from Jesolo to Caorle, itself 30km east around the coast from Jesolo.

In the 1st century BC **Caorle** (population 11,500) was a Roman port, and it remains a busy fishing centre today. Small but proud, it dropped resistance to Venetian pressure and passed under the paws of St Mark's lion only in the 15th century. The centre of the medieval town is watched over by the extraordinary cylindrical bell tower of the 11th-century cathedral. The cheerful streets present a pastel pageant. Although they haven't gone to quite the lengths of the people of Burano (p93), the townsfolk take a special pride in keeping their houses gleaming with fresh coats of paint in an array of bright colours.

The beaches are busy but OK and the whole place has a restrained vibe that sets it apart from the more soulless Jesolo. The old town centre is blessed with a handful of places to lay down your weary head, and restaurants abound.

For Adriatic Coast information, try the **Palazzo del Turismo** (☎ 041 37 06 88) in Piazza Brescia, Jesolo, or the **APT office** (☎ 0421 8 10 85) in Caorle.

TRANSPORT

Distance from Venice Lido di Jesolo 45km; Caorle 65km

Direction Northeast

Boat In summer (roughly June to September), ferry services to Venice are sometimes available but cannot be guaranteed from one year to the next.

Bus Azienda Trasporti Veneto Orientale (ATVO) buses run from Piazzale Roma in Venice to Jesolo (one way/return €3.60/6.40, 70 minutes) and Caorle (one way/return €4.50/8, 1½ hours).

Car Driving up this way can be a nightmare on midsummer weekends and holidays, and even midweek is sometimes fraught because of the intense traffic. Take the SS14 from Mestre.

Directory

Directory

The information in this chapter is divided into two parts, Transport and Practicalities. Within each section information is presented in alphabetical order.

TRANSPORT

AIR

Venice is one of Italy's smaller air-traffic centres. Direct flights from major European centres and New York are available, alongside internal flights from the rest of Italy, but for most intercontinental air travel you will have to change flights at least once, either in Rome or Milan, or at another major European hub.

Look out for budget-airline deals from carriers such as UK-based EasyJet and Ryanair, which between them put on cheap flights from a growing list of UK and other European airports respectively to Venice's Marco Polo airport and Treviso's San Giuseppe airport. These and an array of other budget airlines work on a first-come, first-served basis: as flights fill, the price of a ticket rises.

Within Italy air travel is expensive. In the northern half of the country it makes more sense to go by train, as the time you save in going by air is rarely that great, whereas the economic savings are considerable. Alitalia and Air One are the main airlines serving Venice. Most direct flights into Venice come from Rome and Milan, with a handful from Naples, Olbia and Palermo.

Most airlines, especially the budget ones, encourage you to book on their websites. Useful general sites to search for competitive fares are www.planesimple.co.uk, www.opodo.com and www.expedia.com.

Airlines

Airlines don't bother with shopfront offices in Venice, so you'll need to go online, call the following numbers or try a travel agent (see p263). Most airlines have desks at the airports they serve.

Air Dolomiti (EN; in Germany ☎ 01805 838 426, in Italy ☎ 199 400 044; www.airdolomiti.it) Airline with flights between Munich and Venice, and direct links from Barcelona, Frankfurt, Munich and Vienna to Verona.

Air One (AP; ☎ 199 207 080; www.flyairone.it) Flights from throughout Italy.

Alitalia (AZ; ☎ 848 865 641/2/3; www.alitalia.it, in Italian) Flights from Rome, Milan and other Italian centres, as well as from many European hubs.

Alpi Eagles (E8; ☎ 899 500 058; www.alpieagles.com, in Italian) Has flights from several Italian, Greek and Romanian cities, as well as Barcelona.

Basiq Air/Transavia (HV; in Netherlands ☎ 0900-0737, in Italy ☎ 02 6968 2615; www.basiqair.com) Low-cost flights from Amsterdam to Treviso and Verona.

BMI (BD; ☎ 0870 607 0555 UK; www.flybmi.com) Flights to Venice from London Heathrow and various other UK cities.

British Airways (BA; in UK ☎ 0870 850 9850, in Italy ☎ 199 712 266; www.britishairways.com) From the UK.

Delta (DL; in USA ☎ 1800 241 4141, in Italy ☎ 800 477 999; www.delta.com) Direct flights from New York.

EasyJet (U2; in UK ☎ 0871 244 2366, in Italy ☎ 848 887 766; www.easyjet.com) Flights from London Gatwick, Bristol and East Midlands.

Flybaboo (BBO; in Switzerland ☎ 0848 445 445; www.babooairways.com) Flights from Geneva to Venice.

Germanwings (4U; in Germany ☎ 01805 955 855, in Italy ☎ 199 404 747; www15.germanwings.com) Flights between Cologne and Verona.

Hapag Lloyd Express (X3; in Germany ☎ 01805 093 509, in Italy ☎ 199 192 692; http://book.hlx.com) Flights from Berlin and other German cities to Venice.

Helvetic (2L; in Switzerland ☎ 043 557 90 99, in Italy ☎ 02 6968 2684; www.helvetic.com) Flights from Zurich to Venice.

Jet2 (LS; in UK ☎ 0871 226 1737, in Italy ☎ 199 309 240; www.jet2.com) Budget airline that flies from Leeds and Manchester to Venice.

Maersk Air (DM; in Denmark ☎ 70 10 74 74; www.maersk-air.com) Flights from several Danish cities.

MyAir (8I; ☎ 0931 41 99 37; www.myair.com) A budget Italian airline that appeared out of nowhere after the collapse of Volare. Has flights to Barcelona from Venice.

Qantas Airways (QF; in Australia ☎ 13 13 13, in Italy ☎ 06 524 82 725; www.qantas.com.au) Flights from Australia to Italy in codeshare.

Ryanair (FR; ☎ 0871 246 0000 UK, ☎ 899 678 910 Italy; www.ryanair.com) Flights from to Brussels, Frankfurt (Hahn), Girona (for Barcelona), Liverpool, London (Luton and Stansted) and Paris (Beauvais) to Treviso. Ryanair also flies to Brescia airport, reasonably handy for Verona.

Sky Europe (NE; ☎ 02 4850 4850 Slovakia, ☎ 06 1777 7000 Hungary, ☎ 02 6968 2666 Italy; www.skyeurope .com) Flights to Venice from Bratislava and Budapest.

Snowflake (SK; ☎ 70 10 20 00 Denmark; www.flysnow flake.com) This SAS subsidiary has flights from Copenhagen to Venice.

Thomson Fly (TOM; ☎ 0870 190 0737 UK; www.thom sonfly.com) Flights from Coventry to Venice.

Wind Jet (IV; ☎ 899 809 060; w10.volawindjet.it) Flights to Venice from Catania and Palermo.

Airports

Venice's **Marco Polo airport** (VCE; ☎ 041 260 92 60; www.veniceairport.it) is 12km outside Venice and just east of Mestre. Some flights, notably those of low-cost airline Ryanair, use Treviso's minuscule **San Giuseppe airport** (TSF; ☎ 0422 31 51 11), about 5km southwest of Treviso and 30km (about an hour's drive through traffic) from Venice.

Arrivi (arrivals) at Marco Polo airport is on the ground floor, where you will also find an Azienda di Promozione Turistica (APT) office, numerous car-hire outlets, hotel-booking agencies, *bureaux de change*, *deposito bagagli* (left luggage) and *bagagli smarriti* (lost luggage). Check-in and departures are on the 1st floor. You'll find banks, ATMs, cafés and shops on both floors.

At Treviso's San Giuseppe airport, the arrivals hall boasts a small, thinly stocked regional tourist information booth, a lost-luggage office next to it, a *bureau de change* and several car-hire outlets. Next door in departures you'll find an ATM and a couple of tour and airline offices (including Ryanair). There is no *deposito bagagli* service.

There are several options for getting to Venice from Marco Polo airport, from the super-expensive water taxi to the cheap and prosaic bus. The main problem is with night flights that arrive late. Some people have found themselves at the airport faced with a long wait for public transport and no taxis. All this may change radically in the coming years. A daring €250 million project to build a sub-lagoon rail link from the airport via Murano to the Arsenale in Venice would put the city just 12 minutes from its airport!

Getting to/from the Airports

BOAT

Alilaguna (www.alilaguna.com) fast ferries from Marco Polo airport to Venice or the Lido (€10) and Murano (€5) operate approximately once an hour. The main difference between the *rosso* (red) and *blu* (blue) lines is that the blue line stops at Fondamente Nuove (€5) and Stazione Marittima (€13), but not at Zattere or Arsenale. Travelling to the airport, you can pick up an Alilaguna ferry at several stops, including Zattere (Map pp294–5), San Marco (Map p296), San Zaccaria (Map p296) and Arsenale (Map p298). A free shuttle bus connects the embarkation point at the airport with the new terminal building. Note that, coming from the airport, the *rosso* ferry runs to Murano (the Museo stop), the Lido, Arsenale, San Zaccaria, Piazza San Marco and Zattere in that order. The journey to Piazza San Marco takes one hour and 10 minutes (a few minutes longer on the *blu* line).

A **water taxi** (☎ 041 522 23 03, 041 522 12 65) is luxury. The standard rate for the ride between Piazzetta di San Marco and Marco Polo airport is €45. To/from the Lido costs €55. Watch for night and baggage surcharges.

See Venice Card, p254.

BUS

Azienda Trasporti Veneto Orientale (ATVO; ☎ 041 520 55 30; www.atvo.it) buses run from Marco Polo airport to Piazzale Roma via Mestre's train station (€3, 20 minutes) – they're also known as Fly buses. There are around 27 to 30 departures a day. A separate service runs to Mestre train station from the airport (€2.50).

Azienda Consorzio Trasporti Veneziano (ACTV; ☎ 041 24 24; www.actv.it) city bus No 5 also runs between Marco Polo airport and Piazzale Roma (€1). It makes more stops and takes closer to 30 minutes. You are technically supposed to pay a full fare for major luggage pieces, too.

Eurobus (☎ 041 541 51 80) buses connect Piazzale Roma with flights at Treviso's San Giuseppe airport (one way/return €4.50/8, one hour five minutes). The return ticket is valid for one week only. Alternatively, local Treviso bus No 6 goes to the main train station in Treviso. From there you can proceed to Venice by train.

HELICOPTER

Heliair (☎ 041 269 91 38) has at least one helicopter permanently based at the airport. VIP types in a hurry can hop on for quick transfers to the Lido, nearby cities and even the chic ski resort of Cortina d'Ampezzo (just 25 minutes way).

TAXI

Normal land taxis cost around €35 one way from Marco Polo airport to Piazzale Roma (15 to 20 minutes). From Treviso's San Giuseppe airport (€75) they can take an hour in traffic.

BICYCLE

Cycling (hardly feasible anyway) is banned in Venice. On the Lido and Pellestrina it can be a pleasant option. A couple of places where you can hire bicycles are clustered around the vaporetto stop on Gran Viale Santa Maria Elisabetta (Map pp302–3). You'll pay €9 to €10 per day.

BOAT

You probably know already that, aside from your feet, boats are the only way around Venice. You may not realise that you can also arrive by boat. Apart from Mediterranean cruise ships that call in, Minoan Lines (www.minoan.gr) runs regular ferries to Venice from Greece. Venezia Lines (www.venezialines.com) runs high-speed catamarans between Venice and seven destinations, including pretty Pola, along the Istrian coast (once part of La Serenissima's merchant empire) in Croatia.

Gondola

A gondola ride is the quintessence of romantic Venice, but few people use them for practical transport purposes (like getting from the train station to your hotel). And at €73 for 50 minutes (€91 from 8pm to 8am) the official price is a rather hefty return from the clouds to reality. The rates are for a maximum of six people – less romantic but more affordable. After the first 50 minutes you pay in 25-minute increments (€37, or €47 from 8pm to 8am). Several travellers have reported successfully negotiating below the official rates.

Gondolas are available near main canals all over the city, or can be booked by phoning ☎ 041 528 50 75 or at various gondola

stops (stazi) such as those in Rialto (Map p296; ☎ 041 522 49 04) and at the train station (Map pp290–1; ☎ 041 71 85 43).

Hire

The freewheeling tripper with nerves of steel might want to rent a boat to get around Venice with a dash of panache. Try Brussa (Map pp290–1; ☎ 041 71 57 87; www.brussaisboat.it, in Italian; Fondamenta Labia, Cannaregio 331; ⏰ 7.30am-5.30pm Mon-Sat, 7.30-12.30pm Sun). You can hire a boat (including fuel) for an hour (€20.66) or a day (€130), or make an arrangement for a longer period. Prices include petrol (if you need to fill up there are only four boat petrol stations around Venice). You don't need a licence, but you will be taken on a test run to see if you can manoeuvre and park – if you have no experience, they won't rent you a vessel.

Traghetto

The poor man's gondola, traghetti are used to cross the Grand Canal where there is no nearby bridge. There is no limit (except common sense) on the number of passengers who stand. The ride costs 50c.

Traghetti are supposed to operate from about 9am to 6pm between Campo Traghetto (near Santa Maria del Giglio) and Calle de Lanza (Map pp294–5); Calle Mocenigo Casa Vecchia, further northwest, and Calle Traghetto (Map pp294–5); Campo Santa Sofia and Campo della Pescaria (Map p300), near the produce market.

Several other traghetto routes operate from 9am to noon only. They include Stazione di Santa Lucia to Fondamenta San Simeon Piccolo (Map pp290–1); Campo San Marcuola to Salizada del Fontego dei Turchi (Map pp290–1); Fondamenta del Vin to Riva del Carbon, near the Ponte di Rialto (Map p296); Campo San Samuele, north of the Ponte dell'Accademia, and Calle del Traghetto (Map pp294–5); and Calle Vallaresso to Punta della Dogana (Map p296). Some of these may on occasion not operate at all (as was the case with the latter two in 2005).

Vaporetto

The most common form of transport around Venice, after your feet, are the vaporetti, the city's ferries. Actually, there are at least three kinds of ferry: the standard, ponderous vaporetto (as in line No 1 down the Grand Canal), the sleeker *motoscafo*, which also runs local routes, and the *motonave* – big inter-island boats that head for Torcello and other more distant destinations. Just to complicate things a little, locals tend to call any public-transport boat a *batello*.

The **ACTV** (☎ 041 24 24; www.actv.it) runs public transport in the Comune di Venezia (the municipality), covering mainland buses and all the waterborne public transport around Venice. You can pick up timetables and route maps from the ACTV information office on Piazzale Roma (Map pp290–1) and ticket booths at some stops (such as Accademia).

Something to remember: the vaporetti get crowded, and visitors have a habit of gathering by exits. If you are standing near one, it is common practice on reaching a stop to get off and let passengers behind you disembark before you get back on.

The main night-vaporetto service (N line) does a circuit around Venice and the Lido (see below).

ROUTES

From Piazzale Roma, vaporetto No 1 zigzags up the Grand Canal to San Marco and then on to the Lido. If you aren't in a rush, it's a great introduction to Venice. Ferry No 17 carries vehicles from Tronchetto, near Piazzale Roma, to the Lido.

A route map can be found on p306. Routes and route numbers can change. Not all routes go both ways.

Frequency varies greatly according to line and time of day. The No 1 runs every 10 minutes through most of the day, while lines such as the No 41 and No 42 only run every 20 minutes. Services to Burano and Torcello are still less frequent. Night services can be as much as one hour apart. Some lines stop running by around 9pm, so check timetables.

DM (Diretto Murano) Piazzale Roma– Ferrovia–Murano and back.

LN (Laguna Nord) San Zaccaria (Pietà)–Lido–Litorale del Cavallino (Punta Sabbioni)–Treporti–Burano–Mazzorbo–Murano (Faro)–Fondamente Nuove and reverse.

T Torcello–Burano (half-hourly service) and back from 7am to 8.30pm.

No 1 Piazzale Roma–Ferrovia–Grand Canal (all stops)–Lido and back.

No 3 Fast circular line: Tronchetto–Ferrovia–San Samuele–Accademia–San Marco–Tronchetto (summer).

No 4 Fast circular line in reverse direction to No 3 (summer).

No 5 San Zaccaria–Murano and back.

No 11 Lido–Pellestrina and back.

No 13 Fondamente Nuove–Murano–Vignole–Sant'Erasmo–Treporti and back.

No 17 Car ferry: Tronchetto–Lido and back (extends to Punta Sabbioni in summer).

No 18 Murano–Vignole–Sant'Erasmo–Lido and back (summer).

No 20 San Zaccaria–San Servolo–San Lazzaro and back.

No 24 Mestre (Darsena Via Torino)–Rialto and back. A limited commuter service that runs not more than four times a day and not necessarily year round.

No 31 Pellestrina–Chioggia and back (part of the No 11 bus line from Lido).

No 41 Circular line: Piazzale Roma–Sacca Fisola–Giudecca–San Zaccaria–San Pietro–Fondamente Nuove–Murano–Ferrovia.

No 42 Circular line in reverse direction to No 41.

No 51 Circular line: Piazzale Roma–Santa Marta–Zattere–San Zaccaria–Lido–San Pietro–Fondamente Nuove–Ferrovia.

No 52 Circular line in reverse direction to No 51.

No 61 Limited-stops weekdays-only circular line: Piazzale Roma–Santa Marta–San Basilio–Zattere–Giardini–Sant'Elena–Lido.

No 62 Limited-stops weekdays-only circular line, reverse direction to No 61.

No 82 San Zaccaria–San Marco–Grand Canal (all stops)–Ferrovia–Piazzale Roma–Tronchetto–Zattere–Giudecca–San Giorgio. A Limitato San Marco or Limitato Piazzale Roma sign means it will not go beyond those stops. Sometimes it goes only as far as Rialto. In summer the line extends from San Zaccaria to the Lido.

N All-stops night circuit: Lido–Giardini–San Zaccaria–Grand Canal (all stops)–Ferrovia–Piazzale Roma–Tronchetto–Giudecca–San Giorgio–San Zaccaria (starts around 11.30pm; last service around 5am).

N A second night service (aka NMU) from Fondamente Nuove to Murano – three or four runs from midnight.

N A third night run, this time a nocturnal version of the Laguna Nord service (aka NLN) – a handful of services between Fondamente Nuove and Burano, Mazzorbo, Torcello, Sant'Erasmo and Treporti.

SERVICES

Linea Clodia Venice (Pietà) to Chioggia (same-day return €9.30); operates June to September only.

Linea Fusina Venice (Zattere) to Fusina (one way/return €5/9). There's also a direct summer service between Fusina and the Alberoni beaches on the Lido for the same price. Fusina, on the mainland, has a huge parking lot for day-trippers and several nearby camping grounds. The trip to Zattere (from seven departures a day in winter to 15 a day in summer) takes 15 minutes and the Alberoni run about 20 minutes.

TICKETS

Tickets can be purchased from the ticket booths at most stops. Generally, they are validated when sold to you, which means they are for immediate use. If they are not validated, or if you request them not to be (so you can use them later), you are supposed to validate them in the machines located at all stops before you get on your first vaporetto. You can also buy single-trip tickets when boarding. You will probably be charged double if you have lots of luggage. If you are caught without a ticket you must buy one and pay a €23 fine.

The following tickets are poor value and should only be used if you rarely catch a vaporetto:

Andata e ritorno (Return €6) Valid until midnight.

Corsa semplice (One way €3.50) Valid for one hour.

Grand Canal (Tickets €5) Valid for 90 minutes.

Line 11 (Tickets €5) Boat and bus from Lido to Chioggia; valid for 12 hours.

Line 24 (One way/return €5/10) Multiple tickets are not valid.

Paglia/Fondamente Nuove (Tickets €8.50) Allows unlimited use on LN line for 12 hours from validation.

Return trip using Grand Canal one way (Tickets €7) Applies to lines 3 and 4.

Better value is a *biglietto a tempo* (€10.50), a ticket valid on all transport (except the Alilaguna, Linea Fusina, LineaBlù and Linea Clodia services) for unlimited travel during 24 hours from the first validation (*convalida*). The *biglietto tre giorni* is a three-day version (€22, or €15 if you have a Rolling Venice card, see p254).

If you are staying for a week or more, consider an Abbonamento (period pass). The pass, which you can apply for at the Piazzale Roma ticket office (Map pp290–1) and is valid for three years, costs €8 (you need a passport photo and a residential address), or €5 to renew. With this you can obtain a monthly pass for unlimited use on all ferries (except Alilaguna, Linea Clodia and Linea Fusina) for €25 (or include buses to Mestre for €29).

WARNING

Vaporetto stops can be confusing, especially the bigger and busier ones such as Piazzale Roma, Ferrovia, San Marco and San Zaccaria. At these and some others you will see several jetties, each catering to a line and direction. Study the signs at the various quays carefully, otherwise you might find yourself on a vaporetto with the right number but going the wrong way!

Vessels making for the Piazza San Marco area in particular can cause anguish, as most stop at one of a string of stops along Riva degli Schiavoni (Map p296 & p298). Always keep an eye out for San Zaccaria. If your boat stops here, it is unlikely to make another San Marco stop before heading off elsewhere.

Finally, just to keep you on your toes, some of the main services (most commonly the No 82) are limited-stops jobs. This can mean, for instance, that if you pick up the No 82 with a view to heading for the Lido, you may find it terminating at Rialto instead. Ferry crew cry this out, but in Italian only.

Water Taxi

Venetian water taxis ain't cheap, with a €8.70 flagfall, an extra €6 if you order one by telephone, €1.30 per minute thereafter and various surcharges that make a gondola ride look affordable. Up to 15 people can ride in a taxi, but that can be rather uncomfortable. If you want to take a taxi, make sure the craft has the yellow strip with licence number displayed. If approached by a craft without this sign, don't take it.

WARNING

A special problem on the Isola del Tronchetto is illegitimate water-taxi drivers. These people may wear official-looking caps and badges and approach the freshly parked tourist with stories of having the only vessel available to transfer people from Tronchetto to destinations elsewhere in Venice. This is rubbish, as vaporetti (No 82) call here regularly. Unwitting victims are transported (often to places they did not want to go) for outrageous sums of money. Some have been whisked away to Murano to look at someone's cousin's glass shop!

BUS

All buses serving Venice use Piazzale Roma as their terminus. **Eurolines** (www.eurolines .com), in conjunction with local bus companies across Europe, is the main international carrier. Eurolines' website provides links to the sites of all the national operators. In Venice, Eurolines tickets can be bought from **Agenzia Brusutti** (Map pp290–1; ☎ 041 520 55 30; Piazzale Roma, Santa Croce 497/e). Buses run several times a week from London, Paris, Barcelona and other European centres.

ACTV buses serve the area immediately surrounding Venice, including Mestre and Chioggia, while ATVO operates buses to destinations all over the eastern part of the Veneto. Numerous other companies go further west in the Veneto, across into Friuli-Venezia Giulia (Italy's easternmost region) and beyond. Tickets and information are available at the ticket office in Piazzale Roma (Map pp290–1). As a rule, most of the main destinations are more conveniently reached by train.

Buses (including night buses) run across the bridge to Mestre and up and down the Lido. Tickets cost €1 and are valid for one hour from the time you validate them in the machine on the bus. A carnet of 10 tickets costs €9.

You can buy tickets at the main bus station in Piazzale Roma (Map pp290–1), and from many newsstands and *tabaccherie* (tobacconists). See also Tickets, opposite.

CAR & MOTORCYCLE
Driving to Venice

Venice is 279km from Milan, 529km from Rome, 579km from Geneva, 1112km from Paris, 1135km from Berlin, 1515km from London and 1820km from Madrid.

The main points of entry to Italy are the Mont Blanc tunnel from France at Chamonix, which connects with the A5 for Turin and Milan; the Grand St Bernard tunnel from Switzerland, which also connects with the A5; and the Brenner Pass from Austria, which connects with the A22 to Bologna.

Make sure you have snow chains in winter when crossing the mountains into Italy.

Once in Italy, the A4 is the quickest way to reach Venice from east or west. It connects Turin with Trieste, passing through Milan and Mestre. Take the Venezia exit and follow the signs for the city. Coming from the Brenner Pass, the A22 connects with the A4 near Verona. From the south, take the A13 from Bologna, which connects with the A4 at Padua.

Many of Italy's autostrade (four- to six-lane motorways) are toll roads. You can pay tolls by credit card (including Visa, Master-Card, Amex and Diners Club) on most autostrade in northern Italy. You sometimes have the choice of the toll road or busy *strada statale* (represented on maps as 'S' or 'SS'). These tend to pass through towns and can as much as double your travel time. But they can also be more interesting. The SS11 from Padua to Venice is an example. Smaller roads are known as *strade provinciali* (represented on maps as 'P' or 'SP').

Vehicles must be roadworthy, registered and insured (third party at least). Ask your insurer for a European Accident Statement form, which can simplify matters in the event of an accident. A European breakdown-assistance policy, such as the AA Five Star Service or the RAC Eurocover Motoring Assistance in the UK, is a good investment.

You can pay for petrol with most credit cards at most service stations. Those on the autostrade are open 24 hours. Otherwise, opening hours are generally around 7am to 12.30pm and 3.30pm to 7.30pm (7pm in winter). Up to 75% of service stations are closed on Sunday and public holidays; others close on Monday. Quite a few service stations have self-service pumps that accept banknotes.

Hire

Avis (Map pp290–1; ☎ 041 523 73 77) has an office in Piazzale Roma, as do **Europcar** (☎ 041 523 86 16), **Hertz** (☎ 041 528 40 91) and **Expressway** (☎ 041 522 30 00). They all have reps at Marco Polo airport, too.

Parking

Visitors to Venice who insist on driving their cars right into the city pay a hefty price, and not necessarily just in parking fees. On busy days (especially holiday weekends), day-trippers frequently find themselves stuck on the Ponte della Libertà making little forward progress and unable to go back. It is not unknown for traffic to get so jammed that the police shut the city off from the mainland. Why risk it?

Once over the Ponte della Libertà from Mestre, you can pay to tie up your metallic steed at one of the huge car parks in Piazzale Roma or on Isola del Tronchetto. There is a small area in Piazzale Roma (Map pp294–5) where you can drop a car for 30 minutes free of charge (in practice, people tend to leave their cars longer). Queuing to get into one of these few spaces can be supremely frustrating, but locals generally observe the first come, first served rule. Pay car parks:

Autopark Ca' Doge (Map pp294–5; ☎ 041 520 24 89; Piazzale Roma; per hr €3; ⏲ 7am-1am)

Garage Comunale (Map pp290–1; ☎ 041 272 73 01; www.asmvenezia.it; Piazzale Roma; per day €19; ⏲ 24 hr)

Parking San Marco (Map pp294–5; ☎ 041 523 22 13; www.garagesanmarco.it; Piazzale Roma; per 12 hr €20, per 24 hr €26; ⏲ 24 hr) Guests of certain hotels get discounts.

Parking Sant'Andrea (Map pp294–5; ☎ 041 272 73 04; Piazzale Roma; per 2 hr or part thereof €4.13; ⏲ 24 hr)

Parking Stazione (Map p305; ☎ 041 93 80 21; Viale Stazione 10, Mestre; per hr €2, per 3 hr €4, to midnight €5.50; ⏲ 24 hr) This is one of several car parks, some of them on the same street, in Mestre. They are all cheaper than those in Venice. Nearly all street parking is metered in Mestre.

Tronchetto (Map p289; ☎ 041 520 75 55; www.venice parking.it; Isola del Tronchetto; per 24 hr €18; ⏲ 24 hr)

THE CARRYING TRADE

Getting from the vaporetto stop to your hotel can be difficult if you are heavily laden. *Portabagagli* (porters) operate from several stands around the city. At the train station and Piazzale Roma they charge €15.50 for one item and roughly €5 for each extra one for transport within Venice proper. Prices virtually double to transport bags to any of the islands, including Giudecca. You have to negotiate at other porter stations.

Points where porters can be found include the train station (☎ 041 71 52 72), Piazzale Roma (☎ 041 522 35 90), Campo San Geremia (☎ 041 71 56 94), Piazza San Marco (☎ 041 523 23 85) the Ponte dell'Accademia (☎ 041 522 48 91).

ILLEGAL PARKING

If you return to your car to find that it's no longer there, call the *vigili urbani* (local police) on ☎ 041 274 70 70. They dump towed cars in one of three depots. It'll cost you around €100 for the towing, €40 a day in the pound and the parking fine.

WARNING

Thieves haunt some of the car parks, particularly in Mestre. Do not leave anything of even remote value in a parked car.

TAXI

Land taxis operate from a rank in Piazzale Roma (Map pp294–5). Call ☎ 041 523 77 74 or ☎ 041 93 62 22.

TRAIN

Train is the most convenient overland option for reaching Venice from other Italian cities or abroad. For information on travelling from the UK, contact the **Rail Europe Travel Centre** (☎ 0870 838 2008; www.raileurope .co.uk; 178 Piccadilly, London W1V 0BA). For travel within Italy you can get information at your nearest train station or travel agent. Alternatively, contact **Trenitalia** (☎ 89 20 21; www.trenitalia.it).

A wide variety of trains run on the Italian rail network. They start with all-stops *locali*, and *regionali*, both slow local trains. *Interregionali* cover greater distances and don't necessarily stop at every station.

Intercity (IC) trains are fast services that operate between major cities. Eurocity (EC) trains are the international version. High-speed *pendolini* and other top-of-the-range services, which on high-speed track can zip along at more than 300km/h, are collectively known as Eurostar Italia (ES).

Almost every train leaving from Stazione di Santa Lucia stops in Mestre (€1, 10 minutes). Get your tickets from station tobacconists.

Apart from the standard division between *prima* and *seconda classe* (1st and 2nd class – generally *locali* and *regionali* have *seconda classe* seats only) you have to pay a supplement for taking a fast train (IC and up). You can pay the supplement separately from the ticket. Thus, if you have a *seconda classe* return ticket from Venice to Milan, you might decide to avoid the supplement one way and take a slower train, but pay it on the way back to speed things up. You need to pay the supplement *before* boarding the train. If you know exactly which train you want, the supplement will be included in your ticket.

You can buy rail tickets (for major destinations on fast trains at least) at the station (often crowded) and from most travel agents. If you choose to buy them at the station, there are automatic machines that accept credit cards and cash. You can also buy tickets online or over the phone through Trenitalia, or look for cheaper tickets at www.trenok.com, in Italian. At the Trenitalia number you can also book for ticketless travel on ES and IC trains.

Validate your ticket in the orange machines on station platforms. Failure to do so will almost certainly result in embarrassment and a hefty on-the-spot fine when the ticket inspector comes around.

Orient Express

The **Venice Simplon Orient Express** (☎ 0845 077 2222 in UK; www.orient-express.com) runs between London and Venice via Paris, Innsbruck and Verona on Thursday and Sunday (late April to November), taking about 30 hours. The one-way fare (most people take a plane for the return trip) is UK£1350. You can extend the journey with add-ons to Florence and Rome or do the trip between Venice and Istanbul via Budapest and Bucharest.

Venice Train Stations

Inside Venice's Stazione di Santa Lucia (Map pp290–1) there's a rail-travel **information office** (🕑 7am-9pm) opposite the APT office (see p262). Next door to the APT office is a branch of the hotel-booking service **Associazione Veneziana Albergatori** (Venice Hoteliers Association; see p193).

The **deposito bagagli office** (per piece first 5 hr €3.50, next 7 hr 30c, per hr thereafter 10c; 🕑 6am-midnight) is opposite platform 14, and there are lockers on platform 1.

Mestre station (Map p305) has similar services, including rail information, a hotel-booking office and a **deposito bagagli office** (per piece first 5 hr €3.50, next 7 hr 30c, per hr thereafter 10c; 🕑 7am-11pm).

PRACTICALITIES
ACCOMMODATION

Sleeping options in Venice range from the official HI youth hostel and a handful of other dorm-style places to some of the grandest old hotels in the world, with prices to match. See Sleeping, p192 (in that chapter recommendations are arranged in alphabetical order in each section). The emphasis is on midrange accommodation, but we have slipped in some of the city's great top-end hotels, too. Each section ends with a Cheap Sleeps list for those on a tighter budget.

High season is most of the year for most hotels and many (especially at the cheaper end) do not alter their rates significantly. The depths of winter (from late November to December, except Christmas, and from mid-January to Easter, except Carnevale) are relatively quiet, and many hoteliers cut their top asking prices drastically. The rash of hotel openings since the late 1990s combined with a drop in tourist numbers since the September 2001 terror attacks in the USA has also added downward pressure on prices, so always hunt around.

BUSINESS HOURS

In general, shops open 9am to 1pm and 3.30pm to 7.30pm (or 4pm to 8pm) Monday to Saturday. They may remain closed on Monday morning, or on Wednesday and/or Saturday afternoon. Some shops hoping to do a little extra tourist business open on Sunday, too.

Big department stores, such as Coin, and most supermarkets open from around 9am to 7.30pm Monday to Saturday.

Banks tend to open from 8.30am to 1.30pm and 3.30pm to 4.30pm Monday to Friday, but often vary their hours a little. A few open on Saturday morning.

Bars (in the Italian sense, ie coffee-and-sandwich places) and cafés generally open from 7.30am to 8pm, although some stay open after 8pm and turn into pub-style drinking and meeting places. Pubs and bars in the nocturnal sense are mostly shut by 1am; a few soldier on until around 2am or 3am, especially on Friday and Saturday nights.

For *pranzo* (lunch), restaurants usually open from 12.30pm to 3pm, but few take orders after 2pm. Hours for *cena* (dinner) vary, but locals start sitting down to dine at around 7.30pm. You'll be hard-pressed to find a place still serving after 10.30pm and many stop by 9.30pm.

CHILDREN

Venice isn't just for art lovers and hopeless romantics. Its uniqueness makes it fascinating for children, too. Make it an adventure and they'll soon start wondering as much as you just what lies around the corner.

Kids will certainly enjoy a trip down the Grand Canal. If you prefer not to take a gondola ride, at least treat them to a short hop across the canal on a *traghetto*. They are bound to appreciate an excursion to the islands, particularly to see the glass-making demonstrations on Murano. Older kids might enjoy watching the big ships pass along the Canale della Giudecca, so take them to Gelateria Nico (p144) on the Fondamenta Zattere (Map pp294–5) for a relaxing waterside gelato.

Children of all ages will get a kick out of watching the Mori strike the hour at the Torre dell'Orologio (p62) on Piazza San Marco.

Understandably, most of the museums and galleries will leave the little 'uns cold, but some may work. Kids with a nautical interest should be drawn by the boats and model ships at the Museo Storico Navale (p85). The sculpture garden at the Peggy Guggenheim Collection (p68) may prove an educational distraction while you indulge your modern-art needs.

Climbing towers is usually a winner. Try the Campanile di San Marco (p55) or the bell towers of San Giorgio Maggiore (p91), and Santa Maria Assunta on Torcello (p93).

Parco Savorgnan (part of Palazzo Savorgnan, Map pp290–1) and the Giardini Pubblici (Map p299) have playgrounds.

In summer, a jaunt to the beach – the Lido di Venezia, Sottomarina (Chioggia) or Lido di Jesolo – should win points. If you are using your own transport, remember to leave early to beat the horrible traffic jams. And forget it at weekends (except on the Lido di Venezia) – whether you drive or catch buses, you'll be stuck on the roads for an eternity.

Discounts are usually available for children under 12 on public transport, and at museums, galleries and other sights.

A couple of handy books are *Viva Venice*, by Paola Scibilia and Paolo Zoffoli, and *Venice for Kids*, by Elisabetta Pasqualin. These books are richly illustrated and bursting with games, legends, anecdotes and suggestions on what to do.

Baby-sitting

Some of the major hotels, especially those on the Lido di Venezia, offer a baby-sitting service.

CLIMATE

Midsummer is the worst time of year to be in Venice – average daytime temperatures hover around 27°C but can go higher. Humidity is high, the canals can get a little on the nose and prevailing southern winds (the *sirocco*) are hot.

In spring the weather is often crisp and clear and the temperatures pleasant. That said, quite a lot of rain falls in May and into June. In July and August the humidity can bring cracking storms in the evening.

The first half of winter sees heavy rainfall, with flooding most likely in November and December. On bad days, the city and lagoon are enveloped in mist (which some find enchanting), but every now and then you get lucky and the sky clears.

December and January are the coldest months, with average temperatures hovering between 0°C and 7°C, and often clear skies. Because of the city's position on the lagoon, snow is a rarity.

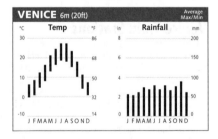

COURSES

The **Istituto Italiano di Cultura** (IIC; Italian Cultural Institute), a government-sponsored organisation that promotes Italian culture and language, is a good place to research courses in Italy. The institute has branches all over the world, including Australia (Sydney), Canada (Montreal), the UK (London) and the USA (Los Angeles, New York and Washington). The Italian foreign ministry website, www.esteri.it, has a full list; click on Diplomatic Representations and then on Italian Cultural Institutes. There are surprisingly few language schools in Venice.

Some suggestions for Italian language and other courses in Venice:

Bottega del Tintoretto (Map pp290–1; ☎ 041 72 20 81; www.tintorettovenezia.it, in Italian; Fondamenta dei Mori, Cannaregio 3400) This former stomping ground of Tintoretto has recovered its use as a hive of artistic activity, as Roberto Mazzetto now runs an old-time print workshop there. Venice was once at the forefront of European printing, but Roberto is one of the last to keep traditional methods alive. To supplement the activity, he and his cohorts run a series of courses ranging from bookbinding to design, from painting nudes to sculpture. Some courses run over a year, with lessons of two to four hours a week (€85 to €120 a month). Also of interest are the summer intensive five-day courses (€360). Mazzetto can also offer B&B accommodation.

Ca' Macana (Map pp294–5; ☎ 041 522 97 49; www.camacana.com; Calle delle Botteghe, Dorsoduro 3172) This mask and costume shop runs a pair of short courses (2½ hours each) in mask-making and, more interestingly, mask decorating. As a rule it only takes groups of between 10 and 55, which keeps the cost at between €23 and €56.50 (plus VAT) per person, depending on the course and number of participants. After the decorating course, you take home your own mask.

Fondazione Giorgio Cini (Map pp302–3; ☎ 041 524 01 19; www.cini.it; Isola di San Giorgio Maggiore) Organises seminars and specialist courses on subjects relating to the city and its culture, in particular music, art and restoration.

Istituto Venezia (Map pp294–5; ☎ 041 522 43 31; www.istitutovenezia.com; Campo Santa Margherita, Dorsoduro 3116/a) Offers language and one- and two-week courses on subjects as widely divergent as cooking, wine and Burano lace. Four weeks (80 hours) of intensive language classes cost €600.

Venice International University (Map p289; ☎ 041 271 95 11; www.univiu.org; Isola di San Servolo) Proposes a vast range of undergraduate courses, aimed mostly at foreign students, with components ranging from Italian language and Venetian churches through to bioethics!

CUSTOMS

Travellers entering Italy from outside the EU are allowed to bring in duty-free one bottle of spirits, one bottle of wine, 50ml of perfume and 200 cigarettes.

Duty-free allowances for travel between EU countries were abolished in 1999. For duty-paid items bought at normal shops in one EU country and taken into another, the allowances are 90L of wine, 10L of spirits, unlimited quantities of perfume and 800 cigarettes. VAT-free shopping is available in the duty-free shops at airports for people travelling between EU countries.

DISABLED TRAVELLERS

People with disabilities have not been completely left out of what is, after all, a fairly unfriendly environment for those with mobility problems.

A map available from APT offices (p262) has areas of the city shaded in yellow to indicate that they can be negotiated without running into one of Venice's many bridges. Some of the bridges are equipped with *servoscale* (lifts), which are marked on the map. You can (in theory) get hold of a key to operate these lifts from the tourist offices.

A **disabled assistance office** (⌚ 7am-9pm) is located in front of platform 4 at Stazione di Santa Lucia.

Vaporetto lines 1 and 82, and the bigger lagoon ferries, have access for wheelchairs. Passengers in wheelchairs travel for free.

Five bus lines are adapted for wheelchair users: No 2 (Piazzale Roma to Mestre train station), No 4 (Piazzale Roma to Corso del Popolo in Mestre), No 5 (Piazzale Roma to Marco Polo airport), No 6 (Tronchetto and Piazzale Roma to the mainland) and No 15 (a mainland service running between Marco Polo airport and Mestre).

The Venice town hall is also developing a project for the sight-impaired, including tactile maps of the city that can be downloaded using special processes. Information (in Italian only) is available at www.comune.venezia.it/letturagevolata.

Organisations

Accessible Travel & Leisure (☎ 01452-729739; www.accessibletravel.co.uk; Avionics House, Naas Lane, Gloucester GL2 2SN) Claims to be the biggest UK travel agent dealing with travel for the disabled.

Holiday Care (☎ 0845 124 9971; www.holidaycare.org.uk; 7th fl, Sunley House, 4 Bedford Park, Croydon, Surrey CR0 2AP) Information on hotels with disabled access, where to hire equipment and tour operators dealing with the disabled.

Informahandicap (Map p296; ☎ 041 274 81 44; www .comune.venezia.it/informahandicap, in Italian; Ca' Farsetti, San Marco 4136) The website has details on hotels that can accommodate disabled guests, getting around the city and other information.

Informahandicap (Map p305; ☎ 041 274 61 44; Piazzale Candiani 5) Mestre branch.

Royal Association for Disability & Rehabilitation (RADAR; ☎ 020-7250 3222; www.radar.org.uk; Unit 12, City Forum, 250 City Rd, London EC1V 8AF) Publishes *European Holidays & Travel Abroad: A Guide for Disabled People*, which provides an overview of facilities available to disabled travellers throughout Europe.

DISCOUNT CARDS

An International Student Identity Card (ISIC; www.isic.org) can get you discounted admission prices at some sights and help with cheap flights out of Italy. Similar cards are available to teachers (ITIC) and nonstudents (IYTC). The cards also carry a travel-insurance component. They are issued by student unions, hostelling organisations and some youth travel agencies.

In Venice the ISIC benefits are limited. A couple of restaurants and half a dozen bars give discounts, along with a couple of cinemas and some shops. As for sights, the card will only come in handy at the Palazzo Querini Stampalia, the Scuola Grande di San Rocco and a few minor sights. You may get discounted travel at the Centro Turistico Studentesco e Giovanile (CTS) student travel agency (p263).

Rolling Venice

If you are aged between 14 and 29, pick up the **Rolling Venice card** (€3), which offers significant discounts on food, accommodation, entertainment, public transport, museums and galleries. You can get the card at tourist offices, ACTV public-transport ticket points and Vela information and ticket stands (see p171). The Rolling Venice map lists all the hotels, restaurants, shops, museums, cinemas and theatres where the card entitles you to reductions.

Venice Card

A much-touted all-inclusive transport and sights card, **Venice Card** (☎ 041 24 24; www .venicecard.it) can save a little hassle but represents no financial saving over alternatives.

There are two types of Venice Card. The blue card gives you unlimited use of ferries and buses throughout the Venice municipality for one, three or seven days. It also gives you free access to the public toilets (otherwise 50c) scattered around town.

The orange version throws in the Musei Civici (City Museums) for free (see Special Tickets, p50).

The junior blue card (for those aged under 30) costs €9/22/49 for one/three/ seven days, while the senior version costs €14/29/51. The junior orange card costs €18/35/61 and the senior version €28/47/68. The three- and seven-day passes are cheaper if purchased online.

ELECTRICITY

The electric current in Venice is 220V, 50Hz, and plugs have two round pins, as in the rest of continental Europe. Several countries outside Europe (such as the USA and Canada) use 110V, 60Hz, which means that some appliances from those countries may perform poorly. It is always safest to use a transformer.

EMBASSIES & CONSULATES

Most countries have an embassy in Rome. Look them up under Ambasciate in that city's Pagine Gialle (Yellow Pages). A limited number of countries maintain consulates in Venice, including:

Austria (Map pp294–5; ☎ 041 524 05 56; Fondamenta Condulmer, Santa Croce 251)

France (Map p296; ☎ 041 522 43 19; Ramo del Pestrin, Castello 6140)

Germany (Map pp294–5; ☎ 041 523 76 75; Campo Sant'Anzolo, San Marco 3816)

Netherlands (Map pp294–5; ☎ 041 528 34 16; Ramo Giustinian, San Marco 2888)

Switzerland (Map pp294–5; ☎ 041 520 39 44; Campo di Sant'Agnese, Dorsoduro 810)

UK (Map p305; ☎ 041 505 59 90; Piazzale Donatori di Sangue 2, Mestre)

The nearest **Australian consulate** (☎ 02 7770 4227) is in Milan, at Via Borgogna 2. The nearest **US consulate** (☎ 02 29 03 51) is also in Milan, at Via Principe Amedeo 2/10. The **Canadian consulate** (Map p226; ☎ 049 876 48 33) is in Padua, at Riviera Ruzzante 25.

EMERGENCIES

There is a **police station** (Map p298; ☎ 041 271 55 11; Fondamenta di San Lorenzo, Castello 5053) a bit of a walk from the centre, and a handy branch at Piazza San Marco 67 (Map p296). The city's *questura*, or head police station, is really off the beaten track in one of the few really quite unpleasant parts of town in the ex-convent of Santa Chiara (Map pp290–1; Santa Croce 500), just beyond Piazzale Roma.

Useful numbers:

Ambulance *(ambulanza)*	☎ 118
Fire Brigade *(vigili del fuoco)*	☎ 115
Military Police *(carabinieri)*	☎ 112
Police *(polizia)*	☎ 113

GAY & LESBIAN TRAVELLERS

Homosexuality is legal in Italy and well tolerated in Venice and the north. However, the city offers precious little in the way of specifically gay entertainment.

ArciGay (www.arcigay.it), the national gay organisation, has information on the gay and lesbian scene in Italy. The companion **Gay.It** site (http://it.gay.com, in Italian) provides listings for bars, discos, gay beaches and beauty centres. The pickings in Venice are slim, as you'll find (see p168). The nearest gay organisation is **ArciGay Tralaltro** (Map p226; ☎ 049 876 24 58; www.tralaltro.it, in Italian; Via Santa Sofia 5) in Padua, a town that offers considerably more nightlife options for gays.

HOLIDAYS

For Venetians as for most Italians, the main holiday periods remain summer (July and especially August), the Christmas–New Year period and Easter. August is a peculiar time as all Italy grinds to a halt, especially around Ferragosto (Feast of the Assumption; 15 August). Travelling to and around Venice in this high holiday period is far from ideal. For information on the city's many festivals and other events, see p10.

National public holidays:

Capodanno/Anno Nuovo (New Year's Day) 1 January.

Epifania/Befana (Epiphany) 6 January.

Pasquetta/Lunedì dell'Angelo (Easter Monday) March/April.

Giorno della Liberazione (Liberation Day) April 25. This marks the Allied Victory in Italy, and the end of the German presence and Mussolini, in 1945.

Festa del Lavoro (Labour Day) 1 May.

Festa della Repubblica (Republic Day) 2 June.

Ferragosto (Feast of the Assumption) 15 August.

Ognissanti (All Saints' Day) 1 November.

Immacolata Concezione (Feast of the Immaculate Conception) 8 December.

Natale (Christmas Day) 25 December.

Festa di Santo Stefano (Boxing Day) 26 December.

INTERNET ACCESS

If you intend to use a portable computer for surfing the Web, make sure you have a universal AC adaptor, a two-pin plug adaptor for Europe and a reputable modem. Wi-fi hot spots remain noticeable by their absence, with the exception of a handful of top-flight hotels. Some hotels are set up with Internet connections, and sometimes just plugging into the hotel room's phone socket will be sufficient (although frequently this will not work, as you have to go through a switchboard). For more information on travelling with a portable computer, see www.teleadapt.com or http://igo.ententeweb.com.

Major Internet service providers (ISPs) such as **CompuServe** (www.compuserve.com) have dial-in nodes in Italy; download a list before you leave home.

Some Italian servers can provide short-term accounts for local Internet access. **Agora** (☎ 800 304 999; www.agoratelematica.it, in Italian) is one of them. Several Italian ISPs offer free Internet connections: check out the websites (in Italian only) of **Tiscali** (www.tiscali.it), **Kataweb** (www.kataweb.it) and **Libero** (www.libero.it).

If you intend to rely on Internet cafés you'll need to carry three pieces of information: your incoming (POP or IMAP) mail server name, your account name and your password.

Internet Cafés

Some of the following places offer student rates and also have deals on cards for several hours' use at reduced rates.

Internet Corner (Map p298; ☎ 041 277 05 15; Barbaria delle Tole, Castello 6661/a; per hr €7; ☺ 10am-10pm Mon-Sat)

Internet Point (Map pp294–5; ☎ 041 71 46 66; Calle dei Preti, Dorsoduro 3812/a; per hr €9; ☺ 9.15am-8pm Mon-Sat) You need to bring some form of ID to use the Internet service.

Mondadori (Map p296; ☎ 041 522 21 93; Salizada San Moisè, San Marco 1346; per half hr €3; 🕑 10am-8pm Mon-Sat, 11am-7.30pm Sun) Up on the 1st floor of this bookstore you'll find a few good machines spaced out over a long work bench.

Planet Internet (Map pp290–1; ☎ 041 524 41 88; Rio Terà San Leonardo, Cannaregio 1519; per hr €8; 🕑 9am-midnight)

Venice Internet Point (Map pp290–1; ☎ 041 275 82 17; www.ve-nice.com, in Italian; Rio Terà Lista di Spagna, Cannaregio 149; per hr €8; 🕑 9am-11pm)

World House (Map p296; ☎ 041 528 48 71; www .world-house.org; Calle della Chiesa, Castello 4502; per hr €8; 🕑 10am-11pm)

LAUNDRY

Self-service laundries are finally beginning to appear in Venice.

Laundromat (Map p296; Ruga Giuffa, Castello 4826; 8kg wash €4.50, dry €6, or reductions on €20 card; 🕑 8.30am-11pm)

Orange Laundry (Map pp290–1; www.laundry.it; Calle Chioverette, Santa Croce 665/b; 8kg wash €3, 12kg dry €2 with €20 card; 🕑 7.30am-10.30pm)

Orange Laundry (Map pp302–3; Fondamenta delle Zitelle 65, Giudecca; 8kg wash €3, 12kg dry €2 with €20 card; 🕑 7.30am-10.30pm)

Orange Laundry (Map p305; Via Piave 41, Mestre; 8kg wash €2.50, 16kg dry €2.50 with €20 card; 🕑 7.30am-11.30pm)

Speedy Wash (Map pp290–1; Rio Terà San Leonardo, Cannaregio 1520; 8kg wash €4.50, 15kg dry €3; 🕑 8am-11pm)

LOST PROPERTY

If you lose your stuff in Venice it may well be gone forever, but check with the *vigili urbani* office on Piazzale Roma (Map pp290–1; ☎ 041 522 45 76). Otherwise, the following numbers might be useful.

ACTV (☎ 041 272 21 79) Public transport.

Marco Polo Airport (☎ 041 260 92 22)

Municipio (☎ 041 274 81 11) Town hall.

Train station (☎ 041 78 55 31)

MAPS

You should be able to get by with the maps in this book, but some of those on sale are also worthwhile investments. The free one handed out by the tourist office is next to useless.

Whichever map you buy, you will find inconsistencies. The *Venezianizzazione* (Venetianisation) of street names has created more problems than it could ever have solved. Most maps take a haphazard approach to using Italian, Venetian or mongrel versions. Which is no surprise, because a good deal of the city's *nizioleti* (street signs) are equally haphazard, frequently mixing Venetian and Italian with gay abandon. Usually it's no great hassle to work out – but occasionally you need to use a little lateral thinking. We too have adopted a mix of standard Italian and Venetian, a compromise between what you'll see on the ground and on business cards, websites and so on. There will be discrepancies (and, as purists of the Venetian tongue will note, grammatical and orthographic inconsistencies), but they are usually minor and easy to work out. The final objective is maximum useability.

Try Lonely Planet's *Venice* map. If you can't find it, another good one is the wine red–covered *Venezia* produced by the Touring Club Italiano (1:5000, €7). The TCI also produces a tiny foldout city-centre map (1:5250) for €3.

If you plan to stay for the long haul, *Calli, Campielli e Canali* (Edizioni Helvetica) is for you. This is the definitive street guide and will usually allow you to locate to within 100m any Venetian address you need – saves a *lot* of shoe leather. Posties must do a course in it before being sent out to deliver the mail.

Online, try the maps on **Ombra.net** (www .ombra.net).

Street Numbering

Venice has its own style of street numbering (introduced by the Austrians in the 19th century): instead of a system based on individual streets, each *sestiere* (municipal division) has a long series of numbers. Thus a hotel might give its address simply as San Marco 4687. Because the *sestieri* are fairly small, wandering around and searching out the number is theoretically feasible but often extraordinarily frustrating. Most streets are named, so where possible we have provided street names as well as the *sestiere* number. Even where this is not the case, using the maps in this book in conjunction with the *sestiere* numbers should clear up any mysteries.

MEDICAL SERVICES

Medical Cover

All foreigners have the same right as Italians to free emergency medical treatment in a public hospital. EU citizens (and those of Switzerland, Norway and Iceland) are entitled to the full range of health-care services in public hospitals free of charge, but you will need to present your European Health Insurance Card (EHIC; formerly the E111). Australia has a reciprocal arrangement with Italy that entitles Australian citizens to free public health care – carry your Medicare card.

Citizens of New Zealand, the USA, Canada and other countries have to pay for anything other than emergency treatment. Most travel-insurance policies include medical cover.

The Italian public health system is administered by local centres generally known as Azienda Sanitaria Locale (ASL), Unità Sanitaria Locale (USL) or Unità Socio Sanitaria Locale (USSL). Just for fun, the Venetian version is ULSS. Under these headings you'll find long lists of offices – look for Poliambulatorio (polyclinic) and the telephone number for *accettazione sanitaria* (medical appointments). You need to call this number to make an appointment – there is no point in just rolling up. Clinic opening hours vary widely, with the minimum generally being about 8am to 12.30pm Monday to Friday. Some open for a couple of hours in the afternoon and on Saturday morning.

If your country has a consulate in Venice, staff there should be able to refer you to doctors who speak your language. If you have a specific health complaint, obtain the necessary information and referrals for treatment before leaving home.

The following medical services may be of use to travellers.

Guardia Medica (☎ 041 529 40 60 Venice, 041 534 44 11 Mestre, 041 526 77 43 Lido) This service of night-time callout doctors (locums) operates from 8pm to 8am on weekdays and from 10am to 8am the day before a holiday (including Sunday) until 8am the day after.

Ospedale Civile (Map p300; ☎ 041 529 41 11; Campo SS Giovanni e Paolo, Castello 6777) This is the main hospital. For emergency treatment, go straight to the *pronto soccorso* (casualty) section, where you can also get emergency dental treatment.

Ospedale Umberto I (Map p305; ☎ 800 501 060; Via Circonvallazione 50, Mestre) A modern mainland hospital.

METRIC SYSTEM

Italy uses the metric system. Like other continental Europeans, the Italians indicate decimals with commas and thousands with points. For a conversion chart, see the inside front cover of this book.

MONEY

As in 11 other EU nations (Austria, Belgium, Finland, France, Germany, Greece, Ireland, Luxembourg, the Netherlands, Portugal and Spain), the euro has been the currency in Italy since 2002. By mid-2005 it had hit record levels against the US dollar.

The euro notes come in denominations of €500, €200, €100, €50, €20, €10 and €5, in different colours and sizes. Euro coins are in denominations of €2, €1, 50c, 20c, 10c, 5c, 2c and 1c.

Each participating state decorates the reverse side of the coins with its own designs, but all euro coins can be used anywhere that accepts euros.

For more information, see Economy & Costs, p17.

Changing Money

You can exchange money in banks, at post offices or in currency-exchange booths *(bureaux de change)*. The post office and banks are reliable. Always ask about commissions. You'll find most of the main banks in the area around the Ponte di Rialto and San Marco.

Keep a sharp eye on commissions at *bureaux de change*, which sometimes exceed 10% on traveller's cheques. A handy bank with ATM for both the train and bus stations is the Monte dei Paschi (Map pp290–1) on Fondamenta San Simeon Piccolo.

American Express (Amex; Map p296; ☎ 041 520 08 44; Salizada San Moisè, San Marco 1471; ⏰ 9am-5.30pm Mon-Fri, 9am-12.30pm Sat) Has an ATM for Amex cards.

Travelex (Map p296; ☎ 041 528 73 58; Piazza San Marco, San Marco 142 & Riva del Ferro, San Marco 5126; ⏰ 9am-6pm Mon-Sat, 9.30am-5pm Sun)

Credit/Debit Cards

Major cards such as Visa, MasterCard, Maestro and Cirrus are accepted throughout Italy. They can be used in many hotels, restaurants and shops. Cards can also be used in ATMs displaying the appropriate sign if you have a PIN. If you have no PIN, some (but by no means all) banks will allow you to obtain cash advances over the counter (a lengthy process). MasterCard and Visa are among the most widely recognised for such transactions. Check charges with your bank. Most banks now build in a fee of around 2.75% into every foreign transaction. In addition, ATM withdrawals attract a fee, usually around 1.5%.

If your card is lost, stolen or swallowed by an ATM, you can call toll free to have an immediate stop put on its use. For MasterCard the number in Italy is ☎ 800 870 866, for Visa it's ☎ 800 819 014. For Diners Club call either ☎ 06 357 53 33 (Rome) or a reverse-charges number to the country of issue (☎ 702 797 55 32 in the USA).

Amex is also widely accepted (although not as commonly as Visa or MasterCard). The office in Venice (see p257) has an express cash machine for cardholders. If you lose your Amex card, call ☎ 800 864 046.

Exchange Rates

See the Quick Reference (inside front cover) for exchange rates at the time of going to press. For the latest rates, check out www.oanda.com.

Traveller's Cheques

Traditionally, these have been a safe way of carrying your money because they can be replaced if lost or stolen. In most respects it is more efficient and less cumbersome to use plastic. Various readers have reported having trouble changing traveller's cheques in Italy and it seems that most banks now apply hefty commissions, even on cheques denominated in euros.

If you wish to carry traveller's cheques, Visa, Travelex and Amex are widely accepted brands. The best idea is probably to spread funds across one or more debit/credit cards and a fistful of cheques for emergencies.

Get most of your cheques in fairly large denominations to save on per-cheque commission charges. Amex exchange offices do not charge commission to exchange traveller's cheques (even other brands) or the cash equivalent of US$500 or above.

It's vital to keep your initial receipt, along with a record of your cheque numbers and the ones you have used, separate from the cheques themselves. Take your passport or ID card when you go to cash traveller's cheques.

For lost or stolen cheques, call the following freephone numbers.

Amex (☎ 800 72 000)
MasterCard (☎ 800 870 866)
Travelex (☎ 800 335 511)
Visa (☎ 800 874 155)

NEWSPAPERS & MAGAZINES

A wide selection of national daily newspapers from around Europe (including the UK) is available at newsstands all over central Venice and at strategic locations like the train and bus stations. The *International Herald Tribune*, *Time*, the *Economist*, *Der Spiegel* and a host of other international magazines are also available.

Italian Press

There is no 'national' paper as such but rather several important dailies published in major cities. These include Milan's *Corriere della Sera*, Turin's right-leaning *La Stampa* and Rome's centre-left *La Repubblica*. This trio forms what could be considered the nucleus of a national press, publishing local editions up and down the country.

Two papers dominate the local scene. *Il Gazzettino*, in business since 1887, brings out separate editions in each province across the Triveneto area (the Veneto, Friuli-Venezia Giulia and Trentino). If you are in Venice and want decent coverage of national and foreign news but with solid local content, this is probably the paper you want. Its competition is the more parochial tabloid *La Nuova Venezia*.

Useful Publications

VeNews, a monthly magazine, has info on the latest events, cinema, music and the like, along with a hodgepodge of articles, some in English.

PHARMACIES

Most pharmacies in Venice are open 9am to 12.30pm and 3.30pm to 7.30pm, and are closed on Saturday afternoon and Sunday. When closed, pharmacies are required to display a list of other pharmacies in the area that are open (on rotation) for extended hours. Information on all-night pharmacies is listed in *Un Ospite di Venezia*, available in tourist offices.

POST

Le Poste (☎ 803160; www.poste.it), Italy's postal service, is notoriously slow but has improved over the past few years.

Francobolli (stamps) are available from post offices and authorised tobacconists (look for the official *tabacchi* sign: a big 'T', often white on black).

The **main post office** (Map p296; ◷ 8.30am-6.30pm Mon-Sat) is on Salizada del Fontego dei Tedeschi, near the Ponte di Rialto. *Francobolli* are available at windows in the central courtyard. There is something special about doing your postal business in this former trading house. Stand by the well in the middle and try to imagine the bustle as German traders and brokers shuffled their goods around on the ground floor or struck deals in their quarters on the upper levels back in the Republic's trading heyday.

Postal Rates

The cost of sending a letter *via aerea* (by airmail) depends on its weight and where it is being sent. For regular post, letters up to 20g cost 45c within Europe, 65c to Africa, Asia and the Americas, and 70c to Australia and New Zealand. Postcards cost the same.

Few people use the regular post, preferring the slightly more expensive *posta prioritaria* (priority mail service), guaranteed to deliver letters sent to Europe within three days and to the rest of the world within four to eight days. Letters up to 20g sent *posta prioritaria* cost 62c within Europe, 80c to Africa, Asia and the Americas, and €1 to Australia and New Zealand. Letters weighing 21g to 50g cost 85c/€1.45 (standard/priority) within Europe, €1/1.50 to Africa, Asia and the Americas, and €1.20/1.80 to Australia and New Zealand.

Receiving Mail

Poste restante is known as *fermo posta* in Italy. Letters marked in this way will be held at the Fermo Posta counter in the main post office in the relevant town. At the main post office in Venice, you can pick up your letters at window No 16 – take your passport along as ID. Poste restante mail should be addressed as follows.

> John SMITH
> Fermo Posta
> Posta Centrale
> 30100 Venice
> Italy

Amex card or traveller's cheque holders can use the free mail-holding service at the main Venice office (see p257).

Sending Mail

Officially, letters sent *posta prioritaria* within Italy should arrive the following working day, those posted to destinations in Europe and the Mediterranean basin within three days, and those to the rest of the world in four to eight days.

Pacchetti (parcels) can be sent from any post office. You can purchase posting boxes or padded envelopes from most post offices. Parcels usually take longer to be delivered than letters. A different set of postal rates applies.

RADIO

There are three state-owned stations: RAI-1 (1332kHz AM or 89.7MHz FM), RAI-2 (846kHz AM or 91.7MHz FM) and RAI-3 (93.7MHz FM). They offer a combination of classical and light music with news broadcasts and discussion programmes.

There are various local stations, two based in Venice proper. Most are not very inspiring, but Radio Venezia (101.1MHz FM) has news and a reasonable music selection. Radio Vanessa (101.5MHz FM) presents anything from operettas through 60s hits to Italian pop. If your Italian is good and you like a little right-on, left-wing, anti-establishment news and views, try Mestre-based Radio Base (93.55MHz FM), part of the national Radio Popolare network.

You can pick up the BBC World Service on short wave at 6.195MHz, 7320MHz, 9.410MHz, 12.095MHz and 15.485MHz depending on where you are and the time of day. Voice of America can be found on short wave at 1593MHz, 9685MHz, 11,835MHz, 15,255MHz and 17,555MHz.

SMOKING

Since early 2005 smoking in all closed public spaces (from bars to elevators, offices to trains) has been banned.

TAXES

A value-added tax (called Imposta di Valore Aggiunto or IVA) of up to 20% is slapped onto just about everything in Italy.

Tourists who are resident outside the EU may claim a refund on this tax if they spend €155 or more in the same shop on the same day. The refund applies only to items purchased at retail outlets affiliated with the system – these shops display a 'Tax-Free for Tourists' sign. If you don't see a sign, ask the shopkeeper. You must fill out a form at the point of purchase and have it stamped and checked by Italian customs when you leave the country (you will need to show the receipt and possibly your purchases). At major airports and some border crossings you can then get an immediate cash refund at specially marked booths; alternatively, return the form by mail to the vendor, who will make the refund, either by cheque or to your credit card.

For more information consult the rules brochure available in affiliated stores.

TELEPHONE

Most of the orange Telecom payphones now only accept phonecards (carte/schede telefoniche). Some card phones also accept special credit cards produced by Telecom – the formerly state-owned telecommunications company – and even commercial credit cards. A few send faxes (see right). If you call from a bar or shop, you may still encounter old-style metered phones, which count scatti, the units used to measure the length of a call. You may also find a handful of phones operated by smaller companies (notably at the train station).

There is a bank of telephones near the main post office on Calle Galeazza (Map p296). Unstaffed Telecom offices can be found on the corner of Corte dei Pali and Strada Nova in Cannaregio (Map p300); Calle San Luca, San Marco 4585 (Map p296); and at the train station (Map pp290–1).

You can buy phonecards (€1, €2.50, €3, €5 or €7.50) at post offices, tobacconists and newsstands, and from vending machines in Telecom offices. Snap off the perforated corner before using it.

Calling Venice from Abroad

Dial the international access code (00 in most countries), followed by the code for Italy (39) and the full number, including the leading 0. For example, to call the number ☎ 041 528 77 77 in Venice you need to dial the international access code followed by ☎ 39 041 528 77 77.

Costs

A comunicazione urbana (local call) from a public phone costs 10c every minute and 12.5 seconds. For a comunicazione interurbana (long-distance call within Italy) you pay 10c when the call is answered and then 10c every 57 seconds.

A three-minute call from a payphone to most European countries and North America will cost about €2.10. Australasia would cost €2.80. Calling from a private phone is cheaper.

Domestic Calls

Area codes are an integral part of Italian telephone numbers. The codes all begin with 0 and consist of up to four digits. You must dial this whole number, even if calling from next door. Thus, any number you call in the Venice area will begin with 041.

Mobile phone numbers begin with a three-digit prefix such as 330, 335, 347 or 368. Free-phone or toll-free numbers are known as numeri verdi (green numbers) and start with 800. National rate (the call rate that applies across the country) numbers start with 848 or 199. Some six-digit national-rate numbers are also in use (such as those for rail and postal information).

To make national directory inquiries, call ☎ 12.

Fax

You can send faxes from post offices and some tobacconists, copy centres and stationers. Faxes can also be sent from some Telecom public phones. Expect to pay around €1.50 a page for faxes sent within Italy, and more abroad.

The main post office operates a fax poste restante service – have faxes sent to you at Fax Fermo Posta, fax 041 522 68 20. To retrieve the fax you will need photo ID.

International Calls

Direct international calls can easily be made from public telephones by using a phonecard. Dial 00 to get out of Italy, then the relevant country and city codes, followed by the telephone number.

Useful country codes are: Australia 61, Canada and the USA 1, France 33, Germany 49, Ireland 353, New Zealand 64 and the UK 44. For international directory inquiries, call ☎ 4176.

To make a reverse-charge (collect) international call from a public telephone, dial ☎ 170. It is easier and often cheaper to use your country's Country Direct service. You dial the number and request a reverse-charge call through the operator in your country. Get hold of the access numbers before you leave your home country.

International Phonecards & Call Centres

Several private companies distribute international phonecards offering cheaper rates on long-distance calls. Some are better than others, but few are available in Venice. Keep an eye out at newsstands, tobacconists and the like.

Planet Internet (see p256) offers cheap-rate international calls.

Mobile Phones

You can buy SIM cards in Italy for your own national mobile phone (provided you have a GSM, dual- or tri-band cellular phone), as well as prepaid call time. This only works if your national phone hasn't been code blocked, which is usually the case, so find out before leaving home. You won't want to consider a full contract unless you plan to live in Italy for a good while, and even then the benefits are not always tangible. You need your passport to open any kind of mobile-phone account, prepaid or otherwise.

Carriers Telecom Italia Mobile (TIM) and Vodaphone-Omnitel offer *prepagato* (prepaid) accounts for GSM phones (frequency 900MHz). The card can cost as little as €10 (with €10 of calls loaded) with Vodaphone. You can then top up in Vodaphone shops or with cards from outlets such as tobacconists and newsstands. Retail TIM and Vodaphone-Omnitel outlets operate in virtually every Italian town. Rates vary according to a galaxy of call plans.

Wind and 3 are two smaller mobile-phone operators with consequently fewer outlets around the country.

US mobile phones generally work on a frequency of 1900MHz, so for use in Italy your US handset will have to be tri-band.

TELEVISION

The three state-run stations, RAI-1, RAI-2 and RAI-3, are run by Radio e Televisione Italiane. Historically, each was in the hands of one of the main political groupings in the country, but media-magnate prime minister Silvio Berlusconi has extended his influence across the entire operation. The appointment of station directors and senior staff is politicised. There is now much talk of privatising (or part-privatising) the RAI.

Of the three, RAI-3 tends to have some of the more interesting programmes. Generally, however, these stations and the private Canale 5, Italia 1, Rete 4 and La 7 tend to serve up a diet of indifferent news, tacky variety hours (with lots of near-naked tits and bums, appalling crooning and vaudeville humour) and game shows. Talk shows, some interesting but many nauseating, also abound.

Regional channels include Telenuovo, Italia 7, Antenna 3, TeleNordEst and Televenezia. Quality is mainly indifferent but all carry more news and cultural items on Venice and the Veneto than the main stations.

TIME

Italy (and hence Venice) is one hour ahead of GMT/UTC during winter and two hours ahead during the daylight-saving period from the last Sunday in March to the last Sunday in October. Most other Western European countries are on the same time as Italy year round, the major exceptions being the UK, Ireland and Portugal, one hour behind.

When it's noon in Venice, it's 3am in San Francisco, 6am in New York and Toronto, 11am in London, 9pm in Sydney and 11pm in Auckland. Note that in North America and Australasia the changeover date to/from daylight saving usually differs from the European date by a couple of weeks.

TIPPING

You are not expected to tip on top of restaurant service charges, but it is common to leave a small amount, say €1 per person. If there is no service charge, you might consider leaving a 10% tip, but this is by no means obligatory. In bars, Italians often leave any small change as a tip, often only 5c or 10c. Tipping taxi drivers is not common practice, but you should tip the porter at higher-class hotels.

TOILETS

Stopping at a bar or café for a quick coffee and then a trip to the toilet is the common solution to those sudden urges at awkward times. Make sure the bar actually has a toilet before committing yourself! Public toilets (visitors 50c, residents 25c) are scattered about Venice – look for the 'WC Toilette' signs. They are generally open from 7am to 7pm.

TOURIST INFORMATION
Tourist Helpline & Complaints

Take complaints to the tourist offices or the **Sportello di Conciliazione Turistica** (Map p298; ☎ 041 529 87 10; complaint.apt@turismovenezia .it; Fondamenta di San Lorenzo, Castello 5050; ⏰ 8.30am-1.30pm Mon-Fri). Note that they don't promise much more than to listen sympathetically.

Tourist Offices Abroad

Information on Venice is available from the following branches of the Ente Nazionale Italiano per il Turismo (ENIT; Italian State Tourism Board).

Australia (☎ 02-9262 1666; italia@italiantourism.com .au; Level 4, 46 Market St, Sydney NSW 2000)

Canada (☎ 416-925 4882; www.italiantourism.com; Suite 907, South Tower, 175 Bloor St East, Toronto M4W 3R8)

France (☎ 01 42 66 03 96; www.enit-france.com; 23 rue de la Paix, 75002 Paris)

Germany (☎ 030-247 83 98; www.enit.de; Kontorhaus Mitte, Friedrichstrasse 187, D-10117 Berlin)

Germany (☎ 089-531 317; Lenbachplatz 2, 80336 Munich)

Germany (☎ 069-259 126; Kaiserstrasse 65, 60329 Frankfurt am Main)

Netherlands (☎ 020-616 82 44; enitams@wirehub.nl; Stadhouderskade 2, 1054 ES Amsterdam)

Switzerland (☎ 043 466 40 40; info@enit.ch; Urania-strasse 32, 8001 Zürich)

UK (☎ 020-7408 1254; italy@italiantouristboard.co.uk; 1 Princes St, London W1B 9AY)

USA (☎ 312-644 0996; www.italiantourism.com; 500 North Michigan Ave, Suite 2240, Chicago, IL 60611)

USA (☎ 310-820 1898; 12400 Wilshire Blvd, Suite 550, Los Angeles, CA 90025)

USA (☎ 212-245 4822; 630 Fifth Ave, Suite 1565, New York, NY 10111)

Tourist Offices in Venice

Azienda di Promozione Turistica (APT; information line ☎ 041 529 87 11; www.turismovenezia.it) Offices have information on the town and the province.

APT office (Map p296; Piazza San Marco, San Marco 71/f; ⏰ 9am-3.30pm Mon-Sat) Staff will assist with information on hotels, transport and things to see and do in the city.

APT office (Map pp290–1; Stazione di Santa Lucia, Cannaregio; ⏰ 8am-6.30pm) Open as late as 8pm in summer.

APT office (Map pp290–1; Piazzale Roma, Santa Croce; ⏰ 9.30am-6.30pm) Next to the Garage Comunale. Operates shorter hours from November to March.

APT office (Arrivals hall, Marco Polo airport; ⏰ 9.30am-7.30pm)

APT office (Map pp302–3; Gran Viale Santa Maria Elisabetta 6/a, Lido; ⏰ 9am-12.30pm & 3.30-6pm Jun-Sep)

Chioggia APT office (☎ 041 40 10 68; www.chioggia tourism.it; Lungomare Adriatico 101, Sottomarina; ⏰ 8.30am-6.30pm, reduced hr winter)

Infopoint (Map p296; Venice Pavilion, San Marco; ⏰ 10am-6pm) Next to Giardini ex Reali, a quick walk from Piazza San Marco.

Terminal Fusina Venice Office (Map pp294–5; Campo di Sant'Agnese, Dorsoduro 909/c; ⏰ 9am-1pm) For those arriving in town from Fusina on the mainland, this office has limited city info, public-transport tickets and a couple of Internet terminals.

The useful monthly booklet *Un Ospite di Venezia* (A Guest in Venice), published by a group of Venetian hoteliers, is sometimes available from tourist offices (and some hotels). Ask also for *Leo*, a monthly free magazine with articles in Italian and English and a handy listings insert, *Bussola*. Another handy listings freebie you may encounter is *VDV (Venezia da Vivere)*.

Informazioni e Assistenza ai Turisti (IAT) offices are increasingly common in the Veneto. These are the places to go for specific information about bus routes, museum opening times and so on.

Useful Websites

Many websites are dedicated to all things Venetian. Some of the more useful sites:

APT (www.turismovenezia.it) The tourist office's website has a search function for tracking down addresses and phone numbers, information on sights and hotels, and a cultural-events agenda.

Comune di Venezia (www.comune.venezia.it) The city's town hall site has links to museum sites and other useful information.

Ente Nazionale Italiano per il Turismo (ENIT; www.enit .it) The Italian national tourist body's website has information on everything from local tourist office addresses, through town-by-town museum details and general introductions, to food, art and history.

Ombra.Net (www.ombra.net) This site is bursting with information, but what makes it special is the interactive map, allowing you to zoom in on the precise location of the item you are researching.

Raixe Venete (www.raixevenete.net, in Venet) An online newspaper in Venet (the language of the Veneto region) with games, news and miscellany from the Veneto community throughout the world.

Rialto: The Venice Marketplace (www.rialto.com) Want to shop in Venice without going there? This could be the site for you. Many of the city's prestigious stores (and some perhaps not so prestigious) have contributed to this site. In many cases you can see catalogues and order online.

Sal.Ve (www.salve.it) This site, prepared by the Italian Ministero delle Infrastrutture e dei Transporti (Ministry of Infrastructure and Transport), is dedicated to Venice's complex urban and environmental problems and the long history of discussion on what to do about them.

Sposarsi a Venezia (www.comune.venezia.it) The town hall's website is the source of information for those who wish to be married in Palazzo Cavalli on the Grand Canal. Search under 'the citizen' and then 'to have a family'.

Veneto (www.veneto.org) Information about the Veneto region, of which Venice is the capital, can be found here, including history, language and local news. You can read it in Venet or English.

Venice Blog (http://veniceblog.typepad.com) A blog site for people who love Venice.

Venice Escapes (www.venicescapes.org) Venice web portal, mostly interesting for its links to other Venice-related sites.

Venice for Visitors (http://europeforvisitors.com/venice/) A general site with reviews, articles and links.

Venice Guide (www.veniceguide.net, not in English) All sorts of practical info and curiosities from the lagoon city.

Venice in Peril (www.veniceinperil.org) For news on restoration going on in Venice and the latest on dangers facing the city, as well as general news.

Vogaveneta.it (www.vogaveneta.it, in Italian) Everything you ever wanted to know about the Venetian way of rowing – standing up!

TRAVEL AGENTS

Venice is not awash with good-value travel agents, but you could try the following.

CTS (Map pp294–5; ☎ 041 520 56 60; www.cts.it, in Italian; Calle Foscari, Dorsoduro 3252) The main Italian student and youth travel organisation.

CTS (Map p305; ☎ 041 96 11 25; Via Ca' Savorgnan 8, Mestre)

Gran Canal Viaggi (Map p296; ☎ 041 271 21 11; Ponte del Lovo, San Marco 4759/4760)

VISAS

Italy is one of 15 member countries of the Schengen Convention, under which all EU member countries (except the UK and Ireland) plus Iceland and Norway have abolished checks at common borders. The other EU countries are Austria, Belgium, Denmark, Finland, France, Germany, Greece, Luxembourg, the Netherlands, Portugal, Spain and Sweden. Legal residents of one Schengen country do not require a visa for another Schengen country. Citizens of the remaining 12 EU countries (including the UK and Ireland) are also exempt. Nationals of some other countries, including Australia, Brazil, Canada, Israel, Japan, New Zealand, Switzerland and the USA, do not require visas for tourist visits of up to 90 days.

All non-EU nationals entering Italy for any reason other than tourism (such as study or work) should contact an Italian consulate, as they may need a specific visa. They should also insist on having their passport stamped on entry as, without a stamp, they could encounter problems when trying to obtain a *permesso di soggiorno* (residence permit).

If you are a citizen of a country not mentioned here, check with an Italian consulate whether you need a visa. The standard tourist visa issued by Italian consulates is the Schengen visa, valid for up to 90 days. A Schengen visa issued by one Schengen country is generally valid for travel in all other Schengen countries. However, individual member countries may impose additional restrictions on certain nationalities. You should check visa regulations with the consulate of each Schengen country you plan to visit. These visas are not renewable inside Italy. For more information and a list of countries whose citizens require a visa, check the Italian foreign ministry website (www.esteri.it).

Permits

EU citizens do not need permits to live, work or start a business in Italy. They are, however, advised to register with a *questura* if they take up residence and apply for a *permesso di soggiorno*. That is the first step to acquiring a *carta d'identità* (ID card). While you're at it, you'll need a *codice fiscale* (tax-file number) if you wish to be paid for most work in Italy. Go to the police station (Map p298; ☎ 041 271 55 11;

Fondamenta di San Lorenzo, Castello 5053) to obtain precise information on what is required. Study and work visas (required by all non-EU citizens) must be applied for in your country of residence.

WOMEN TRAVELLERS

Of the main destinations in Italy, Venice has to be the safest for women. The kind of bravado that has more southerly Italians strutting about in an effort to gain the attention of foreign women seems largely absent here. There are a couple of exceptions. The more popular Lido beaches have a bit of a reputation – local chaps of all ages try it on with local and foreign women. Some are said to 'work' Piazza San Marco. There is apparently even a club of men who compete with one another to pick up women. If you get unwanted attention, the methods you use at home to deal with it should work. Following are a couple of organisations worth noting, especially if you are spending any length of time in the city.

Centro Anti-Violenza (Off Map p305; ☎ 041 269 06 10; Villa Franchin, Viale G Garibaldi 155/a, Mestre) A women's centre offering legal advice, counselling and support to women who have been attacked, regardless of nationality. The service is free and open 9am to 8pm Monday to Friday.

Centro Donna (Off Map p305; ☎ 041 269 06 50; www .comune.venezia.it/c-donna, in Italian; Villa Franchin, Viale G Garibaldi 155/a, Mestre) Located in the same building as Centro Anti-Violenza, this centre has a library and cultural events aimed at women, whether Italian or foreign. Take bus No 2 from Piazzale Roma.

WORK

It is illegal for non-EU citizens to work in Italy without a *permesso di lavoro* (work permit), but trying to obtain one through your Italian consulate can be a pain. EU citizens are allowed to work in Italy, but they still need to obtain a *permesso di soggiorno* from a *questura*. Immigration laws require foreign workers to be 'legalised' through their employers. This applies even to cleaners and baby-sitters. The employers then pay pension and health-insurance contributions.

Doing Business in Venice

People wishing to make the first moves towards expanding their business into Italy should contact their country's trade department. The commercial department of the Italian embassy in your home country should also have information – at least on red tape. In Italy, the trade office of your embassy can provide tips and contacts.

For organising business conventions in Venice, getting temporary accommodation for clients, secretarial services and so on, contact the following.

ENDAR (Veneto Congressi; Map p298; ☎ 041 523 84 40; www.endar.it; Castello 4966)

Venezia Congressi (Map pp294–5; ☎ 041 522 84 00; www.veneziacongressi.com; Dorsoduro 1056)

Employment Options

Work options in Venice are limited. Au pair work, organised before you come to Italy, is one possibility. A useful guide is *The Au Pair and Nanny's Guide to Working Abroad*, by Susan Griffith and Sharon Legg.

Art students and graduates might consider doing a stint for the Peggy Guggenheim Collection. The gallery takes on foreign students to staff the museum, the cloakroom and so on for periods of up to three months. This is most easily pursued through your art school.

The easiest source of employment for foreigners is teaching English (or another foreign language), but even with full qualifications a non-EU citizen will find it difficult to secure a permanent position. Most of the larger, more reputable schools will hire only those people who have work and/ or residence permits.

Translating and interpreting could be an option if you are fluent in Italian and another language in demand.

University students or recent graduates might be able to set up an internship with companies in Venice. The Association of International Students for Economics and Commerce (www.aiesec.org), with branches throughout the world, helps member students find internships in related fields.

Language

Language

It's true – anyone can speak another language. Don't worry if you haven't studied languages before or that you studied a language at school for years and can't remember any of it. It doesn't even matter if you failed English grammar. After all, that's never affected your ability to speak English! And this is the key to picking up a language in another country. You just need to start speaking.

Learn a few key phrases before you go. Write them on pieces of paper and stick them on the fridge, by the bed or even on the computer – anywhere that you'll see them often.

You'll find that locals appreciate travellers trying their language, no matter how muddled you may think you sound. So don't just stand there, say something! If you want to learn more Italian than we've included here, pick up a copy of Lonely Planet's comprehensive but user-friendly *Italian Phrasebook*.

SOCIAL
Meeting People
Hello.
Buongiorno.
Goodbye.
Arrivederci.
Please.
Per favore.
Thank you (very much).
(Mille) Grazie.
Yes/No.
Sì/No.
Do you speak English?
Parla inglese?
Do you understand (me)?
(Mi) capisce?
Yes, I understand.
Sì, capisco.
No, I don't understand.
No, non capisco.

Could you please ...?
Potrebbe ...?
repeat that	ripeterlo
speak more slowly	parlare più lentamente
write it down	scriverlo

Going Out
What's on ...?
Che c'è in programma ...?
locally	in zona
this weekend	questo fine settimana
today	oggi
tonight	stasera

Where are the ...?
Dove sono ...?
clubs	dei clubs
gay venues	dei locali gay
places to eat	posti dove mangiare
pubs	dei pub

Is there a local entertainment guide?
C'è una guida agli spettacoli in questa città?

PRACTICAL
Question Words
Who?	Chi?
What?	Che?
When?	Quando?
Where?	Dove?
How?	Come?

Numbers & Amounts
1	uno
2	due
3	tre
4	quattro
5	cinque
6	sei
7	sette
8	otto
9	nove
10	dieci
11	undici
12	dodici
13	tredici
14	quattordici
15	quindici
16	sedici

17	diciasette
18	diciotto
19	dicianove
20	venti
21	ventuno
22	ventidue
30	trenta
40	quaranta
50	cinquanta
60	sessanta
70	settanta
80	ottanta
90	novanta
100	cento
1000	mille
2000	duemila

Days

Monday	lunedì
Tuesday	martedì
Wednesday	mercoledì
Thursday	giovedì
Friday	venerdì
Saturday	sabato
Sunday	domenica

Banking

I'd like to ...
Vorrei ...

cash a cheque	riscuotere un assegno
change money	cambiare denaro
change some travellers cheques	cambiare degli assegni di viaggio

Where's the nearest ...?
Dov'è il ... più vicino?

automatic teller machine	bancomat
foreign exchange office	cambio

Post

Where is the post office?
Dov'è la posta?

I want to send a ...
Voglio spedire ...

fax	un fax
parcel	un pachetto
postcard	una cartolina

I want to buy ...
Voglio comprare ...

an aerogram	un aerogramma
an envelope	una busta
a stamp	un francobollo

Phone & Mobile Phones

I want to buy a phone card.
Voglio comprare una scheda telefonica.
I want to make ...
Voglio fare ...

a call (to ...)	una chiamata (a ...)
reverse-charge/ collect call	una chiamata a carico del destinatario

Where can I find a/an ...?
Dove si trova ...
I'd like a/an ...
Vorrei ...

adaptor plug	un addattatore
charger for my phone	un caricabatterie
mobile/cell phone for hire	un cellulare da noleggiare
prepaid mobile/ cell phone	un cellulare prepagato
SIM card for your network	un SIM card per vostra rete telefonica

Internet

Where's the local Internet café?
Dove si trova l'Internet point?

I'd like to ...
Vorrei ...

check my email	controllare le mie email
get online	collegarmi a Internet

Transport

What time does the ... leave?
A che ora parte ...?

bus	l'autobus
ferry (large)	la motonave
ferry (speedboat)	il motoscafo
plane	l'aereo
train	il treno
vaporetto	il batello/vaporetto

What time's the ... bus/vaporetto?
A che ora passa ... autobus/batello?

first	il primo
last	l'ultimo
next	il prossimo

Are you free? (taxi)
È libero questo taxi?
Please put the meter on.
Usa il tassametro, per favore.
How much is it to ...?
Quant'è per ...?
Please take me to (this address).
Mi porti a (questo indirizzo), per favore.

FOOD

breakfast	prima colazione
lunch	pranzo
dinner	cena
snack	spuntino/merenda
eat	mangiare
drink	bere

Can you recommend a ...
Potrebbe consigliare un ...?

bar/pub	bar/pub
café	bar
restaurant	ristorante

Is service/cover charge included in the bill?
Il servizio/coperto è compreso nel conto?

For more detailed information on food and dining out, see the Eating chapter, p140–58.

EMERGENCIES

It's an emergency!
È un'emergenza!
Could you please help me/us?
Mi/Ci può aiutare, per favore?

Call the police/a doctor/an ambulance!
Chiami la polizia/un medico/
un'ambulanza!
Where's the police station?
Dov'è la questura?

HEALTH

Where's the nearest ...?
Dov'è ...più vicino?

chemist (night)	la farmacia (di turno)
dentist	il dentista
doctor	il medico
hospital	l'ospedale

I need a doctor (who speaks English).
Ho bisogno di un medico (che parli inglese).

Symptoms

I have (a) ...
Ho ...

diarrhoea	la diarrea
fever	la febbre
headache	mal di testa
pain	un dolore

Glossary

Listed below are useful Italian terms. Some appear in the Venetian dialect (V). In a few instances, words used only in Venice and perhaps elsewhere in the Veneto have been identified (Vz).

abbonamento – transport pass valid for one month
acqua alta (s), **acque alte** (pl) – high water (flooding that occurs in Venice, especially during winter, when the sea level rises)
ACTV – Azienda Consorzio Trasporti Veneziano; Venice public transport (bus and vaporetto) company
affittacamere – rooms for rent (sometimes cheaper than a **pensione** and not part of the classification system)
AIG – Associazione Italiana Alberghi per la Gioventù; Italian Youth Hostel Association
alimentari – grocery shop
alloggio – general term for lodging of any kind; not part of the classification system
andata e ritorno – return trip
APT – Azienda di Promozione Turistica (local tourist office)
arco – arch
autonoleggio – car hire
autostazione – bus station/terminal
bacaro – (V) traditional Venetian bar or eatery
batello – generic term for all types of Venetian ferry

battistero – baptistry
biglietteria – ticket office
biglietto (s), **biglietti** (pl) – ticket
binario – platform
calle (s), **calli** (pl) – (Vz) street
campanile – bell tower
campo – (Vz) square; equivalent to **piazza**
cappella – chapel
carabinieri – police with military and civil duties
carnet – book of tickets
Carnevale – carnival period between Epiphany and Lent
carta marmorizzata – marbled paper
cartapesta – papier-mâché, used to make Carnevale masks
cartoleria – shop selling paper goods
cartolina (postale) – postcard
casa – house
centro storico – (literally 'historical centre') old town
chiaroscuro – (literally 'light-dark') the use of strong light and dark contrasts in painting to put the main figures into stronger relief
chiesa – church
chiostro – cloister
cicheti – (Vz) traditional bar snacks
consolato – consulate
contorno – side order
convalida – validation (of train ticket, for example)
coperto – cover charge (in restaurant)
corte – (Vz) blind alley

CTS – Centro Turistico Studentesco e Giovanile (student/youth travel agency)

cupola – dome

deposito bagagli – left luggage

digestivo – after-dinner liqueur

doge (s), **dogi** (pl) – leader, duke

ENIT – Ente Nazionale Italiano per il Turismo (Italian State Tourist Office)

ES – Eurostar; very fast train

espresso – express mail; short black coffee

fermo posta – poste restante

ferrovia – railway

fiume – river

fondamenta – (Vz) street beside a canal

forcola – (V) wooden support for gondolier's oar

foresto – (V) stranger, foreigner (non-Venetian)

fornaio – bakery

gabinetto – toilet, WC

gelateria (s), **gelaterie** (pl) – ice-cream shop

intarsia – inlaid wood, marble or metal

isola – island

IVA – Imposta di Valore Aggiunto (value-added tax)

lago – lake

largo – (small) square; boulevard

lido – beach

locanda – inn, small hotel

lungomare – seafront road or promenade

malvasia – tavern (named after the wine imported from Greek islands once controlled by Venice)

marzaria – (Vz) shop-lined street in heart of Venice

merceria – haberdashery shop, see also marzaria

motonave – big, inter-island ferry on Venetian lagoon

motorino – moped

motoscafo (s), **motoscafi** (pl) – motorboat; in Venice also a faster, fully enclosed ferry and water taxi

nave (s), **navi** (pl) – ship

oggetti smarriti – lost property

ombra – (Vz) small glass of wine

orario – timetable

ostello (per la gioventù) – (youth) hostel

osteria (s), **osterie** (pl) – traditional bar/restaurant

pala d'altare – altarpiece; refers to a painting (often on wood) usually used as an ornament before the altar

palazzo (s), **palazzi** (pl) – palace, mansion; large building of any type, including an apartment block

panetteria – bakery

passeggiata – traditional evening or Sunday stroll

passerella (s), **passerelle** (pl) – raised walkway

pasticceria – cake/pasty shop

pensione – guesthouse, small hotel

pescaria – (V) fish market

piazza – square

pietà – (literally 'pity' or 'compassion') sculpture, drawing or painting of the dead Christ supported by the Madonna

pinacoteca – art gallery

poltrona – airline-type chair on a ferry

ponte – bridge

portico – covered walkway, usually attached to the outside of buildings

porto – port

posta aerea – airmail

pronto soccorso – first aid, casualty ward

punto informativo – information booth

questura – police station

ramo – (Vz) tiny side lane

rio (s), **rii** (pl) – (Vz) the name for most canals in Venice

rio terà – (Vz) street following the course of a filled-in canal

ruga – (Vz) small street flanked by houses and shops

sala – room, hall

salizada – (Vz) street, the first type in Venice to be paved

salumeria – delicatessen

scala mobile – escalator, moving staircase

scalinata – staircase

servizio – service charge (in restaurant)

sestiere (s), **sestieri** (pl) – (Vz) term for the six 12th-century municipal divisions of Venice

sirocco – hot south wind

spiaggia – beach

spiaggia libera – public beach

squero (s), **squeri** (pl) – gondola-building and repair workshop

stazio (s), **stazi** (pl) – gondola jetty

stazione – station

stazione marittima – ferry terminal

strada – street, road

tabaccheria, tabaccaio – tobacconist's shop, tobacconist

tesoro – treasury

traghetto – ferry; commuter gondola that crisscrosses the Grand Canal

trattoria (s), **trattorie** (pl) – cheap restaurant

Trenitalia Italian State Railways, also known as Ferrovie dello Stato (FS)

ufficio postale – post office

ufficio stranieri – foreigners' bureau (in police station)

vaporetto – passenger ferry (in Venice)

vetrai – glass-makers

via – street, road

vigili del fuoco – fire brigade

vigili urbani – local police

Language

Behind the Scenes

THE LONELY PLANET STORY

The story begins with a classic travel adventure: Tony and Maureen Wheeler's 1972 journey across Europe and Asia to Australia. There was no useful information about the overland trail then, so Tony and Maureen published the first Lonely Planet guidebook to meet a growing need.

From a kitchen table, Lonely Planet has grown to become the largest independent travel publisher in the world, with offices in Melbourne (Australia), Oakland (USA) and London (UK). Today Lonely Planet guidebooks cover the globe. There is an ever-growing list of books and information in a variety of media. Some things haven't changed. The main aim is still to make it possible for adventurous travellers to get out there – to explore and better understand the world.

At Lonely Planet we believe travellers can make a positive contribution to the countries they visit – if they respect their host communities and spend their money wisely. Every year 5% of company profit is donated to charities around the world.

THIS BOOK

This 4th edition of *Venice* was researched and written by Damien Simonis, who also wrote the three previous editions. The book was commissioned in Lonely Planet's London office and produced in Melbourne. The project team:

Commissioning Editors Michala Green, Tom Masters, Tasmin McNaughtan

Coordinating Editor Sarah Bailey

Coordinating Cartographer Natasha Velleley

Coordinating Layout Designer Tom Delamore

Managing Cartographer Mark Griffiths

Assisting Layout Designers Kaitlin Beckett, Wibowo Rusli

Proofreaders Jackey Coyle, Elizabeth Swan

Cover Designer Annika Roojun

Project Managers Fabrice Rocher, Glenn van der Knijff

Language Content Coordinator Quentin Frayne

Managing Editor Bruce Evans

Thanks to Glenn Beanland, Sally Darmody, Ryan Evans, Jennifer Garrett, Mark Germanchis, Laura Jane, Rebecca Lalor, Wayne Murphy, Jolyon Philcox, Paul Piaia, Chris Thomas, Celia Wood

Cover photographs Gondolier's hat, Peter Adams/Alamy Images (top); Fondamenta Navagero, Murano, in the afternoon light, Damien Simonis/Lonely Planet Images (bottom); woman in Carnevale costume, Juliet Coombe/ Lonely Planet Images (back).

Internal photographs by Lonely Planet Images and Juliet Coombe except for the following: p105 (#3), p204 (#2 & #3) Glenn Beanland; p99 (#4) Alan Benson; p203 (#3) Jeff Cantarutti; p105 (#1) Robin Chapman; p104 (#3) Olivier Cirendini; p99 (#3) Jon Davison; p103 (#4), p106 (#2), p203 (#4), p206 (#4), p207 (#1), p209 (#2) Roberto Soncin Gerometta; p51, p101(#2), p205 (#2) Dennis Jones; p102 (#2), p206 (#2) Chris Mellor; p209 (#3) Andrew Peacock; p37, p43, p46, p69, p75, p100 (#3), p102 (#1 & #3), p103 (#3), p104 (#1, #2 & #4), p105 (#2), p210 (#2 & #4), p230, p235, p241 Damien Simonis; p208 (#2) Dallas Stribley; p18 Graham Tween. All images are the copyright of the photographers unless otherwise indicated. Many of the images in this guide are available for licensing from Lonely Planet Images: www.lonelyplanetimages.com

ACKNOWLEDGMENTS

Many thanks to the following for the use of their content: Venice vaporetto map © Actv SpA 2005

THANKS
DAMIEN SIMONIS

Returning to Venice is like coming home, a rich stage whose characters are very real, warm and engaging. As always, Irina Freguia and Vladi Salvan kindly gave me access to their home, a fine base by the Rialto for exploring the city.

Other friends and acquaintances, old and new, all helped render my research time in the lagoon as pleasant as it was profitable. Thanks go (in no particular order) to:

Antonella Bampa (in Verona), Etta Lisa Basaldella (for showing me around 'her' jewel, Palazzo Labia, and the gastronomical leads), Federica Centunali, Caterina de Cesero, Antonella Dondi dall'Orologio, 'Seba' Giorgi, Bernhard Klein, Francesco Lobina, Lucialda Lombardi, Alessandra Magistretti, Lee Marshall, Marta at the Fondazione Giorgio Cini for the personal tour, Thom Price, Federica Rocco, Susanne Sagner, Laura

Scarpa, Michela Scibilia (a local dynamo with loads of tips), Alberto Toso Fei (who has the Knowledge) and Olivia Alighieri, Manuel Vecchina and Angela Colonna (thanks for the meal!), and Ottobrina Voccoli (who came up one foul, snowy day).

In Padua *un abbraccio forte, per bacco!* for Dr Alberto Stassi and Francesca Piro for rolling out the welcome mat. It was good to catch up again.

Thanks to the staff of tourist offices in Venice and throughout the Veneto for their time-saving help, and especially to Luisa De Salvo, who unveiled some secrets (such as the *macchiatone*) I might otherwise never have discovered.

Finally, this is for Janique, who convinced me to buy the mask and tricorn, and whisked me out, thus attired, on forays into Venice of the Carnevale.

OUR READERS

Many thanks to the travellers who used the last edition and wrote to us with helpful hints, useful advice and interesting anecdotes: Alasdair Adam, Cecile Blanchot, Madeline Brown, Ben Coleman, Debra Douglass, Nick Evans, Marjolein Fredrix, Marti Griera, Alison Gyger, Ernesto Hernandez, Iqbal Husain, Paul Lawrance, Nicola McCoy, Frances Rogers, Marianne Stam, Deborah Taylor, Ken Wong.

SEND US YOUR FEEDBACK

We love to hear from travellers — your comments keep us on our toes and help make our books better. Our well-travelled team reads every word on what you loved or loathed about this book. Although we cannot reply individually to postal submissions, we always guarantee that your feedback goes straight to the appropriate authors, in time for the next edition. Each person who sends us information is thanked in the next edition — and the most useful submissions are rewarded with a free book.

To send us your updates — and find out about Lonely Planet events, newsletters and travel news — visit our award-winning website: www.lonelyplanet.com /feedback

Note: We may edit, reproduce and incorporate your comments in Lonely Planet products such as guidebooks, websites and digital products, so let us know if you don't want your comments reproduced or your name acknowledged. For a copy of our privacy policy visit www.lonelyplanet.com/privacy.

Notes

Notes

Notes

Notes

Notes

Notes

Index

See also separate indexes for Eating (p285), Drinking (pp285-6), Shopping (p286) and Sleeping (p286).

Index

000 map pages
000 photographs

000 map pages
000 photographs

MAP LEGEND

ROUTES

Tollway	One-Way Street
Freeway	Mall/Steps
Primary Road	Tunnel
Secondary Road	Walking Tour
Tertiary Road	Walking Tour Detour
Lane	Walking Trail
Track	Walking Path
Unsealed Road	Pedestrian Overpass

TRANSPORT

Ferry	Rail
Bus Route	Rail (Underground)

HYDROGRAPHY

River, Creek	Canal
Intermittent River	Water

BOUNDARIES

International	Regional, Suburb
State, Provincial	Ancient Wall

AREA FEATURES

Airport	Cemetery, Other
Area of Interest	Forest
Building, Featured	Land
Building, Information	Mall
Building, Other	Park
Building, Transport	Sports
Cemetery, Christian	Urban

POPULATION

✪ **CAPITAL (NATIONAL)**	◉ CAPITAL (STATE)
● **Large City**	● Medium City
○ Small City	○ Town, Village

SYMBOLS

Sights/Activities
- Castle, Fortress
- Christian
- Jewish
- Monument
- Museum, Gallery
- Other Site
- Ruin
- Swimming Pool
- Zoo, Bird Sanctuary

Eating
- Eating

Drinking
- Drinking
- Café

Entertainment
- Entertainment

Shopping
- Shopping

Sleeping
- Sleeping

Transport
- Airport, Airfield
- Bus Station
- Parking Area
- Taxi Rank

Information
- Bank, ATM
- Embassy/Consulate
- Hospital, Medical
- Information
- Internet Facilities
- Police Station
- Post Office, GPO
- Telephone
- Toilets

Geographic
- Lighthouse
- Mountain
- River Flow
- Waterfall

Map Section

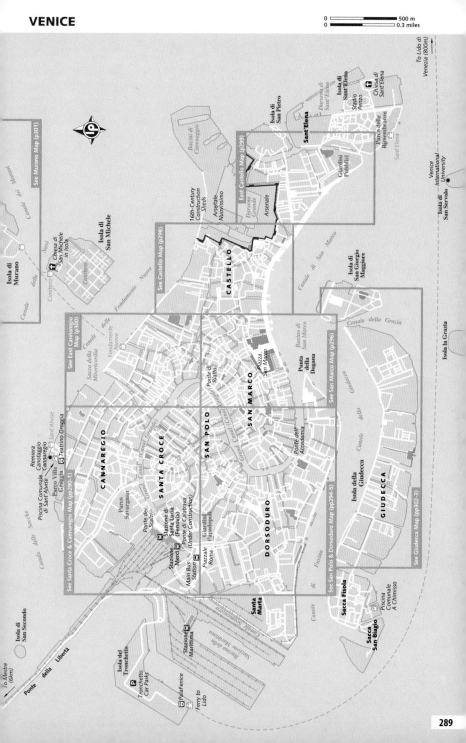

VENICE

0 — 500 m
0 — 0.3 miles

See Murano Map (p301)

See East Cannaregio Map (p300)

See Santa Croce & Cannaregio Map (pp290–1)

See Castello Map (p298)

East Castello Map (p299)

See San Polo & Dorsoduro Map (pp294–5)

See San Marco Map (p296)

See Giudecca Map (p302–3)

To Lido di Venezia (800m)

Venice International University

To Mestre (6km)

Isola di San Secondo

Isola del Tronchetto

Tronchetto Car Park

PalaFenice

Ferry to Lido

Ponte della Libertà

Isola di Murano

Isola di Murano

Chiesa di San Michele in Isola

Isola di San Michele

Canale dei Marani

Canale delle Navi

Cimitero

Canale delle Sacche

Sacca della Misericordia

Fondamente Nuove

Canale della Misericordia

Fondamenta delle Nuove

Remiera Canottaggio Canareggio

Parco Villa Groggia

Sant'Alvise

Teatrino Groggia

Piscina Comunale di Sant'Alvise

Parco Savorgnan

CANNAREGIO

SANTA CROCE

Ponte dei Scalzi

Stazione di Santa Lucia (Ferrovia)

Ponte di Calatrava (Under Construction)

Stazione Merci

Main Bus Station

Piazzale Roma

Giardini Papadopoli

SAN POLO

Ponte di Rialto

Grand Canal (Canal Grande)

SAN MARCO

Piazza San Marco

Punta della Dogana

Bacino di San Marco

Canale di San Marco

Ponte dell'Accademia

DORSODURO

Santa Marta

Stazione Marittima

Bacino della Stazione Marittima

Canale Scomenzera

Canale di Fusina

Sacca Fisola

Sacca San Biagio

Piscina Comunale A Chimisso

Isola della Giudecca

GIUDECCA

Canale della Giudecca

CASTELLO

16th-Century Construction Sheds

Bacini di Carenaggio

Arsenale Nuovissimo

Darsena Grande

Arsenale

Darsena di Sant'Elena

Canale di Sant'Elena

Giardini Pubblici

Isola di San Pietro

Sant'Elena

Isola di Sant'Elena

Stadio Pier Luigi Penzo

Chiesa di Sant'Elena

Parco delle Rimembranze

Sant'Elena

Isola di San Giorgio Maggiore

Canale della Grazia

Isola la Grazia

Bacino di San Marco

Isola di San Servolo

289

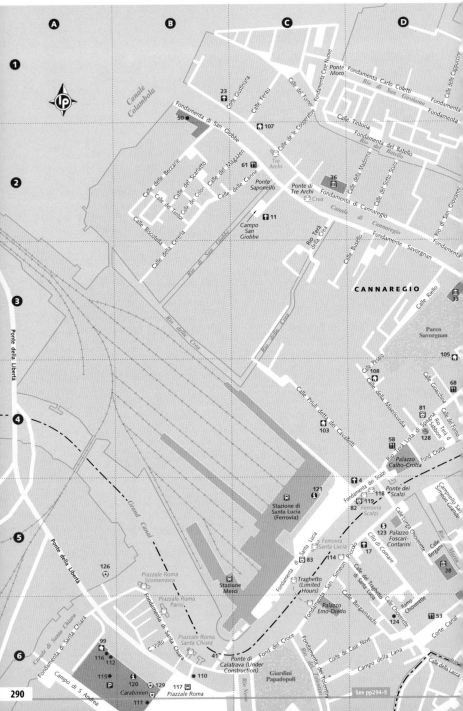

See pp294-5

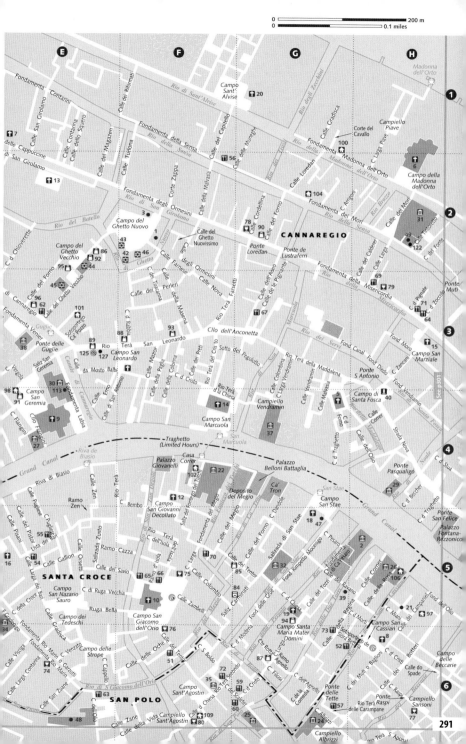

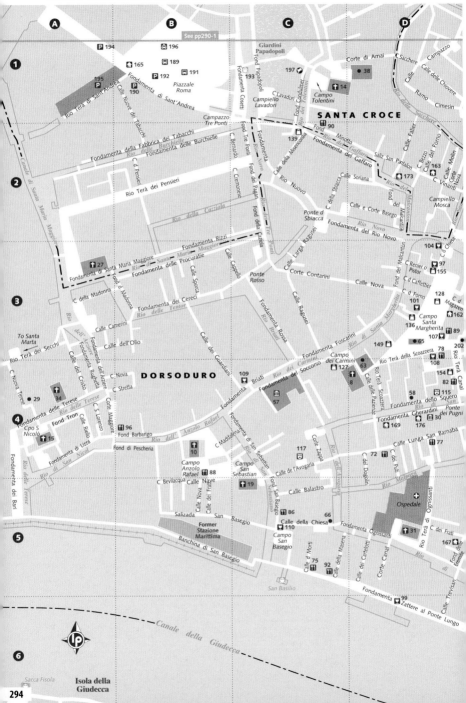

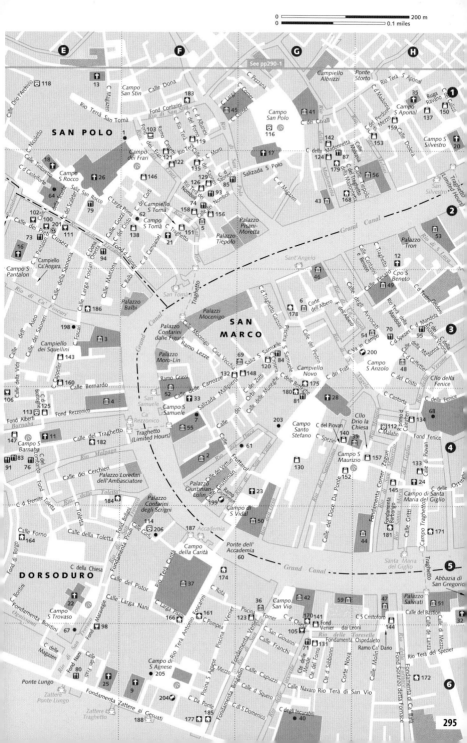

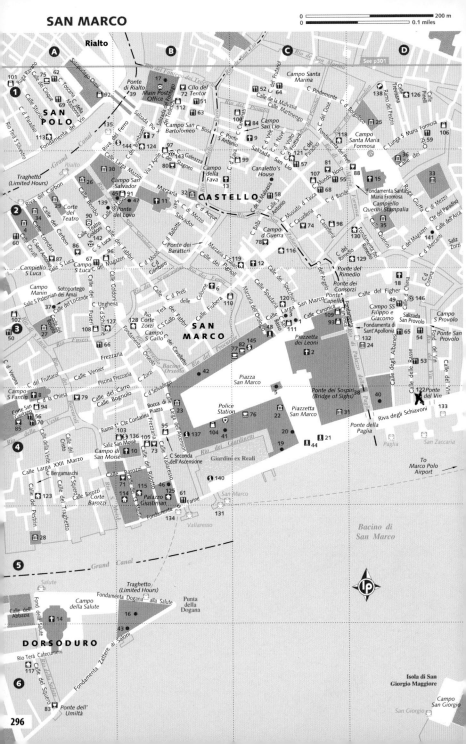

SAN MARCO

SAN MARCO

0 _____ 200 m
0 _____ 0.1 miles

SIGHTS & ACTIVITIES	(pp80-8)
Arsenale Entrance (Land)	1 D5
Arsenale Entrance (Sea)	2 D5
Bucintoro Storage	3 D4
Casa Magno	4 C4
Chiesa di San Francesco della Vigna	5 C3
Chiesa di San Giorgio dei Greci	6 A4
Chiesa di San Giovanni in Bragora	7 B5
Chiesa di San Lorenzo	8 B3
Chiesa di San Martino	9 C5
Chiesa di San Zaccaria	10 A5
Chiesa di Santa Maria della Visitazione	11 B5
Chiesa di Sant'Antonin	12 B4
Museo delle Icone	13 A4
Museo Storico Navale	14 D6
Ospedaletto	15 A2

Padiglione delle Navi	16 D5
Palazzo Erizzo	17 C5
Riva degli Schiavoni	18 B5
Scuola di San Giorgio degli Schiavoni	19 B4

EATING	(pp153-5)
Al Giardinetto da Severino	20 B4
Osteria Ale Do Marie	21 C4
Ristorante Met	22 B5
Trattoria Corte Sconta	23 B4
Trattoria da Remigio	24 B4

ENTERTAINMENT	(pp159-74)
Concerti della Venezia Musica	(see 11)
Piccolo Teatro delle Melodie Veneziane	25 B3
Teatro Piccolo Arsenale Entrance	26 D6

SHOPPING	(pp188-9)
Al Canton del Vin	27 C3
Ca' del Sole	28 A4
Laboratorio del Gervasuti	29 B5
Librairie Française	30 A2

SLEEPING	(pp202-12)
Albergo Paganelli	31 A5
Alloggi Barbaria	32 B2
Foresteria Valdese	33 A3
La Residenza	34 B4
Liassidi Palace	35 A4
Londra Palace	36 A5
Palazzo Priuli	37 A4
Pensione Bucintoro	38 D6

INFORMATION	
ENDAR (Veneto Congressi)	39 A4
Internet Corner	40 A2
Sportello di Conciliazione Turistica	41 A4

EAST CASTELLO

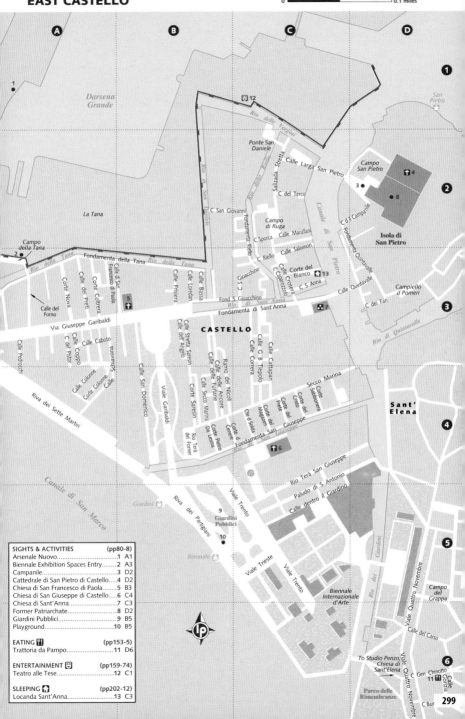

Ⓐ Ⓑ Ⓒ Ⓓ

❶ ❷ ❸ ❹ ❺ ❻

Darsena Grande

San Pietro

Rio delle Vergini

🎭 12

Ponte San Daniele

Campo San Pietro

🏛 4

3 ●

● 8

La Tana

Salizzada Stretta

Calle Larga San Pietro

C del Terco

C San Giovanni

Campo di Ruga

Calle Marafani

Isola di San Pietro

C del Campanile

Canale di San Pietro

Fondamenta Quintavalle

Campo della Tana

2 ●

Rio della Tana

Fondamenta della Tana

Fondamenta Rielo

C Sporca

C Riello

Calle Salomon

C S Gioacchino

Corte del Bianco

C S Anna

🏛 13

Fondamenta di Sant'Anna

Calle Quintavalle

C dei Fàri

Campiello d'Pomeri

Calle del Forno

Corte Nova

Calle dei Preti

Corte Coltrera

Calle di San Francesco di Paola

5 ✝

Calle Loredan

Calle Bassa

Calle Frisiera

Fond S Gioacchino

Gioacchino

Calle Crosera

C Capozzola

🏛 7

Rio di Quintavalle

Via Giuseppe Garibaldi

Calle Caboto

C del Pistor

Calle Coppo

Schiavona

Corte Colonne

Calle Colonne

Calle

CASTELLO

Calle Stretta Saresin

Calle dell'Angiol

Ramo dei Nicoli

Calle delle Ancore

Calle delle Furlane

Calle Cattapan

Calle G B Tiepolo

Calle Correra

Sant' Elena

Calle Pedrocchi

Calle San Domenico

Viale Garibaldi

Corte Saresin

Calle Secca Marina

Cte d Solda

Secco Marina

Corte Solduncea

Corte del Cristo

Corte del Prete

Riva dei Sette Martiri

Riva dei Partigiani

Corte Pietro dal Forner

Corte d Cenere

Corte del Magazen

Corte d Legna

Fondamenta San Giuseppe

🏛 6

Canale di San Marco

Giardini 🚻

Rio Terà San Giuseppe

Paludo di S Antonio

Calle dentro il Giardino

9 ●

Giardini Pubblici

10 ●

Biennale 🚻

Viale Trento

Viale Trieste

Viale Trento

Biennale Internazionale d'Arte

Giardini

Rio dei

Viale Quattro Novembre

Campo del Grappa

Calle del Carso

To Studio Penzo; Chiesa di Sant'Elena

11 🍴

C Gen Chinotto

Calle Gorizia

Viale Quattro Novembre

Parco delle Rimembranze

C Bair

299

0   200 m

0   0.1 miles

A   **B**   **C**   **D**

1

2

To San Michele (5mins);
Murano (10mins)

Canale delle Navi

Sacca della
Misericordia

Fond Gasparo Contarini

Ponte
di Sacca

Ponte
Muti Corte Vecchia

Rio dei Muti

19

Ponte
di Sacca

Calle della Masena

55

C Scuola dei Legnami
Calle delle Cadene

52

72

Fondamente Nuove

Fondamenta dell'Abbazia

28   11

C C Larga Lezze

3

27

54

Fondamenta Santa Caterina

Campiello Calle Matteo Foscarini
S Antonio Calle dei Crociferi
Calle dei Botteri
Salizada dei Specchieri

14

17

Fondamenta Zen

Campo dei
Gesuiti

Calle delle Vida
Calle delle Croci

49

Fondamente Nuove

Fondamenta Santa Caterina

Calle Lunga Santa Caterina

Calle della Racchetta

Calle Zancani

Fond dei Sartori

Calle dei Volti
Calle Venier

Calle del Magazzen
Corte dei
Calle della Pietà
Calle dei Cordoni

30

Calle Larga

Calle del Fumo

Calle dei Botteri

42
Corte della
Carità

Calle dei Volti

Fond d San Felice
C Salamon
Chiesa

48
6
34
74
51

Fond Chiesa
St Martin
C S Felice
Corte dei
Pali

31

Calle Larga Doge Priuli

Calle Zotti

Calle del Forno

Calle degli Albanesi

Ramo degli Albanesi

Sant'Andrea
Fond Corrente

Calle della Vele

Fond dei Sartori

Rio Terà di
Barba

Calle Specchieri

45

63

C dei Reneri

Fruttarol

Calle del Forno

C d Madonna

Calle della Stella

Corte del Squero

Corte del Paludo

Ponte
San Felice

C d Oro Strada
Nova

44

Corte dei
Priuli

Calle del Forno

Rio Terà di S Apostoli

Rio Terà d Franceschi

53

Corte del Verde

Calle Bembo
Salizada del Pistor

68

Larga
dei Proverbi

C d Posta

CANNAREGIO

Cllo
Stella

C Gabriella

73

26

1

Palazzo
Sagredo

Campo
Santa Sofia

Ca' d'Oro

Traghetto

Campo dei
SS Apostoli

Calle Duca
Calle dell'Oca
Calle Dragan

3

Campiello
della Cason

Calle del Traghetto

Calle Varisco

Calle del Pistor

Campiello
della Cason

24
Cllo
Widman

71

Corte
Leon Bianco

69
Ca' da
Mosto

Campo San
Canciano

61

Campo Santa
Maria Nova

5

60
47

Fond
Piovan

43

Larga G Gallina

40

Campo
SS Giovanni
e Paolo

29

Saliz Santi
Giovanni e Paolo

5

6

25

66   Cpo della
Pescaria

12

38

70

Campo
C Battisti

13

33
64

Campo San
Giacometto

39

20

21

Ponte
di Rialto

C d Magazen

Salizada

62   46

36

9

Calle Modena

Calle dell'Aseo

Calle S Giovanni Grisostomo

C d Teatro

56

58

16

Campo dei
Miracoli

C Castelli

Ponte d
Panada

Calle delle Erbe

10

18

73

22

Campo
Santa
Marina

Ponte
Storto

67

CASTELLO

Calle delle Beccarie
Ruga degli Speziali
Ruga degli Oresi

S dei Mori

35
32
41

Ruga Vecchia S Giovanni
C Toscana

57

59

37

15

SAN
POLO

300   Rialto

See p296

Ponte
San
Felice

See p296

See p298

EAST CANNAREGIO

MURANO

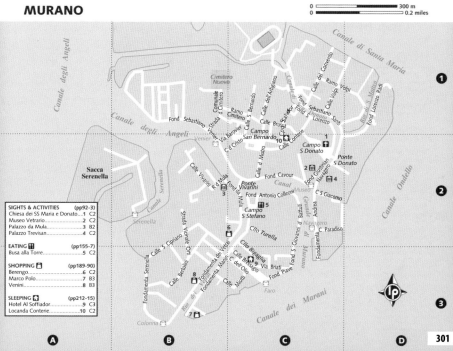

GIUDECCA

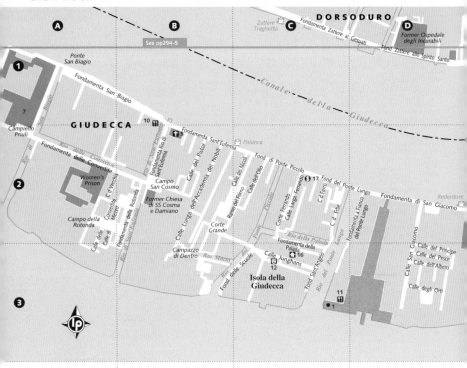

A **B** **C** DORSODURO **D**

See pp294-5

Ponte San Biagio

Fondamenta San Biagio

1

7

Campiello Priuli

GIUDECCA

Fondamenta delle Converite

Rio delle Converite

C d Vecchia

Fondamenta della Rotonda

Women's Prison

Campo San Cosmo

2

Campo della Rotonda

Calle delle Converite di Mezzo

Fondamenta di Sant'Eufemia

Fondamenta Sant'Eufemia

Rio di Sant'Eufemia

10

Fondamenta Sant'Eufemia

Palanca

Calle del Pistor

Former Chiesa di SS Cosma e Damiano

Calle Lunga dell'Accademia dei Nobili

Rio del Ferro

Calle dei Nicoli

Calle dell'Orto

Corte Grande

Campazzo di Dentro

Rio Storto

Fond delle Scuole

Calle Junghans

3

Isola della Giudecca

Canale della Giudecca

Zattere Traghetto Fondamenta Zattere ai Gesuati

Former Ospedale degli Incurabili

Fond Zattere allo Spirito Santo

Fond di Ponte Piccolo

17

Fond del Ponte Lungo

Corte Ferrando

Calle Lunga Ferrando

C d Ferro

C d Erbe

Fondamenta a Fianco del Ponte Lungo

Fondamenta di San Giacomo

Redentore

16

Calle San Giacomo

Calle del Principe

Calle del Pesce

Calle dell'Albero

Calle degli Orti

Fondamenta della Palada

Rio della Palada

Calle Sant'Angelo

12

Rio del Ponte

11

1

LIDO DI VENEZIA

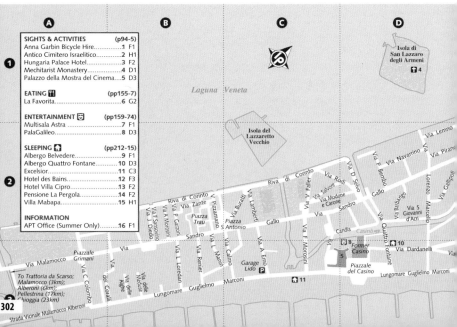

A **B** **C** **D**

SIGHTS & ACTIVITIES	(p94-5)
Anna Garbin Bicycle Hire	1 F1
Antico Cimitero Israelitico	2 H1
Hungaria Palace Hotel	3 F2
Mechitarist Monastery	4 D1
Palazzo della Mostra del Cinema	5 D3

EATING	(pp155-7)
La Favorita	6 G2

ENTERTAINMENT	(pp159-74)
Multisala Astra	7 F1
PalaGalileo	8 D3

SLEEPING	(pp212-15)
Albergo Belvedere	9 F1
Albergo Quattro Fontane	10 D3
Excelsior	11 C3
Hotel des Bains	12 F3
Hotel Villa Cipro	13 F2
Pensione La Pergola	14 F2
Villa Mabapa	15 H1

INFORMATION	
APT Office (Summer Only)	16 F1

Isola di San Lazzaro degli Armeni

4

Laguna Veneta

Isola del Lazzaretto Vecchio

Via Lemno

Via Navarrino

Via Pirane

Via P. Bembo

Via D. Selvo

Gallo

Lorenzo Marcello

Via Callipoli

Riva di Corinto

Via V. Falier

Via Salvore

Via Rodi

Via Modone e Carone

Sandro

Via Bazarago

Via S Giovanni d'Acri

Riva di Corinto

V Pizzamano

Via Zante

Via Bucatti

Via Lamberti

Via F. Morosini

Via

Candia

Casino Sp

Via Quattro Fontane

Via S Sansovino

Via A Morosini

Via J Diedo

Piazza Trau

Piazza S Antonio

Gallo

8

Former Casino

10

Via Dardanelli

5

Via Malamocco

Piazzale Grimani

Via dei Corali

Via L Garzoni

Via L Loredan

Via L Manin

Via Renier

Via A Emo

Garage Lido

11

Piazzale del Casino

Lungomare Guglielmo Marconi

To Trattoria da Scarso; Malamocco (3km); Alberoni (6km); Pellestrina (17km); Chioggia (23km)

Via C Colombo

Via delle Alghe

Via delle Meduse

Lungomare Guglielmo Marconi

Strada Vicinale Malamocco Alberoni

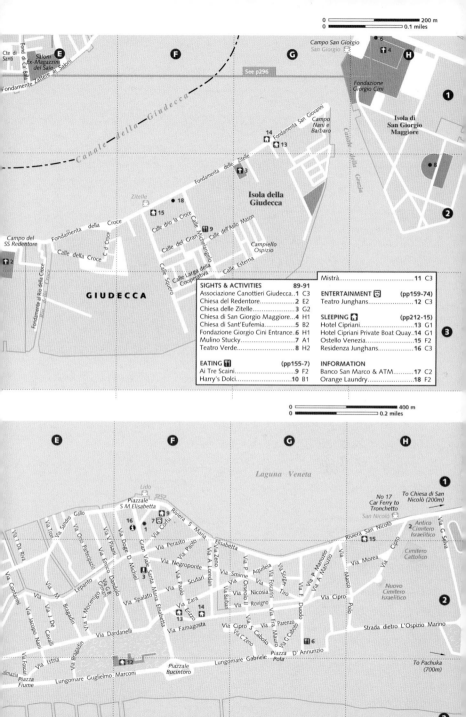

SIGHTS & ACTIVITIES 89-91
Associazione Canottieri Giudecca..1 C3
Chiesa del Redentore...................2 E2
Chiesa delle Zitelle.......................3 G2
Chiesa di San Giorgio Maggiore...4 H1
Chiesa di Sant'Eufemia.................5 B2
Fondazione Giorgio Cini Entrance..6 H1
Mulino Stucky..............................7 A1
Teatro Verde................................8 H2

EATING 🍴 (pp155-7)
Ai Tre Scaini...............................9 F2
Harry's Dolci.............................10 B1

Mistrà.......................................11 C3

ENTERTAINMENT 🎭 (pp159-74)
Teatro Junghans.......................12 C3

SLEEPING 🛏 (pp212-15)
Hotel Cipriani...........................13 G1
Hotel Cipriani Private Boat Quay..14 G1
Ostello Venezia.........................15 F2
Residenza Junghans....................16 C3

INFORMATION
Banco San Marco & ATM..........17 C2
Orange Laundry.........................18 F2

BURANO & TORCELLO

0 —————— 200 m
0 —————— 0.1 miles

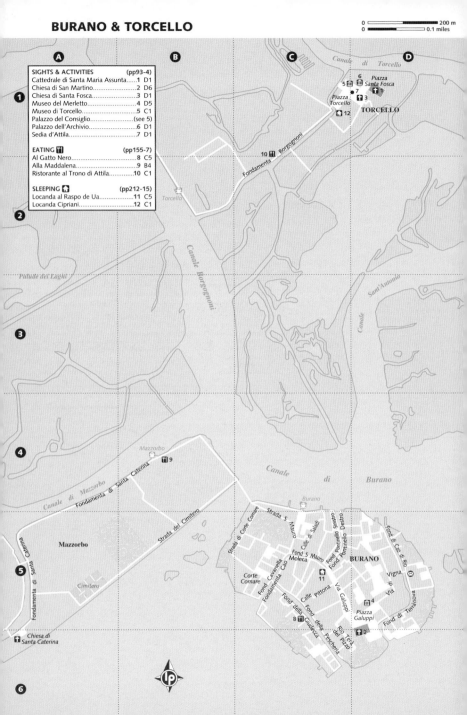

SIGHTS & ACTIVITIES (pp93-4)
Cattedrale di Santa Maria Assunta.....1 D1
Chiesa di San Martino........................2 D6
Chiesa di Santa Fosca.........................3 D1
Museo del Merletto.............................4 D5
Museo di Torcello...............................5 C1
Palazzo del Consiglio......................(see 5)
Palazzo dell'Archivio...........................6 D1
Sedia d'Attila.....................................7 D1

EATING 🍴 (pp155-7)
Al Gatto Nero.....................................8 C5
Alla Maddalena..................................9 B4
Ristorante al Trono di Attila.............10 C1

SLEEPING 🏠 (pp212-15)
Locanda al Raspo de Ua....................11 C5
Locanda Cipriani...............................12 C1

MESTRE

0 — 300 m
0 — 0.2 miles

SIGHTS & ACTIVITIES (pp97-8)
Centro Culturale Candiani...............1 C2

EATING (pp157-8)
Al Calice...2 C3
Brek..3 C3
Osteria La Pergola...............................4 A4

ENTERTAINMENT (pp159-74)
Al Vapore...5 B6
Cinema Dante d'Essai........................6 B5
Metrò Venezia......................................7 B5
Teatro Toniolo.....................................8 C3

SHOPPING (p190)
Le Barche..9 D3

SLEEPING (pp215-16)
Consorzio Alberghi della Terraferma
  Veneziana Hotel Booking Service.10 B5
Hotel Monte Piana...........................11 A5
Hotel Tritone.....................................12 B5
Hotel Vivit..13 C3

TRANSPORT (pp243-51)
ACTV Buses to Venice No 2..............14 B5
ACTV Buses to/from Venice (Nos 6, 6B,
  66)..15 B6
ACTV Night Bus No N2................(see 15)
ACTV Night Bus No N1................(see 14)
ACTV Office...16 D3
ATVO Bus Tickets.............................17 B6
Parking Stazione...............................18 B5

INFORMATION
CTS Travel Agency............................19 D3
Informahandicap...............................20 C2
Orange Laundry.................................21 B4
Ospedale Umberto I (Hospital).....22 C2
UK Consulate......................................23 C3

305

Map

ACTV VAPORETTO MAP

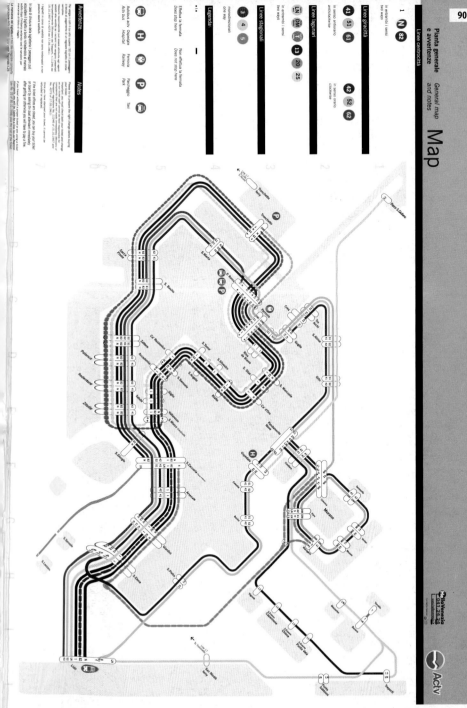

Linee centrocittà

1 N 82
in entrambi i sensi
two ways

Linee giracittà
41 51 61
in senso antiorario
anticlockwise
42 52 62
in senso orario
clockwise

Linee lagunari
LN DM T 13 20 25
in entrambi i sensi
two ways

Linee stagionali
3 4 5

monodirezionali
one way

Legenda

—

Effettua la fermata
Does stop here

—

Non effettua la fermata
Does not stop here

H Ospedale Hospital
Ferrovia Railway
Parcheggio Park
Taxi

Avvertenze / *Notes*

ActvVenezia
041 24 24